Catapulted from totalitarianism to free market capitalism in 1991, Albania emerged from half a century of isolation to find itself an anomaly in Europe: a Third World country economically, but First World in terms of education, literature and the arts. How has Albania transformed since then? Clarissa de Waal here explains Albania's 'transition' from Communism via the experiences of a diverse range of families, highland villagers, urban elite and shanty dwellers – whose lives she has followed since 1992. De Waal shows that whilst the archaic world of customary law continues to pervade highland life, and squatters on state farmland live under constant threat of eviction, members of the ex-communist elite in Tirana embrace rentier capitalism. Albania, it seems, is a country wracked by contradictions.

With unparalleled insights into the region, this book is a unique history told from the perspective of the participants. It will inform and engage all those interested in Albania and south-east Europe, and prove essential reading for students and specialists.

Clarissa de Waal taught Social Anthropology at the University of Cambridge for 20 years. She is a Fellow of Newnham College.

'It was a small shabby sort of place. Land was short, jobs were scarce, politics was unstable, health was poor, prices were rising, and life was altogether far from promising, a kind of agitated stagnancy.'
Clifford Geertz, 1993, *Local Knowledge*

ALBANIA

PORTRAIT OF A COUNTRY IN TRANSITION

Clarissa de Waal

I.B. TAURIS

LONDON · NEW YORK

New paperback edition published in 2014 by I.B.Tauris & Co Ltd
6 Salem Road, London W2 4BU
175 Fifth Avenue, New York NY 10010
www.ibtauris.com

Distributed in the United States and Canada Exclusively by Palgrave Macmillan
175 Fifth Avenue, New York NY 10010

First published in hardback in 2005 by I.B.Tauris & Co Ltd

ISBN: 978 1 78076 484 9
eISBN: 978 0 85773 575 1

A full CIP record for this book is available from the British Library
A full CIP record is available from the Library of Congress

Library of Congress Catalog Card Number: available

Printed and bound in Great Britain by Page Bros, Norwich.

CONTENTS

LIST OF MAPS AND ILLUSTRATIONS

ACKNOWLEDGEMENTS

I am grateful to the Nuffield Foundation for supporting the pilot study, and to the Wenner-Gren Foundation for Anthropological Research, which supported the subsequent fieldwork.

Many thanks are due to Lida Kita who crucially got us off to a good start, and to Ndrecë Loka who helped us so often later. My daughter Soula was an invaluable and (mostly) long-suffering field assistant. The friendship, warmth and spirit of the families who participated in this social history have continued to be a source of happiness over the years.

I am grateful to Ndue Tusha for enabling me to use his map of Mirdita and to Nick James for the professional copy-editing and indexing.

PREFACE TO THE PAPERBACK EDITION

Plus ça change

In the conclusion to the earlier edition of this book I suggested that 'agitated stagnancy' would be a fair assessment of the first dozen years of post-communist life in Albania. Extreme changes had occurred over the first decade. These included the privatisation of cooperative land, the closure of factories and mines, massive unemployment and huge demographic movements as mountain dwellers left small infertile plots for the coastal plains, or emigrated. Emigrants' earnings improved the insides of citizens' dwellings, but outside, municipal water and waste systems continued to leak, roads to be potholed and jobs hard to find. Advances achieved by the independent activity of individuals were not matched by government institutions.

Further upheavals included the collapse of pyramid schemes leading to destitution for many, the raiding of arms depots terrorising the whole population, and a continuing exodus. Only the shock therapists could draw satisfaction from this period of turbulence and trauma. They could congratulate themselves that at least none of these events had led to a rise in inflation, that prime concern of foreign advisors such as the IMF and the World Bank.

The question now is how has the second post-communist decade fared? Are state institutions functioning better? Is unemployment decreasing? Can we talk of productivity rather than stagnancy? Between 2003 and 2009 I visited Albania infrequently. In 2009 I was invited to take part in a social impact survey for a hydro-power project proposed by a foreign conglomerate. Returning to the country after an absence heightened my awareness of changes and continuities as I tried to gauge the prevalent mood and to pick up on people's preoccupations. The nearest town to the hydro-power project was Gramsh in the South, where the level of unemployment is one of the highest in the South country. Prime Minister Sali Berisha (head of government from 1992 to 1997, and again since 2004) had negotiated the concession and made much in his 2009 pre-election campaign of the jobs the project would bring to the area. Gramshiots were more than a little sceptical, having been promised several hydro-power projects in the past not one of which had been realised. Emigration has never ceased to be crucial to the economic survival of Gramsh families.

All over the small towns and rural areas of Albania it is men and young nuclear families who have emigrated. The absence for long periods of so many young and middle-aged citizens, and their resultant non-participation in local affairs, has enabled those in power to avoid addressing the causes leading to out-migration. Re-visiting each place (North and South) where I had done fieldwork between 1991 and 2003, it became depressingly clear over the next 15 months that the leading concerns continued to be unemployment, corruption and the paralysis caused by deteriorating roads.

Improvements in relation to regional development, protection of natural resources, agricultural regeneration and infrastructural investment were not in evidence. On the contrary, the forests had been cut down causing serious erosion and flooding; many hectares of arable land lay uncultivated. Infrastructural decay was widespread, with numerous irrigation systems still unrepaired 20 years later, municipal water systems often polluted, and most households still with only sporadic water supply. It seemed there had been more continuity than change. There had been less agitation but stagnancy was still very much the predominant characteristic economically, socially and politically.

Indeed, the political situation perfectly encapsulated the state of stagnancy. A seemingly inescapable stalemate was established following the June 2009 general election, in which the incumbent Democrats and the opposing Socialists won almost exactly the same percentage of the votes. The results were so close that no official announcement could be made for several weeks. Even when the Democrats were declared the winners with 70 seats they were still one short of the 71 needed to govern in the 140 seat Assembly. In the end, Ilir Meta, head of the LSI (Socialist Movement for Integration, formed in 2004, a splinter group from the Socialist Party) and former Socialist Prime Minister,[1] took his party with its four seats over to the Democrats who were thus enabled to form a coalition government. Meta was rewarded with the posts of Deputy Prime Minister and Foreign Secretary. But the allegations of violations and calls for a recount did not go away and from September to February (the deadline for taking oath of office or losing their mandate), the Socialists led by Edi Rama, head of the Party as well as Mayor of Tirana, boycotted Parliament. Since major constitutional reforms cannot be passed without a three-fifths majority vote in parliament, the government was effectively paralysed. The Socialists returned to parliament sporadically after February but continued to demand a recount. In May they mobilised two massive protest rallies each numbering tens of thousands of citizens from all over the country. The first rally was followed by 19 days of hunger strike in which 200 party members and 20 MPs took part, camping in front of the presidential palace in Tirana's central avenue, the Bulevard. Not for the first time, foreign intervention was brought to bear, this time in the form of the Council of Europe, which tried to reconcile the two sides. No agreement was achieved and the political stalemate continued.

While the vote was equally divided between the two main parties, voter turnout had been low at 50.77 per cent. This was attributed by some to the absence of large numbers of emigrants, potential voters. Others saw it as a reflection of widespread disillusion with politicians and the political process. The spectacular levels of corruption in state institutions, the absence of an independent judiciary, the property laws unclear and contradictory, the non-transparent concessions between government and foreign firms, had understandably left much of civil society distrusting the system as well as disempowered. The question arises why wasn't the populace becoming increasingly restive if not downright rebellious? How could either of the main parties retain any support at all? Here it has to be emphasised that both the Democrats and the Socialists (indistinguishable ideologically) have huge organisational and media clout. Both are in a position to peddle political favours to their friends and state jobs to their voters, enriching themselves while perpetuating the political stalemate. But this in itself does not explain why the great majority of the population, effectively disenfranchised with serious reasons for discontent, has not posed a threat to the status quo; everyone can't have state jobs in exchange for votes.

It is estimated that 1.4 million Albanians, equivalent to half Albania's resident population, live abroad.[2] It is this massive volume of emigration, the highest for any post-communist country in Europe, which has enabled the perpetuation of stagnancy. Emigrant remittances underpin the financial survival of the majority of the population, and enable the state – weak and indifferent – to avoid tackling the main obstacles to economic advance. Successive Albanian governments have been able to maintain the status quo without serious investment in job creation, infrastructure or agricultural regeneration. Emigration and remittances have left politicians and bureaucrats free to pursue policies that increase their power and wealth at the expense of national welfare; free to ignore high levels of unemployment and infrastructural deficiencies regarding roads, irrigation systems and railways, without fear of serious social unrest. The very fact that the teacher who can't afford to pay the sum of money necessary to secure a teaching post (standard practice for entering any kind of employment today, including a government ministry post) can leave for Greece to work in an olive processing factory or become a cleaner, means one less protester, one less person unemployed, and undermines any citizen movement for change. So called civil society, even were it less depleted than it is here, has limited capacity to fight against entrenched levels of corruption in state institutions and lacks the mechanisms to drive legal and financial reforms.

On a Tirana-based television channel, Klan, a regular programme, *Opinion*, brings extended interviews with personalities, such as one in October 2010, when Prime Minister Berisha was interviewed for several hours by a well known journalist, Blendi Fevziu. The topic was the past year of Democrat government. Among the issues discussed the Prime Minister was particularly upbeat on the state of the economy, highlighting when challenged, tourism and exports. 'What exports?' demanded Fevziu. The Prime Minister mentioned minerals and textiles. 'Textiles? You mean ready made materials imported to be returned in the form of shoes and clothes,' retorted Fevziu, adding: 'As for tourists, those were mostly holidaying emigrants.'

Berisha's positive spin on the economy was indeed misleading. Tourism is an area constantly talked up by the government as one where investment is bringing economic rewards. Yet, after nearly 20 years, neither the road south from Tirana to Gjirokaster, a Unesco World Heritage Site, nor the road south to the port of Vlora and the coastal resort of Saranda, are motorways. Much more seriously, having finally reached Saranda, one is confronted by the concrete embodiment of state *laissez-faire*, its failure to uphold the rule of law even where national interest – in this case promoting tourism – is at stake. Anarchic building including illegal highrise in Saranda is degrading the very areas at the centre of designated tourism. The tourist on the way from Saranda to the archaeological site of Butrint passes through one time village, now town, of Ksamil, where vast slabs of slumped concrete – the semi-bulldozed houses – are emblematic of the state's unpredictable arbitrary approach: 'Let them build no matter the expense, then we may or we may not, decide to bring in the destroyers'. But that capital lost to the illegal builders in Ksamil, probably savings from work as an emigrant, could have been put to productive use benefiting both the individual and the state.

Unbridled and unregulated building has also occurred in the port of Durrës with its serried ranks of concrete apartment buildings and hotels, large numbers of which are empty and up for sale. Tourist projects such as Kakome, the bay near Saranda to have been developed by the French company Club Med, have been aborted due to property ownership disputes. The state of the property laws – their lack of clarity, contradictions, hiatuses, the blurred line between legal and illegal – is the most serious deterrent to long-term investment local and foreign, in real estate and in agriculture, and seriously holds back productivity.

Another sector with real potential for the economy, but neglected and undeveloped, is agriculture. Over 50 per cent of Albanians are still rurally based. Fifty-eight per cent of employment is generated through agriculture, which, notwithstanding, only contributes 20.6 per cent of GDP.[3] Even in notably fertile areas more fields are uncultivated than planted. In the southern region of Dropull, which borders with Greece, this is largely due to the majority of the population working in Greece. A draft law of 2009 (yet to be enforced) rules that arable land left uncultivated for three successive years shall be transferred to the commune to be rented out and cultivated locally; the owner would receive rent. In the famously fertile Myzeqea, where depopulation is much less than in border regions, the reasons for lack of activity can be traced directly to government indifference. Here there is real potential for productivity, for agriculture-related industry and export. One obstacle to productivity is the small scale of most farms, which makes the costs of production (seed, fertiliser, machinery, petrol) too high for profit. With government support for the setting up of social associations these limitations could be overcome. Difficult access to markets due to poor roads is a problem in some areas of Albania. But even where roads are viable willing buyers are in short supply since imports are cheaper; in the short term the government gains more from taxing imported produce. The small-scale farming family supplies some of its own food needs and does not add to the unemployment figures, but in reality is largely supported by family members working abroad.

Successive governments over the past 20 years have spent more time enriching themselves than developing the economy. The provincial population in particular has been ignored, with *laissez-faire* only occasionally replaced by intervention when for self-serving purposes the State sees the need for action. The following account of post-communist life between 1991 and 2003 is a portrait of change at the individual level and neglect at the top, a situation that persists to this day. Villagers with tiny plots, officially employed according to government statistics, have taken their fate into their own hands by descending to squat on plains or by leaving the country. The hundreds of thousands facing unemployment who left to work abroad have made the State's task easier in every respect. Their exodus has acted as a safety valve against social unrest, as their remittances have underpinned the financial survival of those left behind.

But this convenient safety valve may be about to shut down if growing unemployment abroad, particularly in Greece, forces large numbers of emigrants to return and remittances to drop dramatically. That may prove the much needed catalyst for ending the self-indulgent antics of members of parliament who, sustained by emigrants, have till now enjoyed the luxury of bickering amongst themselves while leaving the country to stagnate.

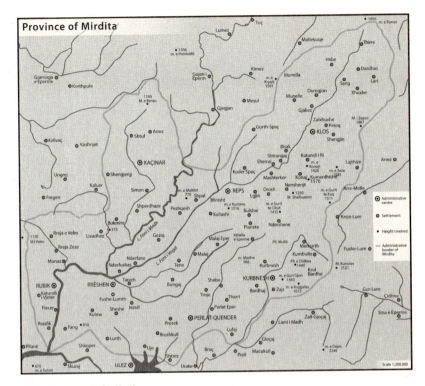

The Province of Mirdita

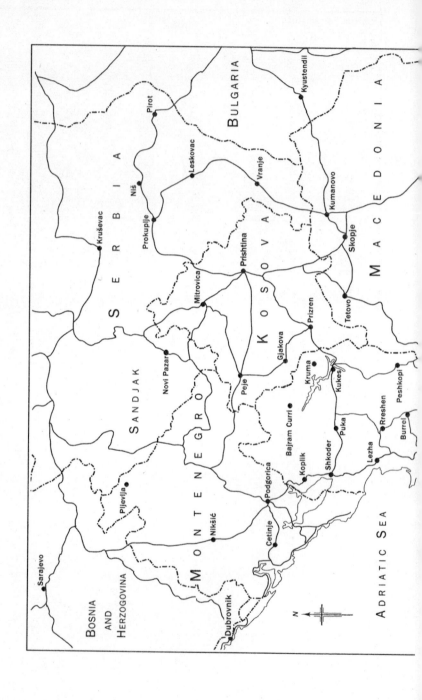

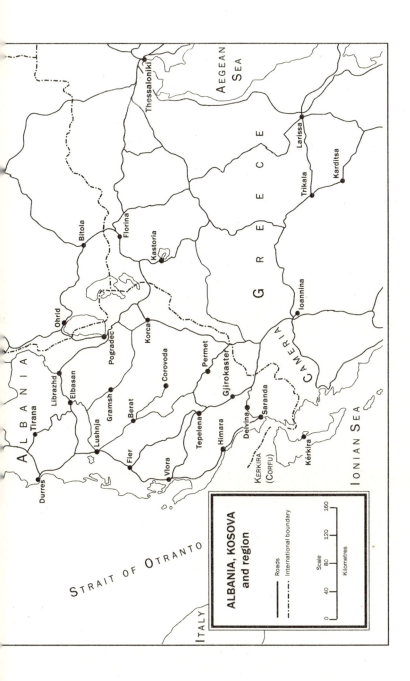

Albania, Kosova and region

Chapter One

INTRODUCTION

i. Doing Ethnography in Albania

T hat must be an anthropologist's paradise,' said a Greek political scientist on hearing that I was working in Albania. The
implication was that formerly isolated and undiscovered Albania
afforded the sort of fieldwork experienced by ethnographers at the
beginning of the twentieth century; the dissolution of the exotic[1]
was not after all complete. The anthropologist George Marcus
discussing early ethnography writes:

> Ethnographies as a genre had similarities with traveller and ex-
> plorer accounts, in which the main narrative motif was the ro-
> mantic discovery by the writer of people and places unknown
> to the reader. To do this, the main motif that ethnography
> as a science developed was that of salvaging cultural diversity,
> threatened with global Westernization, especially during the age
> of colonialism. The current problem is that these motives no
> longer serve well enough to reflect the world in which ethno-
> graphers now work. All peoples are now at least known and
> charted.... (1986:24)

Marcus was writing before the collapse of Communism. Since
1989, Western ethnographers working in the poorer regions of former Socialist Europe have been in a situation which in a number of
respects echoes that of the ethnographers working in the colonial-
ist era. In the early 1990s, numerous foreign 'experts' converged
on Tirana. While they were not colonialists in the sense of holding government positions, they were ideological colonialists come
to teach the locals how to do things the 'right way' according to

the tenets of market fundamentalism. They were extremely highly paid by any standards and stratospherically paid by local standards. Furthermore, they received supplementary pay as Albania was officially a dangerous posting. These experts, some of whom were unscrupulous adventurers, were to assist Albania in the switch from command economy to market capitalism. Their job was to show the locals how to set up institutions, financial and legal, to underpin the changes. Within months, institutions which had taken centuries to build in the West were to be established in a country with hardly an element of capitalist infrastructure – the microwave approach in a country more often than not without electricity.

Attitudes amongst these late twentieth century colonialists towards the locals frequently resembled those of their earlier colonial counterparts; there was a common assumption that isolation from the West meant wholesale ignorance. For instance, many foreigners failed to distinguish between Albania's economic level – on a par with that of some so-called Third World countries – and the educational and cultural (music, art, literature, theatre) standard which was as good or better than that of a number of first world countries. Some American instructors bringing material aid and courses in pedagogy to the University of Tirana and the School of Foreign Languages were surprised to find their instructees skilled typewriter users. 'They thought we lived in trees', several teachers observed bitterly. Similarly, foreign doctors and aid personnel visiting Tirana hospitals were surprised to find that Albanian doctors were well trained. The material conditions might be Third World, but the level of expertise reflected high standards of medical training and practice.

Similarly out of touch were the foreign officials who in the second half of the 1990s were bemoaning Albanians' passivity and aid dependency. This at a time when well over a fifth of the population was working abroad, having had in most cases to overcome the obstacles entailed in illegal status. These 600,000 emigrants were contributing in total at least a million dollars a day in remittances to the Albanian economy (EIU Report, 2000); hardly indicative of passivity or aid dependency. The foreign critics were also ignoring the large numbers of mountain villagers descending to the coastal plains in order to lay the foundations, at least for their children, for prospects unrealisable in remote villages where land and water are inadequate and services non-existent. Of course, as handers out of investment funds and organisers of aid programmes, foreign officials are exposed to individuals who treat the programmes as bandwagons to be jumped on, as opportunities to line their pockets – though even this kind of response suggests activity rather than passivity. That vast amounts of aid investment have sunk without trace or infrastructural improvement is only too true. But it is a consequence of corruption, the absence of an adequate infrastructure to channel aid, and grossly inadequate controls on the part of donors, rather than local passivity.

There were further reasons why the Greek professor was right about the attractions for an ethnographer in Albania. In areas where change is occurring less dramatically, people are often puzzled as to how their lives could be of interest to a researcher. Albanians catapulted from one extreme situation to another saw every reason to be researched. Yes, they would say, what *is* happening to us, how *are* we responding? The nature and effects of these revolutionary social, economic and political changes on their daily lives were quite as interesting to them as to me. Furthermore, many people in Mirdita, the northern region where the greater part of my fieldwork was carried out, saw my research as a means to keeping a record of themselves over this period, a record for the future – 'one forgets so fast, but now it will be written down.' This is of course dangerous ground, as another American anthropologist, James Clifford, is at pains to make clear. He questions the assumption that with rapid change something essential vanishes and is sceptical about the 'mode of scientific and moral authority associated with salvage ethnography', arguing that it assumes the other society is weak and needs to be represented by an outsider.[2] However, he does accept the value of recording disappearing customs in specific cases. In the early post-communist years in Albania it was not a case of an illiterate population whose 'vanishing lore' was being 'salvaged' by a literate anthropologist. The situation was that of a literate population whose desire, according to the Mirditans, was to record a process as it unfolded because memory is unreliable, selective or simply fails; an exercise that might even illuminate the dynamics of social change. The knowledge that there are other people and accounts, equally or better informed must have the salutary effect of increasing the ethnographer's efforts to record as carefully as possible. Where social process is as agitated as in 1990s Albania, the more records from as many angles as possible, economic, political, social, or autobiographical, diary or letters, the more likely we are to make sense of subsequent developments. Rather than imputing weakness or the 'need' for an outsider, the ethnographer's study offers one point of view amongst others.

At the same time, 'romantic discovery by the writer of people and places unknown to the reader' *is* an aspect of doing ethnography in Albania. A country, which has been cut off from the rest of the world for 50 years, *does* have the charm of the undiscovered. The self-imposed isolation, the retention of most of the population in rural areas, the distinctive economic development, did result, particularly amongst the rural majority, in a lifestyle that is unfamiliar to Western Europeans. While rural customs have naturally undergone changes since they were recorded in the nineteenth and early twentieth century by observers such as Nopsca, Hahn and Edith Durham, customary behaviour in the 1990s did strike the Western European ethnographer as exotic; did, in Gellner's phrase, 'titillate our cognitive voyeurism'.[3] Indeed, a common complaint directed by Albanian intellectuals towards foreign writing over the last two centuries centres on foreigners' preoccupation with exoticism. 'Why do they always write about blood feuds, about sworn virgins dressed as men, about the Kanun (customary law), about the rarified aspects of Albanian life? Why don't they write about more important, more central contemporary issues?'

Literature on less exotic topics does of course exist, and the more mundane nature of its content probably accounts for its lesser impact on public consciousness. But there is some justice in the criticism, which could also be applied to 1990s aid agencies and foreign advisers whose focus on the exotic obscured, sometimes with fatal consequences, less obvious but more fundamental problems. In the early 1990s it was usual to hear visiting experts delighting in what they described as the 'incredible laboratory experiment' presented by the Albanian economy. Admiration for the 'miraculous' results of shock therapy and liberalisation policies – low inflation, stable currency, fast growth – seemed to blind the experts to the government's failure to create jobs within the country, to the dependence on (illegal)[4] emigrants' remittances, to the absence of a financial infrastructure. In 1996, only a few months before the collapsing pyramid schemes precipitated a revolt leading to a complete breakdown of law and order, loss of government control and the country's bankruptcy, the World Bank had reported that Albania was a small haven of peace and economic growth.

With a similar lack of attention to underlying factors, foreign aid organisations set up conflict resolution centres and funded courses to try and eradicate blood feuds, which they had identified as a significant social problem. The courses aimed to teach democratic culture, mediation techniques and forgiveness therapy. Well-meaning foreign purveyors of reconciliation attended exotically archaic peace-making ceremonies between feuding families. Shrewd locals were not slow to join this income-generating bandwagon. Unfortunately, representatives of conflict resolution organisations did not investigate the practical sources of disputes such as the hiatus in property legislation – one of the commonest causes of conflict. There was also serious concern amongst organisation members that feuds were preventing boys from attending school. Young males forced to stay indoors for fear of revenge killing are, however, a tiny percentage of those who stay away from school because education has reached a nadir, or because they are having to earn on city streets. In a word, the problems arising from blood feuds are insignificant compared with the problems arising from large-scale unemployment, inadequate legislation, an ineffective police force and demotivated and unqualified school teachers. Blood feuds occur precisely in those areas where unemployment and land and water shortage are most acute, just one symptom of the real problem.[5]

Those aspects of Albanian life that are exotic to an outsider – marriage customs, funeral rites, cradle betrothals, intergenerational behaviour, blood feud, Kanun laws – were the very features targeted with some justification by the communist authorities as 'backward' customs that must be eradicated. However, at the same time as condemning custom and tradition as hostile to communist ideals, a degree of ambivalence towards customary behaviour allowed for its study in the form of '*etnologjia*'. Ethnology was an officially valued discipline initially under the auspices of the Institute of History within the National Academy of Sciences, later a body in its own right called the Institute of Popular Culture. This ambivalence meant that the ethnologist had to walk a tightrope, conveying the richness of Albanian custom which was to the credit of the people, while making clear that all the enlightened members of rural

society had abandoned this archaic *modus vivendi* now that Socialism was their guiding light. Thus, in the journal *Etnografia
Shqiptare*, interspersed between extremely interesting material on
local customs, one typically reads comments such as: 'quite a lot of
the Kanun's norms despite their anachronistic character – the result
of socio-economic relations – clearly expressed the Albanian people's vitality, unconquerable fighting spirit, self-governing skill and
high morals'(1985, ch.9, vol.14). This, given that even mention of
the Kanun in those areas where it had been followed could lead to
imprisonment, was bold. In contrast to the ethnologists forced to
present customary practices ideologically at odds with Socialism
as indicators of a region's earlier 'creative individuality and vibrant
life', folklore festivals were straightforward celebrations of national
pride. A pan-Albanian folklore festival was held every five years
in the southern town of Gjirokastër to which groups from all over
Albania came to compete for the honour of coming first. The festival celebrated the diversity of regional differences in music, dance
and costume wholesomely detached from any 'backward' practices
prevalent in the areas that had produced them. Ironically, archaic
customs and rituals continued unabated through the 1990s when
the folklore festival was on hold.

ii. The 1990s backdrop to the lives of this book's protagonists

The end of Communism

For anyone interested in development, by which I mean the process
of changing economic, political and social conditions, the former
communist countries from Europe to Central Asia provide fertile ground for research. Albania, in particular, whose economy
at the beginning of the 1990s was on a par with that of some
Third World countries despite its situation near the centre of Europe, has been characterised by extremes for the past half century.
Enver Hoxha's dictatorship was the most consistently Stalinist of
the socialist regimes in Europe and, together with that of Romania's, the most brutal. Centralisation was maximal, politically and
economically. Isolation from the outside world, ignorance by the
populace of internal affairs were achieved by a combination of draconian restrictions on movement and a government stranglehold on

the dissemination of information. The introduction through shock therapy to capitalism was equally extreme, exposing the population to massive unemployment, uncontrolled demographic movement and a degree of government *laissez-faire* hard to distinguish from economic and judicial anarchy.

Albania was the last of the European socialist countries to break with Communism. From late 1989, unrest began in the form of strikes, student protests, street demonstrations and, at the end of 1990, mass protests and food riots. The larger protests were suppressed with troops, but bloodshed and loss of life were the exception. Ramiz Alia, Hoxha's successor, had recognised the need early in 1990 for the introduction of measures that for the first time permitted a degree of pluralism and a modicum of free enterprise. These measures included the legalising of political demonstrations, a law allowing for secret ballot and the possibility for independent candidates to stand against those of the party. After two days of mass protests at the end of 1990, Alia's government announced that independent political parties would be allowed, while a number of party hardliners including Hoxha's widow were dismissed from their posts. Some of the very large number of political prisoners were released from prison. Diplomatic links were re-established with the USSR, USA, and some EU countries. Citizens for the first time had the right to a passport (in theory at least), while unauthorised emigration ceased to be a capital offence. Economic changes included some modification to central planning allowing for limited private enterprise. Villagers were now officially allowed to cultivate small plots of land and it was no longer an offence for a producer to sell agricultural surplus. The ban on religion, in place since 1967, was lifted.

These reforms undoubtedly helped reduce pressures and tensions from exploding into an outright revolution. The massive exodus occurring over this period, mainly to the neighbouring countries, Greece and Italy, was an additional safety valve. This was an exodus without parallel in any of the other former communist countries. The most visible exoduses were in July 1990, when several thousand Albanians took refuge in foreign embassies in Tirana, and from March to August 1991, when boats almost submerged by dense crowds of shabbily dressed Albanians, crossed the Adriatic to Italy. Over the same period, thousands of Albanian men walked across the mountains from southern Albania into northern Greece.

Economic breakdown manifested in the empty shops and queues for official food rations was clearly the chief trigger for this exodus. At the same time, the psychological legacy of half a century of incarceration must have been a factor. For the first time it was possible to leave the country without facing border guards with orders to shoot to kill. There was at last an opportunity to see for oneself the Western world hitherto secretly glimpsed on forbidden Italian television channels; a world where private individuals could own cars, shop at well-stocked supermarkets and wear nice clothes.

A series of letters was published in 1996 in a book called *Kapërcyell* – Transition. The author, a school teacher named Meri Lalaj from the southeastern town of Pogradec on the shore of Lake Ohrid, recounts many of the events that occurred over this period when the one-party state was breaking up. She recalls how in December, 1989, Albanians watching television shed tears of sympathy as Romanian women queued for bread. But, she notes less sympathetically, Romanian women were wearing smart clothes, fur coats and warm boots 'while we were dressed like men in drab shapeless garments' (1996:10). In Albania food shortages dominated daily life. Lalaj records that buying a litre of milk involved starting to queue at midnight. In July 1990, a friend of Lalaj, after agonising all night decided that her two sons, aged 20 and 23, should seek asylum in the German Embassy where they joined hundreds of others hoping to be be granted asylum in Germany.

Meri Lalaj's daughter was studying Albanian Language and Literature at the University of Tirana at this time. In October, 1990, students in her faculty demanded that the lecture series on Enver Hoxha's works be removed from the curriculum. In December, protests began against conditions in the Student City where there was no heating, and constant power cuts. On 8 December, students held a meeting to commemorate the tenth anniversary of John Lennon's death. A speaker began by saying: 'At last the day has come in Albania when we can listen to the Beatles at full volume, not secretly with the volume turned down to the minimum.' As Lalaj notes, Albanian citizens had actually been imprisoned on the charge of having listened to, or dared to record, Beatles songs.

In March 1991, the first democratic general election in Albania's history was won by the Communists. The main opposition party, the Democrats, had a majority vote in the towns, but rural inhabitants, 65 per cent of the population, less exposed to the Democrats' campaign and unsure as to the Democrats' policies on land, voted for the Communists. However, the victorious Communist government was forced to resign in June as strikes, demonstrations, riots and – the *coup de grace* – a general strike, threatened complete economic breakdown. An interim coalition government was established with Communist, Democrat and three smaller parties represented. This coalition government succeeded in introducing some effective laws for the privatisation of land, but in the meantime the country's whole production system had begun to collapse. Furthermore, an orgy of vandalism across the country had damaged cooperative buildings and destroyed irrigation systems, greenhouses, orchards and vineyards. The serious weakening of law and order was further manifested in increasing incidents of lootings and robberies.

Finally, in March 1992, yet another election took place, which this time was won with a clear majority by the Democrats who remained in power until the revolution of 1997. Western financial aid and admission to organisations such as the IMF, the World Bank and the European Bank for Reconstruction and Development followed. Distribution of humanitarian aid from the industrialised states, G24, had already begun the previous autumn, under the auspices of the Italian government's Operation Pelikan.

The Beginning of Democracy

Democracy brought changes that were no less radical than those experienced under Enver Hoxha, beginning with decollectivisation and the introduction of free market capitalism. Burawoy and Verdery's robust critique of shock therapy in the introduction to their book *Uncertain Transition* provides a pertinent commentary: 'It is neoliberalism's pious hope that destruction is the vehicle for genesis' (1999:5). In Albania where shock therapy replaced Ramiz Alia's attempts at gradual economic and political reforms, the destruction, which took place in 1991–2, must have gladdened the hearts (if they have any) of the shock therapists who advised the government on economic policy. It was a satisfyingly comprehensive orgy of destruction, which razed orchards and vineyards to the ground, vandalised cooperative buildings and machinery, smashed thousands of greenhouses and irrigation systems and broke factory and apartment building windows. 'Starting from zero' was exactly the catch phrase enthusiastically invoked by the vandals; others, less sanguine than the shock therapy theorists, wondered how without infrastructure and bankrupt the country could possibly get back on its feet. With no opportunities for work in the wake of this destruction and the closure of factories and mines, it is not clear what form of genesis or income generation the shock therapists had in mind for the vast numbers of unemployed. They seem to have been more concerned with the inflation figures than with the jobless humans.

While emigration continued to be the main key to income generation, the initial negative reaction was gradually replaced by a much more constructive popular response to change, and a realisation that to progress 'we must do it ourselves rather than wait for government action'. This was partly the result of a growing consciousness that the state was too weak to be depended on. The despondent phrase '*ska shtet, ska ligj*' (there is no state, there is no law) was heard increasingly often from 1993 onwards as miscarriages of justice increased and hiatuses in the legal system remained unaddressed. No doubt, the experience of the strong hand of the former regime intensified the public's perception of weakness in their post-communist governments. But as the historian Eric Hobsbawm noted at the end of the 1990s in a discussion of the future of the State as an institution: 'It is not clear to what extent we can talk today of a functional state in Albania. The contrast is surprising because, whether we like it or not, there was a state in Albania until the demise of Communism' (2000:36). The refrain '*ska shtet*' in the 1990s may have reflected an element of 'we miss the draconian rule of a police state' but as the years of Democrat rule went by the judgement proved accurate enough. Under Hoxha, life was unpredictable and cruel to those who were seen as a threat to the totalitarian state. The State took a fairly casual attitude to the physical welfare of those who worked in factories and mines, and a ruthless one towards *persona non grata* and workers in forced labour camps. Nevertheless, for the majority, monotony was the dominant feature mitigated by security; employment and modest income could be counted on, as could public safety. Young girls, it is repeatedly claimed, could walk alone across the country at night without fear, so effective was the arm of the law.

In the 1990s, the population's perception of government weakness proved increasingly well founded despite the Democrats' attempt to portray neglect, indifference and inability to control as deliberate *laissez-faire*. As well as failing to organise emigration or tackle corruption and crime, the Democrat government took no steps to organise the growing demographic trend to descend from mountain regions to the coastal plains. In 1995, President Berisha made his '*fytyre nga deti*' (faces towards the sea) proclamation, officially recommending what was already a *fait accompli*. This was a feeble attempt to present the unstoppable bid for economic survival by mountain villagers descending to squat on coastal plains as if it were part of a state instigated programme. The subsequent absence of measures to regulate this influx was defended as a freedom of movement policy (*lëvizje e lirë*), intentionally *laissez-faire*.

By contrast and concurrent with this proclaimed 'freedom', the population had been aware for some time of a creeping policy of intervention leading to the gradual erosion of democratic government. From 1993–4, President Berisha's intolerance of difference of opinion had led to the dismissal of some of his most able advisers. In 1994, the move away from democratic government was manifested in the unconstitutional removal of the head of the judiciary, his replacement by a government yes-man, and by increasing government censorship of radio and television. At the same period, the degree of corruption at ministerial and local government levels was becoming the source of widespread concern and growing cynicism on the part of the population. The referendum held in the autumn of 1994 proposed a new constitution. Despite their limited experience of democracy, the population rejected the constitution on the well-founded grounds that it gave the President excessive decision-making powers. A response that suggests that 50 years of totalitarianism need not lead to ignorance of democratic principles; not, at least, on the part of the populace.

In 1995, a law misleadingly named the Genocide Law was passed. Accusations were not limited to alleged killings, but covered crimes from espionage to having held the post of Minister of Education. The law banned all top communist officials, members of pre-1991 governments and collaborators with the secret police from public office for six years. Berisha, who had been an active member of the Party of Labour and Party Secretary, was unaffected because 'party secretary' was not one of the offices specified. The Genocide Law was transparently a means of purging non-supporters.

In May 1996 the General Election results awarded the Democrat Party a massive majority belying the results of the referendum. The outcome was criticised at the time by the US government, which believed the results to have been manipulated. Europe's reaction, by contrast, was largely supportive of the Democrats, leading to a loss of faith by many Albanians in the European Union's democratic credentials. It was widely felt that cynical political and commercial interests underlay European support. The European Union's conviction that Berisha was the best option for political security in the Balkans notwithstanding his cavalier attitude to democratic procedures engendered a feeling of helplessness amongst many Albanians. These feared that the country would be trapped into years of government by unprincipled individuals whose *laissez-faire* policies provided the freedom to act illegally with impunity, while failing to protect honest citizens from crime and corruption.

The Economy under the Democrats

The income that sustained the country from 1991 onwards came from three main sources: foreign aid, emigration and sanctions busting (arms and petrol smuggling to Serbia and Montenegro with government connivance). Much the most significant source from the majority of the population's point of view was emigrant remittances which, unlike foreign aid and income from sanctions busting, went direct to emigrants' families enabling them to survive in the face of large-scale unemployment and frequent price rises. These remittances, estimated at up to $500 million a year rising to $600 million at the end of the 1990s (Economist Intelligence Unit, 2000), represented the bulk of the country's legitimate income; though because there was no official emigration policy, the source of this legitimate income was largely illegal emigrant labour (70–80 per cent of emigrants had no legal status at the end of the 1990s). The absence of an organised emigration policy was one of the earliest and most persistent sources of resentment towards the government. From the government's point of view, *laissez-faire* meant that Albanians continued to emigrate illegally in large numbers, sustaining the domestic economy and keeping serious discontent by the unemployed at bay. Large-scale emigration obviated the need for policies on regional development, job creation or agricultural infrastructure. The friction it caused between the Albanian government and neighbouring countries was containable. Capture and expulsion by Greek or Italian police led to nothing more apparently serious than repeated clandestine returns by the workers. But resentment on the part of emigrants, particularly long-term ones, grew with each year spent abroad. They saw their illegal status benefiting the economies of both sending and receiving countries while contributing little more than hand-to-mouth subsistence to their families' welfare. As well as exploitative pay and lack of access to social benefits, health insurance or pensions, workers ran the risk of robbery, often with violence, every time they returned home. As illegal workers they could not invest their savings abroad and there was no system enabling them to transfer earnings to banks at home. Moreover, once at home, the inadequate financial infrastructure precluded safe investment within the country.

This situation was a major contributor to the widespread participation in the pyramid schemes whose ultimate collapse led to loss of state control in 1997. A pyramid scheme like the largest, Vefa Holdings, which offered a monthly interest rate of 8–10 per cent and was known to have connections with government interests, was seen to be as good a bet as putting the foreign earnings under the mattress. There was no functioning stock exchange and no private banks. Advice on setting up a business enterprise was almost unobtainable, and raising a loan or supplementary capital from an official organisation automatically entailed giving the official arranging the loan a substantial percentage of the sum borrowed. Furthermore, long-term productive enterprises of a kind to benefit the economy as a whole were far less likely to get loans than quick returns businesses such as buying and selling imports. From 1995, active Socialists and their relations became ineligible for loans. Thus, importers of capital accumulated from five years' earnings abroad were at a loss as to how best to use it once back home, particularly if they already owned an apartment.

At the same time, ironically, the Democrat government's uncritical embracing of 'shock therapy' and 'liberalisation' policies had earned it glowing reports from the IMF and World Bank. These institutions' admiration of the country's economic growth, low inflation and stable currency, seemed to have blinded them to the fact that economic growth was not reducing unemployment; that many products, food and clothing, for example, which could have been produced within the country were being imported; that growth was measured from the economic nadir of 1991. Neither the sources of economic growth, nor the undeveloped state of the country's financial infrastructure, seemed to alarm the foreign financial organisations.

Revolt

In the second fortnight of January 1997, following the collapse of several pyramid schemes, there were anti-government demonstrations all over Albania. The unrest rapidly escalated into serious riots in which protesters set fire to public buildings, ransacked town halls, courthouses, police stations and state banks, and destroyed thousands of official documents. There were pitched battles in several towns between the police and the people. By the end of January the country was almost out of control. Listening to the BBC World Service at this period, if one missed the beginning it was hard to tell whether Albania or Zaire was under discussion. In early February, government measures included mass arrests, brutal beatings and the banning of protest demonstrations. On 2 March the government declared a state of emergency and a curfew was imposed. In the South, arms depots were looted. The following day the Tirana offices of the main opposition newspaper, *Koha Jonë*, were set fire to and members of staff fired at by the secret police. Official censorship was imposed on 4 March outlawing foreign radio and television news programmes. The ruling Democrat Party declared that responsibility for the breakdown of law and order lay primarily with foreign interference; in particular with the BBC, the Voice of America, and the 'communist' English newspaper, The *Independent*. A curfew was introduced and tanks replaced normal traffic on the streets. Thousands of Albanians fled or attempted to flee on boats to Italy. By the eighth, the whole of southern Albania was outside government control and the southern towns had set up their own governments known as Salvation Committees. The European powers became sufficiently alarmed to take action and the former Austrian Chancellor, Franz Vranitsky, arrived in the role of mediator. An interim government, the Government of National Reconciliation, with members from all political parties, was established on 9 March. On the same day, civilians were ordered to hand over their weapons by the end of a week. Instead, all the arms depots in the north were raided and by mid-March every family was armed. On the 13th the prisons opened releasing criminals, political prisoners and the future Socialist government leader, Fatos Nano, jailed in 1993 for alleged embezzlement of foreign aid.

The immediate cause of the initial riots was the collapse of two of the biggest pyramid schemes based in the South. Large numbers of Albanians (as well as some foreigners) had put money into the schemes and many lost everything, including in some cases their apartments, sold to increase investment capital. Reporters and analysts were astonished by what they saw as incredible naivety on the part of the pyramid scheme participants. Some concluded that people had fallen for the schemes because they had grown up in a country innocent of capitalism, lacking financial *savoir faire*. A misconception that ignored the fact that some Albanians including government ministers, profited handsomely, and that plenty of people in capitalist systems, have been similarly conned. The Titan Business Club, for instance, was outlawed in England in 1996, after 13,000 British savers had collectively lost £25 million to its organisers.

The main factors that explain the widespread participation in the schemes were, as noted above, the dearth of alternative income generating possibilities within Albania, itself linked to the absence of a financial infrastructure. The duration of the pyramid schemes over a much longer period than could logically be expected given the nature of such schemes, encouraged people to believe the part truth that some schemes actually had some productive investments. More reassuring still was the well-founded belief by many that the schemes had a base in illegal activities of a highly profitable nature such as arms, drugs and people smuggling. Indisputably, the port of Vlora, as the point of departure for illegal immigrants such as Kurds and Albanians trying to get into the European labour market via Italy, was home to some very rich profiteers. Boat owners (*skafiste*) involved in clandestinely shipping people made huge profits, which formed part of the basis for the southern pyramid schemes and help explain the schemes' long duration. Furthermore, in March 1996, two months before the General Election, President Berisha exempted the pyramids from a banking law, which would have regulated them. In July and August 1996, when growing competition between the schemes would naturally have led to their collapse, the Democrat Party intervened to sustain them. To prevent a massive withdrawal, the myth was promoted that the Democrat Party was an official sponsor, leading investors to believe the schemes were safe. This despite the fact that the Central Albanian bank had demanded the closure of the schemes, and despite the astronomically high interest rates that newer schemes were led to offer in an attempt to oust rivals from the scene.

Reporters and analysts initially interpreted the riots and subsequent anarchy as a response specifically to the fall of the pyramid schemes. In fact, government *laissez-faire*, corruption and indifference to democratic principles had been building up public anger and resentment for much longer than the lifetime of these schemes. The rigged election of 1996, seen by many as the *coup de grâce* for democracy, was a turning point. The fall of the pyramid schemes was a catalyst for a revolt that would have eventually occurred in any case. It was the beginning of a second attempt by the Albanian people to establish democracy.

International peace-keeping troops began to arrive in April 1997, their lack of mandate to do more than be present causing them to be nicknamed 'the world's most expensive tourists'. A new general election was held in June 1997, despite innumerable setbacks and well-founded doubts that it would be held at all (I was present as a media monitor and election observer). It was as democratic as was possible under the circumstances and rekindled hopes for democratic government, economic development and the establishment of law and order.

Despite a brief period of optimism, however, it was clear by the beginning of 1998 that law and order were not under control, nor was the campaign against corruption succeeding. In September 1998, the murder of a member of the Democrat Party, Azem Hajdari, was used as a pretext for an attempted coup détat by the former President, Berisha, now head of the opposition. Fortunately, he succeeded in little more than a few hours take over of the radio and television building.[6] The international community sent representatives to ensure that order was restored, and the head of the Socialist Party was replaced by a man too young to have been 'tainted' by a communist past – the 30 year old Pandeli Majko.

In the spring of 1999, Albania's role in the Kosovo crisis, the readiness to respond unstintingly, the enormous generosity towards so many refugees, brought international acclaim. But once the crisis was over, the flatness of unemployment, the absence of *përspektivë* (prospects) hit the population with even more force than before. The hope engendered by international attention during the war had nothing more to feed on. The dreariness of daily privations reasserted itself. A news item on television in October 1999 struck me as typifying this dismalness. It was announced that the body of a 25–30 year old man drowned off the coast of Vlora had been found and brought to the morgue. The body had not yet been identified. Details were supplied: brown hair, dressed in blue jeans, height, etc. With no change in tone, the newsreader concluded: 'The refrigerator in the morgue is not working.'

iii. Agitated Stagnancy

Ecim, por jo përpara – We're moving but not advancing

'Did you have electricity?' was one of the first questions Millennium celebrators asked each other on 1 January 2000. Every so often in 1999, cheers could be heard in apartment blocks when after several days without water or electricity, these were obtainable again. Albanians would then ask themselves: 'Where are we that we cheer when such basics are restored? Who could have guessed that after eight years of democracy we would be without regular supplies of water and light, without decent roads, without law and order?' The questions that citizens ask themselves daily, which journalists repeatedly ask in the press, are: why after a decade of huge foreign investment have the conditions of daily public life not improved? Why is unemployment still massive? Why are there still constant power cuts? Why is the water supply still wholly inadequate in towns? Why are city streets full of mud and national roads nearly impassable with unmended potholes? Why is violent crime still so common? One common response is once again to cry '*ska shtet, ska ligj*', there is no state, there is no law. The other response is to fill in the form for the Green Card lottery or to risk death by drowning and pay for a place in one of the motor boats (*motoskafe, gomones*) that take people across the Adriatic to Shengen and work.

The trajectory of change has been clear enough. Thanks to emigrant remittances, life inside most flats and some rural houses has become more comfortable with the acquisition of new sofa beds, television, washing machines, fridges, electric cookers and radiators. But while families with members abroad can afford to improve some aspects of their indoor standard of living, the public side of life, the leaking municipal water and waste systems, the overloaded degraded electrical network, is outside their control. The roads, likewise inadequately maintained and unreconstructed, have deteriorated fast under the impact of a massive influx of cars. Since large portions of foreign aid and investment for the renewal and improvement of infrastructure have more often than not been embezzled or spent on substandard materials; the municipal systems, telephone networks and roads, serve citizens less well today than a decade ago. Communications, road, rail and telephone, were literally worse throughout the 1990s than they had been under Communism.

Opportunities for legal income generation within the country have decreased as have salaries in relation to the cost of living. Old age pensions[7] in 1999 were worth half their 1990 value thanks to the huge increase in the cost of living. Unemployment nationwide is at the very least 30 per cent; a more realistic figure for some areas is nearer 50 per cent. This would include the many villagers who, though counted as employed in government statistics because they have land, are in fact unemployed since their land is less than 200sq.m and/or without irrigation, without fertiliser. About a quarter of the population each year, 150,000 families, receives welfare benefits without which they could not survive. In August, 2000, the daily newspaper, *Koha Jonë* (at the time generally supportive of the socialist government in power), reported that in the southern town of Gramsh, 48 per cent of the population were officially unemployed. The non-creation of legal work opportunities means that more and more towns and villages are supported by emigrants. A recent initiative in 'private' work creation near another southern town, Berat, took the form of charging a bridge-crossing toll at a bridge, which is not even on the toll charger's land. Long established 'private' work creation includes: growing fields of marijuana for export; selling girls for prostitution; drug dealing; holding up and robbing buses or cars; falsifying visas and property claims documents; trafficking in people wanting to emigrate; and selling counterfeit telephone cards. In short, we are looking at a population that has far too few legitimate means of livelihood within the country and very little prospect of improvement. Every single Albanian cannot leave the country, but most would if they could.

Despite efforts at the beginning of the twenty-first century to crack down on corruption, judges and building inspectors can still be bribed or threatened, criminals can still pay their way out of prison. Certain banks accept millions of dollars in cash without asking any questions; university faculty deans may take bribes from parents of under qualified students. None of these phenomena is peculiar either to Albania, developing democracies or areas of extreme poverty. Establishing the independence of institutions such as the judiciary and the police has yet to be fully achieved in other parts of Europe. Corruption on a massive scale, as has recently been brought home to the USA and Britain, is alive and well in long established wealthy democracies, viz WorldCom and Enron. But the impact of corruption in a small poor country with a weak government and very high unemployment is more pernicious. An article by the economist Paul Krugman on corruption in several American states (July 2002, *New York Times*) makes the point for the American scene. Reviewing dishonest budgeting in New Jersey, Tennessee and Alabama, Krugman comments that:

> in recent years many states have been run like banana republics. Responsibility gave way to political opportunism, and in some cases to mob rule. The only reason Tennessee doesn't look like Argentina right now is that it isn't a sovereign nation; since the federal budget was in good shape until recently, there's a safety net. And the federal budget was in pretty good shape because the Clinton administration, unlike state governments, behaved responsibly. Budget projections were honest – if anything, too cautious – and boom-year surpluses were used to reduce debt. . . . Now the same governing style has moved to Washington. And this time there's no safety net.

As well as no safety net in Albania, its small size makes those who get rich illicitly more obvious to their fellow citizens. The injustice and consequent economic polarisation lowers morale and ultimately erodes all faith in the country's institutions.

Emigration, Emigration, Emigration

There have been myriad changes since 1991, but as the above indicates, these have not been paralleled by the economic and political progress post-communist Albanians had hoped for. Unsurprisingly, on each occasion when the post office has monitored the US Green Card lottery applications, the numbers have been very high. In October 1999, an article in the newspaper *Gazeta Shqiptare* noted that in the southern town of Gjirokastër post office workers reported applications for the Green Card lottery as running at one thousand a week. Post office officials added ruefully that the actual number of applicants was probably even larger since many applicants would have posted their applications in Greece, having no faith in the Albanian postal system.[8] The weekly magazine *Klan*, 10 October 1999, quoted the Tirana post office statistics: in the first three days of October four thousand Green Card applications passed through the Tirana office. This, the post office pointed out, did not include any applications posted outside Tirana where the economic level is even lower and hence the urge to leave still greater. This exodus, as the writer of the *Klan* article[9] concluded, may be a more individual way of leaving the country than in 1991 when hordes swarmed on to boats, but it reflects exactly the same wish – to leave. 'Now we have finally lost faith in the country's ability to govern effectively',[10] many of my friends repeatedly declared in the autumn of 1999; 'we'd be better off becoming a protectorate.'

The statistician, Professor Ilia Telo, Director of the Institute of Labour of the Community of Independent Trade Unions, estimates that the Albanian emigration rate has been three times as high as that of the highest rate in other former communist countries in Europe (1998:183). The humour section in the daily newspaper, *Koha Jonë* (*Our Time*), on Sunday 11 July 1999, contained this telling anecdote:

The Minister of Labour and Emigration is speaking at a cabinet meeting. He assures the prime minister, Majko, that his ministry is doing its utmost as far as employment goes: 'The motor boats in Vlora are working to capacity transporting emigrants abroad, with the help of course of the Italian Guardia di Finanza. Large numbers of Greek employers in cooperation with our own are enabling emigrants to set off to work in Greece. If there were more visas, more Albanians would be able to work abroad. Thus our Ministry throughout this period has found employment abroad for thousands of Albanians. Our aim has been that no-one should be put to work within the country. And this objective has been realised.' 'Brilliant!' says Majko. 'That shows that my government works night and day for this brave, peace-loving people.'

iv. Fieldwork

Following a brief visit to southern Albania in December 1991, I began fieldwork proper in August 1992, basing myself in Tirana for several months. From 1993 to 1996 I focused mainly on rural Albania because this was the scene of the most radical changes – decollectivisation of land and, subsequently, massive outmigration. Starting literally from the ground up was rewarding because land privatisation was naturally at the forefront of villagers' interest. They were more than ready to talk about a process that affected their lives so directly. Comparing the decollectivisation process in different areas gave me an insight into the very divergent nature of Albania's different regions, both in terms of landscape and cultural character. At first it was difficult to decide where to carry out long-term fieldwork for this very reason; every region was distinctive and fascinating. In the end, I decided to concentrate my research in the north-central province of Mirdita, a province at once economically representative of Albania's poorer regions and one of exceptional cultural continuity and ethnographic interest.

For logistical reasons I worked in several different villages staying with families on a sort of rota basis. What I may have lost as regards a more comprehensive knowledge of each village's population, I gained by acquiring a picture that I could see was representative of Mirditan rural life and developing trends. Since I continued throughout the decade to visit the villages I had got to know initially, I also gained a longitudinal perspective on the impact of economic and demographic change on each community.

Through the ethnography based on this fieldwork I have tried to convey the social process experienced by Albanians during the first decade of post-communism. On the one hand, I was concerned with the effects that the policies and events outlined above were having on households' and individuals' daily lives and survival strategies. On the other, I wanted to provide an ethnographic record of customary practice in a province notable for its cultural continuity where customary behaviour is of outstanding interest.

The basis for customary behaviour and tribal law in the northern mountains up until the communist period had been the body of customary law known as the Kanun of Lek Dukagjin. Seen by the communist government as a symbol of subversion and resistance, the Kanun was outlawed and even reference to the Kanun by locals in those areas where it had been practised could lead to imprisonment. When decollectivisation began, Kanun laws relating to land rights and conflict resolution (inapplicable during the regime) were reintroduced. At the beginning of my fieldwork, a time of economic upheaval, state weakness and legal insecurity, this code of traditional practice acted to some degree as a stabilising factor. But by 1996 when law and order nationwide had been increasingly eroded by government corruption, unemployment and deteriorating communications, traditional law had itself lost its original force. Outmigration was fragmenting village populations, weakening traditional institutions. In particular, community opinion – 'what will people say?' (*opinioni*), arguably the most effective institution of all-had lost its power as village populations diminished. This period, 1996–7 saw the rise and fall of the pyramid schemes culminating in a complete breakdown of both traditional and state law and order.

Between 1997 and the end of 1998, I spent less time in villages, partly because entire village families were beginning to move down to coastal plains or towns, partly because at that period getting to some of the villages was less safe. I concentrated more of my fieldwork on Rrëshen, Mirdita's main town, and on a squatter settlement near the port town of Durrës. Rrëshen was interesting as an example of the unreconstructed nature of state employment. At the same time, it was a stimulating place to work thanks to its large concentration of intellectuals including writers, teachers and doctors, whose resilience in the face of frequent setbacks continues to be notable, as does their commitment to regional regeneration.

Coastal plains are the fastest growing areas demographically and of particular sociological interest. State farm land has still to be distributed conclusively and more and more mountain villagers are moving down to stake claims. A number of families whom I first knew in Mirdita have settled on the plain. This has enabled me to follow the subsequent changes in their lifestyles, as well as to make a study of land rights and property relations, which are particularly chaotic in these plains areas.

In 1999, I was asked by a non-government organisation (NGO) in collaboration with the Ministry of Education to undertake a pilot study on rural education in Albania. As a former schoolteacher and mother of five children, I had taken a close interest in education from the time of my earliest visit to Albania. The bulk of the survey was carried out in Mirdita and provided me with an ideal opportunity to get to know those areas of the province I had not previously visited. During the four months September to December, I worked together with the Local Education Authority and a number of teachers in schools all over the province. I got to know a number of dedicated teachers and heads who were trying to re-inject life against the odds[11] into provincial education. The NGO world was less edifying, but as an integral part of the post-socialist development scene, worth experiencing. Here local and foreign employees, unsurprisingly, were more often fighting for their survival and/or enrichment than for the realisation of their projects. Indeed, some of the projects proved to be no more than a source of false hopes and frustration to the supposed beneficiaries.

I continue to return two or three times a year to all three fieldwork settings, as well as regularly visiting Albanian friends who have migrated to Greece; one can only stop mid-narrative.

Giddens in his discussion of 'the dissolution of the exotic' notes the difference in readership now that anthropologists live in what he calls 'a world of developed reflexivity'. While in the past the ethnographed groups from faraway inaccessible places 'didn't answer back. . . . those who are the subject of anthropological treatises today are likely to read them.'(1995:273). That is exactly what I hope *will* happen in the case of this book.[12]

Chapter Two

FIRST IMPRESSIONS

Towards the end of December 1991 I visited Albania for the first time, together with my 11-year-old daughter. Since we already spoke Greek but not Albanian, I chose the Greek speaking minority of Dropull in northern Epirus for this first visit. Apart from simply wanting to see the country at first hand, I wanted to find out how the land in this area had been distributed since the land reform six months before. An Epirot mayor introduced us to the Kakavia border police at both frontiers so that we were able to walk in and out of Albania freely. The Mayor, who had kindly lent us his vacation house in a nearby village, intended that we should spend the nights in his house and only visit Albanian villages during the day 'since there are no lavatories over there'.

As we neared the border the first time, we made out a lighted up sign round a Christmas tree above the Albanian customs house. It said '*GËZUAR VITIN E RI*' – 'Happy New Year'. On this first visit, the Mayor took us to meet some of the villagers in the border village of Kakavia. We walked up a muddy hillside road from the border post and stopped at the former state shop. This had been bought by the villager who had managed it for the cooperative. The State was selling off shops and cafes cheaply, and this man had paid 250,000 drachmas, about $800. The shop was almost empty apart from some paraffin lamp glass funnels, a water jug from the Korça glass factory, one or two men's shirts and humanitarian aid rations of Italian sunflower oil in a huge tin barrel.

We went on to the coffee shop, which had also been bought by its former manager. On the way we met a large number of sheep coming down the hill accompanied by a man holding two lambs by the scruffs of their necks. It was 5pm, and the flocks were being brought back from the day's grazing just before dusk. Since the end of the cooperatives many of the cooperative shepherds had left for Greece. Some villages had set up a rota system amongst themselves to avoid grazing animals on a household basis. Some had been able to engage shepherds from the newly unemployed central and northern Albanians who had come South looking for work. Here in Kakavia, the six original cooperative shepherds had not as yet left and each animal owner paid them according to the number of animals sent to graze. A count by those sitting in the *kafeneion* estimated that the village's hundred households had over a thousand animals between them. In 1980 all privately owned animals except hens and rabbits had been forcibly handed over to the cooperatives. Many villagers all over Albania had killed their animals rather than give them to the State. Now some families we talked to had sold several of the newly distributed animals in order to buy a television or a fridge. The sales, contrary to my surmise, were not due to a fodder shortage following decollectivisation; animal fodder was said to be plentiful. But there was a shortage, and would be again next year, of food crops due to late planting, poor seeds, and lack of machinery, now either broken or unusable on the smaller plots.

The previous July, the democratically elected coalition government had introduced land reforms as a first step to coping with the economic crisis. An elected village land commission re-established the pre-cooperative village boundaries. The resulting quantity of land was then divided by the number of resident souls (including babies) in each village. Thus the larger the family, the more land it received. State employees such as teachers resident in the village officially received less, though individual villages could exercise a certain amount of discretion. Allocation of land parcels was by lottery; parcels were dispersed to ensure fair distribution of differentially fertile land. All previous ownership was nullified. The distributed land could not be sold (or rented out) but would devolve to the holder's heirs. In Kakavia the land distribution had taken place the preceding September (1991) when every household member had received three *dylims* (one *dylim* equals one tenth of a hectare).

Various factors had contributed to Kakavia's pretty harmonious distribution, not least the fact that before World War II the land had belonged to larger landlords now absent, rather than to individual smallholders. Since the region had been collectivised as early as 1950, only a minority recalled the period following the 1946 land reform when landless peasants had acquired their own land. Moreover, four years only of ownership meant that no strong ties to a particular area had had time to form.

On our first visit, we were struck by how many villagers looked poorly nourished. Compared with Greeks across the border, the villagers were shorter and thinner on average, and there were far more individuals with deformities. Clothes looked poor and threadbare, and were amongst the hardest items to obtain. The list of things now completely unobtainable included salt, pepper, washing powder, nails and paper. There were no newspapers as a result, though, the Greek Minority party political paper printed in Greece, was on sale. The Greek mayor subscribed to the conspiracy theory that these shortages had been deliberately created by the Communists to make the population wish to re-establish Communism. He had yet to comprehend the economic disaster that was largely responsible for the end of Communism.

Lack of materials had brought most production to a halt, though in a few cases the cause was factory workers striking for better work conditions. Those suspended from work for lack of materials were being paid 80 per cent of their salaries. The breakdown of production meant that neither paper nor glass was being manufactured. Prices of those few items still being manufactured or imported had increased enormously, though the government had fixed the prices of certain basic staples such as bread, sugar, macaroni and rice. These had not changed since Hoxha's time. But guaranteed prices did not mean that these goods were always obtainable. Sometimes there was no bread because there was no flour, sometimes there was no bread because there was no fuel for the bakery oven.

After the first visit, we went on our own and quite often spent a night or more in one of the villages. On our second visit we spent the morning at the Kakavia primary school. Looking through the children's books, which were in Greek, I saw that the pupils had gone through their text books inking out every line referring to the party, the cooperative or Comrade Enver. There was nothing subtle about the use of propaganda in the Albanian language primers; the third party, primer was full of paragraphs about 'us children increasing the number of hydro-power stations, railways and factories in our fatherland'. In the second primer you had to fill in the missing clitic in phrases like 'heroine of the people', 'portrait of Comrade Enver', 'cap of the partisan'. The textbooks were just an echo of the ubiquitous use of propaganda outside, where slogans such as 'Glory to the Party', 'Long live Enver' were eye-catching, painted large on the sides of buildings, across the hillsides and factory gates.

The Kakavia primary school building had originally been a church, identifiable by the two cypress trees either side of it. Now a small room at the side of the school had been turned into an Orthodox chapel. There was no priest of course, but a Greek priest now visited from time to time. Indeed the Greeks were wasting no time in rescuing their brethren across the border from the atheist wilderness. Since religion was often accompanied by aid, some of the Greek Minority Albanians were not above exaggerating their spiritual deprivations. One teacher said to me: 'For the first time my son has experienced the joys of Christmas, what a wonderful good religion is'. It was hard not to suspect such comments as motivated simply by the desire to tell the aid givers from across the border what they wanted to hear. It was a double-edged relationship. While there were undoubtedly numerous cases where these Albanian Greeks experienced great generosity and kindness at the hands of Greeks, there were also cases of exploitation in the name of religion. A girl might be taken up by a Greek family across the border and baptised by them. In the name of the close ties of god-parenthood, *koumbaria*, the girl might then find herself working in the family shop under exploitative conditions.

Many of the Greeks who came with a political or religious agenda were apt to sneer at what they found. Italian sunflower seed oil was derided by them as 'substandard stuff', which could only be tolerated by backward people. This may, of course, have simply been an expression of rivalry with foreign aid programmes, in particular with the Italian Operation Pelikan. Whatever the motives, the contemptuous comments about the poor roads and 'Third World people' on the part of visiting Greek priests and officials were not conducive to local self-respect. One result was a tendency on meeting a foreigner, for a Greek Minority worker, whether a barrel maker, metal worker or carpenter, to anticipate mockery or commiseration by deprecating their methods and tools as hopelessly primitive.

At the same time, those members of the Greek Minority who had now been working in Greece over the past months were becoming aware of certain superiorities arising from their communist heritage, not least their schooling. I was struck by the high level of education in Albanian schools and how well informed the Greek Minority school teachers were about other countries. Ironically, in view of their extreme isolation, but perhaps in reaction to it, teachers were often more sophisticated and cosmopolitan in outlook than their counterparts across the border.

One night we stayed with a school teacher who had been a political prisoner in Spaç, one of the notorious northern prisons. His village, Krioneri, was up a roadless mountainside in the woods. From 1974 to 1983 he had done hard labour in the Spaç copper mine. When he returned to his village, no one dared speak to him or attend his daughter's wedding or his father's funeral. He was '*deklasuar*', declassed, stripped of all privileges, including the chance to educate his children beyond secondary school. In a spirit of rectifying past wrongs, he had now been elected mayor of 13 villages. In the evening, we sat with him and his wife roasting popcorn, while he told us a little about the horrors of prison. And some of what he left out could be guessed from his ravaged face. Later we went round to his brother next door; he was due to return the next day to Greece where he had been working for the last six months. There were several men at his house who had been working in Greece, and one setting off for the first time. 'Whatever you do,' said the old hands, 'unless you want to be out of a job or beaten up, don't let on that you are from Albania.' But then these same men started to speak hostilely about Albanian Albanians. Their ambivalence was painfully comprehensive; ambivalence about themselves as a minority versus the rest of the country, about themselves versus the Greeks the other side of the border; about their communist heritage whose educational and cultural advantages they well understood, versus the regime of terror and repression whose suffering and economic deprivations were patent.

The scenes that stand out most clearly from those weeks are walking up mountainsides to roadless villages to be greeted like long lost friends by village men and women kissing us Albanian style; repeated kisses on alternate sides, between each kiss pressing cheek against cheek. The older women wore faded Epirot costumes with embroidered velvet bodices and long skirts dating back more than half a century. The warmth of the welcome, their delight at strangers and incredibly generous hospitality, the remote position of the villages in the middle of woods half way up mountains, and the sheer old-fashionedness of the lifestyle, conveyed a sense of having walked into the past or a fairytale. This was enhanced by an air of festivity as many of the men who had gone to Greece to find work had come back for the New Year celebrations.

As intense as this sense of the past, was a pervasive sense of irony. Many of the people we met who enabled us to do and see so much, had done the same in another capacity during the communist regime. They were quite open about this, laughingly describing visits from fanatical Western fellow travellers. 'We would show them all the triumphs of the regime, the schools, the cooperative achievements, model families in model housing. A moment would come when the foreigners would point to a house and say "Can we visit there?"' The house would contain a normal, non-model family, or worse, a 'deklasuar' family living in direst poverty and misery. At all costs the fellow travellers must be deflected from such glimpses of unedited life.

One of the most amazing and visible aspects of the fall of the communist regime was the orgy of destruction and vandalism that swept through the whole of Albania when the communist government fell. In Dropull we saw broken up cooperative buildings and machinery, burnt vineyards and orchards, smashed school furniture and windows, destroyed school equipment. School buildings stood in a wasteland of litter – the ripped out pages of Enver Hoxha's innumerable works and torn-up photographs of Uncle Enveri. Irrigation systems had been wrecked and looted for the stone slabs, hundreds of greenhouses smashed to skeletal frames. Some of this destruction was the result of theft and pilfering, but much of it was the end of repression run amok. And here there was irony too, because as a basis for a new order this legacy of anarchic destruction was not the best possible start in a bankrupt country. 'We wanted to start again from zero', said some, but others more practical were angry at the loss of so much that was useful.

A more positive feature of the new situation was people's challenging curiosity. On one occasion we found ourselves in a mountain village called Selleio. A Greek Orthodox priest had come to hold the first New Year service since atheism was imposed in 1967, in a church, which had been used as a stable ever since. The evening before the service, the priest accompanied by some villagers, came to visit the family where we were staying. He told us that there had been large numbers of young people at all the services he had held to date in the region. 'Out of curiosity,' said an old and a young man simultaneously. 'Not at all,' snapped the priest, 'they are thirsty for God'. The next day we all trooped down to the cleaned up church for the service. The service went on for a long time, and a lot of people went outside and lit lighted little bonfires to get warm by. I joined them for a bit and they explained apologetically that they were not used to this kind of thing – standing for so long and not understanding anything. When I went back into the church, the priest began a sermon. He was just talking about the Holy Ghost when he was interrupted by a middle-aged man in the congregation calling out: 'Please can you tell us in words that we can understand, what is the Holy Ghost?' It was an electrifying moment to be treasured forever. The priest, once he had recovered from this novel source of irritation, did attempt a brief explanation.

At the end of the service, a wonderful band of clarinet, violin, tambourine and accordion played traditional Epirot music outside the church whilst the congregation danced. Under Communism, they had been allowed to retain their music, though they had to replace the Greek words with anthems of praise to Hoxha. Later the villagers adjourned to the village's House of Culture where they danced until late at night.

After the service I was introduced to a toothless old man from the next village who, for '*diversion*', as a fellow villager put it, had taught himself English and French while in prison. The old man was waiting for a Webster's New World Dictionary to arrive from the United States so that he could learn more up to date idioms. A number of villagers had relations in the United States, a fact which was to have a significant impact on some individuals' lives in the near future. The Selleio area had been one of emigration since at least the eighteenth century, presumably due to a wish to escape from badly paid drudgery as workers for the big landowners. Initially, emigration had not been to the United States, but to Asia Minor where a number of men had established themselves as merchants in Constantinople and Smyrna. In the early twentieth century, emigration to the United States began.

Once the communist government was in power emigration came to an end of course. Even moving away from the village was virtually impossible thanks to the policy of rural population retention. Most of the villagers we met had worked on the cooperative fields in the plain at the foot of the mountain, where tobacco, legumes and wheat were grown. The women described how after working all day in the fields they had toiled back up the mountain to the village, where the household chores of cooking, washing and childcare awaited them.

We were staying with the family of a former cooperative vet who had been responsible for the animals in three villages, and who, like every other vet we met, and indeed most villagers, was now jobless. The family consisted of his parents, his wife, son and daughter Elektra. Less than a year later we ran into Elektra in the plains village of Vrisera. The contrast with her former lifestyle was extraordinary. When we first met, the summit of her ambition had been to acquire a sewing machine in the future and, more immediately, embroidery threads. This girl, for whom the greatest excitement in life a few months before had been a village dance in a village, which could only be reached by foot or by donkey, was now engaged to a young man from Vrisera whose family, thanks to relations in the United States, was very wealthy. Her fiance was successfully running the cafe his family now owned in Vrisera. She appeared quite unfazed by the change in her fortunes.

On several occasions we stayed with a school inspector and his family. Their house was on a bare mountainside above one of the communist government's major local achievements, a huge reservoir. We learnt some details from this family about the degree to which the party had infiltrated daily life. For instance, the cooperative committee had to be applied to for rations for every contingency affecting the family's food intake. Thus, for a wedding or engagement party in the family you received 25–40kg of meat; for a funeral 20 kg; for a visit from a relation from abroad 5kg; for an internal visitor 2kg; a woman who had given birth got 3kg of meat for a month. The New Year allowance was 4kg of meat, 2kg of pork and 2kg of another meat.

Our host, a biology teacher, was responsible as an inspector for the secondary schools in the area, several of which he took us to see. This meant walking across the mountains through scenery which, despite the rather frequent industrial interruptions such as pylons, and still more frequent concrete bunkers (300,000 built under Hoxha for defence), was very beautiful indeed. On these walks we were struck by the rather chilling non-acknowledgement of the few people we passed. No greetings were exchanged even though we were in empty open country and the solitary walkers passed within a few feet of us.

In all the schools we visited we had mutual cross-questioning sessions with both teachers and pupils, as well as attending lessons. Some of the secondary schools, which had survived the wave of vandalism better than others, still had wonderful cabinets full of teaching aids for biology and general science lessons. The standard in the lessons we listened to was high, with lively responses from the pupils and an animated style of teaching by the staff. Some of the lessons may only have taken place because we were there, as there was a general air of suspended activity. Much of the time teachers and pupils seemed to be just hanging around, while the number of teenage male pupils was dwindling by the day as those who could went to work in Greece. In the school at a village called Vouliaratis, pupil numbers had already dropped from 400 to 150. For the same reason, teachers' absenteeism had also grown rapidly, and one of the primary schools had closed for the lack of a teacher. Likewise, in all the villages we visited, the creches, nursery schools and health clinics had virtually stopped functioning for the loss of personnel. At the Vouliaratis health centre, where there had been a doctor and two nurses, there was just one nurse now. She said that formerly they had made daily visits to mothers who had recently given birth, and frequent visits to very young children. Now they did not even have bandages, and 'penicillin had to be given in steel needles from little glass bottles like you Westerners had in the distant past'. Children under three, she said, were not getting the necessary vitamins. Unlike the adults who, as noted above, often did look undernourished and worn, the children looked very healthy. I wondered whether there was genuine concern or whether this was a bit of an 'aid syndrome' act.

In Vrisera, in the area's main secondary school, three inspectors had arrived – to work out a programme for improving methodology, they said. It seemed a rather unsuitable moment to be looking at methodology. The round metal stove in the staff room had been specially lighted for them with scarce coal, and the three of them, in their overcoats, sat close to it toasting their buttered bread; in the rest of the building pupils and teachers sat in freezing rooms often with glassless windows.

The breakdown of production and of health services, not to mention growing unemployment, fuelled the frenetic toings and froings between these villages and the Greek town of Ioannina. There Northern Epirots could hope, as members of the Greek minority, to obtain the necessary documents to work in Greece or to take a sick child for treatment in Ioannina hospital. No wonder that nearly every Albanian immigrant one met in Greece claimed to be Orthodox and from this region. No wonder that the border at Kakavia was thronged each day with open trucks packed with Albanians desperate to be allowed into Eldorado.

Shortly before we had to leave for England, we went to stay with a maths teacher in his village on the main road towards Gjirokastër. We took a bus crammed, as were all the buses, beyond capacity. To reach his house at the top of the village we had to clamber up and over slippery rocks. The hillside was almost vertical and the paths had been washed away in a rain storm two months before. Water had to be hauled from the bottom of the village because the unmaintained water pipes had broken. The teacher's wife was a weaver and had made woven rugs and cloth for the cooperative. The teacher himself had carved a beautiful wooden ceiling in their best room. He was very apologetic for not having a modern lavatory; he was going to build one after earning in the summer vacation in Greece. At the moment it was a case of squatting underneath the house next to the recently distributed cow, sheep and goats. Astonishingly, the teacher was in the middle of reading a Greek translation of A.S. Neill's book about Summerhill, the experimental English school. He was fascinated by Neill's ideas and wanted to hear more about the school.

Chapter Three

TIRANA IN 1992

In August 1992, we flew from Athens to Tirana. Delay at Athens airport gave us the opportunity to talk to some of the other passengers. With the benefit of hindsight it was a pretty typical group of early post-communist visitors to Albania. There were some US missionaries, an Albanian youth on a Saudi scholarship who had just spent some months studying Islam in Medina, and an American and a Greek businessman travelling on a joint mission. On subsequent trips it was easy to work out which passengers were not going to Tirana for the first time. They were the ones who after the meal discreetly transferred paper napkins and tissues into their briefcases. They knew they would not find lavatory paper in Albania in 1992. They also, like us, tended to slip salt, pepper and anything they had not felt hungry for into their cases; they knew the limits of the food shops too.

Tirana Airport, at the time a charming Italianate garden with cypresses and flowering shrubs, was the last well-kempt sight. The rutted road to Tirana between dusty fields was rather empty apart from the occasional bicycle, some bony-shouldered cows, the odd pot-hole and one or two ancient lorries. The city itself in 1992 was dirtier than any South American slum I have ever seen. The level of squalor, decay and dereliction was breathtaking. Empty lots between the infinitely dismal communist apartment blocks of grey cement were dumps where swathes of garbage festered in the stinking mud.

Our block, one of several built expressly for loyal Communists, was right in the centre of Tirana. The filthy staircases with their chipped and broken steps, smashed windows and wrenched-out light fittings looked war torn. At the end of our third floor corridor there was some aesthetic relief where the window with its jagged remnant of glass looked over one storey yellow houses with red tiled roofs – picturesque, if shabby, villagey looking houses in narrow alley ways – a welcome if incongruous antidote to cement high rise.

Our flat was normally occupied by an English teacher called Vjollca who taught at the School of Foreign Languages. While we were in Tirana she and her daughter stayed with her parents. When we went away for a few days they moved back as empty flats might be robbed. Like all the other flat dwellers in the block, Vjollca came from the communist elite. Her parents, both from well off families, had been Partisans. Her mother had become an active Partisan aged 17, one of hundreds of secondary school pupils who joined the Communists in the early 1940s when they had become identified as the main opposition to fascism. Vjollca's father had held a high position during the communist period. Like most officials he had been moved from town to town every few years to reduce bribery, corruption, connections and to keep administrators on their loyal party toes.

Children of the *'privilegjuar'* – party officials – automatically had access to higher education, and when it came to brigade duty or military service (which women had to do too) could get away with less gruelling duties. However, Vjollca's father, a strict, rather puritanical member of the privileged class, had insisted that she perform all the duties that were obligatory for the hoi polloi. Town dwellers who were not manual workers had, from the age of 15 upwards, to spend a month each year doing manual work 'to purify the mind by soiling the hands'. Work ranged from railway construction and road building to terracing mountainsides. An attractive legacy of this policy was that even the most sophisticated urbanites could cope unfazed with the exigencies of rural life, skipping along precipices and down vertical mountainsides to the manner born. Another attractive aspect of egalitarianism, in this case directed at workers but open to all, was the provision of very cheap state subsidised holiday accommodation in seaside and mountain resorts. Now the end of Communism had brought an end both to compulsory rural labour and holidays for workers. Indeed, very few workers in 1992 had work any more since most industrial concerns had either closed down or were working with greatly reduced numbers. The resorts in the meantime had been ravaged by vandalism, theft and the chopping down of trees for firewood.

For the former privileged, however, the end of Communism had brought new opportunities for income generation. The best source of income came in the form of foreigners. The Tiranians who had been in privileged positions were the best placed to take advantage of this influx as hardly anyone else had been allowed contact with the outside world during the Communist period. Most foreigners in Tirana belonged to one of three categories: international aid organisations; would-be investors (few and short-stay only); and missionaries (extraordinarily numerous) who included Seventh Day Adventists, Mormons, Swedish Evangelists, Catholics, Muslims and Bahai. There were also a few adventurers ranging from criminals wanted by Interpol to individuals in search of power, sex and a new arena. Very few foreigners wanted to stay for long in hotels with Third World amenities whose prices were Western deluxe (and whose clients when they ventured out were a prime target for robbers). Most foreigners, therefore, rented flats from members of the former communist elite who were strikingly free from ideological hang-ups about forming a rentier class. At the same time, the Albanian rentier's concept of landlord–tenant relations was quite unWestern. This had its good and less good sides. On the one hand, one was comfortingly nannied, shown how to shop, introduced to numerous relations within the ex-communist elite, taken for walks and visits. On the other, the flat-holder did not consider that he or she had forfeited any rights in the use of the flat just because one was paying to live in it. Experiencing Tirana for the first time, however, the advantages of the nanny service greatly outweighed the occasional inconvenience of finding unknown cousins from Macedonia shaving in one's flat.

There was a small risk attached to renting out a flat since these were still the property of the State and sub-letting was illegal. But the risk of the flat being confiscated was easily eclipsed by the gains of letting it. A teacher who, like Vjollca, had been teaching for 20 years, earned at this time $20–$24 a month. In one night $15–$20 could be earned renting out the apartment. So parents whose grown-up children were working abroad (usually clandestinely in Greece), rented out their offspring's flats, or offspring would move in with their parents for the duration.

Mutual ignorance between locals and foreigners of each other's standards often created problems. Neither the foreign organisations nor the Albanians were clear as to the value of work or money to the other side. Some of the international organisations' representatives were so grossly overpaid that they themselves had probably lost any sense of financial reality; certainly the scale of foreigners' salaries and hardship allowances created resentment locally. But aid organisations and missionaries needed interpreters, drivers and clerical workers as well as flats, and every Tiranian's ambition was to find such employment. During early visits to Albania some foreign organisations paid locals western European fees. Subsequently they paid far less. Interpreters whose skills had been found excellent the first time wanted to know why they were no longer seen as so valuable; while foreigners grew increasingly irritated by the results of the price inflation, which they themselves had triggered.

How to manipulate foreigners' spending was tricky. One strategy was to suggest to the foreigner that he pay whatever seemed to him fitting. While always above local prices, foreigners' initial willingness to pay fees on a par with those abroad dwindled fast as they realised how easily they could find employees. Nor was the Albanian work ethic, generated in response to low salaries and guaranteed employment, always suited to the demands of the Western employer looking for longer hours and greater productivity. Which is not to say that all the Western professionals were distinguished for their work ethic or moral standards.

Unsurprisingly, Albanian views on capitalism tended to extremes. Some enthusiastically supported total privatisation and ceiling-less prices. Others asserted that all capitalists are corrupt. One man recalling presents he had given foreigners lamented, rather hypocritically I thought, given his patent desire for financial gain: 'How hard it is for us to learn to be commercial like you capitalists,' as if present-giving was an exclusively communist custom. Many people were very surprised to learn that not everything was privatised in England (still the case in 1992). I was quite often asked what sort of system we had in England. After I had explained, questioners would exclaim in approving surprise: 'Ah, capitalism with socialist elements, what a good idea!'

Every evening, weather permitting, Tiranians went on the *xhiro* (pronounced jeero), the evening promenade that flourished under Communism and still thrives today in every Albanian town. (Only during the period of chaos in 1997 did the curfew put an end to the *xhiro*.) In Tirana it flourishes most notably in the elegant pine-lined Bulevard, which runs from the central square of Skënderbeu to the university building at the other end. Until 1995, traffic was banned from the main *xhiro* streets in the evenings; unfortunately no longer the case.

On our first evening in Tirana, Vjollca with her daughter and niece – girls of Soula's age – came to take us on the *xhiro*. At the entrance to Vjollca's block of flats there was an ice-cream seller where we stopped to buy ice-creams for 3 lek (3 US cents) each. Vjollca said this was much more expensive than before, a refrain we got used to hearing whenever the price of anything was discussed. The ices were made from powdered milk (probably aid donated), good but short on the anti-melting factor.

On our way to the Bulevard we passed on our right the magnificent hole left in place of a hotel by a Swiss-Albanian entrepreneur, Hajdim Sejdia, representative of Illyria Holdings, who had decamped with the investors' money. On our left, opposite the National Library, was the elegant Ethem Bey Mosque, one of the very few religious buildings left in tact by the regime's anti-religion campaign of 1967. On the threshold at the top of the mosque steps stood little groups of curious onlookers. Inside the mosque men were praying. In the street lots of little girls whose families were evidently being courted by proselytising Muslims were throwing their new white cotton shawls over each other's heads. Each morning around half past four, as the flat dwellers in our block took advantage of the water coming on to do their washing and stock up with water for the day, we would hear the muezzin calling the faithful – mainly tall bearded Arabs in white robes – to prayer.

The mosque stands across the road from the Palace of Culture and opposite the statue of the fifteenth century Albanian hero Skënderbeu, astride a horse. The giant statue of Enver Hoxha, which had previously dominated the centre of Skënderbeg Square, had been pulled down the year before, in February 1991, when the Communist government had begun to seriously lose control. Turning left into the Bulevard, we walked between the headless statues of Lenin and Stalin, decapitated in the name of democracy; Stalin's statue now inscribed with Pink Floyd's name scrawled large in red paint. We saw a lot of Mikel Jaksen (sic) graffiti and T-shirts, though deafening rap was what one heard most. Halfway down the Bulevard we passed the Pyramid designed by Hoxha's architect daughter and built as a museum to him. Little boys were sliding vertiginously down the wide polished marble ribs between the mirror-glass segments of the roof. Every few minutes Vjollca would say: 'Come and meet my uncle, cousin, aunt, sister, friend, colleague'. These former privileged members of society all had jobs under the new regime, having bridged the political gap with remarkable skill professionally despite retaining powerful nostalgia for the former regime.

The people who thronged the streets in the mornings were not so lucky. There were hordes of men mostly shabbily dressed, unshaven with wild haircuts. Tirana pavements are very wide but despite their spaciousness were always crowded in the mornings with groups of unemployed men meeting and chatting, greeting each other with repeated kisses on either cheek. Like almost every man and woman I met outside the charmed circle of former privileged communist families, they were living off their year's *asistenz*. Petty traders sat on the pavements selling an egg-cupful of sunflower seeds for one lek, jumble sale clothes, 1970s foreign magazines, a table knife, a pair of shoes abd second-hand books. Some of the sellers were teachers, engineers and geologists, either unemployed or supplementing their monthly $20 salaries. When school was out young boys sold Hilal chocolate bars imported from Turkey at eight to ten leks a piece. Only gypsies begged, showing off mutilated limbs, or setting a baby down on the pavement and watching at a distance for a pile of leks to accumulate round it. Gambling groups of men would cluster round a man or boy with three cards or matchboxes. Stakes were often high and more than once I saw a loser burst into tears.

Walking in the streets was only for the alert as lidless manholes in crumbling pavements waited for the unwary. Fortunately, hardly anyone stayed in the often unlighted streets after dark. Theft with violence still occurred occasionally as a result of massive unemployment and uncertain law and order following Communism's collapse. If night had already fallen when we reached our block, we would enter the pitch dark stairwell – the perfect cover for ambush – and feel our way up the stairs, hearts thumping, waiting to be jumped out on at each new flight till we reached our door and, shakily unlocking it, hurtled into the flat. But that was the dark side. We were rather lucky, it turned out, to be living on the third floor, because not only did it mean that unlike the floors above, this floor's flats had water in the taps for a short period three times a day (until the summer). It also meant that we were close neighbours with two particularly nice families.

Opposite us lived a widowed geologist, Agim, with his two children and his mother, Aishe, who came from a village in Dibra in the northeast. The 15- year-old son, Artan, was enjoying post-communist educational chaos, loss of school discipline, Western pop music and daily MTV. The 11-year-old daughter played the violin and was more serious. Culturally, the family was Muslim, though Agim at least declared himself an atheist who believed only in the superior power of nature. The following year he managed to send his daughter away to a Greek Orthodox boarding school in Athens, which was offering to educate orphaned Albanian children from deprived homes. Strictly speaking perhaps she would not have qualified; the family was better off than many since the father was still employed. But her mother had been tragically killed in a car accident two years before so that she certainly qualified as a victim of misfortune.

A few weeks after our arrival Aishe asked to borrow some chairs. They were preparing for the memorial service for her daughter-in-law. I was asked to go and pay my respects the next day. The mourners went to the town's cemetery in the morning, crying and calling out laments over the grave. Vjollca and I went to the flat in the afternoon. About eight women, their faces wan from crying, sat in near silence. The men sat in another room. It was very painful and sad. We drank coffee as custom required and said *ngushëllime* – consolation – and other formulaic phrases of condolence.

Our other neighbours, Mark and Prena, came from Mirdita, a Catholic area in the north. Mark was a Moscow educated engineer now in his 60s, who had worked in a high position during the regime, and whose religion, Artan joked, was Communism. Later when I had learnt enough Albanian, we used to have arguments about the pros and cons of Communism under Hoxha. Though passionately committed to its ideals, Mark was clear-sighted about some of its aberrations in practice. But I would never have believed that in 1994 he would become a fan of the television soap *The Bold and the Beautiful*. Or that when I taunted him with its revisionist decadence, he would solemnly assure me that the programme had a serious moral message.

Prena, Mark's wife, had been betrothed to Mark when she was 11 and he was 13, normal at the time in Mirdita. They married when she was 16 never having seen each other; also normal for Mirdita at the time, and not unheard of in 1992. They had four sons and a daughter, all grown up. One son owned a former state shop in Tirana, one was working in Athens where he was joined later by the other two, who remained there for the next ten years. A fourth son lived in the northern town of Lezhë. Their daughter, together with her husband, ran a restaurant in the centre of Tirana, chiefly patronised by the foreign community; few locals could afford to feed themselves at home, let alone eat out.

Prena was Roman Catholic but eclectic in practice. As well as attending the newly opened Catholic church nearby, she often visited the Muslim Dervish Hatixhe, well known for her cures and miracles. Prena and Aishe, who were close friends as well as neighbours, were equally eclectic about evil eye cures. Sometimes they chose verse chanting from the Qur'an while dropping a hot cinder into water; other times they used a cross, oil and water. Albanians were refreshingly fond of pointing out, as they still are, that there is after all only one God.

We met two or three other families in our block of flats, though we never got to know them as well as our immediate neighbours. On the top floor lived a family of professional ballet dancers, the older of whose sons had escaped to a job in Madrid while on tour there earlier in the year with the Albanian ballet. Organised arts in Tirana were naturally suffering, and the father of the family spent a lot of time histrionically leaping about and wringing his hands over the situation. Immediately above us lived a couple who had been cooks to one of Enver Hoxha's right hand men. This had allowed them a number of privileges and a considerably richer diet, they said, than that of the average Tiranian. The wife's sister had recently married a southern Italian. The marriage had been arranged by a go-between, one of numerous recent alliances between Italian men and Albanian women. Albanian women were said to make good wives and many an older Italian in search of a wife enlisted the help of a go-between to negotiate this happy solution. Sometimes a video would be provided to enable the Albanian woman to check the proposed man's appearance; was he bald, ugly, older than claimed? Though as a friend I got to know later who was considering such a match pointed out: 'What guarantee is a video?' Very often the woman was herself older than the average marrying age. In the case of our neighbour's 30-year old sister whom I met when she came back for a visit, the marriage was very satisfactory. Her parents-in-law were very good to her, she said, and she had become proficient at cooking Italian food.

Below us lived a family whose son worked for the state bank. He spoke English fluently and was working on getting transferred to the United States. He used to regret that whereas he and his friends under Communism had shared close friendships, they avoided each other now in order to keep their connections and opportunities to themselves. Perhaps as a result he succeeded in getting to the United States the following year. Opposite his family lived a paediatrician whose husband, like so many now unemployed, had gone into business. All the residents of our block were involved in some kind of business, often in addition to other careers. A second income, whether from renting to foreigners or petty trading, was a valuable supplement now that most prices had ceased to be fixed. The former communist elite was in a better position to launch enterprises than the rest of the population, having had more powerful contacts at home as well as more contact with foreigners. But business dealings were often no more than small-scale petty commerce with perhaps a teenage son selling biscuits and sweets on the street.

Thanks to Vjollca, who acted as voluntary interpreter, we were able to get to know our neighbours before we could speak the language. The central feature of all visits was the coffee grinder. Coffee beans could only be bought unroasted and were roasted at home in a kind of cylinder, which you held over a flame. We had seen these in southern Greece where a few old villagers had kept them as a souvenir of an almost forgotten (though not, in fact, very distant) past. But it was the coffee grinder, a quintessential Ottoman object of brass, which initiated a visit. It would be brought out and various members of the family, men included, would take it in turns to grind. The grinding, which takes some time and effort, the ceremonial formulaic phrases to be uttered before and after drinking by guest and host, were intrinsic to socialising, as were certain questions that were always asked. Amongst the first phrases I learnt as a result of these visits were the answers to: 'How many children have you got? What sex are they? This was the information about one most eagerly sought, the sex of the children as vitally interesting as the number. Having learnt these facts, the enquirer would use whichever formulaic phrase was current in their region to wish one's children well. After that conversation proper could begin.

Preconceptions held by some of Vjollca's relations about different nationalities could lead to comments like: 'But you can't be English, the English are cold.' My daughter, Soula, responded to such comments with outbursts against stereotyping which fell on deaf ears. Years later, she was responding to English comments about tribal primitivism in the Balkans equally forcefully and without much more success. In a country like Albania where propaganda and a stranglehold on information had existed for nearly 50 years, thinking in stereotypes was to be expected, though it was not so very much more pronounced than in the 'free world'; simply that political correctness had not become *de rigueur*. Regional prejudice was entrenched; the image of the North as the centre of backwardness had been a longstanding feature of 'common knowledge' with southerners dispatched to northern villages to teach them civilised ways. By contrast, Western products, English coldness notwithstanding, were in 1992 wholly good. Thus, all Western television programmes from MTV to *Miami Vice* and *Knight Rider* could and should be watched by one's children.

Living conditions for our neighbours were fairly austere. Except in winter when most flats had wood stoves (wood was rationed, expensive, and sometimes hard to get), cooking was done on thoroughly unsafe ankle-level electric plates (*rezistenz*) or foul smelling paraffin stoves. Electricity and water were only sporadically available. Rising at 4am was essential if there was washing to be done. Water had to be stored in buckets and bowls for the long intervals between water shifts. Even when the central power had not gone, the flats' fuses hanging off the wall of the common corridor frequently packed up. And touring the shops for a replacement fuse could be as time consuming and often as fruitless as touring the shops for a replacement light bulb. The period 1991 to 1993 was particularly bad for the uninteresting goods that smooth daily life, such as nails and paper, fuses, light bulbs and glue. One day we were walking behind an elegantly dressed woman who was wearing high heels. When we got closer we saw that she was carrying one of the heels in her hand. You would never have guessed this from her perfectly balanced walk, a skill she may have had time to perfect, since when we tried to get a shoe sole stuck on, the shoe repairers were all out of glue. Albanians were of course quite used to austerities. We went over to Mark and Prena's one day to ask them to lend us a tin opener. They looked blank at the idea that we mimed and opened the tin the normal way, with a knife. Similarly, beer bottles were opened with the teeth or by holding the edge of the bottle top against a table; wine bottles were opened by smacking the bottom of the bottle until the cork came out.

One of the familiar daily sounds of flat life, like the early water users and the muezzin, was the loud hailing from the street to alert a friend in one of the flats above. Instead of walking up the stairs to a friend's flat, one just stood in the street below shouting: 'O, Genc!' or 'O, Vjollcë!' and the summoned would eventually appear on their balcony. Sometimes the summons was to call a friend down, sometimes it was to relay a telephone message. Few people had telephones and it was standard practice to give a neighbour's telephone number as a contact. In 2001, while watching telebingo on television, we saw the presenter ring the winner only to be told that this was a neighbour. 'And what percent will you be taking of the winnings in exchange for providing a contact number?' asked the presenter. In the Albanian comedy film *Edhe kështu edhe ashtu* (*This way and that way*) the telephone-owning neighbour gets so fed up that he eventually has a huge extension cord fitted and takes the telephone ostentatiously down the stairs to his neighbour.

Along the corridor of each floor in our apartment block was a rubbish drop. This had a door like a serving hatch that opened on to a space in the wall down which you tossed your rubbish. It struck us as a surprisingly sophisticated asset until we learnt that it had originally been intended for an elevator before the money had run out. In view of the extreme frequency of electricity cuts, we saw the change of plan as a godsend. The rubbish collecting system was itself a curious mixture of styles. The garbage men came in a very modern lorry from which they jumped down, opened the prison-cage door to the pile of rotting debris, swept out the rubbish with twig besoms into a bin that was then was emptied mechanically into the lorry. It was hard to see, given this daily service, why Tirana was covered in litter unless the litter represented a reaction against the communist regime's emphasis on cleanliness. Apartment blocks under Communism competed to fly the white flag awarded to the best kept. The flag announced *këtu ka pastërti* – here is cleanliness.

There were fines for litter and all night sweeper brigades kept the streets clean. It was part of the jolly avuncular moralism so skilfully propagated by Enver Hoxha – 'Uncle Enveri' to Albanian children – to create invidiousness. Of a kind with Chinese style wall posters: *fletë rrufe* (lightning sheets) for denouncing one's neighbours, colleagues, pupils or teachers, and *fletë lavdërim* or *tabele emulacion* for praising them. Each block had a commission, which held a regular assembly (*mbledhje frontin demokratik* – meeting of the democratic front) to review residents' behaviour. Here in the *dhoma edukimit*, the room for moral education, married couples' difficulties, unruly children, political renegades, would be talked over by the *këshille lagjes*, the ward council. People would make *autokritikë* (self-criticism) if their behaviour had been singled out in a *fletë rrufe*, in the hopes of staving off something worse than simply being reprimanded for lack of ideological maturity – *pjekuri ideologjike*. Even dressing slightly differently, wearing a skirt made in a new style, could be risky. You might be accused of *shfaqe të huaja*, foreign exhibition. Several accusations, and you might acquire a *biografi keq*, a bad biography, and lose all privileges such as the chance for you or your family to enter higher education; you could be removed from your job and sent to work on a cooperative or state farm.

Modernisation had not yet infiltrated the National Bank, which was without computers in 1992. Its circular interior was mayhem with a milling crowd of customers and punters packed literally shoulder to shoulder, all trying to attract the attention of the clerks behind the counters by calling out their names: 'O, Mimosa! O, Liri!'. After finally pushing and shoving one's way to complete the first part of the transaction, one would wait in the middle of this frenetic throng until eventually one caught one's first name being called out across the crowd's heads – the signal to fight a way back to a Mimosa or Liri. (If the clerk's name was unknown, one used the communist terminology: 'comrade' (*shok/shoqe*).)The use of first names for all ages and degrees of acquaintance was normal and partly an indicator of the smallness, egalitarianism and intimacy characteristic of Albanian communist society. It was also, of course, a symptom of a largely rural society where surnames were until recently still being created. In Mirdita, patronymics were more common than surnames, and in 1997 the telephone directory of the region's main town, Rrëshen, still registered telephone numbers under first names. Prominent politicians are known to the populace by their first names. More significantly, Albania is still a 'face-to-face' society in the sense that regionally even if people do not actually know each other, they know *of* each other, or after a short exploration can find common acquaintance. One of the many appealing attributes that goes with this personal type of society is openness to strangers (except as related earlier when passing on a road).

Bank visits, which were both time-consuming and physically demanding, were only necessary if one had travellers cheques. Other transactions were conducted in front of the bank where crowds of money-changers stood. There was an aura of danger about the area where exchangers jostled each other for clients and large numbers of rough looking men were gathered. It was very difficult to decide whom to approach. The exchangers ranged from members of the educated elite to young boys, all crying out: 'Dollar, Marka, Drami'. It was nerve racking not knowing for sure if the notes were false or the exchange too low. We would ask several what the rate was and then from amongst those offering a slightly higher rate, Soula would say 'he looks honest', I would dither and she would get cross.

An article in the newspaper *Koha Jonë* (3 September 2000) quotes financial experts as saying that these exchangers (*kambistet*) in front of the National Bank handle in the course of a year about 400 million dollars. This is the equivalent sum of the National Bank's foreign currency reserves or half the budgeted expenditure for a year. The exchangers have virtually no administration overheads and can make substantial profits, albeit, as news items in 2003 indicate, they are at risk from robbers. At the top of the pyramid are two or three invisible businessmen who put into circulation two to three thousand dollars that are distributed amongst the small businessmen who work for the bosses, taking a percentage of their daily profits. This informal financial trading is a worry for the central bank, and yet the trade goes on openly. Whereas the bank's system is closely supervised, no-one is responsible for the exchangers even though they are working directly in front of the governor's office. However, the bank's then governor, Shkelqim Cani, is reported as saying that for the time being these money-changers serve a useful purpose for the bank; later they can be eliminated. Other financial experts fear that this will be easier said than done as the *kambistet* will simply move elsewhere.

In 1992, Tirana's roads were still nearly as safe as the wide pavements. No privately owned cars had been allowed during the communist period. The influx of second-hand cars imported as migrants returned from abroad had only just begun. With no traffic lights and little past experience, cars behaved as bicycles, swerving to avoid the pedestrians who still saw the roads as people friendly. Less people friendly were the city buses. These were either very decrepit indigenous relics, or nearly as decrepit donations by foreign nations, Greek, Hungarian, Czech, Italian. There were far too few to cater for a population swollen with newly arrived rural migrants. After a long frustrating wait buses would be treated like the only lifeboat of a fast sinking ship. All vestiges of civilised restraint cast aside as 50 Tiranians in unbroken rank tried to muscle through a door just wide enough for two people.

Most people walked or used bicycles, and a common sight was a family of four, a child fore and aft, legs dangling, coasting along on one bike. Sheep were often bicycle passengers too, sometimes uncomfortably slung over the crossbar, sometimes better off tucked under the cyclist's arm. Rules for bicycles seemed to be as for pedestrians, but in the road. It was (and still is, despite heavy traffic in the twenty-first century) normal for bicycles to use whichever side of the road they liked. From our balcony in the Rruga Luigj Gurakuqi, which looked out to the right over the roundabout in front of the Islamic headquarters, we used to watch with bated breath as bicyclists circled counterwise to cars and buses. Bicycles had to accompany their owners everywhere to escape theft; into the office, up to the university lecture room, into the flat whether resident or just on a visit.

Gypsies from the outlying plains villages drove unpicturesque horse-carts whose shoddy orange crate construction echoed the cheap materials and poor craftsmanship present in all local manufacture from the uniform sofa beds and gimcrack coffee tables in every flat, to the exposed electric coils (*reflektor*) used for heating. The effects of long-term poverty were obvious in every form of construction from furniture to buildings.

Farm animals – cows, sheep, horses, donkeys, flocks of turkeys – were a common sight in the streets especially on Sundays, the biggest market day. One day we saw a horse bolting Wild West style the length of the main street from the roundabout down to the Cafe Europa, where it turned right and was lost to view. Sometimes one met sheep on the end of a rope descending the stairs of an apartment block. On Sunday market days it was not uncommon to see a cow's head with lolling out tongue being carried home in a string bag. Much of this livestock could be met with, alive or dead, at the market: rabbits, turkeys, sheep, cows, hens. The meat and cheese part of the market was under cover; hot, foul smelling, fly ridden mud and blood, jam-packed with people. We used to go there with Vjollca to risk our health trying out the different cheeses that sat in vats of dirty liquid. We did not quite have the nerve to buy meat, which like the cheese was expensive for Albanians, though they bought it when they could. (But why is low meat consumption an index of a country's poverty when Westerners are told by their health advisers to eat as little as possible? Is it because poverty measurers know that until you are rich you want to eat meat?)

Outside the covered part of the market one slopped through rank-smelling mud puddles to trestle tables where fruit and vegetables were laid out. In September 1992, there were watermelons at three cents a kilo, onions and peppers at ten cents a kilo, but undersized malnourished looking potatoes costing more than in England. The only eggs were from Macedonia and also cost more than eggs in England, though cracked ones sold for less and broken ones for half price. Much of the produce was imported, recalling the Albanian we had met in Athens who had told us: 'When I saw that villagers were coming into the town in search of food, I thought now it is time to leave'. In winter there were leeks and more leeks. Hoxha had dwelt enthusiastically in speeches on the manifold qualities of leeks that lucky Albanians produced so plentifully. His enthusiasm did not compensate for unobtainable apples and oranges plentifully produced in Albania, but not for local consumption.

Round the corner of the market more villagers squatted behind their produce laid out on the ground: herbs and mountain tea, spices and bottles of wine tamped with torn out pages from books of communist propaganda. On bonanza days Tiranians rejoiced on finding past-the-use-by-date Turkish margarine liquefying in its wrappers, or Greek not-so-frozen chickens. There was occasionally out of date Italian tomato puree or salami guaranteed to make foreigners, less hardened than former communists, sick. Sometimes Soula found out of date Mars bars whitened with age and tasting stale but a reminder of the good things back home.

In a shop beside the market they let us test their honey which, to our surprise, turned out to be horribly bitter. The shopkeeper was a jolly, communicative young man, though he took a bit of winning over as he was fed up with overpaid foreigners from international aid organisations. They were the stingiest customers, he complained, who always asked for the smallest possible quantities. But we eventually got on good terms, perhaps as a result of our keenness to buy up his stocks of powdered milk. Once we spoke enough Albanian, we would have political discussions with him. He asked us what form of government we thought would be best for the time being. I said I thought the country needed a coalition government and a much more gradual introduction of capitalism. He and most of his customers heartily agreed. We were sorry to see his shop disappear in 1993 when the new property law came into being.

Apart from a string bag for fruit and vegetables, you had to take a container if you wanted oil or honey, vinegar, coffee or salt. Glass bottles were valuable, there were as yet no plastic ones, while paper or plastic bags were non-existent. Paper manufacture was almost at a standstill, but pages torn from Enver Hoxha's innumerable works were infinite and acted as containers and wrappers and perhaps catharsis. Salt could only be bought in coarse unground form, and coffee beans were only sold unroasted. By the far entrance to the market, beyond the squatting produce sellers, were the sellers of junk: old shoes open at the seams and so misshapen they could hardly have contained a foot; rusted nuts and bolts; old clothes, probably Red Cross jumble donations.

Donations had a mixed reception. Some argued that none would have been necessary had Communism continued. Others compared Albania with Somalia and complained of donor countries' stinginess. On a visit to the Institute of Environmental Hygiene where one of Vjollca's sisters worked, we spent a convivial hour one morning sitting in the food-testing laboratory helping to test aid-donated peach jam and local raki, which we drank from lab beakers. 'If only we'd known you were coming today, we'd have saved yesterday's delicious tinned pineapple,' they said hospitably.

All the aid food was tested before distribution and much of it sat there for months before distribution. We often saw what were clearly aid donations for sale in the shops and market, sacks of Irish donated powdered milk, Italian sugar in bags inscribed with 'A present from the Italian people'.

Opposite our flat were numerous former state shops that had been divided up and sold off cheaply to the managers. A new property law in May 1993 bewilderingly and contentiously led to many of these premises having two owners, one of the ground on which they stood, one of the shop floor and upwards. These shops looked like storage depots. They sold televisions, Turkish jean dresses, macaroni, watches, plastic bowls, shoes, all jumbled together. There were food shops as well that sold nearly nothing, though occasionally some longed for commodity like powdered milk or margarine would appear, only to disappear after a few days.

The bread shops operated behind bars through which the loaves were passed. Two queues, one male, one female, had to be formed. This had been standard practice throughout the communist period. There were various explanations for gendered queues. One was that no man would agree to stand behind a woman. A more likely explanation was that to establish two queues, a hard and fast category such as male and female eliminates arguments. Even so there was some fighting, and I used to get annoyed at cheating men who would approach the woman at the head of her queue (once it was me), and hand her the money for their order. In 1992 bread cost 20 leks (20 US cents) a kilo. The brown bread was very good indeed, for texture, taste and staying fresh. Albanians call eating a meal 'eating bread', an indication of bread's importance in their diet. I had lunch one day in 1993 with an Englishman who had rented a flat belonging to an uncle of Vjollca. He was a food studies research economist from Oxford come to Tirana to advise the Albanian government on bread pricing. By then bread had risen to 24 leks a kilo. The expert told me that he was advising the government to double the price. For the unemployed, he told me, forestalling my protest, there would be a subsidy. I asked him if he was familiar with Albanian eating habits, their salaries, etc. (For the minority who were not unemployed at the time the monthly salary was $20–30.) I must have slightly alarmed him because eventually he said, apparently quite seriously: 'You don't think there'd be a revolution do you?' After suffering at least two decades of deprivation in silence, the population was not about to revolt now. (It took the loss of their entire savings to trigger a revolution, we now know.) So the price of bread doubled while the quality went by the board. We regularly thereafter found foreign bodies in the loaves, including plastic sacking, stones and other indeterminate weight-making debris.

At the beginning of September the School of Foreign Languages term had not yet begun because the new post-communist curriculum was still being worked out. The Education Ministry's new programme could not have been implemented properly, in any case, since there were almost no books, and paper was virtually unobtainable. However, the teachers were involved in various training courses arranged by foreign organisations. One that I sat in on for a bit took place at the Music School. Hearing a piano, I left the meeting to track it down. Alone at a grand piano in a large hall a young girl was playing Chopin. She played very well indeed, and I listened for a long time, pleasure mingled with homesickness for my own piano-playing daughter away on a gap year in Indonesia. At the end her teacher who spoke some German came in and told me that his pupil had just won a scholarship to study in Germany. The coexistence of a reasonably high standard of cultural development (typical for European communist countries) and Third World living conditions for all classes except the *nomenklatura*, was something a lot of the aid personnel failed to grasp. On the very course that I had been sitting in on, some of the instructors had failed to conceal their surprise that Albanians knew a typewriter when they saw one, and even how to use it.

The School of Foreign Languages where our landlady taught was for 14 to 18 year olds from all over Albania. The dormitory building opposite housed several hundred pupils from the provinces, while a smaller number lived at home in Tirana. The first two floors of the boarding block were not in fact available to boarders since they were being used to house the newly released political prisoners – the '*përsekutuar*' and their families – whose re-housing even by 2002 had not been realised in all cases. There was no glass in the windows either of the dormitory or the school. Every dormitory window was festooned with clothes hanging up to dry, while the ground and the fences round the slummy litter-strewn mud and grass area in front of the building, were draped with dozens of drying sheets. Entry to the building was barricaded and guarded following the worst period of unrest, when a number of break-ins and rapes had occurred. The students slept six to a small bunk-bedded room with nowhere to write. They heated water for washing their clothes by plugging in an electric plate to the light bulb hanging from the ceiling. The meals were poor quality and too small to properly assuage hunger.

On the first day of term Soula and I stood outside the school and watched fascinated as the rural students arrived to register. They came with their families, most of them carrying wooden suitcases. On their feet they wore anything from bedroom slippers or perished rubber flipflops to old sandals with thick woolly socks. Their clothes were wildly assorted in style and uniformly poor looking. One girl had blood stains on her skirt, the nappy style cloths, which were the only thing available, were less efficient than sanitary towels or Tampax. (Some months later, some of the chemists had handwritten signs on their doors advertising newly imported sanitary towels 'the new way to improving the difficult days'.) Teachers we got to know subsequently used to marvel at the speed with which these rural pupils' appearances changed once they were established in Tirana. How they dressed, hairstyles, even way of talking had changed dramatically by the time they graduated. The presence of pupils, some from extremely remote and poor homes, in the School of Foreign Languages highlighted the democratic nature of the former education system, which could reach even the remotest villagers (assuming of course political acceptability).

The standard of language teaching was high at this specialist school which 14 year olds from all over Albania competed to enter. Russian, German, French and English were taught; English by means of J. Eckersley's *Essential English*, despite the irredeemably bourgeois and servanted family who are the book's protagonists. On bus trips to other towns in our first few months we were sometimes addressed by people in instantly recognizable 'Essential'. Certain language teachers' mistakes got reproduced down the generations: 'apple' pronounced 'aipel'; 'time after time' for 'again and again'. A new mistake was 'aids' as in 'these foreigners have donated us aids'. This was unfortunately about to become the literal truth.

A week or so after our arrival, I was at the School when an apparently crazed doctor, parent of a pupil, rushed up to me and surprised me by exclaiming: 'You have been sent by Heaven! Give me a two page summary of this WHO booklet and I will do the rest.' He turned out to be formulating Albania's AIDS policy for an imminent WHO conference. 'We have to have a sociologist, you will be my collaborator. What policy will be successful to prevent AIDS in a country where as yet we have no case?' 'Stalinist isolationism seems to have worked rather well', I suggested unhelpfully. 'Yes, yes, thank you, you have come from Heaven', the irrepressible doctor effused. Undeterred by my claims that I knew too little to contribute he insisted: 'But I will do this part, you must just supply the theory.' I later learnt from an American who attended the conference that despite my refusal to have anything to do with the project, my name was down as a co-contributor.

In 1991 and for a long time to come, there was a paper and book crisis. A number of foreign 'aids' consisted of heterogeneous consignments of miscellaneous school books which, like the donation of computers without manuals, and medical instruments with missing parts, were not much use for practical purposes. These books, like many charitable donations, generally ended up for sale on the streets. Thus, the schools and universities had to manage with very little in the way of books or paper. Our flat overlooked a state book store that supplied school books. All these stores had entrances with metal grilles (like bread shops) to prevent rampaging buyers from overpowering the sellers and running amok in the shop. Even outside the start of school rush when entry to these shops was allowed, the books were cordoned off so that one had to ask to look at a book rather than browsing freely. On the first day of the school year in 1992 and subsequent years, the metal grille in front of the shop entrance was closed save for the small opening through which books were being handed.

Despite the paper crisis there were now newspapers, though not many copies were printed and they had very few pages. In Tirana there were three main newspapers, demonstrating that the constantly invoked '*pluralism*' was more than a fashionable new word. These were the former communist *Zëri i Popullit* (*Voice of the People*), *Rilindja Demokratike* (*Democratic Rebirth*), the new democratically elected government's organ, and the independent *Koha Jonë* (*Our Time*). The new freedom to denounce political opponents meant that the first two were simply polemics against each other; virtually no foreign news was reported. The polemicists preferred to concentrate on criticisms of their opponents' handling of local affairs whose disarray could always be blamed on the other side – past policy or present practice. The introspective isolationism of half a century dies hard. Neither *Rilindja* with its crude and unattractive rantings against the communists, nor *Zëri i Popullit's* stiff formal writing style and propaganda, made for good reading, let alone information. *Koha Jonë* was better for reading, and informative about the northwest coastal region of Lezhë where it was produced.

I wasted quite a lot of time early on talking to people in government offices and university departments: people in Statistics, Economics, Agricultural Policy. Vjollca had friends or relations in almost all of them. (The philosophy faculty, which included sociology, was closed for a year of rethink owing to Marxism-Leninism's no longer being a cool subject to teach or study, particularly if you were hoping for a scholarship to the West.) All the people I spoke to were interested in one thing only, which was to leave. The Foreign Relations Officer at the Ministry for Agriculture and Food said: 'Ah, Cambridge University. If you tell them to give an Albanian a scholarship, we will help you much more.' Others were nicer but rarely failed to ask for a job in England. None of them could have helped me any more than I could have helped them because they did not really know, and certainly did not care, what was happening on the ground outside their offices and IMF and World Bank reports. The one exception to this was the Agricultural University at Kamzë, just outside Tirana, where we went on spec with no contacts. Here some of the people we spoke to appeared really interested in the agricultural situation. So helpful were they that we went back several times despite the hours of waiting for transport, and physical discomfort once on it, which this involved. The buses back were nearly always too full to stop so that in desperation after an hour or so, one would leap into the back of any momentarily stationary van just to get away. Except at Kamzë, I learnt far more talking to our neighbours or visiting the provinces with pupils from the School of Languages. Almost all the officials with whom I had contact, including the Dean of the Agricultural University, had left the country before the end of 1993. All had left by the end of 1994.

Chapter Four

LOOKING FOR A FIELDWORK BASE

First Visit to Mirdita

C hoosing a region for fieldwork was difficult because so many areas sounded interesting, and regional differences were so marked that no one area was like another. We decided to start in the North with a visit to Mark's sister in Mirdita, accompanied by Prena and one of her sons, Pjetër. We assembled at the bus stop early one September morning. Vjollca had taken leave from school to act as interpreter since as yet we could hardly communicate in Albanian. At 9.30am the 8 o'clock bus arrived. All non-city buses had been privatised and arbitrary schedules were one result. Once seated in the bus, there followed another long wait, first for the bus to fill up, then for the conductor to return from scouring the town for tickets – terribly hard to find thanks to the paper shortage. Poor Pjetër, unaware that anthropologists spend half their lives waiting around, was exhausted with apologising for the dreadful effects of the new market economy.

Our destination was only an hour and a half's bus ride from Tirana. The bus let us off next to a steep rock face across from the River Fan i Vogel (Little Fan), which in summer runs between wide expanses of flat pebble beaches. The village of Fang lay across the river. In winter Fang is only accessible by a much longer route via a bridge in the town of Rubik; in summer and early autumn access is by wading through the Fan. We descended a bank and crossed to Fang, which lay about a hundred metres distant. To get to the family's house we had to walk across pathless fields and clamber through holes in fences. The cooperative dirt roads and paths had been annulled and some pretty aggressive indicators such as bramble fences and man-eating dogs ensured that no accidental trespassing occurred. Though we did not yet know it, cooperative land in Mirdita had been distributed on a different basis from the southern areas. Because the terrain is steep and cultivable land very scarce, village houses are not clustered, with family fields outside the settlement, but each house stands in its own land.

At the house we found that a large number of family members had collected from all over Mirdita, and the atmosphere for the next 24 hours was one of an extended party. Nearly all the family members had come, together with their husbands, wives and small children. One daughter and her husband were school teachers, two were ex-cooperative workers. The eldest son had started up a driving school in the nearby copper refining town of Rubik (population 2,800 in 1992). As car ownership had been illegal under communism there was now huge demand for driving lessons. Another son was in the army, about to be discharged and salary less; a third was semi-employed in the copper refining factory. This factory, together with the cooperatives, had been the main source of employment locally. It was now only partially functioning and many workers had been laid off. Those still employed attended work sporadically but continued to be paid their monthly wage of $15.

The family in Fang had been, and still were, devoted Communists. Unlike most people, they had not stripped their walls of the photographs of Enver Hoxha that had been *de rigueur* during the regime. Half self-mockingly, they pointed proudly to a photograph of Hoxha standing with their uncle. Two of the daughters vividly recalled the shock of Hoxha's death in 1985. The girls had been weeding a cooperative wheat field when the brigadier received a message summoning all villagers to the head village of Fierzë across the river. The river was too high to cross and the villagers had to go round the long way. In Fierzë the news of Hoxha's death was received, they said, with near hysterical grief and distress. 'We loved him,' said one of the girls. 'When Enveri made a speech it was like the sun coming out' – a phrase I was to hear from devoted Hoxhaists quite often. I said something about a rule of terror. 'Enveri was a personality to be loved independently of the regime; you don't hate Clinton because the USA has a prison system, do you?' one of the girls retorted, with a logic that defied argument. On a subsequent occasion, the daughters of the family, who had exceptionally beautiful singing voices, sang us the laments (*vajtim*) they had composed on Hoxha's death. One could not doubt the strength of their feelings, which were reminiscent of those for pop stars in the West. Nor could one doubt the impact of the ideological propaganda. When Ramiz Alia started talking of rapprochement with the West, the family told me, they were shocked; surely any contact with the West could only lead to disaster. (A decade later, they may feel that they were right.)

We saw the copper refining town of Rubik the next day on our way to visiting some more relations. The one-street town was thronged with groups of unemployed men standing around talking. The copper refinery, which stands between the road and the river, looked far too derelict to function. The dirt, the dilapidated concrete blocks of flats, the litter-strewn road and shabbily dressed inhabitants made a picture of extreme desolation. Here we picked up a cousin who worked as an engineer in the factory. By coincidence, *Ylli* (*Star*) of August 1982,[1] one of a pile of magazines I had been given in the winter at a school in Dropull, had an article praising this very same engineer whom I recognised from the magazine's photograph.

Ubiquitous gaiety and universal happiness were invariably a *leitmotiv* in these magazines, whether written for grown-ups or children. The style of this magazine was typical of the genre, and is worth quoting for the light it throws on the pervasiveness of propaganda. The article opens with a vignette of young people in a train returning from *aksion*. In every carriage laughter, jokes and youth songs could be heard. The journalist from *Ylli* asks if she may join a group of girls from Rubik. 'What's new in Rubik?' she asks. "Lots, we've just had a celebration because our factory's been made Heroine of Socialist Work. All the workers came to the celebration, including the pensioners." They told us of the amazing changes since they had started work, since their efforts to extract more and more copper.' Later, in Tirana, the journalist meets an ex-director of the factory who recalls that no year ever finished without the factory having exceeded its targets. In 1946 when the factory opened and he was one of the directors:

we had only just emerged from war. No experience, no knowledge. The workers were illiterate, bands of *diversant* (subversives/anarchists) roamed the country and tried to prevent Mirditor workers going to work. The mines and tools were in a bad

state, neglected since the Italian occupation. But the inexperi-
enced workers were conscientious and thirsty to learn. Nobody
watched the clock, they kept working until their comrade came
to relieve them; all that mattered was not to let the furnace out.
These men would attend school after work hours, often took their
children with them (Mirdita had few schools at the time), even
though this might involve several hours walk, in good weather
and bad. But now, 60 per cent of the young workers in the factory have finished secondary school. In the metallurgy section
there are 15 engineers, almost all from Mirdita. Now there are
so many skilled specialists that some have been sent by the Party
as advisors to mines elsewhere in Kukës, Laç, Bulqizë. You had
better go to Rubik and see for yourself.

So the journalist goes to Rubik, where there are so many exceptional workers that the factory head does not know who to single
out. A lot of names are mentioned. Finally, the journalist is shown
to the office of the young Martin, and someone goes to fetch him
from the workshop. Waiting in his office, the journalist notes the
many books neatly stacked on the table. 'The books look as though
the careful hand of a woman has just dusted them. On the left
are technical books in Albanian and foreign languages.' She opens
one book full of sketches, notes and observations written in a fine
clear hand. On the other side is a pile of literary volumes. Martin
enters, a young man of middle size, simply dressed but very tidy
and nice-looking. She and Martin do a tour of the factory. 'You see
those youths over there,' says Martin, 'they all studied metallurgy
at high school, but even so they are taking a course to get further
qualifications.' Wherever she goes in the factory, the journalist finds
happy people. The factory scene in 1992 might have taxed even
this journalist's skills at portraying *la vie en rose*.

In Rubik, nine of us squashed into the driving instructor
brother's Volkswagen Beetle and drove to Martin's village, Vau i
Shkjez, a couple of kilometres beyond Rubik. We stopped beside
the river and, descending a steep bank, came to one of the ubiquitous footbridges (*pasarel*), a suspension bridge with low wire sides
and a footpath of planks, but with more gaps than planks. Maintenance of any kind, bridges, buildings, roads, hillside terraces, had
clearly ceased some years before the end of Communism. Vandalism had exacerbated the problem. The experience of trying to

span the gaps between the planks of Vau i Shkjez's swaying bridge while trying not to look at the drop below, led some of us to wade through the river on the way back. I was not at all surprised to hear that the whole bridge had collapsed into the river a few months later. Travelling through the countryside in the winter of 1992, villages cut off as a result of recent bridge loss were often pointed out to us.

The father of the Vau i Shkjez family, Mark's brother, had six sons and two daughters. Apart from the geologist-engineer son we had picked up, two sons were at university, one at school, one had recently qualified as an engineer, and one was an illegal immigrant in Greece. The daughters, who, like Martin, were both married, had come with their children. The gathering here was even more numerous than that in Fang. Five of the sons waited on the assembled company like medieval pages. After the lunch feast I discovered that one of the sons, Preng, a 24-year-old engineer, had taught himself German. Quite apart from the relief of being able to talk to someone directly, he turned out to be an interesting, if tortured, character. Standing outside the house he indicated the extent of the family's land, a quarter of a hectare. It would have been inadequate even for a small family's subsistence; this family had eight children, six of whom, the sons, would receive equal shares. The fact that in Mirdita families had reclaimed their patrimonial land, while probably the more practical solution given the terrain, did not resolve the problem of population increase. Since the 1940s the population throughout Albania had tripled. Abortion under Communism was illegal, doctors caught carrying out abortions were imprisoned; mothers producing ten children were acclaimed 'Heroine of the People' and awarded a cow. Since all male offspring inherit equal portions of their father's land, since most families had seven to ten surviving children and Mirditans' object was to produce as many sons as possible, the pressure on this newly privatised land may be imagined. All the more so in view of the fact that unemployment, already very high, was increasing as the factories and mines reduced their activities or closed down completely.

It emerged that Preng had had some kind of nervous crisis, that his parents had found him on two recent occasions sleepwalking. He woke one night to find, as he believed, one of his brothers about to strangle him. His parents believed that he was possessed by devils. A wise woman who could exorcise the evil eye had tried to help him. Now he was seeing a Catholic priest in Tirana. He had just become an aficionado of Stefan Zweig and longed to have access to the hitherto forbidden Nietzsche and Freud. It was not necessary to have read Freud to imagine part of the source at least of his frightening mystical experiences where so large a family had so little. He was trying with the help of the Catholic priest in Tirana to get a visa for Germany. With virtually no land and no employment opportunities, emigration was many Mirditans' only prospect. Almost every family in the village with suitably aged males had at least one member presently in, or recently returned from, Greece.

Back in Fang, the situation was the same, though no-one from 'our' family had yet set off for Greece. In a discussion about the distribution of land with the Fang party, a schoolteacher brother-in-law, in an aside to me and Vjollca, said that he feared the situation would lead in the future to conflicts between brothers. I remembered this foreboding when, back in Tirana, I noticed increasingly frequent reports of family conflicts over property in the newspaper *Koha Jonë*, the independent newspaper founded in the northern coastal town of Lezhë. It was not difficult to see why intra-family quarrels were much more frequent than quarrels between non-kin. The tripling of the population over the past 50 years, at once the result of improved health care and the party's pronatalist policy, coupled with partible inheritance, meant more male heirs contending for less land.

The following spring, in the hope of following up an invitation to return to Fang, we asked Mark when we might go again. For two months he and Prena were curiously evasive. We began to feel paranoid; had we made some blunder in Fang and offended? At last it was revealed with some embarrassment that a murder attempt had been made on Mark's sister and her husband by their nephews who lived next door. The wife had been beaten up, but less severely than her husband who had been lucky to survive. After a long period in hospital he was now back home. The affair, like dozens of other assaults and murders reported for the area in *Koha Jonë*, centred on inheritance. One of the nephews was now in prison, the other was on the run. The nephew who had been caught by the police made the defence that his cousins all had employment outside agriculture while he and his brother did not. Therefore, his family should have a larger portion of their grandfather's land. Land disputes continued to dominate the lives of the families we subsequently got to know in Mirdita for several years.

This first glimpse into Mirditan life aroused my interest in the region as a potential centre for fieldwork. From the point of view of decollectivisation it provided a complete contrast with the southern regions. Unlike some of the southern regions, there was no question of the area soon being depopulated by a mass exodus to Greece. The region was representative of much of northern Albania as regards resources. Large-scale unemployment, the result of decollectivisation and gradual shut down of mines and factories meant that alternative survival strategies would have to be found.

While we were in Fang that first time I had asked which part of Mirdita an elderly aunt in Mirditor dress came from. 'From the "depths" – *thellësi*,' I was told. I asked what this meant. It meant a region which was much less accessible, where conditions were much less 'developed'. I said I would like to visit the 'depths'. 'You can't possibly,' they asserted flatly; somehow the depths were beyond the pale and hence, from my point of view, irresistible. By the time we had exhausted our survey of other possible regions for long-term fieldwork, I had made up my mind to spend as much time as possible doing fieldwork in the 'depths' of Mirdita.

From this first venture into the provinces we learnt quite a lot, though sometimes the significance only became clear later. We had only been in Albania for a week or two and knew almost nothing about 1990s Mirdita. I had read Edith Durham's *High Albania*, a fascinating account of the north at the beginning of the twentieth century that includes a visit to Mirdita. But it had not occurred to me that the book might have more than background relevance to my current interest in developments since the fall of Communism and the dismantling of the cooperatives. Nor did we discover until we returned the following spring after visiting several other regions and learning more of the language, how different Mirditans were from southern and central Albanians.

Dropull Again

In October we went back to Dropull to see if I could find a suitable place for fieldwork in that region. We took the bus down to the

Greek border. The bus left Tirana at two in the morning. We made a dawn stop for petrol in the beautiful Mallakastra hills, an area of oil extraction and processing as well as the site of one of the most notorious prisons, Ballsh. All over Albania, the petrol pumps were surrounded at this period of petrol shortage by a cage of iron bars to deflect theft; getting hold of petrol was very difficult, sometimes impossible. The last break before Kakavia was at Tepelenë, birthplace of the cruel Ali Pasha. The stop is between the River Vjosa and a huge waterfall and the place is full of very large plane trees. We walked up to the eating place, which is perched on a steep bank next to the cascade, and naively asked if there was a lavatory. A serving woman sardonically jerked her head in the direction of the trees above.

At Kakavia, there were the usual throngs of Albanians being prevented, for the moment at least, from crossing the border. We asked one of the Albanian customs officers whom we had met in the winter how we could get to Vrisera. In the winter we had walked across the fields but now we were burdened with luggage. Luckily a van was about to return to Vrisera and we got a lift. Where there were so few buses, taking a lift was normal, and hitchhikers simply paid a contribution for the petrol. In Vrisera we found Irini in her accountant's office. We had not seen Irini since staying with her in the winter, though we had met up with her husband in England where, thanks to an aid programme, he and some colleagues had been invited to stay with a family in Wigan. I had gone up to Wigan to meet Vasilis and his colleagues who were finding the set-up there rather puzzling. During my visit their English host insisted on driving me over to his huge warehouse full of old army stores belonging to the Ministry of Agriculture and Fisheries. There he proudly showed me hundreds of odd looking minimalist cast iron ovens and a vast quantity of very unpalatable military emergency rations (I was presented with a sample to test) said to be brimful of essential minerals and protein. The warehouse owner wanted to ship the rations and the ovens to Albania where he was convinced they would be deeply appreciated. What did I think? It was an awkward moment. Food might be short, but it would have taken full-scale famine for the World War II emergency rations to appeal to the Albanians. As for the stoves, all the Albanians I had met were interested in modernising, acquiring the latest Western models in mod cons. Every Albanian family whose house I had visited had a good wood stove with an oven. Later, Vasilis and his friends privately asked me how this quixotic plan might be tactfully deflected. I never learnt what happened to the bizarre shipment.

From Vrisera, a message had been sent to Sofia, Irini's younger daughter, to bring down the donkey to carry our inconvenient luggage. I felt bad about this because Sofia was embarrassed to be seen in public with the donkey. That night over supper, we learnt that almost all the boys over 15 from Sofia's school had left for Greece. Quite a lot of girls had also left for Greece with their families. The population of her school had dropped from 200 to 90. There was a dearth of teachers as well since so many had gone to work in Greece. The local primary school had not been able to open at all this autumn for lack of teachers.

We spent the next day in Vodino while all but the widowed grandfather went down to the plain for work and school. The grand-father reminisced about the different regimes he had lived through. Zog's had been the worst; 1946 to 1949 had been the best. Then the big landowners' estates had been distributed so that everybody got enough land and animals to do well if they worked hard. During these three years before collectivisation they did do well, building houses and outbuildings, getting their fields established. All this was lost under collectivisation, when it was slavery for the state's gain. But at least under Communism they had security, food and safety. The present period, he said, is not as bad as under Zog, but it is worse than under Hoxha. Now people like Vodino's 35-year-old tractor driver who had bought a tractor in Greece, or those with cafes and restaurants in Vrisera, are doing well. The rest simply leave if they can for abroad.

We had been told not to wander around the village as we would be eaten by dogs. We knew this was not the real reason and managed to sneak out while the grandfather was busy with the animals. I wanted to see whether it would be any use making a base here for future fieldwork. Irini had offered us the use of a house belonging to an absent relation. It was a rare case of an available and desirable independent home base. But it was soon obvious that beyond a handful of elderly members of the Greek minority, very large numbers of sheep and goats and very small numbers of herders – unemployed Albanians from further North in search of work – there would be precious little life to research. The able-bodied who had not yet left for Greece were planning to leave.

We set off for Kakavia with Irini who had kindly loaded our luggage on the donkey that Soula led across the hills down to the main road and the border. The guards both sides of the border knew us, and the ease with which we could gain access to Eldorado when so many struggled for days often without success, was embarrassing. The bus for Athens was waiting on the other side. The driver was yelling at the Albanians boarding the bus as if they were criminals, insulting them and complaining about their luggage. Shortly after the bus was under way it was halted for a passport check. '*Falso!*' yelled the customs police every so often as they proceeded down the bus checking to see whether the visas were genuine, and some passengers were made to get off.

Korça

We came back to Tirana in mid-November. Of the things we had brought for Vjollca nothing quite matched the appeal of a roll of plastic bags. For ourselves we had brought instant soups, instant coffee, an electric heater and a pocket torch. For Artan we had brought Bon Jovi. Albanians in winter clothes looked much poorer and shabbier than they had in summer when the women in particular had managed to look elegant. Mass produced communist coats and woollen scarves were more obvious in winter, and you could meet the same scarf on a hundred different wearers. Walking through the streets in November, the biggest change from earlier in the autumn was the proliferation of spit gobbets on the pavements. The schools were still windowless and pupils had to wear their coats in class. There were even larger numbers of missionaries, mainly US evangelical sects. Some of Vjollca's friends and relations whose flats were rented out to Mormon missionaries had undergone formal conversion. Several pupils from the School of Languages had become paid interpreters for missionaries. We frequently found missionaries in the school dispensing bibles and hopes of scholarships to the United States.

I decided to reconnoitre in a new area for a southern fieldwork base and arranged to visit Korça in the southeast where the family of Vjollca's sister-in-law lived. As soon as Tiranians heard we were going to Korça, they applauded us because 'in Korça there is culture'. We took the bus to Korça with the sister-in-law's brother,

Ilo, a 24-year-old school teacher. The road, which is mountainous, passes through the towns of Elbasan and Pogradec. Elbasan was once so beautiful that in the 1930s the English writer on Albanian tribal law, Margaret Hasluck, chose to make her home there. Since then it has become an eyesore as well as polluting – the centre of Albania's rapidly dying steel industry. Pogradec, beside Lake Ohrid, was the aesthetic setting for the 1970s film *Duajë emrin tëndë* (*I would like your name*) in which hypocrite boy woos innocent girl so as to be connected with her father who has just been given an influential party post.

Korça is on a plateau 800m above sea level and, this being November, was cold. Ilo's family was Orthodox, as were most town dwelling Korçans. His father was a retired doctor and his mother had worked in a laboratory. The father spoke a little French. Ilo played the guitar most of the time, and when one of his strings broke, ingeniously replaced it with a piece of telephone wire, which he found after a long search somewhere in the town. During the evenings of our stay Ilo would recline on a divan in the kitchen, the only heated room, and ask me to test him on capitals throughout the world. Though a sports enthusiast rather than a scholar, he evidently found geography tests a stimulating way of getting through the evenings. The alternative (which I rather enjoyed) was watching old television films showing folk singers as they warbled from table to table rolling their eyes in pre-democracy Albanian restaurants. One evening when capital cities were all but exhausted, Ilo astonished me by making references to Homer, Virgil, Dante and Shakespeare, all of whom he had read, he said, at university. A year or so later, I came across one of the textbooks used for the course he had taken, which turned out to be a sort of Bluffers Guide to literary name dropping.

On the first morning after our arrival, Ilo's father took me on a tour of the environs of Korça to help me choose a village for fieldwork. Ideally, he said, we should go further afield to Voskopoja or Vithkuq, centres of culture, but these villages were within walking distance of the town and had some culture. On the tour we saw more countryside than settlements but whenever we did meet a local, the doctor played the feudal, deeply respected doctor-figure benignly greeting benighted peasant retainers. At the end of the tour there was some culture in the form of a derelict though still pretty Byzantine church.

In the afternoon we were taken to meet some relations. The gathering consisted of a dozen or so well-dressed Korçans, and was reminiscent of very dull formal Greek visits. At least the linguistic strains were lessened by meeting several elderly Korçans who spoke Greek having attended Greek schools in their youth. It was a relief the day after to accompany Ilo and some fellow teachers to the village outside Korça where they taught. We took a bus to the bottom of a mountain a few kilometres outside the town. From there we tramped up a hill and across stunning sparkling mountain scenery to a village called Lavdar built on a series of very steep slopes. Talking to Ilo's fellow teachers as much as limited Albanian allowed, I was told yet again to go to the villages of Voskopoja and Vithkuq because 'there you will find culture whereas the people in Lavdar are backward and stupid'. 'But I haven't come to find culture,' I said, exasperated, 'we've got plenty of culture in England.' Luckily they thought this was funny.

At the top of the first slope was the Lavdar school, an eight-year school catering for children up to the age of 14. After a tour of the school I asked if I could go and look at the village. The teachers from Korça said: 'What for?' They had never been beyond the school, there was nothing to see. Eventually a local offered to come with me. We descended an almost vertical slope to a cluster of small houses where we found the headman's brother, the village hodja (Muslim priest) at home. His house was fitted with beautifully made wooden cupboards and he turned out to be a carpenter as well as a priest. He was a charming man in his late 50s who was on a high as a result of a recent plane trip to Saudi Arabia where he had been promised aid both for building a mosque, and, vitally, for installing an irrigation channel. Both were in the process of being constructed. Some relations and neighbours joined us in his house to see two foreigners close-up. The welcoming custom was striking. One would be greeted by everyone on arrival and as soon as one had sat down, each of the people who had greeted us would walk over and go through exactly the same procedure all over again: shaking one's hand, repeating the formal phrases of welcome, and enquiring after one's family and health. I asked the hodja's daughters and daughters-in-law their names. The jolliest one, a pretty girl with red cheeks, was called Borzilok, basil. They thought our broken Albanian was hilarious and laughed in a refreshingly spontaneous way very different from the refined politenesses of Korçan visits.

I asked about the size of their landholdings, which turned out to be very extensive, and their most pressing problems. The biggest obstacle to farming was the lack of a road. Some young men from the village were working in Greece but shortage of labour was not a problem. If they had a road they could start using machinery in the fields.

The hodja carpenter took me to see the half-built mosque and I asked whether women would be going to it as well as men. 'Good heavens, yes, we're not fanatics,' he exclaimed. He asked what religion we were in England and when I explained, he pointed beneficently to the sky and said with an encompassing gesture: 'It's all the same – one god.' Before leaving, I asked whether it would be feasible for us to come and spend some months in Lavdar. Would there be a room we could rent? After some discussion, it was agreed that we could have a room in the headman's house.

We walked down to the foot of the mountain the direct pathless way, the way which ideally would one day become a road linking Lavdar with the outskirts of Korça. Back at Ilo's house, his father asked us what we had thought of Lavdar. We said we had liked it so much we were thinking of spending some months there in the spring when the weather had warmed up. 'You've picked the worst village of all. Why not one of the villages we went to yesterday, why not Voskopoja? The people in Lavdar are dirty, low.' It took me a while, communication channels being rather dimmed by our linguistic handicaps, to realise that what he was objecting to was the choice of a Muslim village rather than an Orthodox one.

To take our hosts' minds off us and our low tastes, we tried to be out as much as possible and went off in the afternoons to explore the town. There were some beautiful but terribly rundown traditional two-storey houses in a quarter at the top of the town just above our hosts' flat. Lower down was the market where there were several narrow streets full of goods for sale, mostly second hand, and one huge central area where the ground was covered with piles of aid donated jumble-sale clothes for sale. There was a rather sinister feel to the place, the presence perhaps of potentially threatening wheeler dealers. The narrower darker streets, more enclosed than Tirana market, made for a more intense atmosphere, much less good-humoured. Perhaps the closeness to the Greek border gave rise to more smuggling and risky activities. In the wide main street there were shops with dusty displays of very nice glass jugs, the famous Korça glass products no longer, of course, being manufactured. Ilo showed us a state hotel building, which was in the process of being reclaimed by some relations of his. The bus ride back to Tirana starting at cold dark six in the morning was memorable for the icy chill due to the glasslessness of the bus windows.

Laberia

After shivering through several nights on the high Korçan plateau, I decided our winter fieldwork place had better be in a warm area. Shortly after our arrival in Tirana in September we had met Agron, a teacher from the former Faculty of Marxism-Leninism with whom I had communicated in mutually partially recalled French. He had taken advantage of democracy, he told me, to become a sociologist in the Western tradition. He was naturally hoping that out of our acquaintance some well-funded international research project would evolve, and he introduced us to several other colleagues with similar unrealistic hopes. He said he could hire a car and driver cheaply to show us his region, Vlora and environs on the southwest coast. The terrain and crops, hilly with olives and oranges, were much the same as in the area where I had worked in southern Greece. I knew something about growing olives and oranges so I would be able to concentrate on the problems contingent to decollectivisation and change of regime. Agron said he would be the ideal guide to the perfect fieldwork village as he had friends in many of the villages close to Vlora and knew the area intimately. The lure of a car, which could be used to look at a number of villages containing known people we could talk to, rather than taking a bus and being landed with no choice, led me to accept.

The car fell through owing to our not having a telephone, but I was so desperate to get to a village and start rural fieldwork in the south that we agreed to meet Agron at 6 0'clock one November morning and take the bus to Vlora. At 5.00am a terrific thunderstorm arose. At 5.30 am, when we were getting up our courage to set out in the pitch dark and the storm, I looked out of the window and saw that the only person in the street was a madman who was careering crazily around hollering. I would have felt cowardly in any one of the contingencies – the storm, the madman or the dark streets, which might be dangerous in November 1992. The combination ensured that we set off in a thoroughly shaky state. Luckily we only got soaked. We met up with Agron who took us along the Bulevard and fearlessly through a pitch dark park beyond which was the bus stop.

As usual we had to wait a long time before the bus had filled up, and we could see that Agron was not happy about the weather or the state of his feet and shoes. About half way through the four hour journey, he got talking to an officer who was travelling with his family to a village inland from Vlora called Vranisht. The officer was going to visit his parents. Agron, who was already tiring of our project, suggested that we go with this man and see if Vranisht suited us. Had I foreseen that this revisionist sociologist was going to be useless even in his native province, I would have accepted what may well have been a golden opportunity. But I had no idea at the time that Agron did not really have close connections with any of the villages, or that he was going to back out of the deal.

In Vlora we went to stay with Agron's sister who lived in a nice old house right in the centre of the town. It was a rundown version of the sort of nineteenth century neo-classical house increasingly rare in Greek towns, with a gone-to-seed garden in the back and a wrought iron balcony overlooking the street where the old man of the house sat most of the day. Agron went out and found a driver who for too high a sum would drive us to some villages. We eventually settled for less money and ultimately a useless route as before long the driver said the road was unsuitable for his car. Not, however, before we had reached the part of the coast road just below one of Enver Hoxha's luxurious villas, Ujë Ftohtë (Cold Water), which the driver, a fervent Enverist (like many drivers), pointed out to us with great pride. Agron, increasingly keen to be rid of us, suggested we look at Kanina, a fortress village on top of a hill right next to Vlora. It was only two or three kilometres and the driver said he would take us, for more money of course. I said we would go by foot, which would give us a better idea of the country besides being pleasant exercise after sitting in buses and cars so long. Agron was dead against this idea but eventually submitted.

Kanina was interesting, set on the mountain overlooking Vlora with a magnificent view of the sea, but interesting more from an historical point of view than a sociological one. It was too small and isolated from any hinterland to provide much activity, social or economic, though it was easy to foresee that in the future, however distant, it would become a tourist centre. I did not feel it would provide enough depth to justify spending a prolonged period there. Agron kept telling us that no village could match it for sheer anthropological and historical interest, and moreover, that he had just remembered he must be back in Tirana tomorrow. By now evening had fallen, it was dark, and we started walking down the deserted mountain road back to Vlora. I was rather surprised that Agron, a short, slightly built man, seemed unworried by this night walking in supposedly lawless 1992 Albania, but his desperation to be rid of us may have made him careless of the odd brigand. Or as a former teacher of communist ideals, he may simply have become so used to guaranteed safety under dictatorship that he had forgotten it could no longer be counted on. Earlier he had told us with a giggle that for several years he had been a most dedicated teacher of Marxism-Leninism in a village school just north of Vlora.

He left the next day and we hired a driver for a more reasonable sum to drive us in a new direction, this time towards Vranisht. Each village we got to, the driver would slow down and ask: 'This one?' It was a mad enterprise to choose a village from the window of a car, but a mixture of disappointment and impatience dictated that we do something. Trawling Tirana University's Economics and English Departments for students from the area had proved abortive, and the School of Languages had produced only town dwellers from this area. At first each village was too flat or too ugly or just did not appeal, and I told the driver to drive on. We crossed an impressively monumental bridge, the Drashovica Bridge, where the driver proudly pointed out a huge statue in Socialist Realist style commemorating a battle won by the Partisans against the Germans. Beyond there was a village to the right of the road on the far side of a river. The bridge linking it to the main road had collapsed. Considering what had been achieved in the field of electrification, the primitive level of bridges not required for monumental purposes was surprising. Where in 1945 not one village had electricity, by 1970 the last village, renamed Dawn in honour of this achievement, was electrified. Although one result was the scarring of the countryside with huge rusting pylons, the cause was clearly a worthy one. It seemed odd that ground communications were so undeveloped by contrast. A couple of years later in the North, we used to be struck by the sight of isolated houses unreachable by road of any kind, sporting Sharp satellite dishes glimpsed through the trees.

Eventually we reached a state farm centre. These are recognisable by the jerry-built apartment blocks standing in mud in the middle of nowhere. As they are usually in the depths of the countryside, the unaesthetic impact was much greater than that of slums on an urban periphery. This one, ironically named Kotë (alb. useless) had a dozen or so derelict high rise blocks of flats, one filthy main street – the road we were on – and hordes of unemployed men, a crowd of whom gathered round us. They were friendly though rough and raucous. Our driver explained that we were English. One man who obviously saw himself as more sophisticated, said: 'I understand; you want to learn about old customs and traditions.' I was ashamed, given the dramatic economic crisis, that he could think an outsider so insensitive to current social upheaval as to be collecting old customs. Eventually we started to climb the foothills. The countryside, now rolling hills, though well furnished with enormous pylons, became more beautiful closer to the mountains. After some time a woman appeared from around a bend in the road spinning as she walked. It was a fatal moment, fully vindicating the state farm man's insight – I was seduced by the promise of the old-fashioned picturesque. The next village, Gjorm, which did not appear for some time, consisted of houses built either side of the road up a hill. It looked rather large for manageable fieldwork so we drove on a kilometre or so till the road ceased to be asphalt. The driver said there was no way he would take his car on the dirt road, so reluctantly we decided to go to the school in Gjorm and talk to the teachers.

Since Soula and I were still far from fluent in Albanian, though we were beginning to understand quite a lot, our spokesman was the driver. All he knew about us was what he had managed to piece together from our broken explanations during the drive. In fact, he did a pretty good job of explaining our aims. We were shown into the staff room where round a large long table we sat down with the Head and about a dozen teachers. One young teacher spoke some French, and we partly communicated through him. The general verdict was that we would be welcome to stay in the village, that Soula could attend the school, which was large and catered for primary aged children and up to 18. At this point I should have accepted the offer to stay the night at a villager's house and later, after some days, made a decision as to whether Gjorm was suitable or whether further into the mountains should be tried. I asked Soula what she thought and she, who had liked the look of the school and was desperate to get settled, begged to fix on Gjorm. So we said we would return to Tirana, get our luggage and move in the next day but one. One of the factors influencing this rash decision was the solid stable atmosphere of the school. In the slightly anarchic situation that predominated, I thought that a large well-functioning school would be a good source of initial contacts. Many of the school teachers I had met in Dropull and in Mirdita had been strikingly intelligent and intellectually lively. But though school discipline in Gjorm was rigorously enforced, I did not in fact meet any teachers like those I had met elsewhere. Either Laberian teachers were different or the liveliest had already left for abroad.

On our return to Vlora the bus did not stop in the expected place and we ended up in the wrong part of town for getting to Gjorm. I had to leave Soula, vulnerable young girl with luggage, in the semi-care of some complete strangers, kiosk owners, in the centre of a town well known for some less than lawful citizens. It may have been self-deception, but I was convinced that no Albanian would harm a child of 12 even in post-communist chaos and she, fortunately, was sure I would not expose her to danger (as opposed to tedium and discomfort). In retrospect I think I was right for 1992; by 1996 it might not have been such a good idea, when the Albanian prostitution rackets across the sea from Vlora had become big business.

In Gjorm we looked for the Headmaster, whom we found in a *klub* (cafe-bar) that had been newly opened beyond the village at the point where the asphalt road ended. He was fairly drunk, and after a longish pause of non-recognition, put his arm round me and suggested we join him for a drink. We rejoined the driver instead and found the man who had originally agreed to house us while two of his children were away. This man, a shoemaker, was in the midst of making a pair of rubber tyre moccasins for a shepherd. His wife had been a nurse in the cooperative creche, and had only three children due to an illness after the third birth. This number of children was so unusual in Gjorm, where many of the families we met had ten or more, that she herself supplied the explanation. The eldest of their children was learning foreign languages in the newly opened language school in Gjirokastër. The second, a boy of 14, had been sent, like several other boys from Gjorm, to a hodja in Vlora to study to become a hodja himself. For the next four years he would be studying the Qur'an and learning Arabic. It was hoped that this would lead to a career in a rich Arab country. When I later asked another Gjorm family with a boy studying to be a hodja in Vlora, whether they had sent him there for religion or money, they said: 'Well, money; we don't have any experience of religion, it doesn't mean anything to us.'

At the shoemaker's gate we called out his name, a custom designed to ensure that any guard dogs are under control, and went down a path to the bungalow, which had a verandah where the shoemaker was working at his shoes. To the right, and facing on to the verandah, was a modern Turkish lavatory, a recent improvement. This had no front wall or door, though we later discovered a short piece of corrugated sheeting that could be propped so that only the upper part of the occupant was visible – an arrangement we found extraordinarily inhibiting since the shoemaker and his friends were nearly always on the verandah.

The next morning we were woken by the arrival at seven o'clock of a kind student doctor offering to give us a lift in the ambulance (which was used to non-asphalted roads) to the next village, Brataj. Brataj was smaller than Gjorm though it had the advantage of housing the district medical and dental centre; a rather dubious advantage we realised after we had inspected it. The dental part was by far the more active, though its activities were necessarily confined to wrenching out teeth, since nowhere in 1992 was there filling material. Even Vjollca in Tirana had asked us to bring material from Greece or England so that she could have her teeth filled. We met a large number of people during our stay in Gjorm with wads of raki-soaked material stuffed into bloody gaps in their mouths.

While we were in Brataj we paid a visit to an army officer who lived at the top of the village, which was built on a series of huge beautiful rounded rocks, a characteristic of the Laberian countryside. Two of the officer's sons were also in the army, and it emerged that the Laberia region was a breeding place for army officers, doubtless an expedient solution to over-population and shortage of employment under Communism, when becoming a priest or a hodja was not an option. Some of the people we met in

Brataj were very forthcoming and offered to help with my study, whose aim seemed much clearer to them than to most people in Gjorm. It would probably have been a better fieldwork base if only because of its greater compactness and smaller size. In retrospect I cannot imagine why we did not move there; I suspect I did not have the nerve to face anger and recrimination from Soula.

Back in Gjorm we made tactful enquiries about alternative living arrangements, which would give us a little more independence. I asked whether there were any houses with just one old person or couple. The headmaster said in a shocked voice: 'We never leave old people to live alone.' Were there any empty houses? Laughter; every house was full of people. Indeed a lot of the houses, we later discovered, contained three or four sons and their families as well as the sons' parents.

At this point a newly married school teacher called Drita, into whose class Soula was to go, said we could live in her house. This turned out to be a partially built bungalow, which you reached by leaping across stepping stones over a broad stream; there was no bridge. It looked an ideal solution providing a modicum of independence. Drita's husband was an army provisions truck driver and worked in Himara on the coast between Vlora and Saranda. I was under the (retrospectively naive) impression that when he was away Drita and Soula and I would share this house. In fact, showing us the house seemed to be a red herring and for reasons never clear we ended up living with her parents-in-law. Her father-in-law, Hasan, had been the village agronomist. Two of his sons were working in Corfu along with half the other young males of Laberia, so their beds were free. His only daughter taught art at the school. As well as the new house for his son and Drita, Hasan had also acquired a building site in Vlora. This certainly lent credence to the popular belief that former cooperative officials had managed to do well for themselves during the communist period by fair means or foul. Hasan's best friend was the former cooperative vet, Sinan, who lived in a new two-storey house, which he was in the process of improving. Their favourite topic of conversation was cars. What would be the best make to buy and what did they cost in England? They were full of unqualified praise for the past era and Enver Hoxha's merits, but they were not letting nostalgia get in the way of present advantages such as car ownership.

It speaks volumes for the open-mindedness and incredibly generous hospitality of Albanians that this family could even consider having two complete strangers to live in their house. From the start they refused rent and only allowed us to contribute minimally to our food costs. As soon as we had moved to Hasan's, Soula started going to school. Unlike most schools we had seen this one still had its windows and classroom furniture intact, although there was no heating except for a wood stove in the infants' classroom to which each infant's family contributed in turn. Drita's class turned out to be run on draconian lines with iron discipline enforced by physical punishment. The timetable also included French lessons until the French teacher emigrated to Italy, and once it was discovered that Soula could sing 'Sur le Pont d'Avignon', she had to go through the torture of endless repeat performances in the playground for those unlucky pupils who were not in her class.

One of the reasons Soula had wanted to stay in Gjorm was the cheerful effect produced by brightly coloured pictures all over the school, painted on pieces of polystyrene and stuck to the walls. These turned out to be bracing admonitions in the communist tradition urging pupils to fulfil their ambitions, work with a will and be good citizens. With the touching stoicism of a 12 year old, Soula went off each day to a toughish time. There were lighter moments occasionally, such as the discovery that her class was reading aloud E. Nesbit's *Phoenix and the Carpet* (in Albanian) in the literature lesson. In Tirana we had met the publisher's reader responsible for the translation of several children's classics into Albanian. Most of the works in question, like the E. Nesbits and the Mary Poppins books, would have been ideologically unacceptable to the communist censor. But one successful ploy for getting past the censor was to arrange for an introduction to be written by a prestigious, politically acceptable Albanian author.

While Soula was at school I was finding out about the recent privatisation of land, how popular it was and what was being produced. As elsewhere in the South at that period, land distribution was regarded in Gjorm as fairly satisfactory. There had been a few disputes earlier on but most had been resolved. The fact that land parcels lay outside the village made redistribution much easier than in those northern regions where land surrounded each house. The chief agricultural activity was stockbreeding, mainly cows and sheep, for which there was ample grazing land. Most of the women I spoke to who had formerly worked in the cooperative fields, said they were much better off now that they could spend more time in their own households. Every evening the road below Gjorm completely filled up for several kilometres with recently distributed ex-cooperative cows, sheep and goats being brought back from grazing to the village by a family member. Sometimes we accompanied Raisa, Hasan's wife, to the family's fields a kilometre or so down the road where their cows grazed for a couple of hours.

Next door to Hasan lived Vera, a woman of 34, with a husband in Chicago. She asked me to teach her English so that when she joined her husband she would find life in the United States easier. Although we wrote many letters and filled in quantities of forms, her chances of getting a visa looked thinner each time we tried and failed. Her husband had escaped in the great exodus to Italy on one of those boats swarming with desperate Albanians seen on television screens all over the Western world. Vera had the chance to go with him but taking a baby was not possible. Having finally given birth to a healthy daughter after a series of stillbirths and the death of a baby son, she could not bring herself to leave the child in Albania and had stayed behind. She was now living with her parents and four of her brothers. Two brothers were married, one with three children, one recently wed with a new baby. Two others, surprisingly, were still bachelors despite being in their 40s. The reason was political. Her third brother had been in prison for five years for having belonged to Balli Kombëtar. His 'bad biography' (*biografi keq*) meant that marrying into his family during Communism would have been death to the career prospects of the family that made such an alliance. Vera and one of her brothers had solved the problem by marrying into families whose own biographies were bad. The others had stayed unmarried and, like numerous older bachelors with 'bad biographies' throughout Albania, were now getting married, usually to women much younger than themselves. One had just got engaged to the daughter of a neighbouring family; there was no restriction in this area on marrying within the village.

The first bride, who wore a kerchief with gold pendants, the customary head dress in her Greek speaking Himara village, had a separate kitchen and cooked only for her family. The newer bride had to cook for everyone else. But she was cheerful about this, explaining that she was used to it as the eldest sister in her own large family. She was always cheerful, even the morning I met her seated side saddle on her husband's motor scooter, wearing a slightly moth-eaten but luxurious looking fur coat (an Italian aid donation the like of which were common in the Vlora area), and heading for the dental clinic in Brataj to get an aching tooth pulled.

No houses in Gjorm had running water inside, but they were much better off than in northern villages, where the water has to be fetched from a spring often at a considerable distance. Gjorm villagers had water in their yards where they did all the washing up. Water for clothes washing was heated in huge cauldrons. Most houses apart from the shoemaker's, with its more sophisticated though geographically inconvenient Turkish arrangement, had a lavatory hut in the yard, on whose floor you squatted. In Hasan's case the hut had a small stream running through it. This might have been an ideal system except that the stream, which ran down from the road, passed just to the left of the squatter; and one would often arrive to find piles of excrement, which had been accumulating all day. However, to clean the lavatory the stream was made use of despite the fact that it ran straight into Vera's garden; an arrangement which must have put a strain on neighbourly relations. In fact, under Communism political differences had virtually eliminated relations altogether. Hygiene was conceived differently in Mirditan villages. There, with a few notable exceptions where lavatories were dispensed with in favour of the great outdoors, outdoor privies were earth closets often with raised seats and lime supplies for killing germs. But unlike Gjorm houses, which were very clean, in Mirdita one often encountered bedbugs and fleas.

For much of the time that we stayed in Gjorm there was no electricity. This was a severe blow to the villagers since some weeks of the blackout coincided with the period when Enver Hoxha's wife, Nexhmija, was being tried in Tirana. The trial was televised and provided entertainment for those with electricity for many evenings. The accusations, which seemed to give greatest pleasure to the public, centred on the luxurious furnishings and unnecessary household goods indulged in at public expense by Nexhmija. In Gjorm we had occasional tantalising glimpses of court scenes when some extra clever Laberian electrician momentarily solved the blackout problem, but the glimpses were fleeting.

Electricity was not the only mod con missing. As the entire tele-phone system had been ripped out and there was no postal delivery service, communication with the outside world was virtually im-possible. Poor Vera would go down to Vlora from time to time to collect a letter from her husband and try to telephone him. More often than not, the Vlora telephone exchange had a sign on the door saying 'out of order'. When the office was open there were huge queues waiting to telephone. As Vlora had no international prefix at the time, Vlora citizens could not be called from abroad. But it was sometimes possible to make international calls and Vera would spend literally hours first queueing, then trying to get through to Chicago.

Sometimes Vera paid a car driver to take her to Vlora and took us with her. Two or three young men in Gjorm had acquired cars with Greek earnings. The cars had no number plates and, since this was an offence, tactics had to be employed to avoid police fines. On one occasion we were stopped by a policeman who after some rebukes and mild threats of impounding the car, started eyeing a snazzy key ring the driver had suspended above the dashboard. This was gracefully presented to the policeman, and fines and impounding were forgotten. Mostly we went to Vlora by bus. These were rare and packed. You could walk up beyond the village in the hope of getting in before anyone else. But two out of three buses were usually too full to stop in Gjorm at all. Sundays was the most difficult day to get a bus because Sunday was market day in Vlora as all over Albania, and a huge animal market was held on the hillside just before Vlora. In the town itself, several streets in the centre became a market so thronged with people that it was literally hard to move through the crowd. On non-market days as well, Vlora was even more a mix of animals and people than Tirana; there were regular encounters with sheep and goats on the stairs of apartment blocks, and always a flock of turkeys being driven somewhere through the town. Turkeys were a particularly Laberian feature. Every yard in Gjorm had turkeys perched in trees.

In the middle of December Drita's husband, Tajar, came back on leave after an absence of three months. We were all in Hasan's kitchen when he arrived. After greeting his parents and grand-mother, he shook Hairja formally by the hand without looking at her. It would have been a breach of propriety to indicate that there was anything more than acquaintance between these newlyweds. Tajar's arrival meant that Drita stopped sleeping at her parent's house and took over the cooking for her husband's family. Hasan's daughter, Entela, helped her but the bulk of the work fell to Drita. 'That's what new brides have to do,' Entela told us with some satisfaction. As the only daughter in a family of boys, most of the housework had fallen to her.

In summer cooking was done in the yard. In winter everything took place in the kitchen, as it was the only heated room. The grandmother's bed was in the kitchen, and Entela also slept there. Anyone visiting was entertained there. At meals if there were visitors, elaborate Laberian drinking ceremonies were observed. Each time one raised one's glass a string of rhetoric and elaborate compliments to someone present or absent had to be delivered before one could drink. Although alcohol was not an issue, the villagers were culturally Muslims with Muslim names, so that at first we were very surprised when the women in Hasan's family told Soula not to knit on Sundays. We remonstrated and said 'why not Fridays, and were they Muslims or weren't they?' Having been atheists since 1967, they were understandably at a loss for an answer. But I later discovered that the Labs had been among the last of the Albanian population under the Ottomans to become Islamicised, having been Orthodox up until about a century and a half ago. The result was a mixture, albeit an unconscious one, of Orthodox and Muslim practices. Everyone could recite the Muslim prayer that begins '*Bismilahi Ramen e Rahim*' while placing a hot coal in a glass of water to test if the evil eye was at work. Vera's brothers next door went through all the Muslim ablutions when washing under the pump in the mornings. Anyone in need of magical assistance would seek out the dervish in the nearby village of Sevaster. Officially, in fact, the Muslims in this area belong to the Bektashi sect. This was resurrecting itself in Vlora as a result of foreign funding, and there we met some enthusiastic born-again, so to speak, Bektashis. In Gjorm people had too many practical preoccupations to pay much attention to religion. However, a young student doctor called Rina came to ask my advice after she had met up with some Swedish Evangelist missionaries during the Christmas vacation in Vlora. 'I am a Muslim, of course, but the thing about Christianity is that it's prettier, the Christmas decorations and the churches are so nice. Which religion do you think is better?' We had met a

Swedish evangelist missionary on the ferryboat to Otranto before Christmas. He was a tall good looking young man who came and asked us if he could borrow our Italian guidebook for a bit. Having mistaken him for an enterprising student hitchhiker, we were taken aback to find that he was an intolerant and humourless proselytiser who aggressively asserted that he 'had the Truth'. I could not recommend his religion to Rina.

Winter in the Mediterranean is always a chilly affair owing to its not being taken seriously either with adequate heating or cold-proof houses. But this winter was beyond the normal discomfort. A freak cold spell had hit parts of southern Italy and southern Albania with two-metre deep snowdrifts. In Gjorm, which had not experienced such weather in living memory, there was a fodder crisis with grazing now inaccessible. At night, even under six or seven heavy cotton quilts, one shivered. After Indrit, another of Hasan's sons, returned from Greece, we moved over for the nights to the new bungalow. Drita and Tajar were sleeping in one of the rooms perfectly happily, but for non-newly married couples the cold was fearsome. At night Soula and I would wear layer upon layer of tights and tracksuits. We took the boarskins off the floor and slept on top of them under piles of covers on top of which we put the carpet, but still lay cold and damp all night. The newly built cement walls oozed water inside the room, and finally Soula got feverish, a heaven-sent excuse to beat a retreat back to Tirana. It was ignominious, but it was worth it.

We never found a satisfactory *modus vivendi* in Laberia, though it was an instructive sojourn and gave us an interesting insight into a region very different culturally from both the Greek minority in Dropull and the Mirditans. One practical drawback was that we were not living in a family with children. In Mirdita we spent most of our time with large families where children ranged from babies to in their 20s. It meant not only that there was a wide range of companionship, but also that it was easier to take part in family life by playing with children and helping with housework. But our lesser rapport with Laberians was not entirely to do with the circumstances we found ourselves in. It may have had something to do with the nature of the terrain and influence this had on local character. Like Mirdita, Laberia had never been a region of emigration, and both had been regions of smallholders rather than large feudal estates. But whereas most of Mirdita is infertile,

Laberia has plenty of rich grazing land to support large herds of cows and flocks of sheep and goats. Yet, despite being far richer agriculturally than Mirditans, and fast accumulating flocks, Labs were forever complaining that they were worse off than Somalians. I sometimes got into ludicrous arguments with Labs met on buses, irritatedly trying to show them how much better off they were than Somalians. To be fair, the fact that they had much easier access to Greece and Italy, had so many young men working there, must have heightened their sense of deprivation relative to Greek and Italian standards, even as it enriched them. And perhaps their comparative ease and prosperity had produced less need for living off their wits. In Mirdita, poverty seemed to have engendered intellectual liveliness and a very developed sense of the comic. The Mirditans' strong sense of distinctive historical identity made them much less vulnerable psychologically to the ideological vacuum and economic upheaval following the fall of Communism.

Chapter Five

MIRDITA AND ITS HISTORY

i. Pre-communist Mirdita

After exploring a number of other regions, and spending several months in the South, we followed up our first visit to Fang with visits to the highland regions of Mirdita. These visits convinced me that the province would be a very rewarding area in which to do extended fieldwork. On the one hand, Mirdita promised to provide a representative picture of survival strategies as practised throughout Albania's poorer regions. On the other, it was clearly an area of exceptional ethnographic interest. The centrality of long-established customary behaviour was striking, as was the resemblance between many current practices and those recorded by some of the nineteenth and early-twentieth century observers of Albanian life such as Nopcsa, Hahn, Durham and Hasluck.

In contrast to inhabitants of the central and southern regions I knew, Mirditans displayed much less ideological disorientation despite the overwhelming political changes, and much more objectivity when discussing the changes. Travel in the over crowded beaten-up buses invariably gave rise to spirited debates in which passengers would bandy back and forth the pros and cons of Communism and democracy with increasing hilarity, as if the freedom to talk openly about political subjects had gone to their heads. In other regions I had visited, one-sided polemics predominated with a tendency, if a foreigner were present, to self-pity and to question why the 'Powers' were not doing more for them. Perhaps because Mirditans had always been poor as well as unpopular with the regime, they had retained their pride and independence of thought; there was no question of self-pity, and their wit and humour were very refreshing.[1]

But probably the main explanation for their difference lies in a clearly defined sense of cultural identity such that the demise of Communism did not leave them with an ideological vacuum. The fact that the region was never conquered by the Turks administratively, and hence did not convert to Islam, has endowed Mirditans with a historical, cultural and ideological continuity which no other region has had. There are two main facets to this identity. One is Mirdita's distinctiveness as the only wholly Catholic[2] region in Albania. The other is its strict adherence to the body of customary law, the so called Kanun of Lek Dukagjin. The Catholics were the main target for conversion since the Porte wanted to weaken their links with its rivals, the Venetians and the Hapsburgs. This pressure was strongly resisted by Catholics, many of whom lived in nearly inaccessible mountain areas, because while their autonomy was not undermined by their Italian links, it would clearly be at risk under the Turks. Mirditans' resistance to the Ottomans likewise appears to have lain in a desire for independence rather than in a desire to defend the Catholic faith. As far as one can glean from limited historical evidence, Catholicism was much more a symbol of cultural distinctiveness than of religious conviction. This in spite of the fact that the clergy, mostly locally born[3] but educated in Italy, were active in Mirdita from at least the twelfth century, and probably much earlier.

Material testimony to the long-term presence of church and clergy can be found in every part of the province. Evidence includes inscriptions on stones dating back to the 1100s, remains from the fifteenth century of over 200 churches plus two bronze bells inscribed with the dates 1436 and 1438, as well as material in the Vatican archives. The Mirditan writer Ndue Dedaj, in his book *Toka e Katedraleve*, provides a list of all the abbots and priests of Mirdita from 1600 to 1930. Many of these, all of whom were educated in Italy, became distinguished scholars.[4] Yet the clerics seem to have made very little doctrinal impact, and much of the evidence suggests that the population was less than fully committed to Christianity. A recently published history of the highland region of Fan by the Mirditan writer N. Loka,[5] includes letters written by clerics during visits to the region. During a visit to Mirdita in 1610, Dom Marin Bici, Archbishop of Tivari, wrote to Pope

Paul V about a recent change in the Church calendar.[6] This, he observes, was suspected by Mirditans of being a Church ploy that would lead to an increase in tithes and a loss in income for them. Without making a connection, he also tells of the extreme poverty of the Mirditans who 'go barefoot all the year round and wear very poor clothes' (Loka, 1996:24–26). A later Archbishop of Tivari, Gjerjg Bardhi, cited by Loka, writes in 1638 that Mirditans not only fail to observe the feast days properly, but say they are too poor to give up stealing. In fact, he says, they would welcome the departure of the clerics who forbid them to steal, making them return goods they have stolen.

Further evidence both of Mirditans' extreme poverty and limited observance of Catholic precepts and practice emerges from a letter written in 1703 by yet another Archbishop of Tivari, Vinçens Zmajeviç,[7] who describes the area of Orosh, which adjoins Fan. Of the 916 inhabitants he says that they are 'of warlike spirit' – '*me shpirt luftarak*' – but with 'such defects as lack of faith and Christian piety' – '*defekte të tilla si mungesa e besimit dhe devotshmëria kristiane*' (Dedaj, 1999:37). A more sympathetic and broadminded cleric, Abbot Pal Duodës, writing at the end of the eighteenth century, observes that Mirdita is:

a mountainous and harsh place – '*vend malor e i ashpër*', but very healthy, with strong people, most able, of good appearance and with customs (*doke*) and virtues of the very best which can be found, and very clever; but they are very poor, their only capital consisting of a limited number of animals, a few vineyards, tiny fields most of which produce less than three months bread.[8]

He goes on to say that they are all Catholic but that they do not keep the holy days regularly and hardly ever go to church. At the same time, they do observe 'superstitious' days such as the Day of the Blackbirds following the winter equinox (that the ice-winds shall not harm the birds), and the Day of the Mouse, (those who work on this day will have their harvest eaten up by mice) (Ibid., 37–8, my translation).

That tithes were still a serious burden in the twentieth century, we learn from Stavre Frasheri's account of a trip he took with the anthropologist Carleton Coon through northern Albania at the end of the 1920s. Frasheri (who was from Korça, a largely Orthodox Christian area in southeast Albania) is surprised, given the respect accorded to clerics by Mirditans, that the clerics have not helped villagers improve their miserable conditions. He observes that cleanliness is of a much lower standard than in neighbouring Muslim areas; living conditions miserable; adherence to principles in daily life are minimal. At the same time, the perceived need to keep on the right side of the priest as their intermediary with God, leads poverty stricken villagers to sacrifice the little they have in tithes. Frasheri meets an old mountaineer so thin from lack of food that he is all skin and bones. Dressed in rags, black from unwashedness and pine smoke, this wretched man has just handed over 25 kg of maize, his annual payment, to the priest's servant. Frasheri, revolted that someone so poor should have to give up the little he has, asks the old man why he does it. The old man replies that unless one pays one's tithes one will not be buried in consecrated ground; nor would the necessary religious rites be carried out by the priest (Frasheri, 1930:98–100).

As these testimonies suggest, Catholicism was neither a source of enthusiasm as a practice nor a model for behaviour. In general, the evidence suggests that Catholicism was more a badge of regional identity nurtured through resistance to Ottoman hegemony than a religious faith.

In the remoter areas of northern Albania, such as the highlands of Mirdita, the mountain dwellers who engaged in pastoralism and transhumance or small-scale agriculture, had never been under feudal or foreign rule. In 1485, in order to gain control over these villagers, the Ottomans tried to set up the timar[9] system. But in many regions village resistance forced Turkish governors to compromise. These regions were left free to govern themselves along traditional local lines on condition that their mountain warriors stopped attacking the Porte's administration. At intervals some regions of Mirdita had to pay the Porte taxes but the intervals were shortlived. In 1571 a memorandum in the Porte's registry notes that 'the inhabitants of Fandi i Vogel,[10] [Fan, the district mentioned above] because they live in harsh land in the mountain peaks, are obstinate and have not come to register.'[11]

Towards the end of the sixteenth century, attempts on the part of the Porte to gain submission in mountain areas by force were abandoned in favour of a new tactic in the form of religious/

economic pressure. This strategy of increasingly heavy taxation for non-converts was widely successful, and resistance to the Porte faded in most areas of Albania following conversion (often purely nominal) to Islam. Only in a few Christian mountain areas such as Mirdita did resistance continue. To overcome this obstinacy on the part of Mirditans, the Turks systematically destroyed the province's churches during the sixteenth and early-seventeenth centuries. However, by the mid-seventeenth century the Porte seems to have realised that there were more fruitful ways to make use of the inhabitants than trying to impose Islam or exact taxes. As a tax source, infertile Mirdita was almost valueless; as a source of fighters, on the other hand, the province was rich. From now on Mirdita would remain independent in exchange for a ready supply of soldiers to be mobilised by the Captain of Mirdita.

Today, Mirditans' names reflect their Catholic culture: for example, Zef (Joseph), Mark, Simon, Gjon, Ndreu (Andrew), Marije, Tom. But Mirditans have always been too independent minded to allow an external influence, whether church dogma or foreign laws, to fundamentally affect their beliefs. Indeed, the very fact that so many Mirditans gave their children Catholic names despite communist disapproval, demonstrates their spirit of independence.[12]

The Kanun of Lek Dukagjin

The second facet of Mirditan identity is the central role played by their system of customary law known as the Kanun of Lek Dukagjin. Up until the imposition of Communism, tribal law based on the Kanun operated throughout the northern mountains. There are conflicting theories as to how the laws came to be associated with the name of Lek Dukagjin, the evidently charismatic fifteenth-century chieftain said to have reformed and codified the laws. Some Mirditan scholars argue that the connection was invented later for political reasons, that the original Kanun was the Kanun of the Mountains, *Kanuni i Malëve* (viz Pal Doçi, 1999:82). Whatever their nomenclature, the laws themselves had clearly been evolving long before the fifteenth century. The twentieth-century recorder of the Kanun of Lek Dukagjin, Shtjefen Gjeçov,[13] annotated his collection of Lek's Laws, pointing out similarities between the Kanun and the Manava Dharmasatra (Laws of Manu), the Old Testament (e.g. Leviticus, Deuteronomy and Exodus), as well as resemblances with Teutonic, Slav, Greek and Roman codes.

The existence of a regional legal code was common all over Albania, and most regions had their own codes.[14] In the north-central regions of Mat, Kruje and Dibër, ruled over by the family of Lek's contemporary, Gjergj Kastriot Skënderbeg, Albania's national hero, the Kanun of Skënderbeu was operative. Unsurprisingly, given the proximity of the regions, this has a great deal in common[15] with that of Lek, and like the Kanun of Lek was still operative in the 1940s. That these codes are more than ancient relics is clear from one of a series of textbooks currently (2000) used in the sixth grade of Albanian eight-year schools by 12-year old pupils – *Edukata Qytetare* (Civic Education) 6. This textbook is devoted to explaining laws, legal systems, human rights and citizens' responsibilities. In the chapter headed 'Different kinds of legal systems', traditional law, religious law and civil law are examined. The section entitled 'Traditional law' explains that this covers customary rights and norms that in some parts of Albania are unwritten, in others written; that traditional legal systems are called kanuns; that a kanun is a collection of laws and norms inherited through the generations. This section of the chapter is followed by one entitled 'Practical skills'. Pupils are required to collect information on customary rights in the area where they live, as well as to collect data relating to whichever kanun once operated in their region. In the revision section of the chapter headed 'Think critically' pupils are asked: 'Can the Kanun of Lek Dukagjin or the Kanun of the Mountains continue to be observed nowadays? Yes? No? Why?' Answers, despite the evident aim of the text to discourage use of local kanuns, were in my experience surprisingly diverse. When asked their opinion, many of the final year pupils I taught in the middle school of Mirdita's administrative centre, Rrëshen, at the end of the 1990s, argued for continuing use of the Kanun of Lek Dukagjin, an issue I return to.

The Kanun of Lek, as noted, was up until 1945 the main repository of legal knowledge in the tribal North. Margaret Hasluck, author of *The Unwritten Law of Albania*, who lived and worked in Albania in the 1920s and 1930s, noted that 'Mirdita was the centre of customary law as laid down by Lek, exemplar for the strict observance of custom, the head and fount of the law' (Hasluck, 1954:146). The centrality of the Kanun in daily practice as reported by observers[16] up until 1945, the comprehensiveness of its moral and ethical tenets defining ideal behaviour, explain why its influence on behaviour was so much greater than the precepts of the Catholic Church; effectively its tenets constituted a secular religion. At the beginning of the twentieth century, the English traveller and ethnographer Edith Durham found the Kanun strongly in force both in the Muslim and in the Catholic areas of the North. She noted that: 'The teachings of Islam and of Christianity, the Sheriat and Church law, all have to yield to the Canon of Lek.' (Durham, 1909:25).

The Kanun provided a complete moral and legal framework for social interaction, covering every area of life from dispute settlement procedure to rules for marriage, division of property, blood feud and rights of way. Its key elements were the inviolate nature of private property and a dispute settlement system by the people for the people. It was unwritten until 1913, when the Franciscan scholar Father Shtjefën Konstantin Gjeçov started to collect the laws in Mirdita. He chose Mirdita as the region where the Kanun was best preserved, publishing his findings in a series of articles. In 1933, some years after his death, the collected laws were published as a book, *Kanuni i Lek Dukagjinit*. Gjeçov's collection contains 1,263 laws divided according to subject: the Church; the Family; Marriage; the House, Livestock and Property; Work; Transfer of Property; the Spoken Word; Honour; Damages; the Law Regarding Crimes; Judicial Law; and an appendix containing examples of laws applied. Naturally, the rules of the Kanun could never be recorded in their entirety as these differed from region to region and from one era to another. This situational flexibility and pragmatism was precisely one of the Kanun's strengths (and partly explains the presence of contradictions as well as omissions in Gjeçov's book). Up to the 1940s the laws were still being modified in line with changing times and circumstances. Frozen on the page they give a false idea of rigid authority transmitted unaltered through the centuries. Nevertheless, Gjeçov's work is of great historical value, providing an insight into the workings of tribal government at the beginning of the twentieth century as well as an invaluable source of material for comparative purposes.

Under the communist regime Gjeçov's book was banned, as were the works of the celebrated Franciscan poet Gjergj Fishta, who had written a long scholarly introduction to Gjeçov's work. Fishta, according to Pollo and Puto, authors of *The History of Albania* published in 1981, was one of the two 'best-known representatives of conservative and reactionary literature' (together with E. Koliqi). 'Their works which are heavily imbued with clericalism together with chauvinist and racist ideas, reflect the conservative, patriarchal mentality of the most backward-looking sections of Albanian society' (1981:223). The communist authorities, recognizing the strength of the Kanun as a regional bond of opposition, targeted it as a symbol and symptom – the 'black spider of backwardness' – the embodiment of a subversive ethos that they were determined to crush. Reference to the Kanun was made a punishable offence and customary practice was officially outlawed.

It is significant that following the change to democratic government in 1991 many Kanun procedures were reinstituted, while religious practice, banned since 1967 in the world's first atheist state, remained dormant. The outlawing of religious expression in 1967 may have been easier to achieve than extinguishing respect for the Kanun. Draconian measures had ensured that both bans were enforced, but religion for Mirditans had been characterised more by quasi magical activities than by prayer and church attendance. By contrast, as the next chapter illustrates, the Kanun is both of practical use and a source of moral authority.

The explanation put forward by one scholar for Albanians' religious indifference centres on their identification of religion with occupying powers; association of a faith with an unwelcome occupier does not lead to wholeheartedly embracing that faith. Stavro Skendi writes:

the Albanians, owing to historical conditions, have never been a religious people. During the Late Middle Ages, their country had become the battlefield between the Catholic West and the Orthodox East. Whenever the West was advancing, the Albanian feudal lords – often followed by their populations – espoused Catholicism; whenever Byzantium was the victor and the West retreated, they embraced Orthodoxy. They lived, one might say, a religiously amphibious life. (1968:86)

ii. Mirdita During the Communist Period

The civil war was largely fought between the towns and rural areas of the South. Mirdita did not become involved until September 1944, when Partisan brigades arrived in the bajrak of Fan. While some young men did eventually join up with the Partisans, more supported the other side. Once the whole country became embroiled in 1944, there was great resistance to Communism in Mirdita, as there was in most of the northern districts, Shkodër, Puka, Lumë. Mirdita, a province that had never submitted to any outside ruler, was certainly not going to succumb without a struggle. Nor was there any obvious advantage for the population as a whole to be gained from supporting the Partisans. In contrast to the South, Mirdita has no large tracts of arable land and hence no landed class. Control of economic resources where these were so inadequate could not provide the basis for a powerful hierarchy. This posed an ideological problem for the 'class war' (*lufta e klaseve*) campaign, though the Communists tried to portray the Captain and *bajraktars*[17] as exploitative landowners; (see, for example, the three propaganda-laden volumes of *Almanak Mirdita*: 1968, 1969, 1975). Gjon Marka Gjon, Captain of Mirdita, was an obvious communist target, as a man who had presided over a largish territory, most of whose inhabitants had chosen to fight against the Partisans. His power, however, had never lain in large estates as communist propaganda claimed, since there was no scope in Mirdita for land-based power. Gjon Marka Gjon's influence arose from Mirdita's geographical position as the link route between the two main commercial, political and cultural centres of the Balkans, Prizren and Shkodra. Mirdita's position as a Catholic area within the Ottoman Empire enabled the Captain to foster reciprocal interests with Serbia, Austria-Hungary, Venice and France, all of whom had stakes in maintaining an influence in this strategically significant territory. Mirdita's strategic position in the Balkans enabled its captain both to negotiate with the Turks when the Porte needed soldiers, and to exploit the vested interests of powers like Austria and Serbia. This had been the source of his wealth and influence; the local population was far too poor to give anyone anything. Indeed, in order to make sure of his fighting men, the Captain had to cultivate the goodwill of the locals. That his influence, like that of the bajraktars, was circumscribed, is confirmed by Hasluck's account cited below, which shows that though the Captain of Mirdita was consulted in certain matters, no captain ever had the right to make decisions regarding local problems on his own.[18]

Another communist propaganda campaign claimed that most Mirditan villagers were in the hands of a few exploitative wealthy bajraktars. Had this been true, one might have expected greater support for Communism as a means of release from enslavement to the bajraktars. Ironically, the clan organisation, which ensured use rights in common land in each district, was more communist in practical terms than the subsequent system of collectives. In place of communal rights in clan land, pastures, forest and water, Communism under Hoxha ensured that the State rather than the locals had a monopoly over the land and its produce. Under the pre-communist system, if a member of a clan needed something that was common property, the entire clan convened to decide on his case at a meeting of the representatives from all the households. The common property was also collectively defended and linked all the blood-related clans into an economic community. Inter-clan disputes were settled by the chiefs of the clans concerned, sometimes with the mediation of a disinterested clan. A clan court passed verdicts based on the rules of the Kanun. Chiefs received no pay but were held in high esteem. Each clan member had to give loyalty and obedience. Serious violations were punished by ostracism or expulsion. According to Hasluck:

> The community sense was fostered by every art the mountaineers knew. . . . The humblest man was encouraged to regard his village or group of villages as his personal property. If home, village or group of villages prospered, he rejoiced as if he had himself been advanced. (1954:11)

In her book *The Unwritten Law of Albania*, a survey of canon law practice in northern Albania, Hasluck writes:

> The Canon is part of the legal framework devised by the mountaineers for every aspect of their life. The Turks never exerted more than a nominal authority outside the chief towns. Every type of unwritten law has been constantly recast, added to, and restated down the centuries by a body of experts drawn from the

rank of rulers. . . [The] close relationship between individual and community was also a curb on dictatorship. The ruling rank had always to respect the individual's property in the community's laws. They could not make any change in an existing law unless they obtained the consent of a General Assembly of their village or tribe. . . . They could not pass heavy sentences like banishment or death unless a General Assembly demanded them, and if it did, they could not resist its will. In short the elders voiced but did not dictate, popular sentiment. They were no privileged oligarchy either. They might sit in the seat of honour or get the lamb's head and eye at a banquet, but they had no official residences, horses or guards of honour provided for them at public expense. They lived in houses that were often meaner than those of their subordinates; they ate the same food and toiled in the same way in their fields and among their flocks. In fact, the self-government of the Albanian mountaineers went far towards being a true democracy in the Anglo-American sense of that much abused word. In its primitive way it was really government of the People, by the People, for the People. (1954:11)

Tribal organisation prior to Communism consisted of several layers of government involving clan chiefs, village elders, minor elders and the people themselves. Depending on the nature of the offence or problem, some or all of these assembled to discuss a resolution. The Kanun says:

Every village has Elders of the clan. The village Elders have the right to gather the villagers together in assembly. The village Elders do not have the right to impose fines or to place anyone under ban[19] without the approval of the minor Elders and the people . . . If a village is oppressed by the Elders of a clan, the Elder of the oppressed village has the right to be defended by chiefs of other clans. The minor Elders represent the people. They have the right to voice their opposition if they see that people are oppressed by judgements and sentences contrary to the Canon. The minor Elders together with the people and sons of the clans (*Djelmni fisesh*) act as imposers of fines . . . those who in the name of the entire assembly enter the stalls of the livestock belonging to the person fined in order to take as many sheep or oxen as have been specified by the judgement of the chiefs, the Elders and the people. If the people do not approve of the decisions of the chiefs and Elders, they have the right to refuse to support them. The chiefs and Elders must then re-examine their judgement of the matters (Fox, 1989:206–208).

From this it is clear that built into the system there were checks and balances to ensure control by the majority over official decision-makers' powers. Clan chiefs' powers were similarly circumscribed. In Book 11, entitled 'Judicial Law' of Gjecov's Kanun, section 151 is called The Chiefs of the Clans:

> The chief of a clan, like any other man, may be fined, may have his house burned, may be placed under ban, may have his property destroyed, may be executed, and may be expelled from the country. *Neither the House of Gjomarkaj,*[20] *nor the chiefs of the clans, nor the village Elders may have any right to the property and wealth of others. The people of the clans have no obligations to pay a tithe or a tribute to the chiefs or to the House of Gjomarkaj.* [My emphasis][21] [Ibid., 206]

Thus, Communism offered little to attract Mirditans either from a political or an economic point of view, and resistance was intense and long lasting. It was not until 1953 that resistance petered out following nearly a decade of terrorisation, arrests, torture, internments, public executions by shooting and by hanging. One indication of the extreme degree of resistance was the communist government's decision to drastically reduce the size of the province by annexing large areas to neighbouring provinces: Fan to Kukës, most of Spaç to Puka, three villages to Shkodër, others to Mat and to Dibër. In many cases this involved Mirditan territory being absorbed into a culturally Muslim area.

Economic Changes

In the early 1960s local mineral resources were opened up, and copper mining and processing, together with forestry and geological exploration, provided salaried employment. This, together with a family's own produce, meant a significant improvement financially. However, it was not long before collectivisation was introduced into

Mirdita, initially appropriating the fertile areas close to the administrative centre, Rrëshen. This step was met with bitter resistance. In 1966, Enver Hoxha declared at the party's Fourth Congress that it was not enough to collectivise those areas that promised an increase in production; all regions must become cooperatives in order to prevent any form of capitalism from burgeoning. He could have added that this measure would facilitate total control over the population through the cooperatives' administrators. Thereafter, even the steepest, least fertile mountainous areas were collectivised. This time, rather than attracting the *sy keq* – evil/bad eye – of the government, leading to internment or prison, there was little resistance. Nor were the consequences so obviously detrimental since collectivisation was not total initially; animals continued to belong to individual households, while retention of up to three dylims of land was allowed. However, within the year the three dylims were reduced to one, the number of animals to ten, and subsequently even these animals were collectivised into state herds.

As well as a natural unwillingness to be divested of their property, villagers' opposition was based on sound economics. Small-scale transhumance and subsistence cultivation of maize and beans had predominated in Mirdita until the forced introduction of cooperatives in 1966. The terrain and poor quality of the soil were quite unsuitable for the government's projected expansion of wheat cultivation.

Small-scale collectivisation of flocks and expansion of fruit orchards would have been much more rational economically. But the regime's still unrealised objective of self-sufficiency in bread provision took precedence over agricultural sense.

Some strong-minded individuals did, in fact, refuse to give up their land. One instance illustrates the inaccuracy of the term 'class war' (*lufta e klaseve*), one of the Communists' main slogans. Martina Doçi was the sister of Mirdita's greatest communist hero, Bardhok Biba. As a result of her refusal to give her land to the cooperative, she and her family were first imprisoned and subsequently interned in Fier, where they had to work on a state farm. The fact that she, a resister of Communism, was the sister of one of its most active proponents, Bardhok Biba, indicates the misleading nature of the official communist line that an exploiting class was an element in Mirdita's resistance. Indeed, Martina and Bardhok were first cousins to the leader of opposition to Communism,

Gjon Marka Gjon, 'Captain' of Mirdita. The province of Mat, to the south of Mirdita, King Zog's homeland, where some of the land had been in the hands of a few landowning beys, might have provided more promising ground for a class war.

As a result of the exploitation of mineral resources in the 1960s and 1970s, copper mining and processing became the region's main source of income. Three-quarters of Mirditan families had one or more members, mostly male, working in the copper industry, with a smaller number in forestry and hydro-electric plants. This meant that the majority of the cooperative workforce consisted of women, with the addition of a handful of males from 'declassed' families. Three small towns were established in the hitherto entirely rural region in the 1960s. These were Rrëshen, the administrative centre, Rubik, a copper refining centre, and Kurbnesh where there was a copper mine. In 1976 another copper refining town, Reps, was created as a processing centre for the copper from the newly opened mine at Spaç nearby. By this time industry accounted for four-fifths of the area's total production, and mining and copper processing in Mirdita constituted 17 per cent of Albania's mining and metallurgical industry. Despite these developments, the area remained rural. Extractive enterprises were all in remote rural highland areas, small scale and labour intensive. The region was without a road network until the late 1970s, early 1980s, when dirt roads were opened with *aksion* brigades to facilitate transport of goods from mines and lumber from the forest. There were still very few metalled roads at the end of the 1990s.

The level of resistance in Mirdita made a heavy party presence in the province necessary throughout the Communist period. Mirdita's initial resistance was largely responsible for its labelling by the government as one of the most 'backward' (*prapambetur*) regions in Albania. In reality, very few regions were not extremely backward if 'backward' means poor in resources, conservative and undeveloped infrastructurally. There were mountain regions in the South that were equally or more backward; but only small areas of these had resisted the Partisans. The combination of a Catholic heritage, clerics who as representatives of the Vatican constituted a potential threat to the regime, centuries of successfully preserved independence and strict adherence to the Kanun of Lek, made Mirdita the target of a vigorous campaign to 'smash the fetters of faith, the Kanun, and old reactionary norms and customs which, like a black spider, have paralysed the Mirditans' moral world (*Almanak Mirdita*, 1975:99). The success of this propaganda campaign outside Mirdita has been long lasting. In addition to being perceived as backward and wild, Mirdita was believed to be distant. This preconception was used to advantage by young men doing their national service who found they could claim the same extra day's allowance of leave to cover the journey from Tirana to Rrëshen, a bus journey of two hours, as those who lived on the northern border with Yugoslavia.[22] In the 1990s, opinion in Tirana as to the negative qualities of Mirdita and Mirditans had not changed.

Backwardness

There were ample grounds for the party's allegations of backwardness, though the same grounds could have been as fiercely targeted in non-Catholic areas where poverty was endemic and the Kanun rules were closely adhered to. The government was understandably scandalised by the alarmingly high level of deaths due to blood feud. Nor was it unreasonable to try to eradicate arranged marriages and cradle betrothals.[23] Kanun rules forbidding unions between couples not separated by at least seven generations of blood relationship, between those related by blood brotherhood, godparenthood or haircutting sponsorship, were likewise not unreasonable targets for reform.

A first step towards reform by the government in the 1940s was the imprisonment, execution or internment of the bajraktars and their families as political traitors and representatives of the traditional discredited order. The Captain of Mirdita and family naturally headed the list as resistance leaders. A priest, Frano Gjini, was arrested in 1947 and executed; a second, Mark Gjoni, was tortured and died in the same year. On the positive side, blood feud was more or less eradicated by the end of the 1950s thanks to new laws and severe sentences.

In 1967 the abolition of religion led in Mirdita to the 'voluntary' dynamiting of the Abbey at Orosh, the church's headquarters in Mirdita and one of the most famous religious monuments in the Balkans. As noted earlier, the outlawing of formal religious expression may have been easier to achieve in an area whose distinctive identity was founded on much more than Catholicism.

Depending on their individual personalities, local priests had more or less hold over their parishioners' actions. Early in the twentieth century, Edith Durham visited the most famous of the Abbots of Orosh, Dom Prem Doçi.[24] During Durham's visit, Doçi was able to prevent the re-opening of a blood feud, a feat he had achieved and continued to achieve as often as feuding parties would listen to him. But the successes were due to the force of his personality and eloquence rather than to any religious conviction on the part of his listeners. As Durham noted, the Kanun carried far more weight than church laws.

The most positive step in the campaign against backwardness was the introduction of night schools for illiterate adults, male and female, in rural areas. Every village acquired an eight-year school (for children aged six to 14). Larger villages also had schools providing a further four years education mainly offering vocational training in agronomy, welding, metallurgy, mechanics, nursing and teaching. One could progress from these to institutions for higher education such as medicine or engineering, with the proviso that one's family was politically acceptable, and families made every effort to educate their children out of agriculture, as wages outside the cooperatives were higher.

The success of Hoxha's campaign to eliminate illiteracy and introduce universal education was an extraordinary achievement given the very high previous level of illiteracy and the extreme poverty of the country. Teachers from Tirana and those parts of southern Albania where the level of wealth and education was higher were posted to schools in the North, just as later, young teachers from Mirditan towns were posted to rural areas of Mirdita. Teachers boarded in the villages' purpose built 'bachelor houses' (*shtëpi e beqarëve*). It was not an easy life isolated from family and friends in a community often difficult to access, where fitting in with local customs and extreme conformism was especially difficult for those from towns outside the province. But talking to former pupils of these 'foreigners' (*jabanxhi*), it is clear that many of the imported teachers were extremely talented and devoted to their work. Indisputably, communist propaganda and philosophy in the form of lessons in Marxism-Leninism took up quite a lot of the schools' timetables. It is worth noting, however, that many intelligent pupils looking back on their schooldays see this flaw as greatly outweighed by what was for the most part a very effective school programme.

Exchange between North and South was an important aspect of Hoxha's programme to civilise the backward parts of the population and reduce regional differences and prejudices. Some southern areas, partly thanks to the influence of migration in the previous two centuries to urban centres of the Ottoman Empire, had developed a more sophisticated culture.[25] Under Communism, women from these more 'civilised' areas of the South were periodically required to spend some weeks in northern villages teaching 'correct' housekeeping, cooking, hygiene and healthcare. It was also policy for state employees to be dispatched round the country outside their own provinces. As well as promoting regional mix, this mitigated cronyism and reduced the risk of opposition bases forming. 'Voluntary' work brigades (*aksion*) of young people would be sent away to work on infrastructural projects such as building railways, roads, water conduits and terracing mountainsides. The young people would meet the locals at the cooperative headquarters and House or Cradle of Culture (*Vatra e Kulturës*) and take part in joint entertainments. Ideally marriages between North and South would result.

It is not clear how effective these attempts to civilise Mirditans were. It is true that in Mirdita cooking was very unimaginative; only a very limited range of vegetables was grown; little other than maize bread, *petulla* (small pancakes made of flour and water) and *fasulia* (haricot beans) was eaten. Nor was the level of cleanliness very high, though this was probably due to the absence of a water source near most houses. Attempts were also made to alter regional costume in Mirdita where the white clothes traditionally worn by women for everyday were considered impractical for work. Headscarves should replace the Mirditan head dress of a black or red kerchief worn over raised plaits. However, traditional costume continued to predominate, as did traditional food.

Once cooperatives were universally established, village conditions changed in as much as there was a clinic in each head village, a bakery, a creche and a school. From the 1970s, electricity and a village telephone and telegram centre further revolutionised village life and communications. Parallel with these changes came the whole administrative set-up required by the cooperatives, the cooperative's agronomist, vet and accountant, often imported from elsewhere. This network gave the government an extraordinary degree of political control over the population.

Government efforts to reform marriage customs more specific to Mirdita and northern regions seem to have had very little effect, despite their reasonableness. Marriage is a central topic in the Kanun, and hedged about with rules. The Kanun stipulates that there must be at least seven generations without common blood between spouses and that spouses should come from different *bajraks* (districts). A person may not marry within their clan. Nor may they marry anyone with whose family they are linked through fictive kinship, that is godparenthood (either baptism or haircutting), or blood-brotherhood. Enver Hoxha, tried to modify these rules, reducing the seven to three generations, discounting fictive kinship as an obstacle and advocating marriages for love. He encouraged young couples who worked together not to feel ashamed of their feelings, not to be unreasonably dictated to by their elders,[26] decrying the customary use of matchmaker intermediaries (*shkuesi*). He succeeded in reducing the number of cradle betrothals, as well as marriages between people who had never seen each other. On the very rare occasions where a couple married for love, or married in spite of fictive kinship ties, Enver Hoxha would personally write them a letter of congratulations, praising those involved for breaking out of the bonds of backwardness. Even so, a case that occurred in the 1980s in an area of Mirdita where I was doing fieldwork was still regarded by locals in the 1990s as shameful. A couple who had married despite being linked by godparenthood had in the eyes of the villagers behaved unacceptably. To my astonishment, when I mentioned this case to a highly educated Mirditan in Tirana, he spoke of the marriage as scandalous. That even a highly educated atheist who had lived outside Mirdita for years and studied abroad should be shocked indicates the extraordinary degree to which the Kanun's rules are entrenched. One crucial contributor to this conservatism was the practice of living in joint households. Shortage of urban housing, poverty and custom in rural areas, meant that several generations, of necessity, continued to live together, thus reproducing precisely the hierarchies and traditional norms the Communists aimed to eliminate.

I came across several instances of marriages approved by Hoxha. One involved a vet from the Mirditan village of Grykë Orosh (a

Catholic) who in the 1970s married a Muslim girl, Hairja, whom he had got to know while he was working in the town of Laç. A chance meeting with Hairja on a bus in the highlands of Mirdita led me to ask her how come she was from Orosh but had a Muslim name. She told me that against her parents' will she and her husband had married for love. Her family broke off all relations with her, but after she had been married for six months they received a letter from Enver Hoxha congratulating them on their daughter's praiseworthy marriage 'throwing aside the intolerance of superstition and faith'.[27] After this Hairja and her parents were reconciled. I asked if her parents-in-law had not objected to their son's marriage. On the contrary, they were delighted to get her for nothing, that is, without the bride-price.[28] 'And I know how they felt,' she added, 'because I've got four sons and their marriages are going to cost us a fortune. Two of them are working in Greece right now to help towards their marriages.' I asked if it had been difficult for her as a Muslim to live in Orosh. She said: 'No, because there were others from elsewhere, and anyhow Enveri was out to mix people from different faiths.' In other words, no one would have wished to be heard objecting.

In fact, mixed faith marriages were rarely a cause of conflict, though the film *Çiftë i Lumtur* (*Happy Couple*), which makes fun of a father who tried to prevent his son marrying into a different faith, suggests that there were some objectors even after Albania had become an atheist state. In Tirana, there are countless cases of marriages between Muslims and Orthodox. In the early days of post-communism, former 'privileged' Communists would draw my attention to this as an indicator of Albanians' religious tolerance. A more accurate representation would probably have been religious *indifference*.

Clearly the advent of Communism, collectivisation, universal education and the opening up of industry resulted in very radical changes to life in Mirdita. Many of the Kanun's laws ceased to apply once land was no longer privately owned, once central government institutions replaced traditional methods of dispute settlement and local decision making. At the same time, those laws relating to intergenerational behaviour within and outside the family, rules relating to reciprocity, marriage arrangements and customary behaviour at life crises, had at the most merely been modified. The very fact of banning so many aspects of local culture probably contributed to cultural continuity, as did the above mentioned living arrangements. In the next chapter the centrality of the Kanun in local consciousness can be seen in the reinstitution of many of its procedures immediately following the end of communist rule.

Chapter Six

THE KANUN IN THE 1990S

It came as a surprise to me to learn that in large parts of the North including Mirdita, land which had been appropriated by the government under Communism was not decollectivised on the basis of state law along the lines we had seen in the South. In the South the land reforms introduced by the coalition government in July 1991, as we had seen in Dropull, nullified all previous ownership. A village's land was divided amongst the residents who received dispersed parcels to ensure fair distribution of differentially fertile land. But whereas in central and southern Albania village houses are clustered with fields outside the village, the steepness of most Mirditan terrain means that houses were usually built at some distance from each other and surrounded by their own land. The portions of land to be distributed were very small and precommunist ownership was well remembered partly because collectivisation had taken place much more recently – 1966–7 rather than 1950. Moreover, unlike in many parts of southern and central Albania, where much of the collectivised land had been in the hands of a few large landowners, here the insufficiency of arable land had precluded such relations of production, and each family had owned their own land. Yet another factor made the state law problematic to implement. As a result of the food crisis in 1987, Ramiz Alia's government had introduced a statute in 1988 to combat food shortages. Despite the ideological reversal this involved, landless cooperative households were thereafter allowed to acquire progressively more land for private cultivation each year. As a result, by 1991 Mirditan families had been cultivating the land immediately adjacent to their houses for the past three years.

For all these reasons, it was clear to northern land commissions that in these areas of mainly steep terrain the official per soul distribution would be both impracticable and unacceptable. The closeness of northern landholdings to the owners' houses, and the owners' intense feelings towards their land, where scarcity imbued it with such value, dictated restoration of the pre-1966 landholdings to the hereditary owners. A majority of the men on the land commissions were older men familiar with the former boundaries, and the commissions followed the Kanun's exhaustive guidelines on boundary recognition and marking. While it was recognized that the official per soul distribution would have been more equitable in as much as family size differed, as did land quality, it would have been unworkable.

The restitution of the Kanun necessitated the re-establishment of the pre-communist council of elders (*pleqni/pleqësia*) and headman (*kryeplak*). The Kanun's rules were, in theory at least, followed exactly; each clan in a village elected a representative to sit on the council. These in turn chose one of their number to be village headman. In some cases, particularly in certain districts such as Orosh and Kaçinar, regardless of political affiliation, Mirditan villagers chose a descendant of a former *bajraktar* or similarly persecuted family to be headman. This was at once a symbolic restitution of the pre-communist order and a gesture of atonement for the sufferings of the *deklasuar*.[1] The headman and his elected council of elders were not however a local deviation from the official administrative structure. As the school text book for civic education *Edukata Qytetare* No.7 explains, the elders and headman (*pleqni* and *kryeplak*) formed the lowest tier in local government:

> The village is run by the *kryeplak* who is appointed by the elders. The *kryeplak* carries out these duties: care for the maintenance of public order; arrangements for usage of drinking water and water for irrigation, usage of pasture land and forest; addresses villagers' demands and complaints, etc.

These are substantial responsibilities for elders and headmen whose powers are obviously limited. But the oft repeated complaint about regional government that it had neither funds nor decision-making powers – *as fond as kompetencë* – applied in some respects less at this level as far as *kompetencë* went. The small-scale face-to-face nature of this assembly of elders and the symbolic reasons for its establishment gave it a moral force that certainly did not exist at any other level. These elements, together with the exactness of the Kanun's laws, were of considerable practical value at a time when central government could not be relied on to enforce its laws and, moreover, had overlooked or not yet recognized a number of areas where legislation should have been introduced.

Despite these advantages, the reintroduction of the Kanun as a basis for dispute settlement was not universally backed in Mirdita. I tried to detect a correlation between disapproval and political affiliation, but could find none. Socialists (the opposition in the early 1990s) might approve because they had no faith in the Democrats' power to establish a functioning legal system; Democrats might approve because the Kanun had been outlawed by the Communists; others, for and against, were simply taking a pragmatic view. There were those who argued that the Kanun had nothing to offer a modernising country, that many of its laws were retrograde, that its stance vis-à-vis women was barbaric. If there was to be a local body of authority, some argued, this should be made up of younger villagers rather than the 'old men' – '*pleq*' – of the traditional *pleqni*. It should be known as a *shoqëri*, 'a company/group of people', to dispel the 'old fogey' image of the word '*pleqni*'. In fact, most of the newly set up councils did include younger and middle-aged villagers. Nor did I ever meet individual members who wished to apply the Kanun's precepts across the board, though the fact that women were still excluded from council membership despite radical social changes indicated an inflexibility perhaps contrary to the Kanun's pre-communist precepts. That is the problem with a written unwritten law.

The majority of Mirditans, however, felt that as long as the state law lacked force and failed to cover all the legal post-cooperative contingencies, the Kanun provided a workable, indeed indispensable framework for village authority, filling a dangerous vacuum. The implementation of those parts of the Kanun that deal with dispute settlement, property division and rights of way was an important practical means of dealing with the existing legal hiatus. Adherence to the Kanun as a symbol of identity and guide to behaviour might, it was hoped, act as a cohesive force in a society whose official ideological basis and practice of half a century had been discredited almost overnight. Disputes arising from contingencies unprovided for by either system stood a chance of being resolved in a face-to-face context by village elders applying the spirit of the Kanun to current situations. This was important because not only were central government's powers weak, its interest in areas outside the capital were very limited. A Member of Parliament for Mirdita, asked in 1992 why he showed no interest in his constituency's welfare or development, said without a blush that in these difficult times one had to think of one's family first. Regional development, still less decentralisation of decision making, was not even under serious discussion until the end of the decade.

In view of the ban on the Kanun under Communism, one might have expected the young to be ignorant of Kanun rules. In fact, I found they had a detailed knowledge of both rules and procedures. Suppression of the Kanun probably contributed to its survival and clandestine transmission to the young (except in the case of prominently communist families). Moreover, two of the regime's policies – rural population retention and pronatalism – had acted to conserve the very features the regime wished to eliminate. As already indicated, the severe housing shortage, partly a consequence of pronatalism, partly an outcome of the country's poverty, meant that most families of necessity continued to live in joint households. The presence of at least three generations in one household inevitably fostered a greater stress on tradition, authority and rules for cooperation than would have been the case otherwise. In fact, the stringent laws restricting internal migration, together with the chronic housing shortage, virtually precluded separation (though in rural areas one of several brothers might build a house of his own once his offspring became numerous). Joint households were also common in towns where the accommodation shortage was even more acute, with large extended families sharing small flats. As a result, the joint family constellation underwent very little modification during the communist period, though in principle the regime was against patriarchy and anything conducive to it. This is one factor that helps to account for the often striking continuity found between pre-communist customary behaviour and that practised in the 1990s in both urban and rural areas of Mirdita.

In Mirdita, as throughout Albania and already noted for Dropull, a massive orgy of vandalism took place once it was clear that the communist government had been ousted. Villagers ransacked cooperative depots and stores, destroyed vineyards and orchards, demolished irrigation systems, dismantled cooperative machinery and buildings, including health centres and creches, broke school furniture and windows, and ripped up textbooks and photographs of Enver Hoxha. Likewise, most of the rural telephone system was destroyed as wires and telephone poles were stolen. Several factors seem to have been responsible for this huge-scale destruction, which gave no thought to future needs. Clearly there was a substantial element of straightforward anger and resentment at the regime's brutal repression, incompetence and injustices, and young *deklasuar* may have been the initiators of some acts of destruction. Distribution to individual owners of former cooperative land still planted with vines or fruit trees would have benefited some but not others; destruction ensured that all started equal. There was also widespread theft of materials by a population fed up with impoverishment, shortages and the State's appropriation of individuals' labour and produce. (Petty theft of state property from factories, for example, had been going on for a long time, a problem the Communists had failed to control.) In addition, there seems to have been a belief on the part of at least one section of the population that a new order could only be successful if it started from what they imagined was a *tabula rasa*, with nothing inherited from the Communist period. As a result much of village life was, and to some extent still is at the beginning of the twenty-first century, semi-paralysed. Many villages, for example, found themselves without functioning irrigation systems as the pipes and concrete slabs forming the channels had been broken up or removed. These constructions, carried out by action brigades, were often engineering feats, bringing water from very large distances over extremely difficult terrain. Moreover, the material infrastructure that was not vandalised was already disintegrating following lack of maintenance throughout the poverty-stricken 1980s. Many bridges in the early 1990s actually fell into the water below, while unmaintained over-terraced mountainsides eroded.

By 1992, all the cooperative farm land in Mirdita had been restored to the hereditary owners. This was a largely successful operation thanks to the Kanun's exact guidelines[2] on boundary recognition and marking, and the fact already noted that some members of the land commissions, and many of the villagers, were old enough to have been familiar with the hereditary boundaries.

Despite the perceived justice (in most cases) of the operation, there was little to mitigate the adverse conditions now facing locals. The policies of population retention and pronatalism between 1950 and 1990 had led to a tripling of Albania's population so that the pressure on land in areas like Mirdita where the lack of arable land had always been a problem was now acute. Family landholdings in most areas of Mirdita (with the exception of the Përlat-Prosek region discussed below) average between 200m^2 and 500m^2, so that very few families had enough land to produce subsistence for more than three months of the year. The quality of Mirditan soil, never very fertile except in small pockets of the province, had been badly degraded by overuse of chemical fertiliser and inadequate rotation during the cooperative period. Lack of pasturage was a major obstacle to the accumulation of animals. Without flocks for manure and with artificial fertiliser prohibitively expensive, it was very difficult for cash-starved villagers to maximise productivity.

Scarcity of land and the uncertainties generated by a weak state were accompanied in the early 1990s by an end to a lifetime of guaranteed employment and staples at symbolic prices. The average wage for those lucky enough to have jobs at this time was $15 to $20 a month. The price of shop-bought bread, as related in an earlier chapter, doubled in 1993 to half a dollar per kilo. Economic deprivation intensified when from 1992 branches of the province's copper industry, including mines and refineries, were partially closed or shut down completely. Most men had already lost their jobs in state enterprises such as mines, copper refineries and forestry. Most women had worked on the now extinct cooperatives. Those dismissed from employment received unemployment pay – *asistenz* – for one year after dismissal. Nearly two-thirds of families in highland villages were receiving unemployment benefit in 1993. For former employees from industry and state administration (as opposed to cooperative workers who received much less) this was about $15 a month in 1993. Social welfare thereafter was about $5 a month. The majority of Mirditan villagers were on the verge, or in the thick of, financial crisis throughout these years.

The general perception that the decollectivisation process had been reasonable meant that conflicts over hereditary boundaries were a less common source of dispute. By contrast, disputes between heirs were very common indeed; as were disputes arising from the fact that houses built during the cooperative period by individual families were now on land that had reverted to the hereditary owner. Similar difficulties arose where buildings, roads or graveyards had been introduced during the Communist period on what was now privately owned land. Initially, an extreme concept of privatisation, an understandable reaction to excessive collectivisation, resulted in rejection by some individuals of any notion of community rights or common good. Thus access roads to graveyards, or even a village school, might be barricaded by the newly restored landowner. There were also frequent cases of linking through-roads and footpaths being closed off, in complete contravention of the Kanun, which decrees that public good overrides private loss.

As a result of the tripling of the population under Communism and local emphasis on producing as many sons as possible, more heirs were contending for less land. Since every male heir is entitled to an equal share, intra-family disputes were very common. Transfer of property rules according to the Kanun stipulate that each son must receive an equal part of the father's land regardless of economic situation or number of children each may have. Equality of division is not limited to land; everything including household cutlery, food and drink, is divided equally between the sons. Today even the household debt is divided, in contrast to the stipulation of the Kanun in Gjeçov's time that 'before the division, all debts must be paid' (1989:48): one example of continuing evolution to fit the contemporary situation. Each brother has the same amount spent for bride-price, though the cost of each's wedding feast may vary according to the family's circumstances at the time. A sum of money is set aside for the brother (usually the youngest) who will live with his parents. If he is unmarried a sum will be set aside for the bride-price as well as for the wedding feast; also a sum for the funerals of his parents, since these will be his responsibility. These rules were being followed in the first half of the 1990s by Mirditan villagers. In most respects these practices tallied with the data collected by Hasluck during the 13 years she spent in Albania from 1926 to 1939, as one can read in the chapter entitled 'The Separation of Brothers' in her book *The Unwritten Law of Albania* (1954:51–72):[3]

As regards daughters, state law allows women to inherit, but in practice only males inherit. Even in the southern region of Laberia where there is no longer any extant canon law, I was told categorically that women may not inherit. Legally this was false, in practice it was probably true. In Mirdita there is absolutely no question of state law overriding the Kanun[4] on this question.

Notwithstanding the comprehensive nature of rules for property transmission, the potential for discord that arises once a household's wealth, including land, has been divided into separate properties is considerable. Not for nothing does an old local saying have it that 'division/separation' (*ndarje*) ruins a family. Traditionally, throughout Albania an undivided family was considered the ideal, both morally and as a source of economic strength. 'The sheep who leaves the flock gets eaten by the wolf' – '*delen që ndahet nga shoqet e ha ujku*'.[5] *Ndarje* was seen as weakening the unit and when it occurred was often assumed to be the result of a quarrel. Prifti cites the proverb: 'Where there are poor people there are quarrels' – '*Ku ka fukarallëk ka edhe sherr*' (1987:125). Moreover, there are practical economic advantages to extended family cooperation. At the end of the twentieth century, the undivided family, which continues to live under one roof in one of the joint households that are still common, enables each family member to contribute to, and benefit from, the shared family budget. Thus, two sons may go to work in Greece. Their earnings can either be used for immediate family necessities or as capital to acquire a bus, lorry or machine with which to set up a business back home. Other members can cultivate the reclaimed family land and look after the animals. Still others can squat on a piece of land on a coastal plain where they can grow the necessary grain for family and animals' use. Once a married son moves his wife and children into a separate household, he may be forced to choose between cultivating his land maximally or trying to get work in Greece. Hasluck makes the point for the pre-communist period:

> it was economically to the advantage of each man that the household should remain together. In a large household all branches of the pastoral and agricultural life were possible, but in a small one activities must be restricted; one and the same person could not tend cows and oxen, ewes and lambs. (1954:52)

Black-Michaud similarly writes of mountain Albanians:

> the larger the male labour force an economically independent unit could command, the more it could diversify production ... Subsistence agriculture could be supplemented by logging, muleteering and transhumant pastoralism, whereas

a man living alone with his wife and children disposed of barely enough time and energy to fulfil their minimal food requirements. (1975:40)

The truth that lies behind the pre-communist saying 'division ruins a family' refers no less to the potential for discord that arises once a household's wealth including land is divided into separate properties. A son with numerous children may feel bitter that his landholding is no larger than that of a brother with only two children. A brother whose property is further away from a water source, or whose property is cut through by a road, may feel that he has got an unfair deal. A brother's wife may incite him to demand what she sees as justice from his brother. The frequency in 1992–3 of press reports of murders and violent assaults between heirs and their families in Mirdita and the coastal plain of Lezhë (formerly part of Mirdita and still inhabited by Mirditans) was striking. The case discussed in an earlier chapter was one of many that I came across personally in the villages where I was doing fieldwork. In the Fang case it will be recalled, the perceived injustice arose from the fact that one family's offspring were still employed, while the others were not. Killed for *një rrip tokë* – a tiny strip of land – was a not infrequent occurrence.

Disputes were, of course, plentiful pre-1945 in this area of land and water scarcity. But whereas some quarrels – allegations of misuse of irrigation rights and accusations of theft – are common to both periods, certain types of dispute in the 1990s were direct consequences of the collectivised past. As indicated above, problems often arose when a house built in the cooperative period was now on private land. Under Communism a married son could get permission to build himself a separate house on cooperative land if his father's home was becoming overcrowded. Following decollectivisation, the owner of the recently restored land on which this 'foreign' house stood would, if he were a reasonable man, offer the house-owner some kind of compensation – a piece of land or a sum of money – in exchange for the house. But many of the landowners were far from reasonable. Some ordered the house owner off the land with no compensation. Others went and demolished the house; in the village of Grykë Orosh, it was the headman himself who did this. In one case, in a village near Rrëshen where I knew both parties, one of the landowner's sons killed the house-owner, thereby starting a blood feud, which so far has led to two deaths, removal of part of the house owner's family to a squatter settlement on the Durrës plain and, six years later, no final solution.

This kind of dispute consequent on privatisation of cooperative land was unprovided for either by the Kanun or by state law. Theoretically it should not have been very difficult for the state to take into account a recurrent problem of this type and to legislate for it. However, in a discussion of comparable situations in Romania, the American social anthropologist Katherine Verdery shows that even where the State does acknowledge such problems, jural nightmares can ensue.[6] When I asked officials why there was no legislation in Albania for this type of contingency, one reason given was that the State could not have afforded to compensate numerous displaced house owners. This does not explain why it could not have laid down guidelines for solutions to be negotiated by the parties involved in such disputes. Presumably, an important obstacle to such legislation was the fact that land distribution in these areas had not been according to official decree. Where land had been distributed per soul – *për frymë* – these kinds of contingencies did not arise. Since land here had been distributed in effect illegally, however impracticable the legal solution would have been, the State could wash its hands of the consequences. Hence it was found expedient to ignore the problem despite the many conflicts, which not infrequently led to murders.

Here it should be mentioned that in the Prosek-Përlat area near Rrëshen, known as Mirdita's *Myzeqea*,[7] the terrain is much less steep and much more extensive. The area of cultivable land means that division according to the state land distribution plan would have been practicable. But the fact that, as in the rest of Mirdita, the landowners' houses stood surrounded by their own land, that collectivisation had taken place recently enough for strong feelings of ownership to have persisted, made this solution unacceptable. Also, it might have been doubly contentious to have different bases for land allocation within one province. Unfortunately, partly as a consequence of the greater extensiveness of land, more houses were built here during the cooperative period on land now restored to the pre-collective owners. As a result, disputes, some murderous, some as yet no more than sources of daily irritation, have been numerous and largely unresolved.

Another type of problem, briefly alluded to above, also arose as a direct result of property changes under Communism. Village cooperative centres, graveyards, public roads and schools became the centre of disputes once the land reverted to pre-communist owners. During the collective period, fields and access roads had to be altered to increase the size of areas to be cultivated cooperatively, and to permit machinery and vehicles to reach the fields. Numerous instances arose following land privatisation, where restored properties included a portion of an access road for wheeled vehicles. In 1993, roads barricaded by the owners were a frequent occurrence; there were cases in every village I visited. Quite often it was not simply a question of access to another part of the village, but a question of an access road between distant villages. I saw cases where wheeled access to a village several kilometres away was being blocked by a few hundred metres of barricaded field, so that the only way to reach the further village was by foot. There were other cases where a track formerly used by wheeled traffic between two villages had been closed off forcing people to follow the river bed, impassable in winter, and in summer only passable on foot and partly wading. Some cases have still to be resolved at the beginning of the twenty-first century.

Similarly, where a villager's reclaimed property included a graveyard established during the communist period, the owner often refused access to the public. This was rather a common occurrence as it was communist policy to replace more distant graveyards with new ones within a village's borders; part of the campaign referred to in the communist propaganda publication *Almanak Mirdita* cited above:

> to smash the fetters of faith, the Canon of Lek, and old reactionary norms which like a black spider, have paralysed the Mirditans' moral world. Religious prejudice still prevents each village from having a systematised and beautified graveyard nearby. (1975:99, my translation)

Mirditans considered it unlucky to have burial places close to a village while communist officials evidently found distance impractical.

The extreme attitudes by those owners who refused, initially at least, to even consider accommodating community rights were at variance with pre-cooperative norms that strongly upheld community rights, as the Kanun makes clear. However, Hasluck's example below shows that resistance to such decisions could also be found prior to the cooperatives. Despite such intransigence, even where the Kanun provided no precedent, the village headman and elders in the 1990s were often able to arbitrate successfully. Much depended on the force of character and diplomatic skills of the headman. Given that the basis for their appointment was quite often their persecuted position under Communism rather than their competence as leaders, not all headmen were equally skilled. Nevertheless, by invoking the spirit of the Kanun, not to mention village opinion, councils of elders quite often did succeed in resolving these kinds of disputes. In fact, the Kanun provided very explicit guidelines for comparable cases. It states that: '*E mira e përbashkët i paravehet damit të veçanët*' – the common good is placed before private damage – (Fox, 1989:81–2) but offers flexible solutions[8] so that where possible both the individual and the community are accommodated.

Hasluck refers to cases where public roads had to be diverted to higher ground because they became too muddy in winter:

The men whose land was taken for the diversion received no compensation. They often threatened to kill the elders, but for sole reply received an exposition of the law; they might shoot as much as they pleased but could not have their way; the village could not be shut up by mud, and the public good overrode private loss. (1954:88–9)

Whenever I came across a case where a villager had flagrantly abused another's rights, blocking off an access path, for example, I would ask why the case had not been referred to a court of law. *Ska shtet, ska ligj* – there is no state, there is no law – was always the reply. Experience had shown that appealing to a court of law rarely brought a solution. The relevant personnel, local headman, police, judge, prefect, might have been bribed to support the other side. Or the opponent would take advantage of the coexistence of customary and state law and its hiatuses, invoking whichever aspect worked to his advantage. Or, if the opponent lost his case, he might take revenge and kill you or one of your sons; and there was no guarantee that even then he would not escape justice. Not surprising then that many Mirditans felt that the community involvement required by Kanun procedures gave villagers more control over the outcome of a dispute; a better bet than the blind eye of the state, the arbitrary decision of a court or potential anarchy.

Chapter Seven

FAMILY LIFE AND POVERTY IN FAN

Cri de Coeur

1993 Letter home after one of many bus journeys to Mirdita:

The terrible thing about Albania is the slumminess and the total absence of system. The bus journey to the provincial town
(starting point for the mountain villages) is a nightmare in itself.
You walk to a horrible terminal out of town. You sit in a disgust-
ing zakaraka for two hours. Around you are filthy wild-haired
passengers, some picking their noses for two hours continuously
unless you are lucky and they break off for a smoke. Meanwhile at raging headache volume the bus radio plays rap fit to
burst. But this was a comparatively good journey once started;
folk music replaced rap and we had seats. Coming back in a
packed bus crouched under the luggage rail after several hours
of not finding a bus at all and several days of minimal sleep, poor
Soula, bus sick as usual, was worse. Then there's the entrance to
our apartment block: the dark entrance, broken steps crowded
with filth including a pile of shit, rubbish, old food, etc. The
entrance to halfway up the first flight of stairs is used by passers-
by as a pissoir. All over Tirana the smells of drains that don't
work are terrible. An endurance test. There are good things;
there's a man who sells delicious home made meringues round
the corner; it is nice seeing sheep and cattle led along the pavement right in the centre where we live, and the climate's mostly
sunny. It's just that the economy's so run down, everything's difficult and dirty. From water rationing, no washing facilities, to

hopeless communications and lack of infrastructure, to DECAY of a mind-boggling degree.

Today Mirdita covers an area of 867 square kilometres. As an area strongly resistant to Communism it was deemed expedient by Hoxha's government to annex large areas to neighbouring provinces: Fan to Kukës, most of Spaç to Puka, three villages to Shkodër, others to Mat and to Dibër. In many cases this involved Mirditan territory being absorbed into a culturally Muslim area. The altered borders also entailed the loss of its coast and the mountains above the coastal plain to what is now the province of Lezhë. The steep rise in population between 1955, when the population was 19,075, and 1993, when the population numbered 55,172, was due to the communist government's pronatal policy and was parallelled by the development of the mining industry. Over the period 1993 to 2001, the closure of mines and high unemployment have led to an exodus from the province either abroad or to other regions, which has reduced Mirdita's total population by about a third. Descent from mountain villages to Mirditan towns has increased its urban population to a little over 15,000.[1]

The terrain is hilly-mountainous, much of it 400m or more above sea level, most of it extremely steep and rocky with large areas of pine forests at the higher altitudes. Since the beginning of the 1990s large tracts of the accessible parts of its beech and pine woods have been felled, mainly illegally. One of the more fertile areas is the Fan River basin into which run the Little and the Big Fan rivers. Mirdita's four towns, Rrëshen (the administrative centre), Rubik, Kurbnesh and Reps were founded in the late 1950s and early 1960s, when mining and copper processing were established as the region's main source of economic activity. Hydro-electric plants and forestry were sources of employment to a smaller number of people. Most of the extractive enterprises were in remote rural areas, small scale and labour intensive. The rest of the population worked on the state farms, the cooperatives and, in the case of loyal party members and their families, in urban government jobs. In Rrëshen there was a copper refinery and some processing of local produce, the main products being wine, raki and jam.

Although the towns are very small, they are recognizably towns by the rows of grey cement blocks of apartments. Immediately outside these urban centres the province is deeply rural with widely scattered settlements in largely precipitous terrain, most of which can only be reached by dirt roads hard to maintain. In heavy rain, mudslides and subsidence can make the roads impassable. Though the province's southern border is only about two hours drive from Tirana, Mirdita's villages are remote in terms of cultural and social distance. (In fact, villages in the Dajti Mountains half an hour from Tirana are no more developed than in the mountain depths of distant provinces. Poor road communications – some villages can only be reached on foot – and undeveloped conditions in villages make for a much lower standard of living than in towns. Enver Hoxha's urban-rural equalisation programme, except in the important respect of education, had limited success.)

Rrëshen had a population in 1993 of 4,000, which had doubled by 1999 as a result of mountain villagers moving down. The copper refining town of Rubik has also increased its population since the 1993 count of 2,800, due to the descent of mountain villagers. Kurbnesh, by contrast, has lost population since its sole *raison d'être*, its copper mine, has been closed down. It is also less accessible and is fast becoming a derelict ghost town where an apartment can be bought in exchange for a sheep. Reps, in the highlands, grew up around its copper refinery supplied by the copper mine a few kilometres away in Spaç. Both mine and refinery, after functioning only sporadically in the early 1990s, had ceased to function at all by 1997. The population is in flux as some families leave for the plains or lowland towns, while others are moving in from the highland villages. The influx is less than in Rrëshen or Rubik, as the advantage of a middle school and administrative offices is counterbalanced by unemployment and the fact that almost the only accommodation is in blocks of flats. Hence a village incomer can no longer grow even the minimal subsistence food he could produce in the village, or would be able to grow as a squatter on the coastal plain.

In the early 1990s all these Mirditan towns, in common with every town in Albania at the time, looked war torn. Most of the trees had been axed, pavements and fountains smashed, litter was ubiquitous, and the staircases of most apartment blocks (*pallate*) were unmaintained and filthy, with many of the staircase steps broken. In the streets, deep mud had to be negotiated every time it rained. Livestock, chiefly pigs and cows, wandered the roads and pavements scavenging in the rubbish heaps.

During the first year-and-a-half of fieldwork I only knew the towns from passing through them or as a place to change buses, since the villages I got to know best were in the highlands in the adjoining bajraks of Fan and Orosh. In 1993, still based in Tirana, we regularly made the bus journey from Tirana to Rrëshen, and then changed into a bus for the highland regions, another two hours travelling. These buses were old and decrepit, and, since there were very few of them, they were always crammed to overflowing. There were very few of them because hardly anyone could raise the capital to buy one. In one case, a former state lorry driver had bought his lorry for a very low price – state property was sold off very cheaply. He worked transporting wood until he had enough capital to buy a bus with the help of a state credit of $5,000, which he paid back very quickly from the profit he made. In another case, two brothers had raised the capital working in Greece. A few buses had been bought with state loans alone. The bus owner, unless he was a former lorry driver, usually acted as ticket collector, while the driver would have gained his license under Communism when, thanks to the ban on private cars, few apart from truck drivers could learn to drive. In the 1990s the number of buses in the mountainous areas was quite inadequate to the number of villagers needing transport, and in any case one could never be sure that a bus would not have a '*difekt*' and fail to run at all. Spare machine parts were one of the crippling dearths of the early 1990s. (To my surprise I learnt that the public transport situation had been no better under Communism when would-be travellers would have to wait for hours in the hopes of hitching a lift with a lorry.) In the 1990s, even if the few available buses were running, they were too full long before their destination to pick up everyone waiting. Occasionally, lorries emptied of their wood loads passed and picked up passengers who stood up in the back and paid slightly less than for the bus. One of the commonest sights along the mountain roads was little clusters of resigned looking people trying to hitch a lift. Since a lot of the journeys were too big to be covered by foot in half a day, one could wait half a day and then have to give up until the next day.

The extreme rarity of foreigners meant that we always got into conversations with people on the buses. Why were we here? What did we think of Albania? Approving guffaws if I said 'poor'. What did we think of the government, what salaries did people in

England get, what other languages did we speak? Sometimes one would have serious conversations with an individual, sometimes it would be a joint performance of bantering exchange and jokes. Sometimes the bus driver would accept no money '*nga respekt*' – out of respect; heart warming if ironic given our relative wealths. The best thing about the bus journeys within Mirdita was the fact that passengers were always discussing the pros and cons of the present and past regimes. They usually argued with more humour than temper, a strikingly different approach to politics from the prejudiced intolerance and lack of debate that was so depressing in Tirana. They found positive things to say about Ramiz Alia, the last communist ruler, and about Sali Berisha, the current Democrat leader. In Tirana objectivity was almost non-existent. There it seemed as though all energy was used up in vilification of the other side with none left over for constructive action or forward thinking. There was also an aid-dependency stance, a 'we deserve foreign help' attitude on the part of Tiranians. For some reason this was absent in Mirdita. Perhaps because Mirditans never had enjoyed any privileges.

Rapidly declining employment and disputes engendered by scarcity of land and water dominated rural Mirditans' lives during the period 1993 to 1995. Alternative survival strategies were essential. One of the best hopes for making ends meet lay in emigration abroad, though it was more difficult logistically and psychologically for northern Albanians to migrate to Greece than for southerners, who were so much closer to the border. Southerners' proximity to Greece had also familiarised them somewhat with Greek culture and lifestyle through television channels not received in the North. Neverthless, at this early period (1993–4), at least 30 per cent of Mirditan village families had or had had a male family member temporarily in Greece. Not all of these found work there and very few managed at this stage to work for more than two or three months before being caught and expelled by the police. The absence of any agreement and legislation formalising migration between Albania and Greece was one of the most serious causes of resentment against the Democrat government. It was a topic repeatedly raised by villagers and town dwellers in 1993 and every year thereafter. Villagers and town dwellers alike thought a good solution would be an official quota allowing each family to send one member. The longer the issue remained unaddressed, the greater the bitterness and anger engendered. Some of the seeds of the 1997 revolt were sown at this period. Resentment was further fuelled by the State's cavalier attitude to property disputes and inadequate legislation as expressed in the phrase '*ska shtet, ska ligj*'.

Yet notwithstanding the problems arising from weak government and massive unemployment, this was a period when rural Mirditans were still strikingly optimistic about the area's potential for development. The initial post-communist wave of crime, vandalism and general anarchy was over. Violent conflicts were chiefly intra-family affairs. It was safe to move around the countryside. Though ideas for cooperative-type management of the forest were shortsightedly rejected by the government, many Mirditans still believed that the area could attract foreign investment. Some felt that the local abundance of medicinal herbs, which had been used commercially during the communist period could be a source of foreign interest and long-term income. Others believed that foreign firms would invest in local forest and mineral resources. There was even a belief that the highland area might become a tourist region despite the infrastructural shortcomings. None of these ideas was wholly unrealistic. But their implementation depended on the State's interest and active support. It was two or three years before disillusionment set in with the realisation that regional development was not part of the government's programme and that out-migration was the only solution to economic survival. Any hope of constructive intervention by local MPs (who, as we saw, did not live in the province but in Tirana) had been abandoned. A member of parliament's duty to his or her constituency largely consisted of, and continues to consist of, arranging for a limited number of his or her constituents to get jobs in state administration.

Fieldwork Logistics

As explained, I worked in several different villages. There was no possibility to live permanently with one family since each household's space was so limited. Independent or semi-independent accommodation did not exist; it would probably have been out of the question to live independently anyway. Even in southern Greece, where we were free to get to know anyone we liked, we would be asked by locals we did not know: 'Whose are you?' and we learnt to give the name of the family in part of whose house we were living. This enabled the questioner to link us with someone they could place who, moreover, would be a source of further information. Otherwise we were an anomaly, difficult, initially at least, to relate to. Where blood relations are the starting point for social relations, the case in both these rural societies, it helps to be able to say 'whose one is' until one is well known enough to exist in one's own right.[2]

By visiting the different villages and families in a kind of rota we gained an insight into variations between villages and families without becoming too burdensome to any one household. In several cases I have followed families down to new lives on the coastal plain, Tirana and Greece. Shorter visits over the decade to a much larger number of villages all over Mirdita have added to the general picture of demographic change and common local problems, ranging from property disputes and the blocking off of public roads to failing schools.

Most of the families whom we got to know best had children covering an age range from very young to adult. This turned out to be a key contributor to establishing long-term relationships. Where there were children, we could play with them or accompany them on errands and chores and contribute more easily to some of the work. This way we got to know a cross section of youth from cradle through teenage life and duties to young adults chafing at unemployment, restrictions on behaviour and family problems. At first, each time that we spent two or three days with a family, good manners, tradition and family pride resulted in us being looked after nearly all the time. A family member took it in turns to entertain us and supply possible needs. This could be burdensome for the family, though for the individual involved doing things with us quite often provided a welcome break from monotonous routine. Once they knew us better they realised that they could get on with their own work, leave us alone or even allow us to be useful: lull crying babies, wind wool, help collect fallen mulberries for raki. What they did not want us to do was leave the house to wander off and talk to other families. It was understood that I was there to learn about property changes, survival strategies, local government and customary behaviour, and everyone thoroughly approved, seeing this as a period of change that they were keen to have documented. But freedom to roam and talk to anyone we came across in the interests of carrying out this research project was always delicate.

One of the casualties of post-communist life, now that there are no cooperatives or houses of Culture for get-togethers, is intensive community interaction. This is especially acute in the northern villages, where houses are usually very dispersed and there is no physical centre such as a village square. There is no replacement for the former cooperative meeting places, no religious meeting place, no village hall. Weddings and funerals are literally the only opportunities for gatherings now that there are no longer cooperatives. The young feel the loss of companionship severely and, less importantly, it is harder for the anthropologist to get a first-hand insight into community dynamics, local government and interpersonal relations. Since the anthropologist must stay with a family rather than living independently, her knowledge of the community is in danger of being restricted to that household's friends and tales of enemies. Where neighbourly relations are as conflict ridden as they often are in these areas of acute scarcity, that may not leave many friends. One's host's feelings ought to be respected, but, if they are, it may be at the expense of getting to know anyone else well.

The barely disguised reluctance of our hosts to let us become too friendly with other members of the community was doubtless partly caused by a wish not to spread their foreign assets too thin. Sometimes reluctance to let us out of their sight would be accompanied by a justification. In Dropull they told us we would be eaten by dogs if we went out on our own. In Mirdita the reason given was more often that the people in 'that house' or 'that village' were bad. Often, if we had been invited to another villager's house, 'our' family would surreptitiously organise an activity to prevent our going. Quite elaborate steps might be taken to avoid our visiting elsewhere. For instance, the normal time for getting water from the neighbourhood spring would be put forward so as to prevent us meeting members of the family who had invited us; or a weeding party or a wood gathering expedition would suddenly be organised. There was more to this attitude than straightforward self-interest or fear of what gossip might be relayed to us about them. One factor may well have been a legacy of totalitarian life – secrecy, fear of neighbourhood spies, the *sigurimi* (secret police) and a general pervasive mistrust engendered by a regime whose power lay in instilling fear and divisiveness. But there were other considerations of a serious kind arising from the local laws of customary behaviour and the importance of conformity in a small conservative society.

Mikpritje – hospitality – the deeply ingrained code of behaviour regarding hosts and their guests as dictated by the Kanun of Lek directly reflects on the host's social honour, and is hedged around with rules. At the cliché level, Albanians, urban and rural, will proudly declare that, however poor, a household will offer you bread, salt and their heart – *bukë, kripë, zemër*. The Kanun has a more practical set of guidelines on hospitality:

At any time of the day or night, one must be ready to receive a guest with bread and salt and an open heart, with a fire, a log of wood and a bed. Upon entering the house, the guest must give you his weapon to hold. Holding his weapon is a) a sign of valour and honour, as well as an indication of your pleasure that a guest has come to you; b) a sign of guardianship, since after you have said 'Welcome', he must have no fear and know that you are ready to defend him against any danger; c) *a sign of prudence*, since, if you hold his weapon, even if your guest has some bad intention, he is unable to accomplish it if you disarm him.

Hospitality honours you, but also creates problems for you. (Hospitality discloses the devil some have said.) ... The Kanun demands that a guest should be accompanied *both* lest he be the victim of some wicked act *and* lest he harm someone while under your protection. *If your guest commits some evil act while under your protection, you are responsible for it.* The person dishonoured or harmed is not obliged to pursue the one who committed the act of dishonour or damage, but knocks at the door of whoever gave him shelter and food. (My emphases; Fox, 1989:132)

In everyday terms this may boil down to a trivial incident such as this. Together with two daughters of the family where we were staying, we went to collect some wheat we had left at the mill to be ground. On our way back we passed the house of a woman who stocks a few groceries. She insisted on treating us to a fizzy drink. Unluckily, I had no money with me to buy anything in return. When the parents back home heard of this encounter they made little of it, but later that day a bottle of home-distilled raki was despatched to the woman. This family with whom we had become close friends always questioned us closely if we had visited without them. Both as to how we had behaved and as to how we had been treated; to check whether we had made any *faux pas* and to ascertain how correctly we had been received.

As a result of these strictures and their consequences, we had to sacrifice a certain amount of freedom of movement and acquaintance. The dispersed housing pattern helped to ensure that we spent most of the time together with our hosts, taking part in their daily lives or going to meet other families and places *with* them. However, in one village where we had got to know several families independently we were able to visit each in turn, thus getting to know the village from several households' perspectives. Amongst these families was one whose life was so full and whose numerous members were so involved in local affairs that staying with them gave us plenty of insight into community life.

We eventually mitigated the problem of independence and accommodation by renting a base flat in Rrëshen, the small administrative town of the fieldwork region. Most of the inhabitants were originally from villages and we could be part of the community without losing domestic independence or being restricted in whom we got to know. Another advantage, now that we were two hours closer to the mountain villages where we regularly stayed, was the chance sometimes to reverse the guest-host relation. Many younger villagers had no experience of town life, and girls would stand entranced at the window gazing their fill at streets full of people. Village life now that cooperatives and houses of culture no longer function is particularly solitary and bleak for young girls who no longer attend school. Visiting villagers brought us village produce, were curious to try our exotic cooking (some met carrots for the first time in our kitchen), joined in our daily activities, and suffered from the same sort of problems with eating, stomach upsets and inhibitions that we experienced staying with them. Instead of us making demands on their hospitality, knowledge and acquaintance in the community, we could sometimes be of use to them in the urban world of bureaucracy and connections. A salutary role reversal.

Once I had decided that I was going to concentrate fieldwork in Mirdita, I arranged through a literature teacher at the School of Foreign Languages to meet those of her pupils who were from Mirdita. We checked with our teacher friend who had taught for several years in a remote area of a neighbouring northern province, Mat, which would be the most welcome provisions to take. In fact, there are established guidelines on what to take when visiting: soap for the young bride or eldest daughter; cigarettes for the head of the house; coffee beans for the household. We also took some staples – macaroni, rice, sugar – to cover the expenses that feeding us would incur. Every Albanian household, rural and urban, was struggling to cope with price rises, and rural Mirditan households would be struggling even more.

The most significant factor influencing rural poverty levels in the early 1990s was the availability of male family members who could be spared for emigration. Thus a family whose eldest son was 15 and studying at the School of Languages was much worse off than two families whose youngest daughters were studying while their elder brothers were earning, even though only sporadically, in Greece.

The Lekas of Bisak

The first family we got to know belonged to Ilir, who was in his first year studying German as his main subject. He was 15, with an open cheerful face, and about five foot tall. He was laid back about being diminutive, pointing out that it enabled him to ride on buses for nothing. We set off with Ilir for the northern bus terminal just outside town. The terminal turned out to be an assortment of ancient buses in an acre of mud and litter. Ilir's smallness did not prevent him from managing the bus trip efficiently or from keeping curious passengers satisfactorily informed about his protégées. After two hours we arrived in Rrëshen, Mirdita's administrative centre, where we got into a much more antediluvian bus to go to the mountain villages. Ilir engineered us seats by telling the bus driver that we were foreigners. Foreigners were very rare in Mirdita, and foreigners who travelled to the highlands by bus unheard of, so Ilir enjoyed a lot of attention as our manager. There were several young men who had spent some time as illegal immigrants in Greece who were pleased to show off their Greek to the rest and exchange pleasantries with us. The bus left full to bursting and we went up and down mountain roads for two hours. When we got near the top of the highest pass, the driver, Preng (a very common Mirditan name), got into a race with another bus, overtaking and being overtaken whenever possible at the narrowest bits where there was a sheer drop of several hundred feet on one side. I began to long for the raki I hoped we would be offered on arrival, in case we arrived.

The asphalt road ends at Reps, the bleak wind-exposed town at the top of the mountain. The bus does not go up to the town but follows the dirt track below the copper refinery whose grey sheds with corrugated iron roofs and broken windows look like a collection of abandoned aeroplane hangars ranged down the hillside. The precipitous dirt track continues high above the River Fan as far as the *Gjeologji* where the road forks. The *Gjeologji* had been the meeting centre, mensa and dormitory for the geologists and workmen working in highland Mirdita. Shortly after the end of Communism two young men from close by had opened a cafe-bar to be patronised, it was hoped, by those walking to or from their villages. But the passers-by were too poor to make the owners any money, and by the time I got there the building was a small pile of stones. However, the spot was still referred to as the *Gjeologji* and marked the junction of the two dirt roads; the right hand road continuing to the highland villages of Orosh; the left hand fork descending to the dismal stony shores of the river, and passing through the village of Mashtërkorë before entering the next bajrak, Fan. Towards Bisak, Ilir's village, the road narrows again and climbs, bounded on one side by overhanging rock cliffs, on the other by the grey-black Fan i Vogel River. Here one might see two or three employees of the province's Road Maintenance Department desultorily shifting fallen rocks or sweeping in slow motion.

The bus stop for Ilir's house was just across a bridge, rail-less in 1993. Looking upwards from the bridge, a mountainside of near vertical bare rock stretched up into the distance. Of the 70 houses in Bisak, only one was visible. To reach the house we had to climb over a pile of rocks between the road and a field. This turned out to be an obstruction designed by the *vllazni* (several houses belonging to brothers) higher up the mountain to discourage the lower houses' inhabitants from crossing the field, which was being claimed by the upper houses. Since the field was the only means of access to both lower and upper houses, the barricade, inconvenient to both parties, was more symbolic than functional. We walked along a progressively narrowing track that ran above the River Fan i Vogel. While concentrating on not looking at the river below, I saw a reception committee coming towards us in single file. We shook hands and kissed Albanian style on the ledge. We passed a spring in the mountainside, the source of the family's water, and continued along the track, which narrowed to a few inches round a sticking out boulder. Beyond the rock was a garden gate and through the gate a small one-storey house, the first part of which we later learnt was the grandparents' quarters. Passing the house we turned up a path into a tiny yard where five of the eight children, aged three to 11, were sitting on a narrow bench in a solemn row. They stood up and gravely shook hands with us in turn. From the yard we entered a short windowless passage at the end of which was a water container and a milk churn. To the left was a small room with a cement floor and two beds. Soula and I sat down on the narrow bed and seven children sat down on the double bed opposite. The father, Mark, sat on the only chair, and the mother, Dava, sat on a low stool next to a wooden cradle, which contained under a ceiling of scarf the swaddled one year old.

For the last few years of Communism the father of the family, a man in his early 40s, had worked as an electrician in the Spaç mining centre, a two-hour walk across the mountains. Most Bisak men had worked in one of the industrial concerns, mining, timber or hydro-electric. The village women, like Dava, had worked on the cooperative earning three cents a day (the price of a loaf of bread or packet of cigarettes at the time). In 1993 the family were half way through the year of *asistenz*, unemployment benefit. Their two biggest problems were getting enough to eat and clothing themselves. The eight children aged one to 18 did not look malnourished. It was only when you knew how old they were that you realised how minute they were for their age.

In the house there were none of the stereotypical signs of poverty; no mess or crying or dirty faces. Without acting as if repressed, the children were still and quiet indoors. Outside they were as active and lively as any other members of their age group. The indoor behaviour was the result of their father's influence. Mark was intelligent, given to longwinded philosophising redeemed by practical application, and well informed, chiefly through listening to the radio – they had no television at the time. He said he had made a conscious decision to devote his energies to bringing up and educating his children. He was a talented amateur teacher who educated his eight children in much more than their school lessons. He put his life plan in a nutshell when we were talking six years later in 1999 about the scholarship his second daughter, aged 14, had just won to study foreign languages in Shkodra:

> Even though I live in a village, I am a *qytetarë* [a citizen, but in this context literally 'a city man']. My long-term plan since 1991 has been to educate all my children out of the village so that they can take up non-village professions. Eventually I will move to the capital myself. I work what little land I've got so as to eat, but I'm not a villager.

That same year, 1999, he and his family had collected three *kuintal* (300) of thyme in order to pay for the children's schoolbooks, a practical illustration of his stated life strategy.

In 1993, now jobless, Mark devoted his energies to finding ways to make ends meet, and to educating his children. He had solved the clothes problem temporarily, by writing to the Catholic organisation Caritas requesting a parcel of old clothes.[3] Cash generation was a constant problem. Occasionally a villager needed some electrical work done; two days work would bring in about a hundred lek, worth in 1993 about a dollar. Whenever herbs of pharmaceutical use were in season family members were mobilised to gather them for sale to itinerant middlemen. Three adults and a child could gather and sort 20kg of thyme in three days. As well as introducing system and keeping control of a potentially demoralising situation, Mark had made a point of planting one small plot in front of the house entirely with flowers – irises, chrysanthemums, roses – because 'beauty is an important part of education too – not everything should be for use'. In Hoxha's time, this plot had been the only land left to them after compulsory cooperativisation, and they had used it to grow tomatoes.

After we had drunk the coffee and raki customarily served on a visitor's arrival, we went with Bardha, the 18 year old, and some of the other children to explore the family's property and 400m^2 of land. In the narrow yard opposite the house was a small pigsty. Next to the sty was a tiny two-storey barn with hay storage space above and animal shelter for the cow and hens underneath. Below the house and the front garden was the earth closet. A steep path above the sty led up to the vegetable garden where in 1993 they could grow enough beans to cover three months consumption, and maize to cover three weeks. Beans were rotated with rye grown for animal fodder. At ten day intervals in summer they had access to irrigation water through a rota of a few hours a day. They also grew garlic, cabbage and, in summer, tomatoes and peppers. Above the vegetable garden was a small patch planted with some grape vines and fruit trees – cherry, plum, quince, pear, walnut. The cow, which two of the children took to graze after school every day, provided them for part of the year with a small supply of milk from which they made *kos* (sour milk), which they diluted with water, and a small quantity of cheese. Out of Bisak's 70 families 30 had already built up small flocks of goats by 1993, but the village has little pasturage nearby and animals had to be taken a long way up the mountain. This family did not have the wherewithal or personnel to build up a flock without sacrificing the children's education.

Late in the evening of our first day, when it was time to eat, Bardha, who seemed to do most of the work, brought a bowl of water and washed our feet. More water was brought for our hands and then a low table was brought for the father and me and Soula to eat at, while Dava continued to suckle the baby. One of the children was instructed to act as a whisk to keep the swarms of flies at bay. The children and Dava would eat separately later. First-time guests are more often entertained alone by the '*zoti i shtëpis*', head of the house. In houses with more than one room the rest of the family, perhaps with the exception of other adult males, might not be present at all.

At bedtime, Soula and I shared the very narrow bed while the mother and six children slept as usual crosswise across the double bed. The baby spent some of the night in his cradle and some in the big bed. The father and Ilir, who would have shared the narrow bed, slept in the hayloft.

The day after our arrival we were taken to meet the head of the clan, a musical instrument-maker *emerituar*; that is, he had been awarded a communist medal of excellence for his skills. He was incomparably better off than Mark thanks to his profession and the current Kosovar diaspora demand for traditional instruments such as the two-stringed *çifteli*, native to Mirdita and Gjakova. He also had far fewer expenses since he had only one child, born after an

18 year wait and hence named Gëzim (Joy). Also his wife earned as a road sweeper for the Mirdita Maintenance Department working on the Bisak stretch of the road. This job, generally performed by two or three locals on each village's section, involves clearing fallen stones and boulders, shifting mud and debris after rain, lighting bonfires to burn the leaves and sticks, as well as to keep warm by in winter.

During our visit, the instrument maker politely urged us to stay with him that night, either because he knew it was difficult for his impoverished cousin to have us or, as he hinted, because he thought we might be uncomfortable there. Or it may have just been customary politeness; it is normal good manners to ask a guest to stay for the night. Once when staying in the same apartment building as the family I had just had supper with, I was invited to stay in their ground floor flat for the night rather than returning to my flat at the top of the building. This situation, which arose often, was rarely a dilemma as usually we felt it would have been insulting to leave one host for another.

During this first visit to Bisak we also met the Headmaster of the eight-year school. (There had been a school in Bisak since the 1940s.) Ilir's scholarship to study in Tirana had been won with the disinterested support of the headmaster who, unlike many teachers, was said to be impervious to bribes from the parents of the less able. Of the 130 children attending the school at this time (1993), about 30 came from outlying hamlets. The ten teachers, three women and seven men, despite lacking higher qualifications, were, according to the Headmaster, motivated and took an interest in the children. A situation that had changed by 1994 when some teachers had become demoralised, while others had descended to towns to be replaced by less qualified and often less able individuals. The Headmaster had had to move with his family into the school since their own house, built on cooperative land under Communism, was now on someone else's land. He and his family were soon to move down to Laç, a town with a population of c. 35,000, on the plain halfway between Rrëshen and Tirana, where they had bought a flat. His wife had been the local nurse, but as a result of political changes in local government was now jobless and keen to point out how underqualified her successor was.

The head was one of those who thought the Kanun was quite unsuitable for a modern state. He claimed that it had not solved a single dispute in Bisak. He was also dissatisfied because, in contrast to the system in other villages where the number of clan representatives on the *pleqësia* was in proportion to the size of the clan, here each clan was represented by one man only. This despite some clans being very much larger. Ironically, the conversation on this first visit was unobtrusively tape-recorded by the head in a reversal of the more usual anthropological situation.

It was not long before we had a chance to experience some of the unresolved disputes at first hand. One afternoon the family decided to show me the grave of their eldest son, who had died when an infant. The graveyard, created under Communism 'to smash the fetters of faith', was halfway up a hill past the now empty site of the cooperative bakery and across some fields. In the last field we had to get under a fence to enter the graveyard. On our way home, on the road near the bridge, an angry young man, a son of the family who now owned the land where the graveyard was, suddenly appeared. Ordering our host sharply aside, he said in threatening tones: 'If you're ever seen on our land again, you'll be in trouble.' No-one had died since decollectivisation, and the villagers had not yet solved the problem of acquiring a new piece of land for burial purposes.

In common with numerous other villages, Bisak had had one of its roads blocked off by the owner of recently restored land. This dirt road linking it with Spaç, the site of a large copper mine as well as one of Albania's most notorious prisons, had been usable by wheeled traffic and saved hours of detour. Not far from the beginning of this road one now came to an impassable barricade. There was nothing symbolic about this fence, which consisted of thick wooden planks ferociously reinforced with thorn bushes. About 100 metres of the road passed through the newly privatised land of a particularly intransigent owner. Since cars and lorries had no means of circumventing this stretch, they had to drive down to Reps and up to Spaç, more than three times the distance. In cases like these it was up to the headman and elders to find a solution. State law was indifferent and probably helpless, and once again reference to it elicited the oft-repeated phrase: '*ska shtet, ska ligj*'.[4]

When we left after that first visit, I wondered why we had not been introduced to Mark's parents who lived next door, or to the brother and his family who lived in a house three metres beyond Mark's yard. We understood on our next visit when we found the garden gate at the end of the path above the river locked. To reach Mark's part, one had to slither down a bank and up again to the far side of his yard. No one made much of this, and when I privately asked Bardha about it she discreetly said that her grandfather was not really himself at the moment. The grandfather had, in fact, physically attacked Mark and Ilir before barricading them out. This was the fruit of yet another inheritance dispute. Following the break-up of the cooperatives, the family land had been regained and divided between the sons. But a dispute between this son and some other family members had resulted in the grandparents taking three rooms of the house and leaving this son with only one. The son who lived in a house beyond Mark's yard was much better off as he had a small house to himself and only three children. Another brother, a music teacher, had a separate house near the village school. The parents were not on speaking terms with Mark's family (though the mother secretly came to meet us on later occasions); nor did Mark's family speak to the next door brother's family. Almost every family we stayed with had cousins in close proximity with whom relations had been broken off. The children had invariably been told on no account to speak to, let alone play with, the children next door. Since the quarrels were all post-cooperative, and hence recent even in the experience of small children, we used to wonder what the children made of these strictures forbidding contact with former close companions who were usually visible through a fence.

Mark's *asistenz* was due to run out in August. Entitlement to unemployment pay lasted for a year after being laid off. Thereafter, *përkrahje sociale*, social support, would be far too little to make ends meet. The fact that the State considered those with land, however small the amount, as employed, meant that even families with many children, a factor in the allocation of welfare, received minimal state help. Numerous ideas as to income generation were being considered by Mark and many other desperate rural dwellers, at least 70 per cent of whom in this area were now jobless. Mark's favourite plan was to become a bread delivery van driver. At this time, the difficulty in obtaining and paying for wheat or wheat flour was such that many families had to buy bread. Since bread was only produced in fairly distant towns – the nearest to Bisak was Reps – one either had to travel by bus or lorry (both rare and expensive) to buy bread, or walk for several hours, or go without. One solution would be delivery service. Mark, who had been a driver at some point in his career, saw himself as a bread deliverer, but without access to a foreign aid organisation's capital input there was little chance of this project being realised. Two years later, when villagers had easier access to flour, the need for bakeries had passed, the more so because home-baked bread costs less than bought bread. However, the Austrian charity Caritas, very likely acting on information received two years earlier, decided to build bakeries in some Mirditan villages. Since the headmen involved stood to gain from the plan, though not in the way envisaged by Caritas, they enthusiastically supported the building. Had Caritas representatives held meetings in the village schools and asked a wide section of the community, they would have discovered that villagers desperately needed local clinics, while there was no demand at all for bakeries. The ensuing ironies, which we witnessed at first hand in the neighbouring bajrak, Orosh, are recounted in a later chapter.

Another project much discussed as a generator of employment concerned the commercial use of medicinal plants in which the area is rich. Under Communism these had been collected and processed in state enterprises; the derelict sheds of one processing centre could still be seen in Rrëshen. Now individual families were collecting and selling thyme and blueberries to middlemen. But the organisation required to turn this into an enterprise, which eliminated middlemen and produced for the sole benefit of the region, was again too difficult logistically. Other projects such as modernising and reactivating the mineral industry were recognized as dependent on foreign investors yet to materialise.

One idea that had been promoted by the school head concerned Mirdita's forests. Much of Mirdita is forested, chiefly with pine, dwarf oaks and beech. Under communism the forest had of course been state property. Some members of the commune (*komuna*) of Fan, the highest regional authority apart from the provincial authorities in Rrëshen, had proposed to central government that the forest should be cooperatively managed by the commune for the commune. This would have had two advantages. Firstly, it would have produced funds giving the local authority more than theoretical powers. Secondly, even more importantly, the self-interest of its local managers and their presence on the ground might have helped to prevent the subsequent uncontrolled destruction. The proposal had been rejected, as the State was not prepared to surrender one of its very few valuable assets. That this response was short-sighted and ultimately irresponsible became ever more obvious through the 1990s. Increasingly large tracts of forest all over Mirdita and the rest of the country were cut down, mainly illegally by private individuals, while no replanting occurred. The Fan proposal included the establishment of a local furniture factory and sawmill business to be operated on a cooperative basis, a measure that would have created immediate employment and benefited the area economically and ecologically in the long term. This proposal to utilise the forest for local enterprises such as furniture production was by far the most practical project suggested for income generation, and with help from the State could have been carried out.

After we had known the family for several months, a more modest possibility for income generation presented itself. The instrument maker's wife no longer wanted her job, and would have handed it over to Dava, but for some reason this change was not acceptable to the maintenance authorities. Whether they had another candidate for the job in mind, or whether this family was not voting for the 'right' party, was unclear. Without mentioning anything to the family, I asked a friend to introduce me to the Head of Works and Maintenance. After some resistance, the Head agreed to the deal, and Dava became a road sweeper. Her state salary was paltry but it provided social insurance and the security of a regular sum of money.

This intervention on my part was exactly consistent with local traditions of reciprocity expressed by the term *miqësia*, friendship or exchange of favours. The derivative word *mik* means both friend and guest. The word for hospitality is *mikpritje* (literally waiting for/on the friend/guest. *Mik* has a different meaning from the other word for friend which is *shok*. *Shok* (masc), *shoqe* (fem) means friend/companion and under Communism meant 'comrade', the normal way of addressing people; (*shoqëria* means society). *Mik* means linked through reciprocity which, of course, includes relatives through marriage, and is the term used to refer to the father-in-law of your son or daughter. *Miqësia* also means 'connections/cronyism', the kind that can be used to get a visa or a place high up on a housing application list; (cf. German *beziehungen*, Greek *meson*). Under Communism *miqësia* was an institution of major importance for obtaining, for example, favours from bureaucrats. By the middle of the first post-communist decade, *miqësia* was becoming complicated by the new need for cash, and hence less reliable. It was no longer certain that one's *mik* on the housing association would not give priority to someone who had offered them money. However, the general understanding, that where you have done a favour you may expect a return, continued.

Xhuxhë (pronounced Jooge)

Through some maternal first cousins of the Bisak family we got to know a village called Xhuxhë, which was about three-and-a-half hours walk northeast of Bisak at the far corner of the bajrak. To get to Xhuxhë you had to pass through Fan's district centre, Klos. In 1993, Klos had the usual handful of rundown blocks of cement flats, in this case standing on a narrow piece of land between the river and a forested mountainside. The first building we came to was Klos' one time church turned into a grain store in 1967. There were some administrative offices, many of whose windows, like the school's, were broken. The school provided secondary education for the whole of Fan. During the communist period, ambitious 14 to 19 year olds would walk from villages all over Fan, for many a walk of three hours or more, to take advantage of the future that secondary school education offered.

Klos also had a small hospital, which in 1993 had no water supply and only sporadic electricity. Here six nurses on full, albeit small, salaries 'worked' their shifts. Occasionally maternity cases appeared bringing their own food and presumably water. One maternity case had tragically died the week before our visit as a result of blood loss. There was a dentist who simply extracted teeth; there were no materials for any other treatment.

From Klos, a dirt road runs beside the river. This road had been built by '*aksion*' in the late 1970s to provide access to the mine at Thirra, the furthest village, and to enable lorries to transport tree trunks from the forest. Across the river is the village of Domgjon, accessible in 1993 only by foot along the river bed. Its access road had been closed by newly restored landowners. This was still more serious than the inaccessible Spaç road, because even those on foot could only get to or from Domgjon when the river was low, leaping from rock to rock and wading through pools. Further on towards the village of Sang, the road runs through a narrow valley with grim enclosing rocks on one side and the cheerless grey river and steep mountainside on the other. The only vehicles using the road in 1993 were the occasional lorry heavily laden with huge tree trunks. In the case of the one lorry we did meet this first time, it had been bought with a government loan plus the money that one of the two young men who owned it had earned in Greece. The men had gone into partnership running a legal wood-hauling business. Until 1995 there was no bus linking Sang with Klos, Reps and Rrëshen. One rarely met anyone on the road though once we met a young man in flashy sunglasses and jeans, recognizably a returnee from Greece.

At the village of Sang the dirt road continues on to Thirra mine and Thirra village. For Xhuxhë one turns off to the right along a path that runs through a long tree-shaded ditch with a few houses on either side, before rising up an almost literally vertical mud slope to the hills above. (I noticed at the end of 1999 that someone had taken the trouble to cut rough steps up this obstacle, and I wondered, as I had so often before, why such minor but significant improvements had not been made sooner. One reason, no doubt, was the hardiness and agility of rural Albanians, who had never known easier conditions. Perhaps later experience of conditions abroad led to improvements such as widening precipitous paths and constructing simple log footbridges to avoid wading.) At the top of the hill one looks down on Dardhaz, the nearest hamlet or quarter (*lagje*) of the several which make up Xhuxhë. Descending the hill in 1993 we passed the new graveyard site. The same problem as in Bisak had been resolved more quickly here because in pre-communist times this hillside had been *vakuf*, church land. Thus, it had not been returned to an individual owner; moreover, it was of little agricultural value. At the bottom of the hill was a narrow wooded valley dominated by the river. Across a short bridge there was a small wooden shack housing the recently privatised water mill where the villagers took their grain to be ground.

Xhuxhë's different *lagje* are at a considerable distance from each other. Each *lagje* had its own eight-year school thanks to Hoxha's campaign to provide education for all, however remote the settlements. Until the Communist period the whole area was one of transhumance. In 1967, the flocks were collectivised and the mine at Thirra opened. Thereafter, 90 per cent of Xhuxhë men worked in state jobs; the majority in the mine, a few for the forestry commission. Most of the cooperative workforce was female. In 1993, following the closure of the mine and the end to most state forestry jobs, Xhuxhë's families had to revert to pastoralism and, where possible, tree felling and selling (mainly illegally). The average landholding in Dardhaz, whose terrain is steep and wooded, is a mere 200 square metres, so that wood and livestock are the only local means of obtaining what is for most a hand-to-mouth existence.

To reach the cousins' house, we passed the eight-year school, crossed back over the river, wading this time, and climbed up a steep bank where it was hard to make out any kind of path. At the time this was a problem because trespassing was likely to call forth a fierce dog or angry owner. The cousins' house, made of stone and roofed with wooden tiles, stands in a tiny patch of land on a wooded slope. In 1993, the family consisted of the parents, the father's mother and five small daughters aged from ten to a few months. In a dank dark room with a bare cement floor we found Ilir's grandmother feeding a swaddled baby tied into its cradle. A two-year-old girl with shaven head, wearing only a ragged skirt, ran into a corner with fright at the sight of us. Ilir's uncle had gone to the district office in Klos in need of some document. The rest of the family was in the forest picking bilberries, which we later learnt they dried to sell to merchants for pharmaceutical use. The mother and the three older children went gathering for three to four hours every day in the short bilberry season.

To fill in time until they returned, we went up through the steep forest to Lari to visit a schoolteacher I had been told to talk to. Lari was the beginning of the pasture-land area. Prior to collectivisation it had been the summer base for transhumants from the lower regions. But after the flocks had been collectivised the Communists had settled an all the year round population there, complete with four-year primary school. We found the teacher's wife at home cooking to deafening music. Only her children, who were out, knew how to operate the new radio-cassette player, so conversation was difficult. But we did learn that her husband had, like Ilir's uncle, gone to sort out some bureaucratic problems. Trying to obtain the necessary documents and records in order to claim benefits had become a major occupation for villagers. Papers showing evidence of one's land size, number of children, number of years one had worked in which kind of job, were essential, but in the aftermath of regime change, many papers had been lost or destroyed, while others allegedly, had never existed.

On our return from Lari, we found the rest of the family had come back, including the father, Nikollë, who had taken a quicker more precipitous cross-country route than ours. In addition to managing his smallholding and selling wood on a small scale, Nikollë was a *çifteli* player and performed at weddings. Kristina, his wife, was from a riverside village in the bajrak of Orosh. She and one of her sisters had both married here. She was a charming vivacious 30 year old, self-assured and intelligent. Nikollë's mother, Maria, was a lament singer (*vajtuese*) and dressmaker of death clothes, *veshje e vdekjes*.[5] The grandmother's own death clothes were said to be exceptionally fine, but I had been told not to ask to see them in case getting them out might be seen as unlucky, that is, might hasten her death. Far from avoiding the subject, Maria herself brought it up having seen my camera, and suggested that she put on the death clothes to be photographed. Then Kristina said that she would put on her best Mirditan costume. So we held a photographic session in the *dhoma mikpritve* (the room for hospitality) as yet half built, so that you could still see the wall insulation material of pine cones.

Later in the evening, when Kristina breastfed Alma, I noticed that she lifted the cradle to feed the baby still tied into it, just as Edith Durham had described for the area nearly 100 years earlier.[6] But if this seemed old fashioned, Kristina's psychology was up to the minute, for she paid far more attention to the two-year-old Mariana, holding her close and caressing her whilst feeding the baby. I commented on this and she said 'it's hard for the youngest when there's a new baby'. (Very likely, Mirditan mothers in Edith Durham's time were just as enlightened.)

We had supper at the traditional *sofra*, the low round wooden table found (like the brass coffee grinder) throughout the former Ottoman Empire. After supper, Maria made Nikollë play us a tape recorded the week before when she had sung laments at the funeral of the young woman who had died in childbirth in the Klos hospital. Kristina, with a grin, whispered that her mother-in-law was very fond of listening to herself. The making of tapes at all struck me as unexpected in view of the extreme poverty and isolation in which they lived. Perhaps it was a direct result of the government racket of 1988–9 when the population was given the opportunity to hand

Election rally in Skënderbeg Square, Tirana 1997

Dardhas 1995: Return at dusk spinning

Mirditan family at supper, 1993

Trying on the death clothes, Mirdita 1993

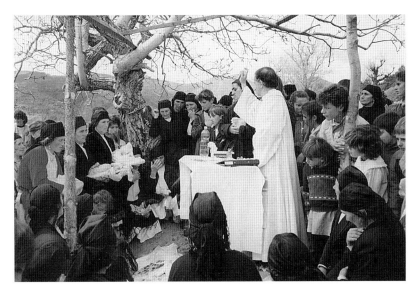

Orosh 1994: First celebration of Easter Mass since 1967

Women's burden: Wood collecting, Bulshar 1996

Spaç prison semi-destroyed 1996. The motto says: 'Through stealing evildoers attack our regime and the economic basis of Socialism.'

Rrëshen 1997: Cows feeding on rubbish

Descent to the Plain: the Gjokas' claim shanty near Shenavlash 2003

Illegal houses Built Into the Old Tractor Factory, Tirana

in their traditional silver jewellery to be weighed and exchanged for tape recorders.

Under Communism, the bajrak of Fan was administratively linked to the town of Kukës, capital of the neighbouring province. Kukës is close to Xhuxhë and much closer for Fan inhabitants than Rrëshen, though post-communism Rrëshen and Reps are the administrative centres for the whole of Mirdita. Linking Fan with a Muslim province may have been a tactical move by the communist government as well as a practical one; part of a strategy to dilute Mirditan and Catholic identity. As Nikollë told us, this administrative link did lead to numerous connections, friends and fictive kin – *kumar i flokat* – godparenthood through haircutting (as opposed to *kumar i pakzimit* – through baptism), as well as commercial and medical (orthodox and magic) contacts in Kukës. Kukës had a famous curer if conventional medicine failed to help. Kristina scoffed at this and said she did not believe in miracle performers or the evil eye. This scepticism was unusual and not a view shared by the rest of the family. The general readiness to have faith in non-religious rites such as godparenthood through haircutting and healing through magic, indicate that the communist government may have overestimated the centrality of religious faith to Mirditan identity. Nor were the attempts to encourage non-Catholic links successful from a socialist ideological point of view. Quite the contrary; Nikollë said that throughout Communism they had done all their black market exchange with Kukës, where the bureaucratic links had greatly facilitated private sales of meat and carpentry goods. Being partly engaged with flocks and wood, as well as isolated, these villagers were in a position to take a rather cavalier approach to communist strictures on markets even after 1980, when all but a tiny plot and a chicken or two had to be handed over to the cooperatives.

The family subsisted on the produce from their small flock of goats (which the two eldest girls took to graze each afternoon), their vegetable plot and occasional income from sale to itinerant traders of their own produce such as walnuts. In addition they gathered herbs and bilberries in season. Five kilos of fresh bilberries made one dried kilo, which in 1993 they could sell for $9. (In subsequent years the price fell until no itinerant middlemen came at all.) Nikollë was able to earn a little cash through *çifteli* playing during the wedding season. Although they were very poor indeed in terms both of cash and nourishment, Nikollë was in the process of finishing the *dhoma mikpritve*, the room for entertaining guests, which he had just built on to the house. Like the pine cones for insulation and bracken for mattresses, most of the materials were free, so that the new room had cost skill and time rather than money.

As one would expect given the traditional pre-cooperative settlement pattern whereby brothers build on adjoining land if they move out of the patrimonial house, the two houses nearest to Nikollë and Kristina's belonged to relations, second and third cousins. Their situations were somewhat different from Nikollë's since in both cases the family heads had had some form of higher education. One family head had been an accountant on the cooperative, while the other had just retired from being head teacher at the eight-year school and, more significantly in terms of income, both families had offspring working in Greece. Throughout Albania, the presence of sons old enough to migrate abroad was a decisive factor in economic level. Since neither the Bisak family nor their first cousins were in this position, they were much worse off than the second cousins. One of the Headmaster's sons was a teacher, one had been a brigadier on the cooperative, one was a builder. Two of the sons had worked for some months in Greece. The youngest daughter had just got her degree in literature at the University of Tirana and was about to marry the Headteacher of the secondary school in Klos. The household was a joint one; the two married sons and their wives and children, together with the household head and his wife and unmarried children, had a common household budget. The sons' earnings from Greece had been handed over to the father, they told me, to be spent as he thought best. Part of the earnings had gone towards house improvements, part towards staple food supplies. In fact, their house indicated that under Communism they had had a higher standard of living than Nikollë; there was a good *dhoma mikpritve* and an indoor lavatory. The fact that the father had been a head teacher under Communism and that his daughter had been able to study at the university indicated an above average level – teachers under Communism were amongst the best paid groups. As a result of this sizeable male workforce and common budget, the family was able to diversify income generation in a way impossible for the neighbouring cousins. The wife of the household head said that families had to work much harder now that they had their own animals to care for and plots to cultivate. Without the cooperative services such as bakery, creche and nursery school, women had far more to do. But she saw the changes as positive because 'now we are working for our own gain'.

There appeared to be far fewer ongoing disputes in Xhuxhë, and various factors differentiating the settlement from other villages were mentioned as minimising conflicts. One source of solidarity may have been the fact that Xhuxhë is one of the few Mirditan villages where intermarriage is permissible. This is due to the presence within it of three unrelated clans who settled at a much later date than the founders. The resulting inter-relatedness is seen as a unifying factor both by the villagers themselves and by those from villages where intermarriage is not permitted. The immediate explanation for comparative freedom from disputes proffered in 1993 was that, as a pastoral village, they had far more work than villagers with only small plots to cultivate: 'We don't have time for quarrelling.' Certainly their joint activities combining wood and flocks gave them more to do, and the fact that there was adequate and accessible pasturage was crucial. Most importantly perhaps, agricultural land was not the main source of income, so that there was less cause for boundary disputes. Also significant as regards one of the commonest causes of dispute elsewhere, families here tended to remain joint, so as to maximise the potential for division of labour, thus avoiding intra-familiar friction over land inheritance.

Chapter Eight

OROSH

Life in Lëgjin

By the summer of 1993, I had got to know several families in the adjoining highland bajraks of Orosh and Fan. Sometimes acquaintance with a family had begun as a result of a chance meeting in a bus or at a wedding; sometimes through going to stay with a pupil from the Tirana School of Foreign Languages; sometimes through meeting a co-villager or relation of one of these. The two bajraks are linked by intermarriage as one would expect given the customary rule that proscribes marriage within a bajrak (except in the infrequent case of a village like Xhuxhë where an unrelated clan arrived at a later date). In Orosh as in Fan, people were much more isolated from each other now that there were no cooperatives, few functioning state concerns, no houses of culture and no regular administrative get-togethers. Moreover, whereas a family's livelihood under Communism, however minimal, had been guaranteed, now it depended on intensively farming one's own minute portion of land, and finding alternative sources of income such as emigration. And if a family head was not cultivating his land, he was probably touring the administrative offices in Reps or Rrëshen trying to claim benefits or rectify bureaucratic muddles. People were too preoccupied with subsisting to socialise except at funerals or weddings. Hence, the families I visited in one bajrak were always interested to hear any news and gossip I had come across during visits to the other. They, in turn, were able to supply me with detailed background histories of the families I had met elsewhere.

The first time I visited the Deda family of Lëgjin I had already decided that as soon as I could I would give up research in Albania.

It was too much of an endurance test physically and psychologically. This time, rather than inflict the exigencies of old buses, new people, and fresh entomological discomforts on Soula, I had left her with friends in Tirana. I set off with Dila, a pupil at the School of Foreign Languages in Tirana, a tomboyish 18 year old with blustery rough manners. We left the mountain bus below the small town of Reps, and walked for three-quarters of an hour along the track from the copper refining factory. The track runs beside a precipice several hundred feet above the river, wide enough not to be alarming except at the edge. Lëgjin is a wooded settlement of very dispersed houses above the River Fan, and run through by rivulets. The Deda's house lies just below the dirt road that runs between Reps and the upland village of Bulshar. No other houses are visible, though within a radius of a kilometre or so a dozen houses are hidden amongst the trees. This dispersedness and lack of centre make it harder to imagine daily cooperative life. In fact, underlining the unsuitability of the area for collectivisation, brigade members were often required to go for *aksion* to other parts of Orosh. This joint activity was part of the much more intensive social life of villages under Communism; an aspect greatly missed in the 1990s.

The nearest settlements to Lëgjin, apart from the town of Reps, are Grykë Orosh and Bulshar. Bulshar, an hour's walk up the dirt road and somewhat nearer by precipitous mountain tracks, had been the cooperative's administrative centre. In Bulshar there was an eight-year school and a middle school (catering for 15 to 18 year olds). Children from Lëgjin of eight-year school age went either to Grykë Orosh School or Bulshar depending on which was nearer their house.

Below the Deda's house at the bottom of a steep bank ran the River Fan i Vogel (Small Fan) where one of the sons later showed us how to catch fish using only one's hands. Across the river was a flat beach of grass and tall cherry trees beyond which was a grassy bank where the family's cow was taken to graze. As well as having a larger house than anyone else we knew, the Dedas had more than average land for highland Mirdita – five and a half dylims (10 dylims = 1 hectare). In the time of King Zog the grandfather had made a considerable sum of money serving in the army. In addition to building the house, he had bought quite a lot of land as well as some forest. He had also bought land and a house on the Lezhë plain where this family's cousins now lived. When the local land commission of seven men in their 60s confirmed the former hereditary borders, this family gave away a piece of their inherited land which did not adjoin the rest of their property. 'We have a bit more land than most people anyhow, so we gave it to a needier family.' One can imagine that a piece of land nearer to another house might be more of a liability than an asset, so that it was probably prudent to be generous. Moreover, the increase in Lëgjin's population had been even higher than average; there were now over 50 households where in pre-communist Lëgjin there had been seven.

Those families who had owned a part of the forest in Zog's time were unable to reclaim it, as the forest continued to be state property. This was a source of annoyance to the family, but at least it applied to all pre-communist owners. Unfair distribution of cooperative animals, by contrast, was a source of bitterness amongst all those villagers across Albania who had lost out. Ignoring the official basis, the cooperative officials gave the best and the largest number of animals to their cronies. Cooperative officials, accountants, agronomists and vets had been in a stronger position to enrich themselves throughout the regime, and this final act of injustice over the distribution of animals caused a lot of resentment.[1]

Local sources of income other than tiny land parcels were shrinking fast. Of the 300 individuals who had worked in state jobs rather than on the cooperatives, only 15 were still employed by the State, most in the Reps factory, a few in the police force. A potential source of income for this family was believed to have been lost when the grandfather was killed in his 60s by a falling tree. He had hidden a hoard of gold for his heirs but had unfortunately not revealed its whereabouts before his unexpected death. Under Communism any asset of value would have been confiscated by the State, and it was common for people with money to hide it. A number of newspaper reports in the 1990s told of finds and the ensuing dramas involving multiple claims and the return of hopeful émigrés.

The Dedas might have lost the gold but they possessed another asset of great value in the stream, which ran through their land. Agricultural work was central to their life in 1993, and the abundance of water vital to production. They grew maize, white beans (*fasulia/grrosh*), peppers, cabbages, garlic, onions, tomatoes, and some potatoes. (Only the highest villages can grow good potato crops.) They grew grapes, not in vineyard type bushes but as climbers (pergola). The mother and father saw to all the irrigating work, channelling the water to the relevant pieces of land in rotation. They also took care of the grazing (they had one cow and a calf) and of the animals, which included a pig and hens. The rest of the family did the sowing, hoeing and harvesting. One obstacle to cultivation was the extreme steepness of their fields. They had no access either to draught animals or to a small-scale machine such as a rotivator. For ploughing they hired an itinerant ploughman from the plain who ploughed with horses. Their small number of animals meant that to increase productivity they would have had to acquire artificial fertiliser, but this was prohibitively expensive. Maximising productivity was thus impossible. Because of these obstacles the family had decided to gradually reduce the area devoted to maize and beans – labour-intensive crops requiring hours of tedious weeding. They reasoned that it would make more economic sense to reduce labour input and thereby release two brothers for work abroad. Foreign earnings would provide the cash for staples and for the accumulation of animals, and in place of maize and beans they would concentrate on forage crops such as clover, as well as planting more vines and fruit trees. The married brother planned eventually to move down to the plain, leaving the patrimonial house and property to his two younger brothers.

In 1993 the household consisted of the head of the house (*zoti i shtëpis*), his wife, their three sons, the eldest son's new wife, and two unmarried daughters. The other surviving children were married daughters who lived in Reps, Rrëshen and Rubik respectively. The father's most recent job had been with the forestry commission. Before that he had worked for 12 years in a mine. The documents testifying to his mining years had disappeared, which meant that he could not claim the pension for those years. This was all the more distressing since the pension for work in a mine was higher than most. Not because the likelihood of early death from silicosis was admitted, but because the work itself was both risky and heavy.

The eldest son, Gjergj, aged 33, had been a foreman in the mine at Spaç for seven-and-a-half years. One day when he had been absent due to illness, a man was killed in the mine. Gjergj was fetched to the scene and then summoned to Tirana where he was reprimanded despite what he saw as his innocence. Whether he quit this job in anger at the lack of recognition for seven years of satisfactory service, or was dismissed for dereliction of duty, was not clear. But it is the case that under communism foremen, doctors, midwives, and so on, were held responsible for the lives of those under their charge. A doctor whose patient died had to appear before a commission; if he or she failed to convince the commission that they had taken every possible step to prevent the death, they were gaoled. Gjergj was now jobless with his year's *asistenz* due to finish shortly. The family had decided to take out a state credit of 4 million lek (c.$4000 at the time) with which to buy him a visa for Italy. This was a risky business since there was no guarantee that once in Italy you would find yourself a job. No job and your property, the collateral, would be forfeited.

The second son, Tom, aged 26 in 1993, had learnt welding in secondary school and had since become a self-taught and skilled stone mason, barrel maker and carpenter. That he was skilled was proved by the work he had been doing inside and outside the house, building some new rooms on the ground floor, and stone walls surrounding part of the yard outside. On leaving school he had worked on the cooperative until 1991. In 1992, he had walked to Greece where he had worked picking olives and oranges, and doing some carpentry. After six months he was expelled for having no visa and returned to Orosh. Some of the money he had earned was spent on tools, seeds and fertiliser. Some was set aside for necessities like sugar and coffee, dental treatment and bus fares. When asked who decided how his Greek earnings should be spent, the family said it was by general consensus; in contrast to the family in Xhuxhë, where it was said the father alone decided. Shortage of food was not a real problem though they almost never ate meat. The main problem was shortage of cash. As soon as the bulk of the autumn agricultural work was over, this son was going to return to Greece.

The third son, Gjon, aged at this time 21, had learnt agronomy at secondary school. Agronomy was the most studied subject throughout Albania as most middle schools (for 15–18 year olds) offered no alternative. But this son was a genuinely keen horticulturist and agriculturist, systematic and experimental, and aesthetically conscious. He was also a fledgling carpenter.

When Dila and I reached the house I found everything quite different from my dreaded expectations. The stone house looked like a French farm house, its long façade covered with roses. The inevitable steep enclosing mountains would have been dreary but the family and the house itself, spacious and aesthetic, more than made up for scenic deficiencies. The *dhoma mikpritve* was upstairs, a nice large room with arched windows and a vaulted fireplace. There were no pictures on the walls now that the obligatory portraits of Enver Hoxha had been removed and there was nothing to replace them with. Downstairs was a large living room-kitchen. Surrounding the house there were tall trees, walnut, cherry, quince and plum. The roses planted by Gjon four years before, were pink with a delicious smell and this was May, their peak month. The family made lemonade with the petals, picked them to smell on the bus and chewed the petals. They brought a rose to one for company if one was reading or writing alone.

The mother, Mrika, in her early 60s, came from Bisak and was related to the Leka family. She wore the beautiful Mirditan costume which is a dark blue (or black) headdress over two long plaits looped round the head, circular silver earrings with a bell shaped pendant, black jacket over white embroidered blouse, white very full skirts over white trousers and a wonderful coloured woven cummerbund (*qemer*) tied with the decorative tassles hanging down at the back. As noted earlier the communist regime had tried to enforce more practical clothes. The very large number of women who still wear traditional dress in spite of the campaign suggests that poverty and clothes shortages made a change unrealisable. But perhaps continuing to wear traditional dress was a form of protest, or maybe just conservatism. One still saw young married girls from 'fanatik' families looking ravishing and exotic in an even more beautiful red version of this costume with red head-dress. Most girls shunned this costume as '*prapambetur*' – backward. A few of the older men still wore Turkish baggy dark blue trousers and white felt fez type caps, either flat on top or domed, called kësulë.

Mrika had not even seen her husband on their wedding-day, due to the head and face-covering duvak worn by brides at the time. She had borne 11 children, eight of whom survived, five daughters, three married, and three sons. Dila showed me a photograph of the absent daughters, naming all but one. 'What about her?' I asked. 'We don't talk about her. She married without consulting my father, and we are not allowed to say her name. My father has never seen or spoken to her since she left.'

Gjergj's wife, Zina, aged 20, had been educated from the age of 14 to 18 in a school for accountancy in Vlora. She was from a village in the Zadrimë area of the Lezhë Mountains and hating the isolation of Lëgjin, yearned to move down to the plain. I asked her why she'd married here and she said: 'I liked the boy'. She'd seen him at an arranged meeting once. It must have been particularly difficult for her as she had boarded for four years in the busy coastal town of Vlora where she had studied accountancy. There she had had the freedom of living in the school *konvikt* away from her family. Now she had come to a house so isolated that the nearest was out of sight, a kilometre's scramble up and down steepnesses through the woods and over streams.

Liza, the 24-year-old daughter, was the only waged worker in the household in 1993. She worked in the copper refining factory, and was engaged to be married to a young man from Reps. Her marriage meant that she would soon be leaving to live in her husband's household in Reps. At least she would be in the rare situation for a village girl of having her family within easy walking distance.

The day after we arrived, the 26 year old, Tom, took me to see the ruins of the Abbey of Orosh, vividly described prior to its destruction by Edith Durham. Below the abbey stands one of Albania's earliest schools, started by Franciscans in 1899. The Abbot in Edith Durham's time, Prend Doçi, was said to be the wisest man in Albania, and people had come from miles around to get his advice on disputes as related in an earlier chapter. In 1967, the year atheism was enforced, the Communists had got the villagers to dynamite the abbey. Some, either out of fear or devotion to the cause, ostentatiously testified to their loyalty by burning the church paintings and smashing the statues.

The ruined church was at the top of a cliff on a plateau reached by a more or less vertical goat path, a nightmare to negotiate even when gripped fore and aft by Tom and a villager called Pjetr. There was a spectacular view of distant blue mountains in one direction and a beautiful village, Grykë Orosh, on the hill behind the abbey the other way.

Unlike in other Mirditan villages, Grykë Orosh houses are built close together. One result of this cosy proximity is that everyone is at loggerheads, quarrelling over inadequate irrigation water, land boundaries, and real or imagined offences. In Edith Durham's time blood feud had been a serious problem, one of the reasons a peacemaker like the Abbot was so sought after. On this occasion with Tom and Pjetr, things seemed to be reverting. The 50 year old, Pjetr, who had a hut at the foot of the cliff where he kept his wood, was just talking about the terrible relations between villagers in Grykë Orosh when we saw a man below approach a pile of planks that Pjetr had stacked beside his hut. Pjetr, who was carrying a gun, disappeared down the cliff while Tom waited to make sure there wasn't a fight. It was very Edith Durhamish; all the more so standing in this spot, which she had described so graphically.

On the way back by a marginally less vertical route, Tom talked about his time in Greece. Amongst other things whilst he was there he had bought a camera, being careful to keep the receipt. But when expelled by the police as an illegal immigrant, the camera was taken off him at the border as if he'd stolen it. 'They thought because I'm Albanian I must be a criminal,' he said sadly. 'They can't understand that though I'm a poor person, I'm a person of culture.'

When we got home we found that another sister, Roza, had arrived from Rrëshen with her two children. Talk of the abbey led to Liza saying she thought it would be good if a new church were set up to provide a focus for socialising. Now that there's no cooperative or House of Culture there's a real lack of company. 'We weren't allowed religion before, you see,' she said to me, 'because it was opium.' She didn't say this as though it were a quotation. Ironically, Roza started recounting how some Italian nuns were going around trying to missionise the small children in Rrëshen, the town at the foot of the mountain. 'We don't need that kind of propaganda religion,' she said crossly. From religion we got on to magic. I asked if there was a lot of magic in Lëgjin. Tom said it was rife, 'but you musn't think it is in our family.' At first I thought he meant that his family didn't believe in it, but he meant that his family didn't cast the evil eye on people. Later, Liza said she believed that only older people were witches, '*shtriga*'. While Roza said that there were no witches at all in Rrëshen.

The father was away until the last day of my first visit. One of the grandchildren caught sight of him coming round the mountain and exclaimed: 'Lala!', the word used for 'Grandpa'. Gjin, the father, was a tall, impressive-looking man of 67, upright and handsome, with as much charm as his sons; a good conversationalist and wonderful teller of stories. When his wife returned from adjusting the irrigation channel, she strode up to greet him looking pleased and warmly shook his hand.

There was an interesting discussion in the evening between Gjin, the father, and Gjergj, the eldest son, about whether the Canon of Lek should be used today. Gjergj said that it was quite unsuitable for modern life: 'Look what it says about women.' But his father and Tom argued that as long as the new government's laws didn't function properly, didn't even cover some of the new situations, the Canon was much better than nothing.

By June, which is called *qërshor* (cherry month) in Albanian, the roses were over, but there was now an abundance of different kinds of delicious cherries, small, large, light red, dark red. The 18-year-old tomboy, Dila, climbed to the tops of the highest trees and gathered basketfuls. Zina, the bride, had gone home to her village for a rest – *për pushim*. A bride moves into a household of people she has probably never met, into a part of the countryside she has usually never seen before. Zina's life in Lëgjin was typical of a young bride's. She helped in the fields with hoeing and harvesting; she did much of the household cooking, washing and cleaning. She was lucky, as she told me, that she got on well with her parents-in-law and had such congenial brothers-in-law, but there was no denying that she missed home, the more so because in Lëgjin there was little opportunity for contact with the world outside the household. Fortunately, a young wife's sufferings – homesickness and work in strange surroundings – are recognized both by the Kanun and by society in general. The Kanun has exact rules for mitigating it. After one or two weeks of marriage the bride is accompanied home, usually by her father-in-law, to 'learn the way' (*zgjedhudhë*). She stays at home for one night. After one month, accompanied by one of the in-laws who did not go the first time, she goes home for two weeks. The in-law leaves after a night, and two weeks later a member of the bride's own family takes her back. Travelling only occurs on Wednesdays and Saturdays (*dite të pastër* – clean days); Tuesday is '*ters*' – unlucky, and so is Friday, though less so. Subsequently, the bride seems to go home as often as she can. I very often found a married daughter of the house at home '*me pushim*' – on holiday, or a daughter-in-law absent on leave.

Liza and I went over to Reps one day so that she could show me her workplace. Reps was created as a town for workers at the copper refinery. The asphalted road up from Rrëshen stops just before the town, which consists of about 30 cement apartment blocks on top of a barren hill. There were no roads then, just mud, pigs and, from 1994, the ubiquitous Sharps – satellite dishes – sprouting from every apartment block. There was nothing in the way of greenery, plan or aesthetics. A dreadful dusty wind blows almost continuously through this bleak setting. The tower blocks in the early 1990s were in a state of severe disrepair, with rusting railings round the balconies. In the mud streets one had to keep jumping across channels of water while large numbers of pigs rooted among the rubbish which lay all over the place. The factory buildings, grey sheds with broken corrugated iron roofs and broken windows, lie below the town, ranged down the hillside on a steep bank of earth and copper residue. Here Liza had worked since leaving secondary school.

The factory, like all state concerns where night duty was necessary, ran on three eight hour shifts: 6am–2pm, 2pm–10pm and 10pm–6am. To get to the part where Liza worked we had to scramble up the steep pathless banks till we reached the sort of metal ladders found in the engine rooms of large ships. In Mirdita it seemed, even away from precipitous goat paths and swaying suspension bridges, there was no escape from vertiginous challenges. Once inside the factory, we climbed up to a platform on what would have been the second storey had there been solid floors, and watched a co-worker doing the work done by Liza when on duty. The work involved walking slowly back and forth three or four metres alongside some rotating machinery which from time to time and for reasons unclear to me, had to be poked with a long metal rod that the worker held in her hand. 'It requires constant vigilance you see,' said Liza. 'But surely you can't be constantly vigilant for eight hours at a stretch?' I asked. The workers had explained that they had no breaks during their shifts. Moreover, in addition to the official responsibilities, the machine carer had also to be vigilant as to where he or she trod, since a number of the metal slats forming the platform were missing. Since the factory was open plan in the sense that there were no solid floors or walls dividing the different areas of machinery, one could look down at the drop 30 feet or so below, this level being near the top of the hill. We did a tour and saw that much of the machinery, all of which was Chinese, was stationary and broken. No one seemed to be working intensively; presumably most of the labour was there to check that nothing went wrong rather than to actively direct it. The entire building was in semi-darkness; there was a constant loud noise from the machines; whatever one touched was filthy and there was always dust blowing around. None of the machines had safety guards to protect the workers. If you stumbled into one you would be caught up in its motion. In winter, Liza said, her work was freezing; in summer boiling hot.

We went outside and perched in the glaring sun on a small level area at the top of the slope. Some of the workers, most of whom had rougher manners than the people working on the land, and a beaten, lined look in their faces, gathered round to talk. They earned 20 dollars a month. I asked the brigadier, the foreman, if the factory had made a profit under Communism and if it did today. He said he did not know for either case. He claimed that there had only been three fatal accidents in the last 20 years, a testimony to quite remarkable skills of self-protection and vigilance on the part of the workforce, and apparently a true claim. After half an hour or so of talking to at least two-thirds of those on duty, I asked them what they meant by eight hour shifts without breaks. 'I thought you couldn't leave your machines; but you've all been away from them for the last half hour.' It turned out that constant vigilance was a relative concept.

They started asking me to guess some of the workers' ages. I privately subtracted ten years from every guess. And even so, in almost every case, I guessed too old. There was simply no comparison with the men and women I had met who had worked on the cooperatives or in other non-factory work. Nearly all of the factory workers, young and old, seemed to have lost more teeth than the rest of the population. Their faces were haggard, their cheeks sunken, their complexions pale and faded. I started subtracting 15 years. For a woman who looked 45 I diplomatically said 30; she was 28. Why did they challenge me to guess their ages? If it was because they knew that the factory work ravaged them and they wanted recognition of their sufferings, it might have given more satisfaction if I had said the ages I really thought they looked. But telling a 28 year old woman that she looks 45 could not have given *her* much satisfaction even if her co-workers had been pleased. For some reason, Liza did not suffer from this aged look, presumably because at 23 she had not worked for long enough yet to be affected; also perhaps because her household was better off nutrition-wise than many.

We went down to the laboratories at the bottom of the hill. These had walls and floors, and were on the level. There were several rooms, in most of which no one was doing anything at all. At last someone offered to show me some work, which took the form of a rather desultory juggling of test tubes to determine the purity of some liquids. 'So which bit do you like best of the factory?' they asked me. 'This bit,' I said, and Liza looked rather hurt. I hastily explained that the combination of the height and not understanding her job was the only reason I preferred the labs. On the way home, Liza revealed which of the older women she had introduced me to was a witch.

Back at home, she showed us her modest trousseau. Unusually, her marriage had not been arranged. She had met her future husband in the Reps factory and was marrying him from choice. Her trousseau included a few items of costume jewellery touchingly treasured, a packet of black hair dye and a makeup set. She had made some embroidered cushion covers and napkins, and a small rug for the bridal chamber. Two weeks after her wedding, I saw that as well as wearing the smart clothes, makeup and jewellery, which current convention for brides demands, her hair had been dyed black; she had done exactly as the brides described by Edith Durham in *Tribal Customs* had done. Dying one's hair black as a bride had survived as a fashionable practice here in Orosh for over 80 years.

Spaç mine, where Gjergj had been a foreman, was attached to one of the grimmest and most brutal of Albania's prisons. The prison had been closed down at the outset of democracy and much of the place vandalised, but the copper mine where the prisoners during Communism had worked was still functioning up until the last years of the decade. Although I did not visit Spaç until 1996, I describe it here because geographically it fits into the landscape of Lëgjin and Reps.

A lorry driver who had worked for 12 years delivering the prison supplies drove us up from Reps to Spaç. The narrow road follows a precipitous track between a steep rock face and a ravine. When we reached the site of the prison we saw a crowd of people standing around who turned out to be miners on strike. Their brigadier was holding a list on which were written their monthly salaries. Most of them were earning about 20 dollars a month, while he was the best paid with 34.

The landscape was ideally suited to enhancing the horrors of prison life. Between the steep mountain slopes and overlooking a ravine, the site had no more than two hours sunlight a day in winter when the extreme cold and grimness of the scenery must have accentuated the psychological and physical sufferings intolerably. Gjon, the lorry driver, pointed to the spot across the ravine where some 70 prisoners had been buried with identification; some failed escapees, some suicides, some prisoners who had simply succumbed to death while in prison. The dead bodies could not be restored to the families until their prison sentence had expired, after which date they could be disinterred. Dead or alive the sentence was fixed. A good example of totalitarianism's thoroughness.

Gjon showed us a row of what appeared to have been outdoor showers. Here prisoners who had misbehaved had to stand chained with a constant drip of cold water falling on to their heads. There had been soldiers posted all round, and Gjon reckoned that during the entire period not more than 12 prisoners had succeeded in escaping. Although parts of all the buildings had been destroyed, the shells remained, with moralistic slogans inscribed large on the walls: 'By stealing, evil-doers are attacking our regime and the economic basis of socialism'. Or 'The party's work educates people and draws them away from the nets of intriguers, of the lazy and the malcontents'; or 'indifference is worse than criticism', an odd one given that criticism frequently led to prison.

To get to the mine one had to cross some high bridges, rail-less and wobbly, so I stayed to read the slogans and talk to Gjon. He told me that one of the supplies he had brought daily was milk, large quantities of which were given to the mine workers to enable them to absorb the mine dust with less immediately fatal consequences. (Several of the ex-miners I met in the villages now had silicosis.) They were also given good meat rations to ensure productivity in the mine. The rest of the prisoners had miserable food, mostly bread and jam. Chlorine was added to all the prisoners' liquid intake to reduce their sex drive. A dentist we knew had been the prison dentist for nine years. He was horrified, retrospectively at least, at the state of his patients' health and degree of malnourishment. Political prisoners were kept separate and treated appallingly, made to work in the worst part of the mines, tortured, underfed, never allowed meat.

A teacher friend from Fan told me subsequently that he had also worked for a period in the mine, though not as a prisoner. Everyone who had been trained for a non-manual profession, doctors, teachers, engineers, and so forth, had to spend a year working with their hands 'purifying the mind by soiling the hands'. Silicosis, he told me, was by no means the only hazard. He recalled an occasion when he had been asked by the brigadier in charge to go up an obviously rickety ladder. He had asked the brigadier: 'If it breaks, will you take responsibility for the accident?' The brigadier said no and our friend refused to take the risk. A refusal meant the loss of half a day's pay, so that a married man with a lot of children to feed would be unlikely to refuse.

According to Gjon, there had been a good library with a lot of foreign books, classics of a politically acceptable kind and the chance to learn foreign languages. Intellectuals could be seen regularly, he recalled, at the bridge over the River Fan (*Ura e Fanit*) just outside Rrëshen. They were waiting, often for hours, to hitch a lift in a lorry up to the turning off point for Spaç where they were going to visit their relatives who were political prisoners.[2] One of our best friends had often been to Spaç to visit a cousin imprisoned there. She told us how depressing it was walking up the long Reps-Spaç road; several kilometres overhung by high enclosing rocks, a grim foreshadowing of the prison to come. You had to go through a huge forbidding portal, now destroyed, where you were checked in a body search while all the food that you had brought was opened up, pies examined and eggs shaken. It was essential to bring food as an important aid to the prisoners' survival. No letters were allowed in. There were armed soldiers at every step; you were surrounded by them in the public meeting room where you met with your imprisoned relative.

Some thought the prison should have been preserved as a museum to a reign of terror. I preferred to imagine the exultant feelings of those who had vandalised the buildings, able at last to defy brutal authoritarianism. However, in an essay called 'Nostalgia for Bitterness' the writer Fatos Lubonja, who was imprisoned for 17 years, 11 of which were spent in Spaç prison, has recently written of return visits to the prisons where he was held. [23 June 2002, *Shekulli*] He found himself regretting the changes. Bricks and concrete slabs, barbed wire fencing and sentry boxes had been taken by locals for building purposes. He was particularly disappointed to find that the punishment cells in Spaç where he had been kept for several months in 1979 had gone. Puzzled as to why the disappearance of those reminders of terrible suffering should trouble him, he attributes his disappointment to a yearning to re-evoke the most intense emotions of his experience.

Chapter Nine

THE BAJRAKTAR AND THE
HEROINE OF THE PEOPLE

On several occasions when staying in Lëgjin, I had suggested to Dila that we walk up to Bulshar and meet up with Etleva. Etleva was in the same class as Dila at the School of Foreign Languages in Tirana. 'It's a long way,' or 'The people in Bulshar are bad,' Dila would say. So nothing ever came of the proposition. Finally, I decided that I really had to see another village in the area, so one day I explained that Soula and I would go and visit Etleva's family on our own. The family sense of honour and good manners dictated that a family member should accompany us. As noted: 'The Kanun demands that a guest should be accompanied, both lest he be the victim of some wicked act and lest he harm someone while under your protection.' Because: 'If your guest commits some evil act while under your protection, you are responsible for it. . . '. So together with the youngest brother, Gjon, we set off up the track to Bulshar where he had attended secondary school, about an hour's walk above Lëgjin. Unlike the other villages where we stayed, Bulshar was much more open. Most of the other highland villages were in narrow enclosed valleys with no views and a feeling of inescapable gloom. From the upper part of Bulshar, as well as views to the South of distant mountains, there was a very beautiful view of the ruined abbey of Orosh, which lay below. And even though few of the houses were close together, you could at least see enough from afar to ascertain that there was a community.

On reaching Bulshar this first time we ran into the only person we already knew right at the entrance to the village; the very Etleva whom we had met at the School of Foreign Languages in Tirana. She was in the act of filling a pitcher at a water source beside the road, the prototype beautiful damsel from some myth or biblical story. We arranged to go to her house later and continued up to the school with Gjon. In 1993 Bulshar school, a substantial two-storey building, combined an eight-year section with a four-year *shkollë e mesme* attended by 15–18 year olds from all the villages around. Things seemed pretty riotous at the school, parts of which had been damaged during the spate of vandalism of two years before. We went and sat with a lot of the teachers round a large table in the staff room where a lively, at times heated, argument ensued about the pros and cons of post-communist village and school life. At the end of the morning Etleva's brother Artan, a literature teacher, accompanied us with Gjon to his house.

Artan and Etleva's mother, Athina Milo, was from Përmet, a southern province bordering with Greece. To diminish regional differences and prejudices as well as rural-urban distance, work brigades (*aksion*), mostly consisting of young people, would be sent to build roads and railways or to terrace mountains in some distant province. This was how Athina had come to Orosh when a young girl. Should a marriage result, the couple would receive a letter of congratulation from Enver Hoxha himself, and acquire certain privileges as a reward. Propaganda publications would often mis-represent such occurrences so as to increase the impressiveness of the act. In Athina Milo's case, she herself told me that she had gone as one of a brigade of school pupils from a village in the province of Përmet and fallen in love with a tractor driver in Orosh. The author of the article in Almanak Mirdita, however, writes that she had been a teacher in the capital town of Përmet. As a reward for her conduct, Athina was made a heroine of the people. She and her husband were enabled to take a correspondence course to qualify as teachers of geography and history and both became teachers at the school in Bulshar. A local joke had it that Athina's husband, an enthusiastic communist supporter rather than a scholar, used to teach that Skënderbeu (the fifteenth century Albanian national hero) had fought with the communist Partisans. The couple's three children, as offspring of loyal party members, were entitled to go on to higher education.

At the house, we found Athina and Etleva. The father was in Tirana for a few days, and Athina told us that the family hoped to move to the capital as soon as possible. She had taken early retirement from teaching at the school because, she said, there was no longer any discipline. She was very hospitable, and made a point of cooking us a Përmet speciality. But when Gjon left us to go home we began to realise how different life was in a household without the family structure, duties and routine of a more typical rural household. The lack of country chores meant that most of the time was spent watching films on television at a volume that made conversation difficult, or looking at family photographs.

In the late afternoon I went with Artan to see something of the village. Before long we ran into the village headman, Gjon Ndue Prenga, or Gjon Bajraktar, as he preferred to be known. His grandfather had been the bajraktar of Orosh before the Communists came to power. The bajraktar's relations, as representatives of the discredited traditional order, were condemned by the communist regime, along with the families of bajraktars all over the North, as political traitors. The headman's father had been shot dead in Shkodër by communist sympathisers in the 1940s. All members of the family were then interned for a year in Tepelenë in southern Albania. When they returned to Bulshar they faced the social isolation, which was the fate of all those who had opposed the regime. This family was doubly disgraced since Gjon's brother had managed to escape from Albania across the Yugoslav border, eventually settling in the United States.

Anyone who had been reported for having expressed criticism of the regime or of life under the regime, overheard complaining of food shortages or watered milk, risked becoming *deklasuar*. Anyone with a close family member in prison for political reasons, or with a relation who had escaped the country or fought against the Communists, had a *bigrafi keq* – a bad biography – and was *deklasuar*. Socialising with those classified as *deklasuar* was to invite official criticism and throw doubt on your devotion to the party. Should you out of clan loyalty, for instance, attend a *deklasuar* relative's funeral, you would be summoned to make *auto-kritikë* (self-criticism) by the local party commission. A man of spirit might defend himself by declaring: 'I didn't go to eat, I didn't go to drink, I didn't go for politics, I went to cry.' But it was always risky and most people, however badly they felt about abrogation of clan duty, preferred to play safe. So village life for the *deklasuar* tended to be one of isolation and humiliation.

It was of course possible for such families to act as ingratiatingly as possible to the communist authorities. One simple measure was to pay to change your name from a *deklasuar* one to an acceptable new one, demonstrating to the regime your readiness to put the past behind you. Thus one family whose name was Markagjon, relatives of the Captain of Mirdita's family, changed their name to one without political associations. Some fourth cousins of Gjon, stripped of the chance for higher education or political office, concentrated on practising their skills as carpenters and cabinet makers when they returned from internment camp. To affirm their ideological enlightenment in the eyes of the authorities, the father of this family went with another family member in 1967 to help burn the icons and break up Orosh Abbey. (According to Almanak Mirdita, Athina in her position as a Heroine of the People also set an example by destroying church symbols at the abbey.) Such diplomatic behaviour somewhat reduced the unpleasantnesses of the carpenter family's position. It may have helped that several members of this particular family were exceptionally intelligent and gifted as craftsmen, and that their products were in demand.

As a direct descendant of the Bajraktar and brother of an es-capee, Gjon experienced particularly harsh treatment by the au-thorities throughout the period. After complete collectivisation took place in Mirdita in 1967, he and his family became herders for the collective. This was a job often assigned to those families who symbolised the most discredited group in pre-communist society; a job well suited to the social isolation and loss of all privileges. Such treatment had no doubt contributed to the family's demoralisation and lack of discipline.

Gjon had been chosen as headman in recognition of his past sufferings and direct connection with his grandfather, a greatly respected and exceptional character. Unfortunately, perhaps as a result of his past, Gjon was quite unsuitable for the job. In fact, at the time when each clan was providing representatives to make up the council of elders (*pleqni/pleqësia*), some of the most able men were unwilling to be chosen even as elders. Still fewer were willing to become headman, and though there were several candidates in Bulshar who were far stronger characters than Gjon, no one else was as eager to be headman at the time. Even when new elections came up two years later, the group of elders discussing who should be appointed for the next two years concluded: 'Gjon will be very sad if he isn't headman again, might as well let him be it.' The repercussions of this indifference, discussed later, were ultimately seriously damaging to the welfare of the community.

Gjon insisted on my agreeing to stay at his house the next day. Unsurprisingly, there was no love lost between the household of the Heroine of the People and that of the ex-bajraktar; the one having enjoyed all the privileges reserved for loyal Party members, the other '*deklasuar*'. Despite dire warnings that we would regret it, we accepted the invitation, and found that there was a good deal of truth in their neighbour's criticisms. The family *was* feckless; one son was in prison for theft, not for political reasons as it was glossed, and the household was somewhat haphazard. On the other hand, they were generous and hospitable and lively, which compensated for direr features that had not even been mentioned, such as the absence of *any* lavatory, even in the yard. Above all, they were more interested in conversation than in watching television.

Gjon was a diminutive rather clown-like figure with a puckish face. His much larger wife, Maria, was from a Catholic region near Shkodër. She and Gjon had eight children, the eldest of whom, a daughter, had been betrothed at birth, 28 years ago. Maria had liked another woman giving birth at the same time in the clinic at Reps, and they had agreed that their respective infants should marry on reaching a suitable age. This they did despite the Communist Party's understandable disapproval of cradle betrothals. Three of the sons were now in their twenties. Apart from the eldest who was in prison, one was away in Greece and the other was working as a forest policeman. The 13-year-old son took the animals to graze every day after school and sometimes during school hours. As he said, concurring with Athina, school was pretty much a waste of time now. The 18-year-old daughter, Roza, was the fifth of the eight children and unluckily for her, since her eldest sister was married and her three older brothers unmarried, had most of the chores to do on her own. Her mother worked hard as well cultivating the vegetable garden, taking care of the pig and the hens and doing the main part of the cooking. But the clothes washing, house cleaning, milk, butter and cheese preparation, care of the youngest siblings, often including visiting nephew and niece, serving coffee to visitors, and doing chores for her elder brothers, fell to Roza.

On the morning of the first day Gjon decided to take us up the mountain to his cousins who lived near the site of the Captain of Mirdita's *saraj* (*seraglio*/palace). The cousins were the descendants of the former Captain of Mirdita, and their houses lay an hour and a half's walk above Bulshar. The Markagjons had commanded a largish territory, though as explained earlier, their power had not lain in large estates, Mirditan terrain precluding land-based power. Pre-communist Mirdita provided a direct route through from Prizren to the west coast (Lezhë) as well as to the then capital, Shkodër. It was this strategic position that enabled its Captain to exploit the vested interests of powers like Austria and Serbia. Manipulating the different powers that subsidised them in order to gain their support had been the source of the Gjomarkajs' influence and comparative wealth. Once established in the province (according to some sources, they moved to Mirdita from the north-eastern region of Has in the eighteenth century), the Gjomarkajs began to intermarry with bajraktar families who had been gaining influence for centuries as a result of leading successful military campaigns under the Turks.

In 1993, the four brothers who occupied the area where the *saraj* had been, lived off their modest fields and animals and the earnings their young men brought back from Greece. Like the inhabitants of the village of Grykë Orosh, which lay immediately below them, they were miles from any viable road, and all heavy articles had to be transported by donkey. The *saraj* itself was now rubble, but its position on top of the mountain commanded a fine lookout point. One of the households insisted that we stay to lunch, part of which was a test of faith. 'You probably don't eat pork,' they said, offering us some slabs of pork fat. We promptly took some, explaining as we chewed that England was not predominantly a Muslim country.

Back in Bulshar that evening, the first thing that caught my eye in the *dhoma mikpritve*, was a mimeographed copy of the Kanun of Lek Dukagjin. In Gjon's case, using the Kanun was both an ideological assertion that pre-communist laws were better, and a practical attempt to cope with the legal vacuum since the end of Communism. A written 'unwritten law' is obviously unsatisfactory even when many of the principles are still valid; all the more so when the unwritten laws have not been in operation for nearly a century. While the unwritten laws were able to adjust to regional and temporal variations, this flexibility was lost once the laws were frozen on the page. Though in Gjon's case, flexibility where particular interest groups were involved was not lacking.

Asked what sort of disputes occurred most commonly, Gjon cited some relating to closed-off access roads. Thanks to the Kanun's guidelines, some of these had been resolved. He seemed much less interested in the present than in the past and I failed to get any insights through him of current community relations. I understood his nostalgia for pre-communist institutions when on subsequent occasions conversing with Maria I learnt about some of the deprivations and discrimination the family had suffered under Communism. For instance, for many years they did not get their fair entitlement to irrigation water. Eventually, someone interceded for them. Surprisingly, if you were sure of your case and could demonstrate a breach of law to the communist authorities, a complaint of this kind would be addressed even in the case of the politically non grata. Whatever the injustices suffered, Gjon's preoccupation with the past made him a poor informant on the present.

Throughout the next day, villagers, mostly women, kept arriving at the headman's house to collect their humanitarian aid rations provided by the Italian government. To load the sacks, which contained flour and sugar, they had to crouch down on the ground while someone else fastened the woven ropes and secured the sack on their back. Since it was always women who went to the woods for firewood that they brought back in huge bundles on their backs, this kind of donkey work was nothing new. Very few families had donkeys or mules because even when offered one free, as happened to a family we got to know later, they could not afford the fodder necessary to maintain one.

Inevitably, aid distribution was regarded by many as unfair. A headman was always suspected of taking the best of the clothes handouts for himself and his cronies, of holding on to some of the food provisions, or giving less to some families and more to others. No doubt these suspicions were often justified. I certainly knew of several concrete instances where headmen used their access to charitable resources for their own advantage.

During our stay we had a lot of opportunities to talk to Roza and much of the conversation turned to marriage, a subject of burning interest to village girls of her age. We learnt that not only were all respectable marriages in her circle arranged, but that this was considered desirable by the girls themselves. Marriage arranged by a couple's parents was not just the conventional way, it was the way one's role models did it. It seemed as if the very fact of not knowing the groom added a thrill to the procedure. Getting married combined the frisson of drawing lots with the glamour of new clothes and increased status; something exciting that every girl was eagerly waiting for. Roza gave us sound reasons as well why arranged marriages were better than marriages '*si të themi ne, me dashuri*' – 'as we call it, with love', whispered embarrassedly. An arranged marriage means that there is no cause for gossip or bad feeling between bride and parents-in-law or parents, she explained. 'I'll show you my '*pajë*' – trousseau, but not when my brothers are around *se e kam turp* – because I am ashamed.' Her bridal suitcase contained some clothes and trinkets, as well as some embroidered articles.

The day that we left, we were walking down the road towards Reps when we came across a young woman sitting near her grazing cow. We got talking, and I asked her if she was married. 'Not any more,' she said, so that for a moment I thought she must be the .01 per cent divorce statistic for Mirdita. But her husband had been tragically killed in the fire in the northern town of Puka in 1991, when a large number of people broke into a government warehouse full of provisions such as groceries and oil. It was night time and dark so someone lighted a piece of cardboard to see where the provisions were. The oil caught fire and more than 60 people were burnt to death. Now the young woman lived at home with her widowed mother and some of her brothers and sisters.

At the crossroads beside the former *Gjeologji* we found a girl sitting next to a small suitcase while a group of young men, one of whom was her husband, stood talking nearby. Like us they were heading for Fan, and hoping that a lorry with room in the back would pass. We sat down with the girl, whose name was Dilora, and as nothing at all passed for two hours, had plenty of time to talk. She was a young bride from a village above Bisak, married into Bulshar. She had never seen Bulshar until her wedding day and she had been dismayed by it. 'Fan is a much better region than Orosh,' she said. She was elated at going home for a three-day visit. Like every young bride I met, she suffered dreadfully from homesickness. At the same time she was immensely proud of being a *nuse* – bride. She showed us the clothes in her bridal suitcase, and which she would put on to help in the house at home. 'You see here on the road I'm dressed like this because I am a bride.' A bride when she goes out for the first year or two of marriage must be recognizably a bride and dress accordingly. Instead of the skirt over trousers, which all village women who do not wear the Mirditan costume wear at home, a new bride wears a smart dress or blouse and skirt, with necklace, earrings, rings, lots of makeup and a dressy hairstyle. Often the dress will be silver or gold lamé, or brightly coloured shiny satin. Brides married into '*fanatik*' (strict patriarchal) families wear the beautiful Mirditan bridal costume and red head-dress, but this is rarer now, and most girls hope to avoid the fate of marriage into a '*fanatik*' family.

'How do brides cry where you live?' she asked us. 'Do you cry '*me lot*' – with tears – or with a noise?' And seeing me hesitate: 'We cry like this: ohee, ohee,' a ritual sob. 'When it is time to leave we go through the neighbourhood with a handkerchief to our eyes.' In Mirdita there are two weddings for every marriage, the first at the bride's home for all her relations, on a Saturday. On the morning of the Sunday the groom's representatives, the *krushq*, come to fetch the bride. One of Hoxha's reforms led to the groom himself coming with them as well as his sister (or female cousin) to keep the bride company. The bride is taken off by the groom's party while her relations must stay behind. The only exception to this rule is when a girl marries in Mirditan bridal costume, in which case her mother accompanies her. The logic here is that formerly brides wore a head and face covering (*duvak*) that prevented them from seeing and being seen. This was good for modesty purposes but sometimes led to mix-ups when two bridal parties converged on the road. The Kanun gives instructions as to what to do if two groups of bridegroom's men meet in a village or a bajrak to which neither belong. It obliges them both to leave the road and to settle the matter with honour and without argument (Gjeçov and Fox 1989:34). It was in this kind of situation that the brides sometimes ended up with the wrong group. To avoid such mistakes it was found expedient to send the mother along with the bride. The mother's presence was not of course a guarantee against deliberate deceptions where, for example, a family substituted an ugly sister for the chosen one. Today it is more usual for the bride to wear the '*velo*', the Western style white wedding dress, and she leaves home unaccompanied by any friends or relations. She often has good reason to cry; she is leaving her family for one she has probably never met. Not only is she a stranger amongst her husband's family, but she usually has to work very hard at the most tiring jobs, such as fetching water, washing clothes, cleaning the house. If there are several brides or teenage sisters-in-law already in the household, the work burden will be less, but the newest bride gets the most tedious jobs.

Dilora seemed somewhat ambivalent about being married. She was overtly regretful that she had married instead of studying. She said she thought her groom was all right, but declared that it was impossible to live in Bulshar, and that they would move to the plains town of Laç as soon as feasible. At the same time she was obviously very taken by the external trappings of marriage, the trousseau, the bride's clothes, the status as a source of kudos and pride.

At last a lorry came in sight and we climbed into the back. The passengers, like the lorry and the dirt road, were rough. Most of them had come from finishing a shift at the Reps copper refinery. As I looked at their faded heavily lined faces, sunken cheeks, their beaten look, the desperate state of their teeth, their ragged clothes, and then at the unrepaired bridges, the dismal stony shores of the River Fan, I thought I could sense the regime of terror that had enforced acceptance and patience in these inhuman conditions. Or was it more than the presence of a massive secret police that made a people as educated as many Albanians were under Communism, put up with so hopeless a regime? Perhaps the majority had really believed the propaganda. When shown pictures of Third World poverty and told 'this is what capitalism does', did they feel grateful that they were better off? I know plenty of intelligent younger people who recall being convinced by the propaganda. We stopped to let a man get down; there on the wide lonely beach beside the dreary grey river were two women working with long-handled tools shifting stones for no apparent reason in a desolate landscape. The man who had got down said something to the lorry driver who started haranguing him for being a Communist, half bantering, half really angry, leaning out of the cab and working himself up while others started joining the fray. As the lorry started up again, another man arrived on the scene just in time to hurl a pig squealing and yelling up into the back. For the last 20 minutes of the ride political debate was drowned by the anguished squeals of the frantic pig. It was almost a relief to arrive at the precipice path in Bisak.

Chapter Ten

DEVELOPMENTS: UPS AND DOWNS

Tirana

The disadvantage of no longer being continuously on the spot to follow developments was counterbalanced by the greater awareness absence gives to changes that have occurred. Returning in March 1994, we found a good many things had changed since September. The headless statues of Lenin and Stalin had been removed completely. For the first time stray dogs roamed the streets. Imported pumpkin seeds in packets were replacing the egg-cupfuls of local sunflower seeds. More citizens wore sunglasses, the obligatorily retained label partially obscuring their view. There were more books (as well as more porn) for sale. It was not quite so hard to get basic groceries if you could afford them. Quite a lot of windows had glass in them, and some open manholes were now partially covered by a crosswise smaller lid. Missionaries were no longer allowed into schools to proselytise. People stayed out a little longer after dark. But there were still electricity and water cuts.

In the market next to the rows of leek sellers, there were now rows of stalls selling mechanical parts. There were also bicycles for sale, many new. There were still cracked eggs to be bought, but for the first time bananas were being sold on street corners. A few traffic lights had been installed. There were more cars, many windscreenless and at night lightless. But at least the windscreenless ones had better visibility than the even more numerous cars with spider-webbed windscreens. Sheep and cattle still grazed on any available patch of grass, but there were fewer available patches.

This was due to the mushrooming kiosks, quite elegant prefab constructions providing bases (albeit illegally) for outdoor bars and cafes, which had quadrupled in number since August. Some had been put up on the very wide pavements in the centre of town; too many were taking over the parks. As well as kiosk restaurants and cafe-bars, there were some kiosk barbers. One advantage kiosks had over permanent premises was avoidance of the highly confused property laws. Contradictory laws had resulted in many urban premises having two legal owners, one of the ground on which the property stood, one of the property itself. One law enabled those who had been renter occupiers under Communism to buy the properties. While a later law, which did not however nullify the earlier one, restored these same properties to the pre-communist owners.

The other very visible change was the arrival of satellite dishes known as *sharps*. Now, as often as one saw someone leading a sheep or cow along the pavement, one saw someone carrying home a *sharp*. These enabled their owners to watch a vast number of channels including Turkish, Spanish and Dutch, as well as the Albanian and Italian channels they had had before. The effects of MTV could be seen on the new Albanian television programmes and the cassettes on sale. An ideological development was the new addiction by former staunch Communists to the US soap *The Bold and the Beautiful* shown on Italian television. Televised beauty contests on the Albanian channel were new and hugely popular. These contests were unusual for featuring men as well as women. Muscular men in miniscule bathing trunks would flex their biceps while posing precariously on rocks above seascapes. Widely watched and strongly reminiscent of past practice as well as supremely tedious, was the programme on Easter Monday showing the sentencing of Fatos Nano to 13 years imprisonment for alleged embezzlement of Italian aid. Nano had been Prime Minister for three months during the brief Socialist reign in 1991. He had been kept in prison since the previous autumn without trial. Viewers were now treated to the entire 90 minutes it took the judge to read out his verdict. Imprisoning the head of the opposition Socialist Party was a satisfactory way of keeping democracy under control. In similar evocations of the past, some once prominent Communist Party members had recently had their telephones confiscated. The familiar phenomenon of giving your neighbour's telephone number as a point of contact continued, though now it might be that of a different neighbour, with different political affiliations. Telephone charges had increased fourfold, and increases in the charges for electricity had also been introduced.

Foreign remittances helped to mitigate the austerity of Albanian daily life and rising costs. Growing numbers of families in Tirana had one or more relatives working abroad, usually in Greece, mostly illegally. (There were estimated to be at least 300,000 (about a tenth of the population) Albanian migrants in Greece at this period.) At the same time, there seemed to be just as many unemployed men filling the streets as before. This was due to an influx of villagers, primarily from the mountainous areas in the North of Albania. To the north of Tirana outside Kamzë, there was now a growing number of wooden shacks erected by northern villagers. The buildings, which were neatly constructed on an unlittered grassy plain, looked quite unlike the makeshift constructions of shanty dwellings on the outskirts of Medellin or other Colombian towns I knew, but they indicated a similar trend. The government at this period was wisely letting them stand. Given that Albanian cities were very small under Communism thanks to the policy of rural population retention, there was plenty of scope for urban expansion. The extremely serious housing shortage in Tirana might as well be alleviated by self-help as by a bankrupt government.

Corruption, mainly government corruption, loomed larger in the public consciousness than before. Engineers complained that they could only get contracts for public works if they agreed to hand over a sizeable percentage of the funds to the relevant government personnel. Foreign aid funds were producing more luxury villas than new roads and municipal water systems.

Our former Tirana base flat was now occupied by missionaries. The acquaintance who took us to our new base was a mechanic with a large minibus acquired through a sister in Germany. Albania, now known as the graveyard for Europe's used cars was the right place for a mechanic, he told us. 'Before, I was making very little money indeed. With all these imported cars in very poor condition I have as much work as I like.' We told him we were going to Mirdita and he said: 'Ah, like in Kadare's *Broken April*; I love that book. I like reading prose. I can't get on with poetry easily, but prose I love.'

The effects of easily accessible cheap books under Communism had not yet been extinguished. Books were still cheap, and many of the proliferating kiosks were book stalls.

Our new lodgings were not in a block of flats but on the first floor of a pre-communist house. The family letting the rooms did not own the house but was waiting in suspense to see how the pre-communist owner progressed with his restitution claim. Across the landing from our rooms a widow and her son lived in similar suspense. The house was close to the US Embassy, which meant that there was water continuously. The area was one of rundown but quite picturesque houses and gardens whose potential was quickly realised by the international community. By the late 1990s the area had virtually been taken over by embassies and NGOs.

Although whenever we stayed in this house we paid as if for exclusive occupation, it was no secret, from us at least, that an Italian firm's representative had taken it on an annual basis. Moreover, very often during our absences in Mirdita the rooms would have to be cleared of our belongings for the sporadic visits of a German businessman. Sometimes we would return from Mirdita to have the landlady throw up her hands in relief at our having been away the night before. The strain involved in making sure that the German and the Italian remained unaware of the box and cox nature of their respective contracts (there was no telephone and they would arrive unexpectedly) was more than compensated for by the financial rewards.

Tenants were by no means the only source of income for this resourceful family. One daughter was married and lived and worked in Athens, which facilitated the other daughter's import business, though this did not always run smoothly. A Russian entrepreneur had recently decamped with their joint profits from a Greek oranges deal. The daughter was now trying to recoup her losses by importing teabags. In subsequent years one of her ambitions (never realised) was to import the round boxes of Vache Qui Rit type cheeses, which had become popular particularly amongst foreigners. Her biggest success came with washing powder that she and a male friend would drive from Greece over the Kapshtica border to Korça and up to Tirana. As she put it in March 1997: 'The thing about washing powder is that however bad the crisis [and March 1997 was rather serious] people still have to wash their clothes.'

Mirdita

On Good Friday we set off for Mirdita to stay with the Dedas in Lëgjin. There we found that Gjon had gone to work in Greece, while Gjergj and Zina now had a baby son. Easter was to be celebrated for the first time since 1967 at the Abbey of Orosh. Italian Roman Catholics had established a base in Rrëshen where there were now two Italian priests and several nuns. On Easter Saturday Soula and I walked up from Lëgjin to Bulshar, where we found the headman's wife, Maria, baking special Easter bread to be taken the next day to be blessed at the service. Despite the 26-year interval during which all the Easter customs had been forbidden, they were now being practised as though there had never been a break: bread for blessing (*bekim*); coloured eggs; the exchange of ritual Easter phrases; gathering at the site of the Abbey. Gjon, the headman, ever keen to revert to pre-communist ways, said he would be fasting, not eating meat until Sunday evening.

On Sunday morning Tom Deda and I set off for the Abbey of Orosh. We took a route that brought us out just above the site of the Abbey. Streaming down from the villages above, men, women and children, the women mostly in Mirditan costume – black and white for the old and red for the young – converged on a spot just in front of the outdoor altar that had been set up by the Italian priest and his helpers. The women approached the altar and, kneeling down, held out their loaves to be blessed. Several girls were baptised. The atmosphere of the proceedings was a little undermined by the fact that everything the priest said in Italian had to be repeated by an interpreter in Albanian. A more serious problem was the priest's growing impatience at what he saw as unsuitable behaviour on the part of the congregation. Had he said to himself these people are quite unused to religious services, not to mention religion; had he rejoiced in the fact that so many people had come; had he taken this as an opportunity to initiate them benevolently and gently into the authoritarian hierarchical ways of the Roman Catholic Church, he would probably have won a lot of hearts. Instead, he became more and more irritated until, losing his temper completely, he started yelling at no one in particular one of the Albanian words he had learnt: *jashtë* – out. Three times he yelled 'out' in tones strongly reminiscent of devil exorcism. Worst of all, instead of ejecting the

men who were the chief perpetrators of the noise, he weakly picked
on three little girls and had them removed.

The coming together of about 200 Mirditans to the spot described by Edith Durham nearly a hundred years earlier was nevertheless an impressive scene, though more as an evocation of the
past than a resurrection of faith. At the end of the service the congregation drifted off to their villages. On our way back, Tom told
me that he had managed to prevent lots of people I did not know
from coming to talk to me. This is the kind of misunderstanding
that leaves the anthropologist close to tears; I explained that talking
to all sorts of people was exactly what I wanted to do. We came to
a wood where at the top of a steep bank was a house belonging to
some cousins who called to us to come up. To make up for my earlier disappointment, Tom accepted. His father, who had suddenly
appeared through the trees, initially said not to go, but for some
reason changed his mind and gave us permission.

In the house a number of relations and neighbours were gathered. None of them had been to the service, said they had not
known about it and were not interested in religion anyhow. Easter
visiting was, however, an established custom, which was why they
were all there. When we got up to leave, a cousin of the host invited
us to his house, where we found his uncle, the head of the house,
zoti i shtëpis, very drunk. After some befuddled speechmaking, obviously embarrassing for his wife, he was silenced more or less, and
the dozen or so men seated round the table began to talk about the
Kanun. Apart from a boy of 13, most of the men were in their
20s and 30s, born and bred, in other words, under Communism.
I asked whether they had known about the Kanun during Communism, when even talk of it was supposedly banned, or had they
only become familiar with it since 1991. They said they had known
about it all their lives.

Today with 'no state or state enforced law' (*ska shtet, ska ligj*)
the Kanun was the only way to manage local affairs. It worked
well because it encompassed the whole community and every case
raised and each decision made, involved a meeting with representatives from each family. A person judged to have done wrong had
to put the wrong right; a thief must return a stolen good as well as
pay a fine for committing an offence. If two men were disputing
the boundary line between their lands, the elders must be called
in and either a compromise reached or the elders must convince

the one that the other's claim was just. In other words, unlike non-customary justice, it was not a case of one person being wrong and punished; the solution had to be acceptable to both sides and serve the community's interests. The Kanun's strength lay in the fact that its laws were invoked and applied on the spot by a community whose members had face-to-face relations with each other. State institutions were distant, out of touch, frequently corrupt; court decisions were liable to leave burning resentment in their wake, leading to further crimes. I only discovered two years later that in the very house where we were sitting one of the drunken uncle's brothers was in prison for killing a third brother. The year before they had quarrelled over '*një rripë tokë*' – a (mere) strip of land. The murderer was in prison (to this extent state law had functioned) while the widow and the murderer's wife and their families continued to share the house.

The young men got on to the question of oaths, efficacious they said, because everyone is afraid to perjure themselves. In the case of theft, for example, a suspect might have to swear an oath that he was not the thief. I asked what would happen if the oath taker were lying. He would be punished by God in some terrible way, they said. Yet these very same people had said that religion meant nothing to them, that they had never learnt anything about religion, being too young to recall anything before 1967. 'But how come you believe that falsely swearing an oath will be punished by God if you're all atheists?' I asked. There was a moment's incomprehension. The 13 year old successfully explained what I meant to them. Two things emerged; one was that believing in God was not the same as Catholic religious practice; the Kanun had God built into it and embodied an ethos to which all subscribed. The other point was that they could enumerate several instances of perjurers who had met terrible fates. They cited the case of a man from Bulshar whose son had died shortly after the father had perjured himself. There was ample evidence that perjuring oneself led to supernatural retribution.

Back at the Dedas, people were coming to pay Easter visits. One did not work in the fields over these days because it would be anti-social if visitors found the members of the household away in the fields. On Easter Monday evening most of the family watched the televised trial of Fatos Nano. The next morning it was raining and we all sat in the kitchen. During talk of past times one of the family recalled the inspections made in each village by a hygiene commission consisting of a brigadier and two helpers. At each house they would run their fingers over surfaces, check the sheets on the beds for cleanliness, count the spoons, forks and plates to see if any were lost or broken, and check the children's heads for lice. Should the house fall short of the required standard, a *flet rrufe*[1] would denounce the household publicly and a fine might be imposed. In Rrëshen we had been told that cradles had been banned under Communism, but if this was true the hygiene and health brigades had been ineffective. In every household we knew (and still in 2003) babies continued to be tightly swaddled and tied into cradles, which were then covered with thick scarves in much the same suffocating way that had worried Edith Durham a century earlier.

The talk moved on to magic. Gjin told how the 25-year-old mother-of-two in nearby Mashtërkorë had been paralysed by a witch. Then he mesmerised us with a true tale about a man who had taken two wives. This man was visited by a gypsy who told him: 'You've done something bad. I'm coming back next week and you'll see that something will happen.' The gypsy went away to Tirana and fetched an enormously fat gypsy woman – the width of this window, Gjin indicated. Then the two gypsies drove in a Benz[2] back to the man with two wives. The fat gypsy was '*bektashi*'. A feature of Gjin's stories was the use of Ottoman Turkish vocabulary like '*vakuf*[3]' and '*bektashi*'; in the case of the latter with altered local meaning, so that by *bektashi* he meant not a member of the Muslim sect, but a person with supernatural powers.

Despite the moral condemnation made clear in this story, it was not in fact all that rare for a man to have two wives in certain circumstances. I subsequently learnt of several cases in Orosh where a husband lived with two wives. In one case the first wife had failed to produce children; in two others, the first wife had produced only girls. In each case, the first wives were treated respectfully and, following an official divorce, continued to live with the family. In the first case, the children of the new young wife called the first wife 'Granny' (*Nëna*) and everyone involved was said to be happy with the situation. In the other cases, the first wife and her daughters lived away from the new family for a year, after which, following the birth of the required son, the two families reunited. A daughter of one of the latter families told me that the village never spoke critically of them – *nuk na kanë sharë* – but respected the family. At midday we left Lëgjin and walked to the Gjeologji to catch the Klos bus on its return from Rrëshen. From the bus window as we neared Bisak, we saw Dava and her two fellow road maintenance workers each armed with a bezum walking along the road. The path to the house was not barricaded this time, and we found Mark with Bardha and some of the children at home. Two were out grazing the cow a little way up the mountain above their house. The four younger children, who were at home, looked listless; the stuffy atmosphere of their only room where they cooked and slept, and the contrast with the cold outside, was conducive to colds and coughs. The youngest girl suffered from asthma and often needed medicine. Winter clothes were hard to get, and there were not enough coats and shoes to go round.

A major preoccupation was how to find a suitable family for Bardha to marry into. From time to time *kërkesat* (enquiries) had been made by families seeking a bride, but none as yet had been considered suitable by Mark. His principles ruled out a *fanatik*[4] family; he was proud that his eldest daughter had short hair and did not wear Mirditor dress or earrings, that she had attended middle school in Klos. Ideally, the groom's family should live in or near a town. How this family could possibly manage without Bardha, given the extreme youth of so many of her siblings, did not seem to be a consideration. Even before becoming a road sweeper, Dava was busy with bearing or suckling babies while Bardha got on with many of the chores. I never saw Bardha look discontented, and she obviously adored the babies, but now that she was no longer at school, she literally never saw any girls her age. Their house was so out of the way that even the spring they went to for water was not used by girls from other families. It was fortunate that Bardha was exceptionally sweet natured and patient as well as a good housekeeper, nanny and teacher.

There was sad news about their cousins in Dardhaz. In January, Kristina and Nikollë's third daughter, Pashka, aged five, had become ill with a mysterious illness that had resulted in one of her arms being paralysed. Kristina and Nikollë had taken her to see a doctor in Kukës who told them that medicine could not cure her. He told them to try a miraculous cure; they should go to Laç, the pilgrimage centre. Despite Kristina's scepticism and Ilir's father's advice to go straight to Tirana hospital, Pashka was taken to Laç, but to no avail. Eventually, after fruitlessly visiting several folk curers, Pashka was diagnosed in Tirana as having a brain tumour. In case she died during the difficult operation, she was taken to be photographed beforehand. One of the parents' worries had been that the surgeon would demand a substantial sweetener (*ryshfet*), which they would be quite unable to raise, thus preventing Pashka from getting the necessary treatment. Fortunately, in this case, the surgeon seems to have been a humane man who recognized the family's desperate economic situation. He said that Pashka was now blind and there was no guarantee that the tumour would not recur.

Usually, no sphere of hospital life functioned without bribes. Just to get through the entrance of an individual clinic within the hospital, one had to bribe the doorman. When the son of Rrëshen friends was operated on the following year, they had to bribe the operating doctor, the anaesthetist, the ward nurse and the guard at the entrance to the wing. The doctor never came near the patient after the operation; 'unavailable' medicines materialised only on production of a monetary inducement. Though Pashka's parents had been spared doctors' bribes, their expenses had forced them to borrow from every possible source. They had had to find cash for the buses to Tirana, for medicine, for their own subsistence costs in the hospital as well as the strengthening meat broths essential for Pashka's recovery. Some days after the operation, Pashka was just strong enough to be taken home by her exhausted parents, who had had to sleep on the floor or propped on the end of Pashka's bed every night for over a week. On top of their anguish over Pashka, they had been worried about the rest of the family. The elderly Maria, and Kristina's mother, were in sole charge of the other four children, including the seven month previously unweaned baby, and the seven animals. On learning that Pashka was now blind, some relations said it would have been much better had she died; blindness was too serious a handicap to contend with.

A Communist Family

Through an acquaintance met at a wedding party in the first Mirditan village we visited, we got to know another Fan village, Sang.

The grown up sons from this family had been educated at Tirana University and now lived in Rrëshen. Their parents and youngest siblings lived in Sang, a village close to Xhuxhë. This family was also connected to a heroine of the people, though in this case the title was awarded during the 1940s and the young girl in question could really be said to have behaved heroically. Born in Mirdita, she moved with her family to the town of Laç, where she became an active Partisan. As a volunteer worker on the railways being built in 1947, her merits and dedication to the cause were noteworthy. *The Fjalori Enciklopedik Shqiptar* notes her outstanding capabilities, revolutionary optimism for women's education and emancipation from backward customs, the Kanun and religion. These qualities led to her appointment as leader of Mirdita's youth organisation. Courageous and undaunted by enemy threats, she was tortured and killed when she was only 18 by opposition forces in 1948 (Fjalori Enciklopedik Shqiptar 1985). Inspired by her example, the succeeding generations of the family, into which she had married, continued steadfastly Communist, some attaining important government posts, others remaining in the village but sending their children to university. The summer of 1994 when we had just established our base in Rrëshen, one of the brothers told us that his family was expecting us for a visit.

Armed with 100 eggs, numerous cans of beer, and several kilos of tomatoes, this brother met us the next day with a small truck, in the back of which we made the three hour drive up to the village. Bearing eggs and tomatoes, we walked along a narrow muddy track to the house, where the family greeted us with undisguised astonishment and barely disguised dismay. They certainly had not been expecting us. The yard, in which the plaque to the Heroine of the People had been allowed to start fading, was overhung with tall trees making it dark and gloomy. Not a single prettifying touch relieved its dismal aspect. After a moment or two while we sat on a low wall in the yard and wished ourselves a thousand miles away, the family rallied. We went into a kitchen even darker and gloomier than the yard, where there was no furniture apart from a couple of low three-legged stools and, pushed away into a corner, a table. In the fireplace were cold dead ashes. To make the coffee, compulsory arrival hospitality, a fire had to be kindled. To this purpose an Economics textbook was produced and I noticed that the pages being torn out were from a chapter on capitalism. As nieces and nephews of a distinguished heroine of the people, they had naturally all been very devoted supporters of the Communist Party, but the brother who had brought us had become an entrepreneur, and I couldn't help exclaiming: 'I thought you were all pro-capitalism now,' as the pages merrily burned to ashes. 'Oh, we are; but this book was written under Communism and it presents capitalism from a biased point of view,' said the coffee-making sister who had studied accountancy in Tirana.

The house was divided between two brothers and the cousins had grown up as siblings. The eldest unmarried cousin, Fran, a boy of 20, came round to greet us and practise his Greek on us. He had been a '*refugjat*' in Greece for several months but said that we spoke a different dialect of Greek from the one he'd learnt. He was a mixture of genuine goodheartedness, considerateness, and infuriating cockiness. Like most Albanian young people he was wonderful with little children – two small nephews lived in the household – playing with them in real delight and treating them with tenderness. But he was maddening when accompanying us on visits, because he was certain he knew what I wanted to talk about to villagers and would officiously 'manage' the conversation just when I wanted to let the villager talk, give a topic its head, or talk about something quite different.

While drinking coffee, we talked to the mother of the family, Prena, who was justifiably proud of having brought up ten children all of whom had survived, and most of whom had had, or would have, a university education. All this studying and training had cost the family continuous sacrifice, and the austerity of the house testified to privations on the part of those who had stayed at home. The entrepreneur brother to a large extent supported his siblings' upkeep and studies. He also contributed substantially to the provisioning of the house, and had recently bought a carpet for the room of hospitality. Prena and her third daughter, a girl of 16, were the slaves of the house. Much of their time was spent collecting dwarf oak branches for animal fodder and wood for the fires; they cooked, cleaned, washed, and laboured without end.

In the afternoon three more family members arrived: the father, an unmarried daughter, Marta, and a new sister-in-law. The father and daughter had been in Tirana on a mission, which afforded a new insight into marriage customs. It emerged that Angjelina, the eldest daughter, was engaged to be married to a former army officer. Marta and her father had gone to Tirana together with the groom's father to acquire the bride's entire wardrobe, which is always paid for by the groom's parents as part of the brideprice. 'But doesn't Angjelina want to choose her own clothes?' I asked. It would be immodest (*turp*, literally 'shame') for the bride herself to go, they explained, and, in fact, strict convention dictates that the bride should act as if she knew nothing of the imminent marriage. Even when I asked Angjelina point blank if she were to be married soon, she replied: 'How should I know?' Fortunately, consistency did not require that the bride-to-be waited till her wedding to see the clothes. That evening we repaired to the girls' bedroom (one of two ground level rooms recently added) for a delightful orgy of trying on. It was interesting seeing what sort of clothes were deemed suitable for bridal attire after the wedding, and even more so to learn the size of the financial outlay – about $1,000. All the clothes were Turkish imports, and most of them were very dressy. Angjelina's mother came to watch and in some cases to exclaim at the lowness of a neckline. But on the whole, Marta seemed to have done the job to everyone's satisfaction.

The sister-in-law was a telephonist in Reps. She had recently married one of the sons, a road maintenance worker in Reps. They were both hunchbacked and exemplified the tradition that dictates that a disabled person marry another with a similar disablement – a match in the literal sense of the word. We had come across another example in Domgjon where the spouses were both deaf and dumb.[5]

The next day we went to look at the village school, reached by a practically vertical path that dropped down 50 feet to the playground. The school was almost totally vandalised; it could hardly have served as a stable. The furniture had either been broken up for firewood or left unusable. All the windows were broken. One or two homemade posters shipwrecked forlornly on the walls hinted at past use for education as opposed to animal shelter. It was in a far worse state than the other schools I had been in to date. So bad, that a year later the school was closed for reconstruction.

Across the river, planks were being sawn and loaded on to a truck. Apart from small numbers of animals, the forest was the only local source of employment, and income was mostly contraband. The non-local source was Greece. Almost every youth had made at least one foray across the border. A few had found work for long enough to make good money, such as the two young men who had given me and Ilir a lift in their timber-laden lorry the year before. But many returned with little more than flashy sunglasses and memories of ugly confrontations with the Greek police.

One afternoon we walked up to the hillside above where small children grazed the family animals – a cow, a couple of sheep or some goats. The hillsides were so badly eroded that it was hard to imagine what there was to graze. In the yards of the houses were bell-shaped oak-branch stacks (*mullar*), the local form of haystack. All the houses and yards we saw were as bleak as our hosts' – unbeautified in any way. Was this simply dire poverty or was it the demoralising effect of living in a particularly dismal place?

In Xhuxhë and Bisak, likewise poor villages, householders had made an effort to lighten the gloom with small improvements as well as flowers. Ilir's father, poorer than most, had just built a stone fireplace and bread oven in his tiny yard. Kristina and Nikollë, still poorer, had flowers in their garden and a newly built room for guests – *dhoma mikpritve*. Perhaps the real reason for the gloom in Sang was that in a village where the majority had been loyal Communists, higher education had drained resources and perhaps removed many of the more dynamic individuals.

Back at the house we found Ded Gega, a man in his 50s referred to as 'one of ours', which I supposed indicated cousin or uncle, sitting in the yard. He had a house in Xhuxhë but had recently moved down to the plain of Lezhë, where he had built a shack (*barakë*) in the middle of a plot of land, which he was cultivating. He was a conversational man, full of information about the Kanun, old times and present gossip. Originally, he told us, this area had been one of transhumance, with the families taking their flocks up to the higher mountain slopes for the summers. The flocks had never been large, for even before the population increase the region had been a poor one, with its steep terrain and harsh winter climate. Under Communism, 90 percent of the population had worked in state jobs, mainly forestry or mining. Most men had worked in the neighbouring Thirra mine, now closed, and though all had now accumulated a few animals, the only long-term prospect for survival was down on the coastal plain. Already 20 percent of Dardhaz's inhabitants had managed to raise the cash to build a *barakë* and pay the necessary bribe to the headman on the coastal plain. Eight families now owned lorries, vital for the transport of tree trunks to the plains towns. The only sources of income for most people were their animals, seasonal fruit and herbs, and the wood from the forest. Virtually every family except the mill-owner was in debt. They struggled to make ends meet and, while there was still timber, to pay off debts and save, but any setback such as illness in the family left them eclipsed yet again by debt.

We talked about the Mirditan villagers' greeting formulae. Whenever a passerby comes within range of people working on their land, he or she must call out: '*A u llodh?*' Are you tired (i.e. from working)? To which those working will call back: '*Nga pak,*' – a little. You never call out 'Good day' or 'How are you?' When you meet at close quarters a villager you know, you probably ask: '*A je burri i fortë?*' Are you a strong man? You then proceed to ask: '*Nga shtëpi?*' literally 'from the house?' that is, 'How are those at home?' followed by an enquiry as to health, and a string of at least six other versions of the same questions. In towns, the procedure tends to come across as meaningless ritual. In villages, it is asked in serious sincere tones. But in both settings, the formulaic quality and the repetition of the same enquiry differently worded with hardly a pause between each phrase, had often struck us as slightly comic. Ded told us that the pre-communist formula had been: '*A ke pas buk?*' that is, 'Have you had bread (food)?' a poignant reminder of the poverty prevailing in the region. Subsidies for staple requisites throughout the communist period had eliminated the need for this enquiry. Now it seemed likely to resurface.

In the old days, that is up until the 1940s, when feud was still rife, a charitable custom prevented, for a time at least, an immediate outbreak of killing. A man meeting another not known to him when journeying between villages might offer a cigarette. If the other accepted, and in the course of conversation it was discovered that their families were in blood, the Kanun forbade that any action be taken. In effect, they were bound by the laws and ties of hospitality, exempted from the exigencies of feud dictated by the code of honour until another meeting.

After Ded had gone, I asked Angjelina how he was related to the family. 'By blood-brotherhood,' she replied. It was a relationship that we had come across surprisingly often. A man we had met at a friend's house in Rrëshen shortly before had mentioned a blood-brother in Dibra whom he had met on military service. They had liked each other so much that they had decided to *pi gjak* – 'drink blood' together. Each pricked their thumb over a glass of raki and in drinking became brothers. Members of their respective families and their children would not be able to intermarry because they were now related. Given that one of the most important unspoken reasons for marrying one's children outside the immediate district was to extend potentially useful connections to other areas, this rule made sense.

For some days after this it rained relentlessly. At one point, I was wading through the mud to the lavatory, which was raised on stilts with a short ladder up to it, when I heard the eight-year old calling: '*Mama e Sulës* (Soula's mother)!' She came splashing after me with some more pages from the multi-purpose economics book now to be used as lavatory paper. The use of technonyms in Mirdita means that children do not address other people's mothers by their first names but as so-and-so's mother. So a mother of ten children would be addressed as the mother of whichever of their children was contemporary with the child speaking to them.

On the first dry day I asked if I could walk over to Dardhaz to visit Kristina and Nikollë and find out whether Pashka was as ill as Ilir's family feared. Angjelina was happy to join us since she had spent the year teaching at the eight-year school and this was a chance to visit some of her pupils. No accountancy job had been available, and the school had been pleased to have an educated, albeit unqualified, teacher at a time when many of the qualified teachers had left the village. Fran had been told to look after us, which, when he was not misdirecting conversations, he did very considerately. He and Angjelina were cheerful companions, full of stories about ghosts and fairies and Mirditan customs. At Dardhaz we negotiated the usual difficult steepnesses and, leaving Angjelina at the house of one of her pupils, went on to Kristina and Nikollë's house.

In the *dhoma mikpritve* we found Kristina's mother and sister, Nikollë and his mother and, sitting on the bed, Kristina holding the hand of her little daughter while fanning her face. Pashka, now blind, her head shaven, twitched convulsively and continuously. The silent agony and self-control of the mother and the grim sadness of the fellow watchers was heartrending. I sat with them for a time, cursing my failed efforts to procure morphine for Pashka to mitigate the pain and Kristina's anguish. The hospital had insisted that Nikollë come in person to collect the pain killing drugs. When we left, Nikollë and Kristina accompanied us to the end of their property as custom requires. Nikollë asked if I thought the medicine would cure Pashka. I knew that Kristina had no such false hopes. We had left them a few provisions knowing that Pashka's illness had run them into debt, and their gratitude and charming good manners, picking apples from their tree by the path and pressing them into our hands, were all the more poignant a testimony to their self-control in these days of wretchedness.

The day we left Sang, we had to set off at four in the morning to catch the Klos bus for Rrëshen. Fran and Angjelina angelically insisted on accompanying us. It was pitch dark, and Fran started on the most alarming ghost stories he could recall, none of which frightened us at all. Unlike our encounters with ravening raging dogs. Halfway to Klos there are several houses near the road ferociously guarded by large homicidal dogs. The moment you are in earshot, bloodcurdling barking breaks out, and before you know it monstrous dogs hurtle out of the darkness. Fran, who is slightly built, was ready with a hefty stick, and without turning a hair or even putting on heroic airs, kept them at bay in Herculean fashion. I have seldom been so impressed. He and Angjelina had made the two-hour trek to Klos every school-day 'such was our thirst for and dedication to learning', they said. 'Then there were no dangers on the road day or night; a young girl on her own even at night was not at risk.' No doubt the strong arm of the party did keep a good deal of crime at bay, though it is hard to believe that Albania was the perfect haven of security nostalgic Communists are so fond of recalling.

While waiting to get on the Klos bus we learnt that Caritas was about to open a bakery as well as repair the school and restore the church. The bakery would employ 15 people, which would have two small trucks for delivery. The church was subsequently restored, but the bakery never functioned.

The following spring I spent Easter in Sang. On Easter Sunday we watched the Pope making a speech in a snowstorm. It turned out that this was actually an illusion caused by the television that went on to show Easter services in Shkodër Cathedral and the Roman Catholic church in Tirana also in snow. Abandoning the snow for the bookcase, I tried to immerse myself in the works of Enver Hoxha. The unflagging attention paid by these formerly dedicated Communists to the luminaries of the Roman Catholic Church was striking. I couldn't resist teasing them by asking whether they were so addicted to personality cults that as long as a charismatic leader figure was on offer, it didn't matter whether it was Jesus, Hoxha or the Pope. The eldest brother, always ready to laugh at himself, gave a mock dramatic rendering of a poem lauding the virtues of Enver Hoxha. And admitted that there might be an element of truth in the thought.

Also watching the Pope was a charming great aunt. She was wearing her beautifully embroidered waistcoat inside out – in order to protect it from wear and tear, she said. I asked her to reverse it for the camera, which she thought was funny. We discussed the laments sung at funerals. What happened, I asked, if the person who had died had had some awful characteristics? She roared with laughter. 'Oh, there were lots of cases. The laments would still say good things, but if they mentioned generosity when we all knew how stingy the person had been, we'd meet each others eyes and have to hold back the laughter.'

We went over to Dardhaz, this time to congratulate the family on a great joy, the birth of their first son. When we got to the bank of the river below Fran and Kristina's house, access to the land below their house had been barricaded off so that for all but trapeze artists swinging out over the river, approach was impossible. Luckily, the author of the barricade, the ex-Headteacher's son, was working nearby and agreed to let us walk over his land. The barrier suggested that village relations were not quite as harmonious as previously. One factor which may have started to undermine peaceful relations was the gradual depletion of the timber stocks, the only significant source of income.

At the end of the summer of 1994 we found the Lekas and the Dedas in a state of depression. The Lekas now had better relations with the grandparents but they were afraid that Dava's sweeping job was under threat. The latest marriage proposition for Bardha was not really suitable. Standards at the school were falling. They were worried about Ilir who, despite being only 15, had gone to find work in Greece. This worry at least was somewhat allayed when Ilir sent a message to say that he had found work fruit picking. When he returned he brought much needed cash as well as a present from his employer of a rug for the family's one room. His youth and small size, combined with some knowledge of German and readiness to work hard, had been much appreciated by a northern

Greek farmer who had himself in his youth been a *gastarbeiter* in Germany. This man had treated him very well and asked him to return the following summer.

In Lëgjin morale was even worse than in Bisak. Gjon had been in Greece for several months, but they had had no news of him and were worried. Mrika, the mother, had broken her arm. Tom was planning a return to Greece. Gjergj was particularly down because he had just failed to get a state loan to buy a lorry for the wood-selling enterprise he had planned. He explained the economics of it, showing how the profit would have been more than sufficient to cover the necessary police bribes. He was determined to emigrate, but was not prepared to go to Greece, where he rightly believed anti-Albanian feeling to be stronger than in Italy. At the same time he was afraid that without a guaranteed job in Italy, he risked being sent back to Albania and losing the money raised with such difficulty to get there. To get to Italy one paid a considerable sum (at the time up to $750) to one of the small boat operators crossing clandestinely between Vlora and the east coast of southern Italy. These boat owners (*skafiste*) were making a fortune ferrying Albanians and lately Kurds, all hoping to gain a foothold through the backdoor into Western Europe. Alternatively, one could buy a false Italian visa, but this was even more expensive. 'If you haven't got a long-term goal, ambitions, a life plan, working is pointless,' Gjergj said gloomily.

To make ends meet in the meantime, the family was selling wood (illegally), sharing the profits with the lorry driver who sold the wood to middlemen in Laç at $30 a cubic metre, in winter up to $40. They also sold wood occasionally to locals needing wood for house repairs or building on rooms. No-one was putting any faith in the rumours that the Italian firm currently making a study of the Reps copper refinery might be going to invest so as to make it profitable; nor in the rumour that a French firm was interested in opening up tourism in the area. As for the rumoured asphalting of the road to Fan, scepticism was fully justified, and none of the rumoured improvements had yet occurred a decade later.

Gjergj's comments about having a life's purpose were significant. The family was better off materially than many other villagers. Gjergj had dismissed the idea of applying for *përkrahje sociale*[6] – social welfare benefits – as degrading and useless. Tom, in addition to some barrel making, was doing welding work, but said that he only took on welding work if he got paid at twice the average. I asked him who had that sort of money. 'Well, most people will pay me when they can.' Now he was hoping to return to Greece, but if that proved impossible, he planned to earn by making barrels for an uncle's business. Having started from a somewhat better level, feeding themselves was less a problem than overcoming the obstacles to leading pointful lives. The frustrations of these early post-communist years for the better off stuck in rural depths with no outlet for ambition, were in a sense no less demoralising than the survival struggles of the really poor for whom every day was a challenge.

One day, while we were all sitting outside in front of the house, a Deda cousin, a policeman, son of the brother murdered the year before for 'a strip of land', arrived with a telegram announcing the death of an elderly relation in a distant village. This was a severe blow, not for the loss of an 83-year-old man whom no-one had seen lately, but because family duty, honour and social obligation necessitated attendance at the funeral. Getting to the village would involve painful expense, but clan duty could not be shirked. After a long and worried discussion it was decided that it would not be construed as failing in respect if only the eldest son went; this would at least reduce the transport costs.

Later, Soula and I went down the precipitous bank to the river below the house, and seeing some young boys of 12 or 13 on the other side, each with a cow, waded across to talk to them. They were sitting down playing with catapults (*lastiçe*, the latest craze) but stood up as we approached and shook hands with typically graceful Mirditan manners. A passenger on a bus in Mirdita will still half rise from his or her seat to greet an acquaintance seen boarding the bus. The communist regime put great emphasis on good manners and respect to elders. But Mirditan manners had a special quality perhaps because respect and hierarchy were so strictly enforced within the family. Even where brothers are grown up, a younger brother will never smoke in front of his eldest brother, or raise his glass before he does. One of the boys, whose father I later discovered was commune secretary in Reps, asked us if we liked Orosh. We said we did. 'Yes,' he said ironically, 'the country *is* nice for town dwellers.'

Bulshar

From the gloom of Lëgjin we went up to Bulshar. On entering the village, the first person we came across was once again a beautiful young girl filling a pitcher at the spring. This time she was Gjelina, a cousin of the headman's family. The families were not on speaking terms, and Gjelina, knowing that we would be prevented from visiting her family if we proceeded on to the headman's house, urged us to accompany her up to her house right away. Her family, who ran one of the mills for grinding flour, lived right at the top of the village. Up here had been the former cooperative office buildings, the house of culture and the storehouses for crisis reserves and weapons in case of invasion. All that now remained of this centre of authority, fear and punishment, entertainment and companionship, was a pile of rubble.

We found Gjelina's mother in the house and two of Gjelina's sisters-in-law and their children. No men were at home, and we sat in the room for guests with the mother while the daughters-in-law went to make coffee. I asked Gjelina's mother how the women of the house divided the chores in a household where there were several in-married brides at home. She explained that initially it is the female head of the house who does the skilled jobs, while the young in-married brides do the more menial tasks such as the daily bread making, house cleaning, water carrying and clothes washing. Everyone has to work on the family's land. Where there are daughters old enough to help, the duties are shared with them. The more women, the more the burden is shared, though as children accumulate so work increases until the children are old enough to help. I subsequently learnt from a different source that one of the married-in brides regularly did more than her share of the work. It was not clear whether her greater work burden was due to laziness on the part of the other girls or victimisation by her mother-in-law. This bride did not come from a similar mountain village in a neighbouring bajrak as most Bulshar brides did, but had come from near a plains town. Her parents had been assured that her husband would be moving down to the plain a month or two after the wedding. It was a wonder that anyone was still taken in by such an old ploy; many a bride had been lured to the mountains by similar promises of soon moving to the plain. A middle-aged friend had been caught the same way. Her parents had been so incensed that, amazingly, they had told her even if she were already pregnant they would find her another husband. But she had stuck it out.

Before we left, Gjelina's mother showed us the married couples' rooms. Each had a double bed decorated with cushions worked by the bride, and on the floor brightly coloured rugs also made by the bride. We learnt that one of Gjelina's married brothers had descended two years before with his bride and baby to squat on the plain near Lezhë. The baby had died, perhaps because of the difficult living conditions on the plain. A second married brother was planning to follow the elder shortly.

Gjelina then took us a little way down the hill to her uncle's house, a two-storey house with an impressive indoor staircase and strikingly superior conditions to the average village house. The reason for this very different appearance was that here lived the talented carpenter family mentioned earlier who had held their own under Communism despite being *deklasuar*. Upstairs, their room for guests was furnished with their own work, including some magnificent heavy pieces of furniture and a beautiful inlaid chess table. The head of the house was a tall aristocratic-looking man with rather formidable manners. Under Communism they had worked hard, and their skill and industry as master carpenters meant that their work had been in demand on the cooperative. Thus their position had never been on a par with that of their miserably off fourth cousins, the *kryeplak's* family. The eldest son, Nikollë, aged 38, whom I got to know later, combined the skills of a first-class carpenter with a sharp mind and the sort of nervous, potentially irritable energy of a race horse. Everything he did, he did frenetically and successfully. He had learnt Italian and taught it at the school until the 14–18 year old part closed at the end of 1994. Soon after the end of Communism, he and his brothers had taken out a tree-felling licence, bought the sawmill, and set up a private carpentry business and lorry repairs workshop. The carpentry business, which sold all over the province and beyond to the Lezhë plain, specialised in doors, window frames and bridal furniture. Out of their initial profits from furniture sales they had bought a lorry for transporting the furniture. Another brother, a mechanic, ran the repairs business, useful where there was a ready made clientele amongst the local lorries transporting timber. They sold most of the timber, apart from that needed for the carpentry business, to the towns of Laç and Lezhë. The success of this joint venture was largely due to Nikollë's energy, intelligence and business flair. He was one of the earliest car owners, and drove like a racing driver on the mountain tracks. Eventually, in 1997, he moved his part of the business to the coastal plain of Durrës, while his brothers continued to work in Bulshar.

The Headman's Household

At the Headman's house we found a number of changes. The eldest son was out of prison. The third son had returned from Greece with a beaten up car. Roza was unmarried, but there was talk of a suitor from Rrëshen who was currently away working in Greece. On a visit to Bulshar, he had caught sight of Roza fetching water from the spring, and on making enquiries through a go-between, his parents were beginning negotiations. Roza disclaimed much knowledge of the proceedings, pointing out that she had not been and would not be consulted. But she was clearly interested, as it was every village girl's hope to marry into a town. In a town there was far, far less work; there was the daily *xhiro* when the weather was warm, and constant opportunity for seeing people outside one's immediate household. As we had seen, Roza's duties were particularly heavy, since her only other sister at home was too young and probably too wildly brought up, to do any chores other than take the animals to graze. Her brothers were many and inconsiderate and certainly did not help.

One afternoon, sitting with Roza's mother, Maria, sorting beans, I asked her about some magical beings (*ore*), which I had read about in Edith Durham's account of northern Albania. Maria had heard of *ore* but was more interested in humans' supernatural powers than spirit or fairy types, and explained that just as some people are witches who can cast the evil eye, others have a 'good eye' effect. 'Look, for instance, that boy sitting in the car Mark brought back from Greece; he doesn't know anything about mechanics but he has a "good eye" and can make it go.' At supper that night when we had finished eating, Gjon asked for the chicken carcass to be brought to the table, and showed us how to read the future from it, one part for government, another for personal fortune. Edith Durham also mentions reading the future in the Highlands, though from parts of the breast bone only. I wondered if this was a case of ethnographers influencing the descendants of the ethnographed, but Gjon, unlike numerous Tiranians, had not heard of Edith Durham or her books.

Our stay coincided once again with the arrival of villagers to collect aid, 80 per cent of the village was now jobless. We talked to one woman, who looked years beyond child-bearing age, who had come with her fourth child, a two-month-old baby. Another woman told us that she had six children and a husband with three legs. We learnt later that the husband had had a lorry accident after which one leg had had to be amputated. After a long wait he had finally acquired an artificial leg, which in conjunction with crutches made him mobile. This woman had an abundance of brown curly hair and a face which made an impression on Soula as we were to discover two days later when we walked down to the Gjeologji very early in the hopes of catching the Fan bus to Rrëshen. (There was no bus as yet in Bulshar, and the walk to Reps even by the precipitous short cuts was over an hour away.) The bus must have had a '*difekt*' because none came. As we walked on to Reps we caught up with a very tall thin curly haired boy of about 20. 'He looks just like the woman whose husband has three legs,' said Soula. We accosted him and he was indeed the three-legged man's son. His name was Simon, and he was on his way down to the plain of Lezhë, where the family, like Gjelina's and numerous other landless mountain dwellers, had appropriated a small piece of land and planted it with wheat.

A week or so later back in Bulshar staying with the headman's family, we found to our surprise that they were paying a worker the equivalent of $5 a day to install a water system that would pipe water direct to the house. They were vague about this project and it was not until several months later that the reasons for the project became obvious. Meanwhile, unknown to us, Simon's parents had sent him up to ask us to a meal. His coming was concealed from us, however, and we only discovered the next day when we ran into Simon in the village. To convince his family that we really had not got this message, we accepted their suggestion that we should go and stay with them. This was the beginning of a close friendship, which eventually extended to a coastal plain near the main port of Durrës, as well as to Athens.

Chapter Eleven

VILLAGE LIFE

Through our friendship with Simon's family we became familiar with the routine, rituals and crises of 1990s village life. In the process we also got to know the village itself well. All these villages of dispersed houses are divided into named neighbourhoods, *lagje*, which are often far apart from each other (cf. hamlets), so that a village may cover an area of four or more kilometres. Within a *lagje* the houses are scattered unless they are those of one family, in which case three or four houses may be built next to each other and the group known as a *vllazni*, brotherhood. The *vllazni* may consist of a row of houses down a hillside, or be built in terraced house form on flat ground with a brother and his family in each section. In other cases, the solution takes a vertical form with each family occupying a floor of a *kulla*, a three-storey tower-like building. Within a household there would often be several married sons each with his own marital bedroom, but sharing everything else: the kitchen and *dhoma mikpritve*; the household budget and the work (field and household). When more brothers than there is room for marry and start families they build a house close by if there is family land available. During the cooperative period houses were built regardless of former land ownership; one of Enver Hoxha's projects was to cluster houses in northern areas along the southern pattern. But before the cooperative period, the distance that separated one *vllazni* from another meant that the land of each same name group – *fis* (clan) – was adjacent to its houses. Since land shortage and competition for irrigation water were common sources of feud, distance between *vllazni* was desirable, as well as dictated to a large extent by the terrain. Under Communism competition between villagers for land and water resources ceased to be an issue, so that even had feuds not been outlawed, they would probably have been rarer.

Since 1993, members of some families, particularly professionals such as teachers, have left to live in Reps or Rrëshen. But even when a brother has moved to a town, owns a flat and has established a family, he still has a right to one room of the patrimonial house. Unless, that is, he has made an agreement resigning his right in exchange for some kind of compensation, a piece of land or a sum of money.

As the head village for a cooperative, which comprised several smaller villages, Bulshar had cooperative buildings, offices and storage depots. These were at the top of the village near one of the flour mills, and their ruins could still be seen. Here had been the House of Culture, the bakery, the creche and the storehouses/depots for crisis reserves and weapons in case of invasion. The House of Culture, initially vandalised and subsequently dismantled by villagers in need of building materials, had been the venue for dances, film shows, plays, sketches (*estrada*) and concerts put on by cooperative members and visiting groups. The one post-cooperative shop was nearby, a room in what was now the private house of the former cooperative shopkeeper. Stocks had to be brought from Tirana and were expensive. By the mid-nineties, stocks included drinks like Fanta, Coca Cola and beer, Danish feta cheese, sugar and macaroni; the sale of imported cheese in an area of stockbreeding a sad reflection on local productivity.

At the bottom of this hill near the sawmill, on land restored to Gjon the *kryeplak*, had been the village clinic, which by 1993 was a pile of rubble. The road from Lëgjin passed between the former clinic and the spring serving this part of the village, continuing up past the school to the *konvikt e beqareve*, boarding house for the unmarried. Here the unmarried teachers and cooperative employees from other parts of Albania had been lodged. It was now on private land, semi-vandalised and lived in by two recently married sons of the owner's family. The school itself, a two-storey building, stood partly on property belonging to the carpenter family, who had resigned their claim on the land. One part, however, stood on the land of a former brigadier. In 1994 she converted her part into a *bilardo* (snooker hall) conveniently placed to take advantage of demotivated pupils and teachers. Until 1994, the school was both an eight-year school and a middle school catering for 14 to 18 year olds. After that the middle school closed, many of the qualified staff left, the level of teaching and discipline fell, and the building was progressively vandalised, doors and windows broken, classroom furniture broken up. By 1999, the whole structure had become unsafe, and lessons for the small number of remaining pupils had to be held elsewhere.

A second dirt road had linked Bulshar with Grykë Orosh, the village above the abbey, and the Gjonmarkagjon *saraj* we had visited the year before. This road now came to an end at the bottom of Bulshar where the shallow wide rocky River Fan flows down to Lëgjin. Here there is a wide log bridge originally built for vehicles, but as no-one post-cooperative was responsible for its maintenance, by 1993 it was only usable by pedestrians. This was a problem for lorries collecting lumber from across the river, and finally some villagers who needed to transport tree trunks to be sold in Lezhë repaired the bridge at their own expense. The maintenance and repair problem was a serious obstacle to economic progress throughout Albania. It was not simply that the past history of *aksion*, so-called voluntary work, had turned people off any communal activity, though this was a factor; or that, lacking a competent leader, there was no ready organisation. It was to a large extent a case of literally not having the material wherewithal to mend anything. Foreign visitors to communist Albania in the late 1980s remarked on the preponderance of semi-broken machinery and the makeshift nature of repairs where these had occurred. The material infrastructure of the country had literally been falling to pieces for a decade at least.

The steep hillsides on the far side of the river are forested with pine and dwarf oak. The leaves and young branches of the dwarf oaks are used for animal fodder; the pine, progressively depleted, for sale. There is no longer a viable road beyond a few metres on the other side; Grykë Orosh is inaccessible now except by foot. Walking up the mountainside in the direction of the Saraj and Grykë Orosh, one can see the irrigation system built by *aksion* brigades to bring water from a distant source in the mountains. But it no longer functions because most of the materials that channelled the water – metal pipes and stone slabs – have been stolen or vandalised.

The houses close to the river are better off in respect of water than those higher up the village, as they can use the river water for washing and cleaning and watering of vegetable patches. But their nearest drinking water source is a spring several hundred metres away from any of the houses, reached via awkward terrain. Girls from all the neighbourhood families from either side of the river assemble at the spring in the evenings to fill up plastic containers or wooden barrels with straps carried like rucksacks on their backs. There are springs in different parts of the village but few households have drinking water closer than a hundred metres.

The mountainside on which the village is built itself comprises numerous up-and-down individual slopes. No houses have more than a metre or two of level land nearby, and many can only be reached by scrambling up and down over steep rocky ground and negotiating almost invisible precipitous paths and frequent irrigation streams. Lean cows are taken to graze up nearly vertical forested slopes, negotiable one would have thought only by goats. On the near side of the river grow thorn, cornel, blackberry bushes, mulberry, plum, walnut, cherry and fig trees. In 1993 there were almost no wild flowers or birds, their absence the result of heavy use of chemical sprays and fertilisers during the cooperative period. (By 1996 there were noticeably more flowers and birds.)

The cooperative had grown wheat, maize and beans. After 1980, cows, sheep and goats were herded collectively, and hens (except for a couple allowed to each household) were bred in the *puleria*, the cooperative hennery. Now that subsistence farming had replaced the cooperative system, no family could feed itself from its village land alone. A household would grow small quantities of maize and beans, leeks and cabbage, garlic, peppers, cucumbers, tomatoes and onions, depending on the season. The two *kuintal*s (200 kgs) per month of wheat required to feed a family of eight and its animals had to be bought at a cost of $40 a month (prohibitive for most families) or grown in the plain.

By 1992, all the village services except for the school had come to an end; there was no creche, no medical, pre-natal or dental service, no vet, no bakery, no communal meeting place, no transport. Aid in the form of food rations and clothes parcels was collected, as we saw, from the *kryeplak*, who also saw to the distribution of welfare benefits. Administration involving documents relating to pensions, invalidity benefits, identity cards, necessitated villagers walking to Reps, or for certain documents, catching a bus from Reps down to Rrëshen. Until the end of 1994, Bulshar's telephone *centralë* still functioned sporadically, linking Bulshar with Reps and Rrëshen.

A resident postwoman, whose family ran the telephone exchange, still delivered letters, also sporadically. This service ended when she married an elderly man in Fier, central Albania, thanks to the matchmaking initiative of an employee at the Fier telephone exchange.

Apart from cooperative officials and some teachers, very few families initially moved away from the village. For one thing, they could not afford to move; simply finding the cash for the bus trip down the mountain from Reps to Rrëshen when some administrative problem had to be dealt with was a problem. But also there was still at this stage, as we had already observed in Fan, some optimism about the future of village life. This was a period, 1993–4, when many foreign firms (Italian, Canadian, German, Austrian) as well as aid organisations, were rumoured to be interested in investing in the area. The firms were said to be considering investing in the mines and copper refining industry; the aid organisations were said to be about to construct asphalt roads, repair irrigation systems and build clinics. Smaller entrepreneurs were thought to be considering setting up business in herbs, furniture manufacture, tourism. Some villagers considered that if a proportion of the population, or of each household, moved eventually to the plain, there would be adequate land to support those remaining. There was still a slight hope that the government would introduce organised migration with quotas such that one household member would be granted a work permit and visa to work legally abroad for a period. The net result if even some of these hopes had been realised would have been more jobs locally, legal though rationed migration, and a road network that would have revolutionised communications as it reduced village-town distance and facilitated business and transport for entrepreneurs. These were not unrealistic hopes, though none of them have been realised. Nor did the population sit back and wait for outsiders to improve their situation. In fact, their needs were far too urgent to allow for inactivity.

In 1994 there were 60 households in Bulshar. Middle-aged couples had on average seven to eight surviving children. There were 34 households living on *asistenz*, the unemployment benefit, which those dismissed from their jobs received for one year. A few Bulsharites still worked in the copper refinery in Reps. A handful had jobs as forest policemen, licensed lorry drivers, teachers. The best off, such as those who had worked in the depots where reserve provisions had been stored in case of war, had moved out after helping themselves when the cooperatives fell apart. Likewise, those with official positions in the cooperative, who had had chances throughout the cooperative period to enrich themselves, were amongst the first to leave the village.

The commonest survival strategies for the rest of the villagers after the end of communism and the decollectivisation of land were three: emigration, usually to Greece or Italy illegally; descent to squat on a piece of land on one of the coastal plains near Lezhë or Durrës; sale of timber from the forest. Families with enough members of the right age practised all three strategies simultaneously. By 1994, all but one family, which only had small children, had at least one member abroad or returned from abroad – the most effective way to generate the cash to cover costs of dentists, bus fares, medicines, fertiliser and household provisions such as sugar and coffee.

At the same time, in order to meet household wheat needs – the staple and biggest drain on income – a number of families had started cultivating wheat on ex-state farm land just outside Lezhë. To have a meal translates as 'eating bread'. Food, as explained in an earlier chapter, is known as *buk* (literally bread) because bread is a major part of a meal. The parcels of land in the mountain villages were too small to grow enough maize and beans (staple foods), let alone wheat, to feed a family all the year round. The average landholding of a middle-aged couple was two to five *dylims* (one *dylim* = a tenth of a hectare) and the quality of the land was extremely poor. The cooperatives in these villages, despite huge inputs of artificial fertiliser, had had to supplement local production with imports of grain. In the post-cooperative period, supplying a family's wheat needs involved either buying wheat, almost impossible for these cash-starved villagers, or somehow acquiring more land. The only available source of supplementary land was the as yet undistributed state farm land on the coastal plains.

Descent to the plain ideally involved a married son. An unmarried son, if he could be spared, could be used more profitably earning as an migrant worker abroad. It would be much more difficult for a married couple to get abroad, and their living expenses would be higher. A married son on the plain would have the company of his wife, who would probably welcome independence from the joint household despite the difficult conditions involved in squatting. The couple would build themselves a shanty (*barakë*) next to a few square metres of land, and hope that next time an election came up they would be allowed to settle there permanently.

The forest is the only relatively abundant natural resource immediately accessible to villagers in northern Albania. As we saw, the forest remained state property, but just as the official land distribution policy had been ignored in this part of the world, and hereditary land boundaries restored, so traditional ownership and usage rights in the forest had been reasserted. However, whereas the local solution to land privatisation superseded the State's, the forest situation through the 1990s involved the coexistence of two parallel systems. In October 1992, a new law governing forest management was passed. While the forest continued to be owned by the State, exploitation of timber was transferred to individual licensed operators who had been invited to tender for forest parcels. In exchange for an annual rent these operators were granted usage rights in that part of the forest allocated to them. The ex-forestry commission sawmills were sold off cheaply to these operators, thereby relieving the government of costs such as machinery maintenance and teams' salaries. A proportion of the sawmill owners' profits from wood sales went in taxes to the government.

At the same time, villagers reverted to implementing forest usage rights as set out by the Kanun. According to the Kanun, a household had ownership rights up to half an hour's walk from where its land met the forest. Up to two hours into the forest after this point the whole clan has rights; beyond this the forest is held in common by the whole bajrak till it meets the border with the next bajrak. In the case of an individual household's rights in the early 1990s, the rules were widely, perhaps surprisingly, adhered to. If a woman cut down part of a tree in an area belonging to her clan on the basis of Kanun rules, she could safely leave it for subsequent collection. She simply marked the branch by cutting a cross on it or by placing a stone on it; or she could mark it with two pieces of wood in the form of a cross. This made it clear that it belonged to someone and she did not risk losing it even if unable to return for several days. It would be *mëkat*, sinful, to touch it, and sanctions based on fear both of human and supernatural reprisal ensured that theft was exceptional. Firewood was essential for villagers since without it they could not bake bread or, in winter, heat the kitchen where everyone gathers. Collecting firewood is women's and older girls' work though it is backbreaking and could more practically be done by men.

Sanctions apart, supernatural or human, these rules were presumably adhered to in recognition that one's own community is more likely to thrive if there is not a war of all against all. War between neighbouring bajraks, by contrast, did occur and punishment for theft would be meted out by the wronged bajrak inhabitants, not by the forest police. For example, in 1995, some boys from Kthellë Eperm came to Orosh and started to fell some trees, when they were caught in the act by some Bulshar boys. An argument began, in the course of which an Eperm boy hit an Orosh boy who, in returning the blow, knocked his assailant unconscious. It was not until the next day that the Orosh boy who had knocked out the Eperm boy learnt whether his victim was dead or alive. It may be imagined what sort of a night's sleep he had knowing that he might have to tell his father that he had involved his family in a blood feud. Although the Eperm boys were acknowledged to be in the wrong as regards the attempted theft, the family of the boy who had been stunned threatened reprisal against the Orosh boy. To avert a feud, a go-between, *ndërmjetës*, came to see the Orosh boy's father and a meeting was arranged at which tension was defused and a peaceful solution was found. The incident highlighted the absence of a state role in forest protection and the easily ignited conflicts in an area of acute scarcity.

Gjeçov's collection of the Kanun's laws does not include the minutiae of rights and usage, but it does outline the basis of rights in common property (*kujrija*):

> Common property is the area held in common by a village or a bajrak for pasture, timber, firewood, hunting, and for other needs.
>
> Common property is not divided, but every inhabited house in the village has the right to the common property of the village, and every inhabited house in the bajrak has the right to the common property of the bajrak.
>
> One person without the others may not sell the wealth of the common property; its loss and profit belong to all the households of the village or the bajrak.

No one may plant a field, a vineyard or a garden on the common
property without the approval of this work by the entire
village or by the bajrak.

Whoever has planted a tree on common property has the right
to its timber and may cut it down when he wishes, but no
one else may put an axe to it.

The tree or wood planted on common property belongs to the
person who planted it, but the fruit may be eaten by anyone
able to pick it, without being hindered by the person who
planted it. (1989:72)

Initially, many villagers limited felling to wood for household use.
But eventually most became involved in some way in clandestine
commercial felling and selling. This usually took the form of small-
scale ad hoc joint ventures involving a person with customary usage
rights in a particular area of the forest, the owner of an electric saw –
often a returnee who had bought it abroad – a tractor and a truck
driver. A tractor owner/driver with a winch was required to get the
felled trees to a lorry. The most expensive member of the venture
was the lorry driver because it was he who ran the risk of having
the load sequestered by the police and possible imprisonment. In
1994 a load could make 22 million lek, of which 7 million went to
the driver. (A cubic metre of wood sold in Laç in 1994 for $30
in summer and up to $40 in winter.) A sizeable proportion of the
venture's costs went in bribes to the road police encountered on
the way to the towns (Laç or Lezhë) where the wood was sold. By
1994, there were 12 lorry owners in this area involved in timber
sales; some had licences, most did not.

Had individual households restricted their felling to household
needs, forest capacity would have been adequate to cater both for
state licensed fellers and villagers. But the growing need for cash
by unemployed villagers, combined with an increase in large-scale
felling by illegal commercial fellers, led to severe depletion of the
forest over the decade. Nor was the depletion in any way halted
by forest police who, depending on their interests and their in-
tegrity, collected fines or bribes. In fact, sometimes quarrels broke
out between forest police when one was overstepping the boundaries of his area in an attempt to extract bribes from more people.
Occasionally a policeman would act humanely though still at the
expense of the forest, as in this case in Fan. The policeman caught

a 17-year-old boy in the act of cutting down a tree. He accompanied the boy back to his house to collect the fine of 500 lek from the parents, but on seeing the extreme poverty of the household, ended up handing the family a 500 lek note. Meanwhile, in addition to failing to police the forest, the state was undertaking neither replanting nor disease control; the epidemic of caterpillars, which threatened to kill any trees left by fellers, was left to develop unchecked.

Young male villagers who could be spared from their families walked to Greece where, at least for a few months, an illegal migrant was likely to find work either in agriculture or construction. Migrants would get across the border by one of the mountain paths. Northern Albanians in the early 1990s usually crossed near Kapshtica in Korça and stayed in the north of Greece, where seasonal work such as picking fruit was the commonest source of employment. Some ventured further into Greece and got jobs as plasterers, painters, welders and masons in towns. Their daily wage was usually considerably below that of a Greek labourer, and they had no job security or benefits since they were illegal. This made them vulnerable when employers were unscrupulous. Not many migrants during this period in the early 1990s succeeded in staying for more than a few months before being caught by the Greek police and sent back to Albania. Nevertheless, the money that most brought back was critical to making household ends meet.

For the young men of the mountain villages, going to Greece combined the elements of a heroic adventure and a rite of passage. It was an endurance test: walking to the Greek border; getting across without getting caught; finding a job and, more often than not, suffering physically at the hands of the police before being expelled. Those who were successful in finding work came back with the means to contribute to their family's welfare and an enhanced sense of self-respect. Most of those who had not gone, however sound the reasons for not having gone, felt that they were failing until they did go. In Greece or in Italy, a *refugjatë* experienced another culture and perhaps for the first time realised how different his was. The extent to which rural Albanians, few of whom had televisions, had been closed off from knowledge of life outside Albania is almost unimaginable for a Western European. A Greek villager might well have stayed near his village all his life, but television, films and EU subsidies would have given him some inkling of life beyond the *kafeneion*. For most Albanian villagers the standard of living in Greece, the level of prosperity that was immediately discernible even in the fields just across the border, must have been astonishing. Crossing, for example, from northern to southern Epirus, one is struck by the southern Epirot mountainsides because they are not suffering from erosion, by the roads, which are luxuriously asphalted and smooth, by the supermarkets, which are richly stocked.

A member of a family I knew well said to me in 1994: 'My brother and I work on our small plot of land even though it's a waste of time, because doing nothing is even more dispiriting; but there's no future in these mountain villages.' In this boy's case, as the eldest in the family whose father had been ill, he had been obliged to stay at home. All his contemporaries were in Greece or had been and would be returning. His next sibling, two years younger, had worked for several months in northwestern Greece before doing his military service. The elder brother could no longer fully share the companionship and past experiences of his contemporaries. He yearned for a sight of the unknown, knew that he could learn Greek quickly, that he would be able to help his family far more substantially earning a Greek wage than digging the family's two dylims of land to grow a paltry amount of maize and beans. So it hardly came as a surprise, following his brother's return from military service a few months later, to hear that he had left a note for his family saying that he had set out for Greece with two other young men from the village.

I was staying with his family when one of his companions returned from Greece bringing both earnings and longed-for news. A *refugjatë*, the word used to refer to an Albanian migrant, was usually incommunicado for months at a time, partly because he was afraid that writing or telephoning might lead to capture by the police, often because the family had no means of reaching a telephone. This was terribly stressful for families used to hearing reports of *refugjatë* being killed in fights, traffic accidents and occasional border shootings. The news brought by the friend was reassuring and the earnings very welcome indeed.

Staying with Simon's family, the Gjokas, we learnt a great deal about post-communist life in rural Mirdita, as well as about the Kanun and its influence on the realities of everyday life. One reason we learnt so much was that the six children, three boys and three girls, spanned an age range from seven to 22, so that they were all involved in different village activities. Also, their mother was not Mirditan but from a village near Shkodër, which meant that she had grown up in a region with different traditions, and had a standard of comparison. Her sense of cultural difference had communicated itself to her children who were more cosmopolitan in their outlook as a result. In 1994, three attended the Bulshar school. Two worked in the village, sometimes with timber fellers, sometimes on their own land, sometimes cultivating their plains plot. The eldest girl was most active at home and on their land but had former school friends in the village whom we visited from time to time.

Family discipline was strong; the young's manners extremely respectful; the 22-year-old son would ask permission to express an opinion when his father was talking. The younger children were expected to stand up when their elder brothers entered the room. Getting permission to go somewhere not part of the regular daily routine was an ordeal for the daughters, and the outcome never sure – the proprieties were closely observed. On one occasion, when the 17-year-old daughter was staying with us in Rrëshen, she had to wait for her brother to accompany her home to Bulshar. It would not do for her to travel alone in the Rrëshen-Bulshar bus, though it was driven by a respected friend and neighbour of the family. One might have thought this rather less risky than the proposition that her father was at the time seriously considering, of engaging her through a go-between to an unseen Italian. But *opinion* – what people might think – was clearly more at stake than any real risk to virtue.

Given this background, it was impressive that all the children had strongly developed individual views on life and thoughtful opinions that they could and did express – though not always in front of their parents. The fact that their father had had to spend almost a year in hospital following an accident, and that he had finally had to have one leg amputated, had made the older ones grow up faster as they had to take on more responsibilities. They were very good teachers of village life because they were all closely involved in its daily practicalities and, in the case of the older ones, could compare present-day life with that under Communism. Most usefully, they explained local customs and practices directly, without the longwinded preambles or moralistic lectures tangential to the topic so dear to many of their male elders.

The eldest son had been a weekly boarder at secondary school in Rrëshen till, at 17, he had to give up his education to look after his father in hospital in Tirana. As the eldest, the biggest burden of the household's work fell to him once his father was out of hospital. It was he who saw to the planting and harvesting of their plot in the plains; he who did many of the agricultural chores at home. The second son, Gjin, had worked for several months in the northwest of Greece as a *refugjatë* doing agricultural work. He was now doing his military service at a frontier post in the North where the bribes relating to smuggling, particularly of petrol and arms, could occasionally bring gain even to green young soldiers like him. Doing military service had ceased to be a serious affair, discipline was sporadic, and many young men left before the official number of months was up. In addition to limited profit from frontier post service, Gjin had brought back an electric saw from his Greek foray, an extremely useful entry into earning locally. In the intervals when he was on leave from military service, he and his brother or a friend went to work for a villager who was selling wood to the plains towns and needed fellers.

The eldest daughter, Elda, who was 17 when we first knew her, differed in some ways from other village girls of her age in that she was interested in public affairs and had formed strong opinions, which she did not hesitate to express forcefully. She saw the closing down of the last four classes of the school as a catastrophe, and repeatedly lamented the breaking off of her education, seeing her lack of access to further education as a source of shame, as well as a tragic end to any hope of a career. Once while she was staying with us in Rrëshen, two friends of ours who had not met her before, a journalist and the secretary of the region's Socialist Party, came round. In the course of the conversation, which included some political discussion, Elda expressed strong views with complete self-assurance. Our friends were visibly impressed and later enquired who she was, evidently recognizing political potential.

Like all village girls of her age she worked very hard at home. On a rare visit to a cousin in the port town of Durrës, she and her cousin were chatting to some of the town girls of the same age about how they spent their time. One of the town girls had a job working for an

Italian company sewing shoes. Her salary was $60 a month. 'Good heavens,' exclaimed Elda, 'that's more than twice as much as my family of eight gets a month.' She was asked what she did in Bulshar. 'Well, now the middle school's closed, I'm at home.' 'So you've got nothing to do all day,' the others commiserated. 'On the contrary, I work all day long,' Elda exclaimed indignantly. 'Housework, I suppose,' said one. 'There's water fetching, clothes washing, wood collecting, all the field work: planting; hoeing; harvesting; daily care of the animals, and breadmaking, as well as housework,' listed Elda in exasperation.

One effect of emigration was the extra work burden it put on those family members left behind. In this family, it fell to the disabled father to take care of their claim on the plain when his elder sons were away. This left the oldest girl, together with her mother and younger brother, to take care (in addition to their regular work) of all the chores including irrigation, plot cultivation, planting, weeding, harvesting, taking the wheat to be ground and making the year's supply of raki.

Taking the corn to be ground at the mill was a particularly wearisome procedure that had to be gone through every fortnight. In the absence of her brothers, jobs like this fell to Elda and her mother or younger brother. The younger brother was in charge of grazing their cow, and could be spared less easily. So one day I went with Elda instead. First two sacks for the grain had to be found. It is hard to imagine without having experienced Albania in the early 1990s that finding a sack was in itself a challenge; sacks were rare and invariably had holes that had to be mended. Eventually we found two which we took to the top floor of the *kulla* (three storey tower-like house with a room on each floor) where the family stored their grain. Once filled, we had to manoeuvre the sacks down the ladder from the top floor. The sacks were terribly heavy and one of them turned out to have a previously unnoticed hole in it, which we had to sew up. Meanwhile a small boy cousin had been sent to ask for his family's mule. Unfortunately, the mule's saddle turned out to be in the house of someone who was up on the mountain with his flocks. An hour and a half of toing, froing and waiting went by before the mule, saddle and sacks were united. We set off for Gjelina's mill at the top of the village. On the way, one of the sacks came loose as Elda had little experience of loading and making them fast. Luckily we were near the sawmill, and one of the workers came to the rescue. On finally reaching the mill we learnt that a vital part of the machinery could not be fixed until the next day. For a moment I was afraid we were going to have to take the grain away, but this we were spared, and the next day the correct weight of flour was collected without mishap. Before we left, we had weighed the sacks on the miller's weighing machine in front of Gjelina, the unspoken assumption being that otherwise cheating might occur. Making sure that not a grain was lost was understandable in view of the role wheat played as a family's staple food and the huge proportion it took from their budget; this family required two quintal of wheat a month costing 40,000 old lek ($40). The whole procedure encompassed many aspects typical of early 1990s life.

Elda's 14 year old brother, Fran, took their cow to graze every afternoon after school. He and his friends would take their animals up towards the *saraj* high above Bulshar. In good weather, the grazing was fun since the herders had company and could play football on one of the flatter stretches. If one boy could not go for some reason, a friend would take his animals for him. The following year, when there was no longer a middle school, Fran and his friends could choose the grazing time to fit in with other chores. Older Bulshar boys were said to be lazy about cultivating and still more reluctant to take on animal grazing, which they considered demeaning, so the job was always done by boys in their mid teens. Two years later this created a problem, and those families that had run out of younger boys sold their animals or butchered them.

Wood for cooking and bread-making is needed all the year round, but in winter, when wood is also required for warmth, it has to be collected even more frequently. It is woman's work, and it is backbreaking. One winter's day that I went with Elda and her mother, we started off walking along the river leaping from rock to rock until, crossing over, we started up the eroded mountainside to a part within this clan's area where there were trees. A partially rotten tree was selected first, and, after some strenuous hacking with an axe, some substantial pieces of wood were detached and collected in a pile. We continued up the steep wooded mountainside till another suitable tree was given the same treatment. When as much wood had been collected as could be transported back, we retraced our path, picking up the piles as we passed them. The wood was piled and tied with a woven rope that was then passed round the front and back of the woman while she crouched down. She had to be helped to stand up as the burden was too heavy for her to right herself alone. At intervals the women would stop and rest, propping themselves against a steep slope. The last part, leaping from rock to rock bearing the weight of the wood, was the worst except that it was near home and relief.

A regular summer job was the fortnightly six hours of irrigating; channels for the water had to be dug and vegetable garden or maize field thoroughly saturated. Weeding the grass out of a field, together with several members of the family including a maddish uncle, was interesting because we could converse as we moved along in rows. The uncle was wont to make jokes about cooperative authorities and brigadiers checking the work, and I was struck by the palpable *frisson* discernible through the children's bursts of laughter, as though they had not quite adjusted to such jokes no longer being risky.

One of the major annual chores in late summer, on a par with spring sowing and autumn harvesting, was raki making. In the same way that bread is the staple food, raki is the staple of hospitality, to establish, preserve and not infrequently to restore relations with those who come to the house. A visitor on arrival is offered a cup of Turkish coffee and a liqueur glass of raki. A bottle of raki may be given as a present or used to reciprocate a favour. It is a very effective disinfectant for wounds and bites, and, indeed, the only one available. In a word, raki is an indispensable household commodity. To make it, virtually any fruit in season at the time can be used: white mulberries, *thanat* – cornel, plums, blackberries or grapes. The Gjokas usually burnt their raki twice, making it extremely potent. It was a long hot tedious business that involved constantly keeping the fire below the cauldron stoked and making sure that the water supply did not run out. It involved frequent tasting, and on one occasion when the mother of the family had to do most of the work in the absence of all the males, I was surprised that though dead tired, she was stone cold sober at the end of the day.

While less intensively gruelling in terms of heat, concentration and hours required, collecting the fruit for raki making is also a major undertaking. Sometimes we helped collect *thanat*, which are also used for a syrup to cure stomach upsets. But one occasion when we picked up fallen mulberries made more of an impression.

The fruit had fallen off a tree next to the patrimonial *kulla*, a tree whose fruits by rights, it was claimed, belonged to our friends and not to the cousins who still lived in the *kulla*. The cousins were believed to have been at the mulberries, both on the tree and on the ground. As a result, there was an angry atmosphere amongst the pickers, enhanced by the fact that if a member of the *kulla* family had to pass nearby, they ostentatiously turned their backs on us. The other memorable feature was the level of need that dictated that fallen mulberries had to be retrieved, even including the least attractive. Or was this need partly dictated by a desire to make sure the cousins found nothing left? On a different occasion, the mulberry tree, which stood in our friends' own yard, was shaken so that the pig could be let in to enjoy a special treat.

Other chores of a seasonal nature involved preserves. Some of the meat from a pig, usually killed in late autumn or winter, was smoked. Surplus tomatoes and cucumbers were pickled. Once Coca Cola and Fanta had arrived in Albania, pickles (*turshi*) were preserved using one and a half litre plastic bottles. Fig jam was sometimes made. But little preserving for winter occurred, for the simple reason that there was rarely a surplus. When the maize was harvested, the helpers who came got a meal.

One of the more agreeable regular chores from the point of view of young girls, was the evening water-fetching time before dusk, when half a dozen or so girls from this family's neighbourhood at the bottom of the village would converge on the spring. Some carried wooden barrels strapped to their backs, others brought plastic buckets and bottles. While waiting for the vessels to be filled all sorts of fascinating conversations would take place. Most of the girls, all of whom were unmarried, were aged between 17 and 28 (though the 28 year old pretended to be younger out of embarrassment at not yet being married). Younger sisters and an occasional brother often came along too. Subjects varied depending on recent village events, seasonal work, or what the girls had been doing outside the village. Some of the girls were daughters of family enemies and, although the girls all spoke to each other, there were restraints on gossip and choice of topics.

I heard animated discussions about what careers the girls would like to study for; one girl was already studying in Shkodër to become a French teacher and was only in the village during the vacations; some were in the middle of correspondence courses. A

large number of people in Albania at this time, young and middle-
aged, in towns and villages, were taking correspondence courses in
subjects ranging from law to accountancy to primary school teaching. In the case of men and women in towns, they usually had jobs
which they combined with study. In the case of village youth, some
were completing the middle school classes, which school closure
had prevented them from attending; others had finished school
and hoped to gain teaching diplomas. The water collecting girls
were immensely communicative, keen to question and to tell; what
would I advise – literature or journalism? What did I think of the relative merits of psychology versus sociology? These conversations
took place in a scene so desolate that one wondered why anyone
had chosen to settle here. Yet these girls living in Third World
rural conditions were discussing the relative merits of psychology
versus sociology. While it was not long before the quality of the
correspondence courses and the corruption prevalent in the exam-
inations became a cause for concern, the interest in education was
alive and flourishing. The incongruity of the education level with
the underdeveloped landscape was breathtaking. In these villages
virtually nothing had been done to modify the natural obstacles
and hazards. No houses had indoor water or water in their yards.
None of the villages were served by any form of public transport
until later in the 1990s; nor had there been transport under Communism. Yet two communist achievements – education (with 100
per cent literacy) and electrification – had reached every village
however remote.

   A further incongruity was the conformity to tradition despite
the achievements in the field of education. Marriage, a favourite
topic amongst the girls, was a good example of the entrenchedness
of custom. One day the talk was about a 22 year old from this
neighbourhood who had got married the week before. She had
not wanted to marry the groom, though she thought him good-
looking, because his family was *fanatik* like hers. His parents would
insist on her wearing traditional dress. The older brothers' brides
had rebelled and their families were now living separately, but her
husband was the youngest son and would always share the house
with his parents. But she had said: 'If I don't marry this one, I
may never get married'; an assessment these girls concurred with.
Her crying and that of her six brothers had been heard all over

the neighbourhood the Saturday before. Crying is tiring, and she had cried so much that she had fainted twice. Custom requires that as the groom's representatives (*krushqet*) enter the house the bride starts to cry aloud. The groom's men drink coffee, raki, and eat, while in another room the bride continues to cry out loud. She cries until she and the groom's men have crossed the village boundary at which point all the men except for the groom start singing. Like almost all marriages this had been arranged through a go-between. 'But it's not like it used to be when children were betrothed in the cradle,' exclaimed one of the girls. 'Today the girl and boy can refuse the proposition; they see each other.' 'But how well might you know a boy when you marry?' I asked. 'Well, one *bisedë* (conversation).'

In fact, there were still cases of brides marrying their groom unseen. I met Drania, the daughter of a family in another neighbourhood of Bulshar, while she was home on a visit to celebrate a younger sister's wedding. She told me that she had not been allowed to be present at her formal engagement in 1990, and neither had the groom been allowed to see her even from a distance. In her case, the marriage had been arranged by the two fathers, who were friends. Luckily, her husband had turned out to be both nice and good looking, and she liked him very much.

Normally, nowadays, once the engagement has been negotiated, the groom accompanies his father to meet the girl's family. The girl is then led in, with eyes downcast. The groom stands up, an aunt holds out the girl's hand and the groom slips the ring on to whichever finger it fits and then puts a gold watch on the girl's wrist. Then the brideprice inside an envelope (originally it was in a large baking tin), together with the clothes and presents for the bride's family, are handed over to the father while the girl leaves the room. Festivities follow but are not attended by the girl who, alongside the helpers (*hismetçaret*), stays behind the scenes. Contrary to what one might think, the girls pointed out, she is enjoying herself as much as everyone else since she is with her own village friends and relations.

One evening a group of us were standing round the spring waiting for someone's containers to fill up when the talk turned to funerals. A discussion arose as to how foreigners bury their dead. One girl said as if it were obscenely scandalous: 'There are some peoples who bury their dead in a shroud.' 'Muslims?' asked another. 'Oh, no,' said Elda's brother: 'Muslims aren't uncivilised.' In a region where so much care goes into the burial clothes and ceremony, the idea of a shroud was genuinely horrifying.

Demoralisation

On the way to Bulshar in the spring of 1995 we stopped off at Lëgjin, where we learnt that Tom and Gjon were both in Greece, working in Athens as stone masons. Gjergj's attempt to get to Italy had got no further than the southwestern port of Vlora where at the last minute the boat had failed to set sail. He said the mafia were very visible in Vlora driving around in huge expensive cars. The traffic was fearsome and he and his friends had been robbed. But the police were impressive, had acted fast and competently. He was now planning to enter Italy as a Bosniak, aiming to get to Germany via Italy. If you get caught in Germany, he said, you are returned to Italy where if caught as an illegal alien you have 15 days before you must leave. This gives you a chance to try again for Germany.

On the road up to Bulshar we met the middle-aged man who for three months had run a much-valued bus service between Bulshar and Rrëshen. His bus was now a write-off, having recently fallen over the precipitous side of the track not far from the Dedas' house. Miraculously it had met an obstacle that prevented its falling several hundred feet, and the passengers had not been badly injured. 'How did it happen,' I asked? '*Kisha pirë* – I had been drinking.' This was the second bus aiming to provide much needed transport from Bulshar to Rrëshen that had run into trouble. The first belonged to a man who had taken out a *kredi* of several million lek. The bus rapidly proved to have a defective engine, leaving the poor man with a useless bus and a huge debt.

In Bulshar we learnt that the Heroine of the People's son, now Headteacher, was taking his duties so lightly that he was away working in Greece. The teachers who were there, with one or two honourable exceptions, were doubling up the classes and taking it in turns to come in to teach. The state of repair of the classrooms, which could be used at all, was miserable. Half the school had by this time been turned into a *bilardo* (snooker hall) by the former cooperative brigade leader mentioned earlier. The secondary section of the school, for children over 14, had closed down. This was hardly a loss since standards of motivation and discipline had been such as to virtually rule out learning. It was becoming clear that the children growing up in a democratising country were going to miss out on the educational opportunities their elders had received under totalitarianism. There was no more school for the 14-year-old Gjoka boy, but the two younger girls continued. History and geography, they reported, were being taught with some difficulty by the Heroine of the People's daughter, now back in the village having completed her French studies at the School of Foreign Languages.

That summer, a serious blow to the Gjoka family occurred when government bulldozers razed the shanties and plots of the mountain villagers squatting on the Lezhë plain. For three years now members of families from northern provinces such as Puka, Kukës, the Lezhë highlands (Zadrimë) and Mirdita had been cultivating wheat in small plots on the coastal plain near the town of Lezhë. One reason for their ejection was the forthcoming 1996 general election and the government's need for the votes of the local landless from the Lezhë area who were also contestants for the land.

The Gjokas were one of thousands of families suffering from the absence of a planned internal migration policy. Despite this lack of policy to organise the descent of unemployed mountain dwellers, President Berisha had suddenly declared that the coast should be populated by mountain dwellers; *fytyre nga deti* (faces seawards) was the catch phrase he was trying to popularise. It was ironically reminiscent of one of Enver Hoxha's favourite 1960s slogans: 'Let us take to the hills and mountains, and make them as beautiful as the plains.' In Hoxha's case, the slogan highlighting regional equality and expansion of arable land surface was subsequently modified to 'in the lowlands, but also in the hills and mountains'; with a concomitant reduction in attention to hill and mountain areas. Berisha's object was to make the unstoppable mass descent of mountain villagers look as if it were part of a government plan, a deliberate policy – 'freedom of movement' (*lëvizje e lirë*); the Democrats' liberal response to communist rural population retention. At the same time, the *laissez-faire* approach signalled by the phrase 'freedom of movement' alternated with arbitrary authoritarian intervention based on electoral interests. In theory descent from the mountains to the coastal plains was favoured by the government; in practice, squatters were at the mercy of the government's electoral interests. Thus, the Gjokas together with numerous fellow squatters lost out to the bulldozers. It was small comfort to them that the government had experienced a humiliating defeat earlier in the year at Bathorë, close to Kamzë just outside Tirana. There squatters had held out for right of occupation and installation of services until, in the face of government refusal, they had briefly captured a government minister, Tritan Shehu, and refused to let him go unless their demands were met.

The loss of their wheat plot was not the only source of trouble for the Gjokas. A long-running boundary dispute with a neighbour was reaching crisis level. The boundary contestants, two brothers, only one of whom lived in the village, had been waging a campaign of provocation for the past year, putting up fences and ploughing over access paths. The neighbour flatly refused to discuss an amicable solution. For the last six months it had become almost impossible to negotiate the path leading to the Gjoka house. A fence had been erected so that one either had to manoeuvre oneself along a very narrow and slippery strip of grass above a stream cum irrigation channel or wade through the stream. The headman whenever appealed to said that he was taking steps. He and the Gjokas had always been on friendly terms as the wives came from the same area. But in this particular case the headman was in league with the obstructor, whose brother was in a position to help him in another affair. The father of the Gjoka family made repeated appeals to the commune head in Reps to instigate a police enquiry into the affair. Nothing happened until the following January, 1996, when the district head, the village headman and three old men arrived to look into the question. Legally the contestant had no basis for his claim since the boundaries in question had been re-established to everyone's satisfaction in 1991 by the land commission and elders. But not only did these five men now decree that access to the house should be by a much longer way round, they unexpectedly added insult to injury by decreeing that a sizeable slice of the family's yard was actually the property of the neighbour's brother. This brother lived in Rubik and had no practical interest in the land whatever. Having duly sworn the requisite oaths, the five departed leaving my friends digging up their fence and shifting it a couple of metres into their yard.

Women are not allowed to be present when oaths are sworn and I was indoors with the other women during the action. While it was obvious that however just the Gjoka's case, they were helpless in the face of this group's united front, it riled me that they had put up no resistance to the decision. Was it a case of a disabled man with only two grown-up sons losing out against an able-bodied man with four grown-up sons? I asked why they had not argued that either these or the 1991 oath swearers were perjuring themselves. They replied that people who swear falsely will ultimately be struck by some calamity.

While things were looking dismal for the Gjoka family, the household of the headman, Gjon Bajraktar, was experiencing the benefits of a connection through a cousin based in Shkodër with Austrian Caritas. To our surprise, on our way to Gjon's house we found a brand new building on the site of the demolished clinic. For a moment I thought it was the longed for replacement clinic the villagers had wanted. It turned out to be a bakery built with Caritas funds. Roza took us on a guided tour. As impressive as the magnificent machinery for preparing and baking was the bathroom. This had a Western style lavatory, possibly the only one north of the Hotel Tirana and, miraculously, indoor running water with a shower and a hot water heater. Now we understood the reasons behind the surprising introduction earlier that year of pipes to bring water to the house; surprising because no other house had the luxury even of water in its yard. In addition to the baking area itself, there was a bedroom. Here, Roza explained, the bakery guard would sleep. The bakery would soon employ 14 people, Gjon told us, and his sons would soon be learning how to bake bread. No one but some Caritas innocents believed that such a plan was really being considered. (The projected bakery in Fan likewise produced no bread.) From Gjon's point of view, however, the advantages of even a non-functioning bakery on the premises were indisputable. One was the newly installed water system, which now brought water to his house. This would at least lighten Roza's work load, though it would prevent potential suitors from spotting her as she fetched water from the spring beside the main road. Further benefits were enjoyed the following summer when unsuspecting Caritas donors kindly ensured that a large quantity of flour was donated to the bakery. The flour was then very profitably sold off by the headman's sons.

Bulsharites were furious that a foreign aid organisation had embarked upon such an enterprise without holding a meeting with assembled villagers to ascertain the community's priorities. A bakery was never going to be patronised by villagers for whom it was cheaper to bake bread at home. (Nor had the headman's family ever seriously imagined that it would function.) What Bulshar needed and what the villagers most wanted was a health centre with a regular visiting dentist and midwife.

The next surprise in the village was the elopement of one of the headman's sons with the daughter of the Heroine of the People, class enemy of the ex-Bajraktar. Etleva's parents and brothers were furious about the inescapable marriage, and Etleva was now living at the headman's house. However, what would have been seen as a shocking transgression of moral standards had it occurred to most other families, seems to have been regarded more as an absurdity in this case. Perhaps it was thanks to this moral laxity that the wedding party was a lot more fun than most wedding parties. There was a comic act put on by some of the villagers dressed up like mummers and wearing stilts. The band, which was excellent, with clarinet, accordion, drums, guitar and singer, made for an exuberant atmosphere, and a huge number of guests were present, seated at trestle tables over the extensive garden area. Significantly, all the headman's cousins, none of whom were normally on speaking terms with him, helped to organise the proceedings, determined that even though their cousin's family had breached all the rules, the clan's honour should be upheld with regard to the correctness of the public procedures.

The brilliant carpenter was seated at a table in the middle of the yard entering the amount given by each guest against their name in a notebook. Reciprocity in the context of ceremonial events is calculated with precision. Various factors determine the amount: how closely related you are; how good friends; how many members of your family have come; how much the hosts gave when attending one of your ceremonies. The notebook provides a record so that when the host-guest roles are reversed a suitable sum can be reciprocated. This reflects the influence of the Kanun, which is always clear regarding costs. For instance, if the bride should die on the way from her home to the groom's before the halfway mark, her parents are responsible for burying her and for the funeral expenses. If the death occurs after the halfway mark, these duties fall to the groom's parents.

Other cousins were busy at the outdoor oven cooking vast amounts of meat. Some within the house prepared quantities of subsidiary dishes or bustled round the yard serving the hundreds of guests. The bride, despite being dressed in the white wedding dress, the *velo*, only appeared for public view on two short walks around the company. Each appearance was greeted with the gun shots, which are a regular feature of weddings, as is also now the filming by an official video cameraman. The rest of the time she sat upstairs in the recently built bridal chamber. This was contrary to custom, which says that the bride remains largely secluded only if she is dressed in traditional Mirditor costume.

Less dramatically, but more seriously for the victims, one of the headman's sons went the following month to the commune office in Reps to collect the state welfare benefits to be distributed to Bulsharites. Instead of returning with it to Bulshar, he decided to use the money to take a trip to Shkodër. Those families who had as a result received no money at all for more than a month went to the authorities in Reps to complain. 'What can we do?' was all they got for reply. Whether the authorities were too afraid of the headman's sons to demand repayment, or whether they were simply indifferent to the plight of those on welfare, is not clear. The next time the welfare payments were due to be collected from Reps, Gjon asked the headman from the village above to collect the money for him, perhaps embarrassed to appear himself following his son's aberrant behaviour. Perhaps afraid that he would have to replace the lost funds. This time the Reps office refused to hand over anything until the Bulshar headman came in person.

On another occasion, when he was not able to sit in the seat of his choice, one of the sons had broken the window of one of the two recently introduced Bulshar buses. He was said to have been drunk. One reason for not taking steps against these hoodlums was the knowledge that they were armed. But a major obstacle to dealing with them may also have been the lack of unity amongst Bulsharites. Even if the law and state machinery let them down, united threats of action by the villagers themselves might have coerced the headman's sons into behaving more correctly. But some families needed to keep in with the headman, whose position gave him some influence as to which way disputes were settled. Overall there were so many quarrels going on between neighbours and within families that unified action or solidarity was not to be expected. The complete absence of any gathering place, even a physical centre such as a village square, made for isolation and an increase in enmities. As we had seen on our first visit to Gjelina, all that remained of Bulshar's communist centre of authority, fear and punishment, entertainment and companionship, was a pile of rubble. Now that there were neither cooperative duties in the fields nor communal organisation of socialising, villagers met rarely. True, the older boys, nearly all of whom were unemployed, could play and gamble a little along with the male teachers in the newly established *bilardo*. There was also the council of elders, but in Bulshar these met rarely and were men only. This lack of centre and socialising opportunities meant that people probably got on worse with each other than if they had had a chance to congregate. It was easier to be unscrupulous about someone else's property if you saw them rarely and had convinced yourself that they were insignificant or in the wrong. It was also easier to magnify insults or imagine slights and harbour resentment. In an area of very severe unemployment, infertile and inadequate land, where the law barely functioned, scarcity led to a hardening of hearts towards others and a tendency for might to be right.

General demoralisation was intensified by some of the effects consequent on an end to cooperative controls; bears were said to be more numerous and causing damage to the crops. The reappearance of wolves now that no measures to limit their numbers were being implemented meant that increasing numbers of cows and sheep were being attacked and killed. Where before the state had controlled both delinquents and wolves, the villagers were now on their own. As hope for employment dwindled and poverty increased, relations between villagers worsened. Suspicion was endemic. If dogs disappeared it was believed they had been stolen; mother chickens were tied up to prevent them wandering with their young to be trapped by malevolent neighbours. Anyone taking wheat to be ground at one of the mills assumed that unless they were hawkeyed and weighed their sacks before and after, they would be cheated. In a neighbouring bajrak the murder and dismemberment of a young boy while herding his goats made Bulshar parents fearful for their own children. Young boys taking the animals to graze stayed in groups, girls never went anywhere alone.

Between 1994 and 1996, as can be seen from the foregoing, conditions in many respects deteriorated. The school got worse, the forest was being depleted, relations between neighbours tended to be disputatious. At the same time, earnings from *refugjate* meant that immediate material conditions got better. For example, new sofa beds replaced the collapsing old ones; some people acquired a television for the first time; better tools for agricultural work were bought. These modest improvements were greeted with huge appreciation. Following the initial destructive phase, there was until 1995 a general recognition that to advance a period of reconstruction must take place. The general situation seemed calm, and the entrenchedness of custom was a significant stabilising factor in these early years of weak government and ideological vacuum. But while the population was finding its feet and trying to be constructive, it was not getting any support from central government, and the local authorities were helpless – without financial or decision-making powers – *as fond, as kompetencë*. Roads were not improved; increasingly, only untrained teachers were available to fill rural school vacancies; legal hiatuses were not addressed. By the end of 1994, corruption, whether in the form of misdirected aid or bribery of police and lawyers, was growing alarmingly. Bureaucratic incompetence and dishonesty made every undertaking, from formalising land-ownership to getting a loan to set up a business, an expensive odyssey and, as often as not, an abortive one. A gradual loss of faith in the law was paralleled by a growth in chicanery. Descent to the plains increased both in response to the realisation that neither roads nor support for small enterprises were going to be forthcoming; and thanks to foreign earnings, which enabled families to cover the costs of building a *barakë* and paying for the passportisation documents the move entailed.

By 1996, there was a worrying growth in robbery with violence. In July, two masked men armed with machine guns had appeared in the woods above Bulshar and forced two Bulsharites who were felling trees to hand over their motor saws and all the money they had on them. We were in the (new) Bulshar-Rrëshen bus with one of the victims when he was regaling the passengers with his experience. He had just bought the saw with a loan. Though the attackers had stockings over their faces, he thought he recognized one of them. Most of them, it was thought, were fugitives from blood feud in need of money to buy provisions. From another village a shepherd returning from the plain where he had just sold his lambs was ambushed. On refusing to hand over the money, he was beaten unconscious and robbed. In neither case had the police taken any steps.

That many villagers were close to the edge of survival was brought home by the pretty desperate offers made by the less scrupulous to the poorest. The head of the Gjoka family was approached by two young men who, in exchange for one thousand dollars, wanted to make use of his one-leggedness as a beggar in Athens. This kind of offer had also been made to him in the town of Durrës. We began to wonder whether with such a valuable asset he was not at risk of being abducted.

Another chance to make money was to be a *kepucar*, acting as a decoy so that a man targeted to be killed could be ambushed more easily. For instance, a man in blood with another family, duty bound to carry out a revenge killing, might offer you a substantial sum of money to keep track of the proposed victim, and engineer his appearance at a given moment so that he could be dispatched. Or, as in the case of a feud in a village near Rrëshen where the man in blood was said to be afraid to do the killing himself, you might earn by doing it for him. I was shocked at these developments and expected Rrëshenites to be amazed by such goings-on, but they were familiar with it all and their only surprise was at my ignorance.

Chapter Twelve

RRËSHEN: ECONOMIC SURVIVAL AND RELIGION

I n the summer of 1994 we went to stay for the first time in Mirdita's main town, Rrëshen. Due to a misunderstanding we were collected a day early, before we had shopped for provisions unobtainable in Mirdita. We threw things into bags at breakneck speed, Soula fighting tears but acting brave and packing kitchen stuff. The drive was fine – a fine illustration of consummate skill on the part of the driver. We were stopped four times by police. Road police surprisingly did seem to have some effect on reducing the appalling accident rate. The driver was proud because even when the police were not acquaintances, his papers were found to be in order. His smashed spider-like windscreen was not considered a problem. During the two hour drive, most of which was either dusk or dark, times when even locals try to avoid being out on the road, we avoided hitting horses and carts, bicycles, cows, unlighted cars.

In Rrëshen (population c.4,500) a Mirditan friend had found a flat for us to rent. It was in the usual slum-type block with broken steps amid a wasteland of garbage. Poor Soula was depressed as the flat was a bit slummy, sticky in places, with cockroaches and bedbugs (I realised when I woke up with swelling red marks in the morning). But as always, things arranged themselves. Though not very clean, the flat was comparatively luxurious: two rooms, a fridge, a television, Turkish lavatory and occasional water. A wedding was celebrated on our first night, which involved a day and a night of electric band playing and singing in front of the groom's apartment block. The music was nice, luckily, as it lasted most of the night, and helped distract from bedbug bites.

On our first evening we sat in our landlord's flat, which adjoined ours. A visiting teacher had a heated argument with our friend about Kadare whom the teacher considered a traitor. Our landlord, a former public prosecutor (from the next door province of Mat, which is traditionally Muslim, unlike Mirdita) dwelt on the betterness of Enveri's system. The teacher recited Byron in Albanian with passion, while the four- and eight-year-old grandchildren watched a naked Turkish couple making frenetic love on the television in our midst. The family had a *Sharp* (satellite dish), which meant that, amongst other things, they could watch soft porn from dozens of different countries. One of our landlord's sons-in-law was a guitarist with a group of musicians that travelled regularly to Switzerland, where they earned well playing to the emigré Kosovar community. The sons were working in Greece, in Tripoli. For most people the only source of money was abroad. Outside, *Sharps* proliferated on every building, while below them pigs rooted around in the garbage.

The Albanian Encyclopaedia (*Fjalori Enciklopedik Shqiptar*, 1985) tells us that Rrëshen was founded in 1949 on the site of a small village, Fushë-Lumth. In becoming Mirdita's chief town Rrëshen replaced Shenpal, St Paul, (halfway up the mountain to Reps), which had for centuries been the site of the traditional assemblies (*kuvend*) of tribal chiefs. Rrëshen lies in the confluence plain of the two rivers, the Big and Little Fan. During the communist period it became an 'important administrative, educational and cultural centre' whose population in the 1980s was 3,221. At this time it had a copper refinery, lorry and tractor park, a middle school, two eight-year schools, a history museum, library and palace of culture. There was also a creche and kindergarten, a puppet theatre, an acting ensemble, a group of folk singers, a cinema, a hospital and a dental clinic. In the central square there were the busts of three Mirditan heroes and a monument to four Partisan heroines. By 1993 the copper refinery, lorry and tractor park, cinema and puppet theatre had ceased to function. The trees lining the streets had been chopped down, the parks, fountains and statues destroyed. The Palace of Culture, state bookshop and museum were still extant but rarely open. The director of the Palace of Culture at the time was a talented and dynamic young musician. His job involved organising folk performances in Rrëshen and leading the Mirditan ensemble of folk singers and dancers abroad, mainly to countries with a Kosovar diaspora, occasionally to other former communist countries such as Bulgaria. While studying the trumpet at the music lyceum in Tirana in the 1980s, he had supplemented his scholarship by playing in the dance orchestra at the Hotel Tirana despite the communist government's ban on such income-generating initiatives. To his intense irritation, entrepreneurial initiatives were still out of place in the 1990s when the Palace of Culture was in urgent need of income generation. Its few remnants of culture included an upright out-of-tune piano, a theatre, most of whose seats were falling apart, and a collection of extremely valuable folk costumes and musical instruments whose sale was enriching some unscrupulous individuals, despite all the director's efforts to prevent theft. The public library, also in the Palace of Culture, employed several librarians whose duties involved putting out newspapers on rickety tables and, very occasionally, disappearing into dark recesses when some demanding member of the public requested a book. The books were kept in a hinterland safely out of reach of readers. In summer the library was stifling, in winter so cold that even a short read of a newspaper resulted in numb limbs. The librarians toasted their feet behind the desk with the help of an electric coil.

The town itself presented the usual scene of urban devastation and ravaged countryside typical of Albania in the 1990s, though on closer acquaintance one could see that the actual setting, on a hill beside the River Fan i Vogel, was potentially beautiful with its views of the surrounding mountains. Before the Communists came to power, the area around the village of Fushë-Lumth had been densely populated with oaks interspersed with dwarf oak. The trees were all felled to make way for a state farm growing wheat and maize that, due to the unsuitability of the soil, never gave good yields. Across the river the state farm had grown vegetables with better success. The post-communist scene was rundown, slummy and filthy, with wastelands of garbage, broken pavements and steps, unmaintained buildings. The apartment blocks were shoddy constructions of exposed lopsided bricks, unpointed, with uneven gaps between the bricks. In front of each block there was a standpipe in a wasteland of mud where groups of people would stand around waiting to fill buckets on the numerous occasions when the town water pump had a defect or was immobilised by electricity failure. Water inside was rationed to a few hours a day. Fourth and fifth floor flat dwellers were mostly beyond the reach of water pressure and regularly had to descend to standpipes outside. Breakdowns in the water supply were common and the water was, and still is in the twenty-first century, impure. The electricity supply was equally unreliable, with frequent blackouts. Cows, pigs, chickens, donkeys and horses wandered the roads and grazed on the rubbish in the wastelands. The bottom of the flight of stairs leading to the basement in each block had been turned into a rubbish dump.

The inhabitants in 1994 wore shabby clothes ranging from village costume in the case of older women, to ancient flares in the case of youths. In winter everybody's clothes looked shabby; in summer the women, especially young ones, were often elegantly dressed. In the summer evenings between seven and nine the whole town came out for the *xhiro*, walking up and down or sitting on low walls conversing. On our second evening in 1994, the inhabitants of our apartment block, who were gathered in front of it chatting, started talking to us about the lack of maintenance. Every flat was now privately owned, sold by the state to the inhabitants at symbolic prices; whereas the public part of the building was no one's. Some of the flat dwellers were keen to tell us that they knew the terrible impression the dirt must make; at the same time, they were equally determined that there was nothing they could do about it. 'Couldn't you each clean your own bit?' I asked. 'How do I know which is my part?' said one. Ironically, given the number of flat dwellers taking part in the discussion, one woman said: 'You see there's no communal spirit.' One man said he felt ashamed for foreigners to see it now; it used to be perfectly clean. No doubt the white flag of cleanliness and desire not to be criticised at the *Mbledhje Frontit* meetings had made a difference. But I had heard that under Communism, the least privileged, often gypsies, were allocated ground floor apartments while the privileged got higher floors, the advantage of which was that one could hurl one's rubbish off the balcony. However, there certainly would have been far less rubbish before the advent of democracy and Western goods – potato peelings and melon rinds rather than containers and wrapping.

In 1994, the population (c.3,500) had not changed radically since pre-democracy times, and it quickly became clear that as administrative centre for the region, Rrëshen still largely consisted of former loyal Communists. The town had been created by Enver

Hoxha when plans for developing the area's mineral resources were in the process of being realised. In the 1950s one of the more ghoulish methods of inspiring locals with party loyalty (Mirditans for the most part had been reluctant Communists) was hanging traitors from a mulberry tree near the river and leaving the bodies there as a warning to anyone foolhardy enough to consider criticising the regime. An elderly couple who had themselves been devoted communists showed me the tree, recalling one occasion when there had been not one but three bodies. During the regime, while many of the officials in the town administration were from other parts of Albania, the majority of the population originated from villages within the province. Some of these had studied in Tirana, returning once qualified to work in Mirdita as doctors, teachers, engineers. A few had managed to overcome restrictions and descend direct from rural areas. Since movement from one place to another was subject to very strict regulation, those who were granted passportisation to an urban residence were those who had proved their commitment to the party. Thus, most Rrëshenites were not simply Communists in the sense that almost all Albanians were communists – participants in a regime which allowed no choice – but convinced Communists and often party members.

Like the 'privileged' Communists we knew in Tirana, the privileged families in Rrëshen in the early 1990s would dwell on the positive side of the regime: guaranteed work; affordable food; public peace and order; strict liability for results by those in positions of responsibility such as doctors,[1] midwives, foremen; equality across the board. Present problems such as joblessness and high prices were not considered to be linked in any way with the past regime's policies, but blamed exclusively on the present government (from 1992 to 1996 the Democrats were in power). Intelligent, morally upright members of Rrëshen society would assure one that prisons under the regime had been humane, that political prisoners had been well treated. If one mentioned that for most years of the regime, the country had been financed by foreign money, Russian, Chinese, German, one would be assured that Albania at no point ever had a foreign debt. Pressed on the example of the German loan in the 1980s, the answer was that it had not been a loan, but an exchange for goods. This initial uncritical praise of Communism modified as time went on, but unconsciously, so that these people never realised they were changing their accounts and memories; if you told them some of the things they had said several years earlier, they denied ever having had such views.

At the same time, in 1994, there were also some formerly devoted Communists who had become equally fervent supporters of the Democrat government. For instance, a man who had been head of a large cooperative was now the director of privatisation of land and buildings for the area. Some of these individuals were obviously genuinely convinced of the merits of the new economic philosophy. Others who had been demonstratively committed to communism were apparently in denial about their ideological volte face and loud in their condemnation of an ideology that they had so recently warmly acclaimed. These were enthusiasts of free market capitalism, committed to total privatisation and ceilingless prices. A minority of Rrëshenites, some of whom felt that they had been unjustly disadvantaged under the regime, were wholehearted supporters of the Democrat government from conviction rather than ambition. Others, together with early Democrat supporters all over the country, had initially had real hopes that the Democrat Party would transform the political and the economic scene. Many of these were already disillusioned and had joined the Allianza Party, whose leaders had once been members of Berisha's government, subsequently either dismissed for disagreeing with Berisha, or withdrawing voluntarily.

In 1994 there were still a number of families in Rrëshen from other parts of Albania who had not yet managed to move away either to Tirana or to their place of origin. It had been communist policy to post officials to provinces other than their own, partly to avoid nepotism and cronyism, partly to promote regional mixing, partly to maintain centralised domination. Most of these 'foreigners' – *jabanxhi* – had either held administrative positions in local government, or professional posts such as teacher, public prosecutor, army officer, state shop manager. In 1994, those who had not yet left were planning to leave. The difficulty for those 'foreigners' who hoped to move to Tirana rather than their place of origin was the housing problem. Lack of housing was one of the communist regime's most conspicuous failures, one that the Party had openly referred to as a problem that must be tackled. Its non-resolution meant that for the first two or three years of post-communist freedom of movement, the urban and rural populations were hardly less restricted as to mobility than before. Privatisation of urban apartments had taken place in 1993, when flat occupants had bought their flats at symbolic prices. But whereas ownership of a flat in central Tirana bought for $100 or so was now an extremely valuable asset, selling a flat in Rrëshen would cover only a fraction of the price of one in the capital. Nor at first were there any buyers for Rrëshen flats. Few village families could even afford to build a shack to squat in on the plain. Many villagers who had moved to Rrëshen were squatting in the buildings of former state enterprises such as the copper refinery and the now defunct railway station offices (and are still in these makeshift quarters nearly a decade later). Only when emigration abroad had begun to bring in substantial remittances several years later was there any significant movement in the housing market. Members of Rrëshen families living in crowded flats – seven or more to two rooms and a kitchen was usual – were also quite unable to raise the cash to divide joint families. Moreover, had they been able to find the cash, most would have chosen to save up until they could afford to move to a larger town, Lezhë or Laç or, ideally, Tirana. The virtually universal view held by Rrëshenites in 1994 was that the town was future-less, *pa përspektivë*. The town's productive enterprises, its copper refinery, medicinal plants, wine, raki and jam processing, had all come to an end. Its hinterland, it was believed, would inevitably empty out since no new investment was coming into the province's mines or forestry; the existing mineral enterprises were already virtually defunct, while the forest, as the only source of income for jobless villagers, was rapidly disappearing. The majority of villagers would probably move to the coastal plains of Lezhë or Durrës. As an administrative centre with a depopulating hinterland and no production within the town, Rrëshenites were convinced that their town was fast on its way to obsolescence. Lezhë, a much bigger town with the advantage of being very close to the coast with tourist beaches at its port Shëngjin, a fishing industry and a fertile coastal plain, had a future and would become a thriving centre. Laç, a town of 37,000 was not only far bigger, it was half way to Tirana. In the meantime, Rrëshenites must survive as best they could.

Income Generation

Initially, economic survival took four main forms often practised simultaneously by different household members: emigration, petty commerce, a job in the state sector and opening a cafe-bar. By

1995, when Rrëshen had a population of between 4,000 and 4,500, there were 84 cafe-bars in operation in Rrëshen. Some admittedly were on the verge of bankruptcy, but the number reflected the limited scope for generating income, as well as the number of men with time to spend in cafes. While some doubtless saw the time spent in cafes as important to the making and maintaining of networks, which might ultimately produce work and valuable political connections, the majority were there simply to escape from overcrowded flats and monotony. Over the period 1995 to 1999, some cafes were replaced by snooker halls, bingo and fruit machines. It was not until 2000, when a small number of long-term emigrants began to return, that there was a slight shift in or around Rrëshen to more productive enterprise in the form of small-scale greenhouse businesses or activities linked to the building boom, such as tile manufacture, manufacture of door and window frames, soldering.

Petty commerce was the only other readily accessible means to earning. In 1994 there were large numbers of family-owned kiosks selling a few groceries and, less often, fruit and vegetables or milk brought in by villagers. There were even larger numbers of market space holders. The bazaar is situated on the other side of the river. In 1994, at the entrance to the bazaar at the far end of the bridge, two or three money changers stood calling out: 'Anyone want to change *drami*?' (drachmas). By 1996, they were offering to change *dollar, drami, lireta, marka*, reflecting the fact that migrants were much more widely dispersed. In the bazaar in 1994 there were no stalls; all the goods were laid out on the ground; if it rained, selling stopped. Some sellers specialised in old clothes, others in grocery dry goods, some in electrical spare parts. There was a place which sold brides' wear: dress materials and jewellery for when a new bride was travelling between villages or going on visits within the village. Here you could find velvet, gold brocade, silver lamé and costume jewellery. A few stalls also sold handmade cradle ties (*baç*) and the woven cummerbund (*qemer*) worn with traditional Mirditorë dress, together with children's T-shirts, socks, plastic coloured dustbins (used for storing water in the bathroom). On average, a bazaar seller could expect to earn about twice as much a month as a state salary earner. Some clothes sellers in 1994 tried selling new children's clothes exclusively but this was quickly found to be unprofitable; almost no-one could afford them. Secondhand clothes, on the other hand, sold very well, particularly in the early 1990s, when there was a real dearth of clothes. Even before clothes manufacture ceased, people had owned very few clothes; only a handful of the small elite could have afforded to buy more than essentials; and now there was almost nothing to buy as well as almost no money to pay with. The sellers of secondhand clothes bought them by the sack from Tirana middlemen who bought up mass quantities of clothes, mostly aid donated and not intended for the market at all. By 1996, so many people were selling secondhand clothes (which required only a very small capital outlay) that no-one could make much profit, and several sellers changed profession. Clothes sellers apart, however, there was minimal flux with a stable number of sellers working fairly harmoniously together. They would come to an agreement on prices for goods and only make reductions without consultation towards the end of the day. All the sellers got their goods en gros in Tirana. These had to be brought to Rrëshen by bus from Tirana. Almost no one in 1994 had their own transport, and much bus floor space would be taken up with crates of beer and sacks of dry goods on their way to some village shop or provincial market.

Villagers would come in to Rrëshen to sell tiny amounts of seasonal produce at prices which, if they managed to sell everything, might bring them half a dollar (50 lek in 1994) on a good day – a very substantial help to eking out expenses. A friend who sold secondhand clothes had spent a short time testing the market in the highland town of Reps, where villagers from all over the highlands had to come periodically to get documents from the commune offices, visit the dentist or buy essential groceries. It was a hopeless business our friend discovered; no villager had cash to spare for secondhand clothes.

The economic situation of the average Rrëshen household was indeed significantly better than that of village households; an urban-rural distinction that held for most of the country. One reason for greater wealth was the greater accessibility to jobs in both the public and the service sectors. Furthermore, emigration had generally started sooner in towns than in the villages. It had been easier for urban males to cross to Italy or Greece early on, partly because they had easier access to communications – personal networks, roads, coast and news; partly because they could find the money for visas or bribes much more readily than village families.

Early access to news and less distance to the coast resulted in many young men joining the first mass exoduses by boat from the port of Durrës to Italy. Most of the earliest migrants to Italy were more urban and educated than those who walked across the mountains to Greece. Many had already picked up Italian from Italian television programmes, since far more urban households owned televisions than did rural ones. These migrants earned more money, more quickly than those who went to Greece. They were able to invest in flats and shops back home much earlier. Their experiences led to the accurate perception that migration to Italy, though more difficult to achieve, was preferable to working in Greece, where wages were lower and prejudice against Albanians greater. From the beginning of democracy, the Italians had received boatloads of immigrants with humanitarian aid; had made arrangements for refugees' accommodation, and managed the Pelikan aid programme of food to Albania. For the first few years of the immigrant wave, Italians treated Albanians with greater respect than Albanian immigrants to Greece encountered. The fact that crossing the mountains to Greece made access easier to larger numbers partly accounts for differences in reception. Moreover, Italy was more used to migrants than Greece, and for Albanian Catholics, the religious link was a help. (Being a Catholic in Greece cut no ice; if you were not Orthodox, you were alien.) Since Italy was so much larger than Greece, with a much more developed industrial sector, there were far more opportunities for work. It was only later, in the mid 1990s, when the Italian labour market was beginning to be saturated with Albanians, when Albanian-run prostitution rackets had flooded the country, that even those equipping themselves expensively with legal entry documents risked failing to find work and a friendly reception.

Once the remittances, whether from Italy, Greece or, in fewer cases, Germany and the USA, started coming into Albania, there was some change in the makeup of Rrëshen's population. The non-Mirditans were able to move away, while some highland villagers who already had relations in Rrëshen moved down to the town. These were initially more likely to be 'intellectuals'[2] in the Albanian sense of the word, meaning people working with their heads rather than their hands. Thus, teachers would be amongst the first to move out of villages to a town, since their profession would enable them to find work. A non-'intellectual' villager, such as a former copper mine or cooperative worker, would at this period be more likely to try to move to a coastal plain where there would be some land to cultivate and hence a source of immediate food supply. For this type of villager with no specific marketable skill or profession, securing the wherewithal to eat and escaping a prospect-less isolation were the primary concerns. We saw that villagers from Fan and Orosh might be able to send one or two family members to the plain or abroad, but the rest for the present had little option but to scrape by on small plots and *asistenz*. Work in construction or a related area would be sought by those families who eventually found the means to descend to squat near an urban centre.

A private construction firm started building a large block of flats in Rrëshen in 1994. The flats could be bought with a form of mortgage. But many Rrëshenites were shocked by a system that led to paying so much more for a property than buying it outright. When I referred to someone who in 1996 had moved into one of these recently completed flats as the 'owner', some friends exclaimed: '*çfarë pronar*! What kind of owner! He's paying every month for the next 20 years.' Most families continued to live in the crowded conditions they had always known. Towards the end of the 1990s, more village families whose members had been earning abroad were able to buy flats in Rrëshen. Indeed, those Rrëshen families whose members had spent the decade working in state sector jobs found that apartment prices were affordable only by *refugjate*. Emigrant remittances enabled some families to leave Rrëshen for other towns, thus freeing flats for villagers to buy. But young married couples hoping to set up in a flat of their own were forced either to rent or to try to raise the money to build somewhere.

Early on during our first sojourn in Rrëshen we became friends with a family who enabled us to experience many features representative of provincial town life, including making the best of confined living quarters. They were a non-intellectual communist family, eight of whose members lived in a two-room-with-kitchen flat. This in itself was not unusual, and provided an insight into how families managed large numbers in a small space – 'overcrowding' is obviously a relative concept. Order was achieved in the same way as it is living in a small boat, with system and neatness. This family consisted of the parents, two unmarried daughters in their 30s, a married son in his 20s, his wife and son, and the small daughter of a third sister who lived in the south of Albania. The family were past masters at space management; the table in the small room where they entertained and did the wood stove cooking opened up to seat eight people; the table in the room where the mother and daughters slept, opened up to reveal a sewing machine. As well as a single bed and a double bed, this room also contained a fridge and a sink for washing up. The young couple and their son slept in the bedroom where the wardrobe for the whole family's clothes was. The father slept on one of the divans in the cooking-eating-television room with the wood stove. The shower and Turkish lavatory room doubled as kitchen and laundry room; the divans doubled as beds, and the beds were shared. A small balcony outside the bedroom provided storage space for onions, garlic, wood, as well as for people to sit in warm weather. A vine planted by the ground floor flat dwellers now provided dwellers up to the third floor with grapes each autumn. Across the landing from this family, lived a widow with six of her children, four adults and two teenagers, and two grandchildren whose parents were in Germany.

Public Sector Employment

Three members of one of the families we knew best were state employees, which gave us an illuminating entrée into the Post and Telecommunications Office, the Centre of Health and Hygiene, and the state bookstore for schoolbooks. The first thing we discovered about state employment was that despite all the hype about market economy and the new order, most of the state sector was still firmly in place, and much of it remained unreconstructed up until the early 2000s. Pressed to explain in 1996 why these urban jobs remained when rural jobs in factories and mines, no more uneconomic, were abolished, Democrat government representatives would explain that complete rationalisation would have been inhumane. Their literal words were 'we can't take away their *bukë gojës*' – the food from their mouths. They argued that Mirditan village dwellers are not jobless; now that there are no cooperatives, now that the mines, factories and power plants are closed, villagers work their land. The tripled population of villagers with an average of half a *dylim* of infertile land, with no money for fertiliser, with no functioning irrigation systems, with no agricultural or marketing infrastructure can, these Democrat officials claimed, feed themselves. In 1996 the then mayor of Rrëshen told me in true conservative tradition that it is simply laziness that prevents the villager from getting rich. However, emigration and internal migration trends from rural areas provide ample evidence that either those responsible for employment are hypocrites (control over sinecure jobs is an MP's best urban vote catcher), or completely out of touch with reality. Although the Socialist government, which replaced the Democrat government in 1997, was theoretically aware of the need for reform, it took a long time before their accession to power led to any reconstruction of the public sector in the provinces. Towards the end of 1999 a reform was being discussed such that public sector workers should compete through public exams for civil service posts. It was not until the autumn of 2001 that the telephone service was automated and most of the numerous underemployed staff dismissed with two years pay as compensation.

Thanks to our close friendship with a telephone employee, we became very familiar with the service during the 1990s. At the central telephone exchange, as in the factories, shifts were eight hours long. Contrary to expectations, the night shift (*turni i tretë* – third shift) from ten to six was the favourite, because it usually involved an unbroken night's rest. The telephone service was patchy throughout the 1990s. It frequently happened that someone had stolen part of the telephone wires somewhere along the line so that no telephoning was possible. The telephonists would leave a scribbled note in the office window curtly announcing non-function; this left them free to chat to friends and colleagues undisturbed by the frustrated public. Even when breakdown meant that for months on end one could only telephone within Rrëshen, the entire numerous staff continued to 'work' their shifts despite having nothing to do other than knit, embroider or crochet, kept warm in winter by *reflektore*, the lethal-looking unprotected electric coil heaters. Despite worries that the threatened privatisation of telecommunications would put most of them out of a job, the summer of 2000 saw the situation of overstaffing unchanged. The introduction of several automatic telephones with telecards had left staff with even less to do, though they now sold telecards when these had not run out due to underproduction or non-arrival in the provinces. A new development arising from the existence of telecards was the *kontrabandistë* as he was jokingly known, who illicitly sold you 'impulses' from his card; useful for a short call if you did not have the cash to buy a full card, but more expensive. By 2002 a *kontrabandistë* hovered close to almost every public telephone in Tirana ready to sell you impulses.

Sitting with telecom worker friends at the telephone exchange provided some insight into the emigration situation. In 1994 there were constant calls to Greece, and on a smaller scale to Italy. In the summer of 1995, there were far fewer calls to Greece, a large number of the illegal immigrants having been rounded up and sent back across the border. In 1996, calls to Greece were frequent again. Telephone conversations had to be held publicly, the individual booths having been vandalised along with much else early on. There was something very poignant in the way the Greek-speaking Albanian *gastarbeiter* would politely ask to speak to so and so, an *Alvanos* (an Albanian), knowing as we did from first hand experience the contempt with which many Greeks view Albanians. The very word '*alvanos*' had become a term of abuse equated with 'criminal'. Usually the line was bad, so that conversations had to be held fortissimo. Anxious parents would have to shout their tender enquiries for all to hear and listeners were numerous since so many wanted to ring on very few lines. It was touching listening to the way a village father or mother would keep repeating: 'How are you, are you well, are you all right, are you managing?' when you knew they really wanted details of the absent one's life but were rendered inarticulate by the emotion, the expense, the public situation, or simply native custom, which habitually goes through these enquiries. The worry that the callers patently felt about the absent was saddening because it was not unjustified. Cases of deaths in accidents, disappearances, theft or violence by compatriots or foreign police were sufficiently common to justify anxiety.

We were able to gain further insights into the unreconstructed nature of the public sector through another sister, who was employed by the Centre for Health and Hygiene. Attendance at the centre was very sporadic indeed; not even the physical presence of the kind required at the telephone exchange was necessary for its 27 employees to draw the regular Health and Hygiene salary. A day's work when it occurred involved little more than an hour or two's calling in to see how one's colleagues were. In theory the 27 busied themselves analysing water samples, faeces and dubious restaurant meat, to test for dysentery, giardia and salmonella. There was a deep freeze with some samples in it, but as the Centre no longer had a water supply, nor anything except very antiquated equipment, its work was sheer farce. Part of the building had been privatised and taken over by an entrepreneur in whose office were the necessary chemicals for testing recently acquired Turkish rings and necklaces to determine whether they were really gold or not. This at least gave the 27 Hygiene Centre employees something to do.

The overmanning and inefficiency characteristic of Communism (and non-communist bureaucracies such as Greece's) was no less evident in the public sector administrative jobs as the 1990s advanced. Absenteeism was brazen, and underemployment on the part of those who did turn up was unavoidable because almost nothing worked, and if it did, no-one was responsible for results. It was ironic to recall that '*parazitizëm*' under Communism had not referred to these kind of sinecure jobs, but to the tiny minority who did not do state work. The post-communist politicking involved in securing these jobs closely resembles the situation in Greece where the ambition to '*piastei sto dimosio*' – to grasp state employment as a meal ticket for life – has persisted hardly diminished since the nineteenth century. Many of Albania's politico-economic institutions are not legacies of Communism, but the product of the country's Ottoman and post-Ottoman history, its south-eastern Europe heritage. A member of parliament's power to distribute jobs among his/her voters, the need to bribe the doctor (cf. Greek *fakelo* – envelope) or to oil (Gr. *ladonei*) the lawyer, are some examples of this heritage. There can be few if any contemporary Greeks who have undergone an operation without first handing over a very substantial sum of money (the *fakelo*) to the doctor.

Another state institution we were able to study at close hand was the state schoolbook shop, run by the daughter-in-law of the family. This was interesting for rather different reasons. Again the job involved underemployment, in this case for three-quarters of the year since the main period of activity was limited to two or three months at the most – preparation for school opening and distribution of books at the beginning of the school year. Quite a lot of the schoolbooks I was able to peruse reflected a stimulating approach to teaching; an approach echoed in the methods of many of the teachers I listened to, particularly those of the older teachers. Access to the newly published books also gave one the chance to follow ideological changes as prepared for pupils' consumption. For example, in 1995, when the Democrat Party was in power, it emerged that the newly rewritten history text book for the final year of secondary school presented the members of the nationalist movement of the late 1930s and early 1940s, the Balli Kombëtar, as national heroes. Their exploits were dwelt on admiringly and for several pages, while E. Hoxha (sic) got one page; a minimalism which, given Hoxha's role from the 1940s till his death in 1985, looked a bit biased. In 1999, when the Socialist Party was in power, the history text had changed again.

Another source of interest, or rather concern, was the changing price of schoolbooks and its impact on parents. In 1995, the prices of the new books for the coming year had risen by 200 per cent. In the 60 eight-year schools of Mirdita a lot of families were unable to pay these prices. Perhaps it was no coincidence that for certain age groups only half the necessary books had been printed. Or perhaps the government was hoping that the trend to move down from the mountain villages would obviate the need for schools in some areas of Mirdita. Though the 1995 price rise put books beyond the reasonable reach of unemployed villagers who were the majority, yet villagers made huge sacrifices rather than deprive their children of the chance to learn. This was all the sadder given the demoralised state of most of the village schools, where dedicated or qualified or competent teachers were increasingly rare. Various scams were open to the unscrupulous initially; for instance, a teacher could come down from a mountain village, acquire a number of books at state prices and then sell them to pupils for more. Canny parents realising this, would come down themselves, but at the cost of the not insignificant bus fare.

The inefficiency of the still centralised but partially liberalised management was noteworthy. Each autumn, stocks sent by the Ministry of Education were insufficient to provide books for all. Each September saw some of the textbooks arrive late, often weeks after school had started. Some schools went without the books for certain age groups or subjects for a year at a time. The Ministry of Education always had an excuse for the delay – the paper shortage, absence of cash to pay the publishers, the unpunctual Italian publishing house, the recent privatisation of banks, the Kosova crisis. This combination of negligence, poor organisation, late-starting projects, ensured that education was not equally available to all, even to those who could afford to buy the books.[3] In 1999, the state schoolbook shops, while still being managed centrally, became semi-independent enterprises such that individual bookshop managers could make a profit if they distributed the books efficiently. This was a more complex job than might appear. If the books delivered to the schools were handed over to the pupils and paid for, the money had to be transported back to a bank with all the risks of being waylaid and robbed that this involved. Even if one cleverly managed to get the money delivered by some other means, the highwaymen might shoot one before realising that the money was elsewhere. Furthermore, not all the pupils could pay at once for the books; should one take unpaid books back or risk leaving them at the school? Teachers who in the past had paid for books pending repayment by parents, had lost money too often to repeat this solution. In September 2000, contradictory notices appeared simultaneously in the newspapers; one proclaimed that books could now be bought at the central store and the provincial shops; the other advised that books would not be obtainable until school opening when they would be distributed by head teachers. The confusion for parents, teachers and bookstore managers was par for the course.

Local government administration, the town hall offices, political parties' offices, the hospital and the schools were further sources of state jobs. The hospital staff of over 30 doctors seemed at first glance disproportionately large given the size of Rrëshen's population. In fact, the staff catered for the whole province of 54,000, since there were no longer any doctors in posts outside the town. The team included a heart surgeon, several gynaecologists, general surgeons, a pathologist and a psychiatric specialist. Clinics in the smaller administrative centres might have a dentist (increasingly unlikely towards the end of the 1990s when most would have settled in Rrëshen) and some nurses for minor emergencies. But it was Rrëshen hospital that dealt with most cases from all over the province. Many patients until the end of the 1990s would be sent on from Rrëshen to Tirana because even the most basic equipment was lacking. One missionary group had set out to refurbish the hospital, but this well-meant undertaking ultimately consisted of little more than a lick of paint here and there. A donation of beds had ironically led in 1996 to having to close the front entrance of the hospital so as to provide storage space behind the doors for the unused beds. The beds were not needed because the absence of almost all medical apparatus such as an Eko, for example, meant that many of the patients could only be treated in Tirana. A certain amount of 'junk aid' such as diabetes measures missing the vital testing paper, reminded one of the miscellaneous school books and computers without instruction manuals received by schools in Tirana.

Rrëshen has two eight-year schools and a middle school, *Shkollë e Mesme*, for 14 to 18 year olds. The conditions: glasslessness, cheerlessness and run down draughty corridors with cold class-rooms, were to be expected. In freezing temperatures everyone wore as much as possible under winter coats. Teachers were earning $40 a month in 1995, and none had contracts. There were talks of strikes to gain a 35 per cent wage increase, but the risks of being replaced by a less qualified, less demanding teacher were usually felt to be too big, though once or twice a strike went ahead with limited success.

On several occasions in the early 1990s when I was spending a day in a school, a dozen or so teachers would get together for brainstorming sessions in which their informedness about re-mote ex-imperialist islands such as England amazed me. They fired questions at me like: 'How is England managing its overaged demographic problem? What about pensions? What is the nub of the Irish problem? What are the obstacles to resolving it?' We discussed the pros and cons of capitalism and socialism, the pitfalls of full blown deregulation, teaching methods, ideologies. They asked what ideology we had in England, and I told them that people in England do not even know that they have ideology, have not been brought up with the concept; but that of course there is ideology in consumerism, in advertising, in history books. They thought it was extraordinarily naive to be so unconscious of influential ideologies.

During the 1990s many teachers from Mirdita (as from all over Albania) moved abroad, unable to cover family expenses on their salaries. A Ministry of Education report estimated that at least 5,000 teachers had left the country by 1994. Women teachers clean houses in Greece; male teachers do manual work in order to save money to educate their children in the future, or to buy a flat in Tirana so that their children can attend school in the capital, where the standard of teaching may be higher.

Non-productivity and parasitism, as one might have expected in view of past full employment goals, were endemic, not only as demonstrated by absenteeism and underemployment in state jobs, but also as exemplified in the attitude to state provision of, for example, benefits and electricity. Many of those state employees who in fact lived at home, claimed to live on their own in order to pay less tax; students claimed to be separated from their parents so that the State paid the university fees; people who were actually working in private sector jobs claimed unemployment benefit. Many of those registered as homeless (*pastrehur*) lived with their parents; many of those registered as living in Rrëshen for voting purposes, actually lived in villages. Almost every Rrëshen household manipulated their electricity meter. Petty corruption was, of course, widespread under Communism, but the nature of the dictatorship meant that it took a different form. *Miqësia* (cf Greek *meson*, German *beziehungen*, connections) was an institution of major importance for obtaining, for example, favours from bureaucrats, but it was not a cash-based system. A person able to procure one a desired job in a hospital or office might be given scarce goods in exchange. Who one helped or sought help from was based largely on kinship links – blood, affinal, fictive or friendship. Post-communist *miqësia* has an added dimension arising from the new centrality of money. It is now a question whether your *mik* (friend) on the housing commission might not be tempted to support your rival if he or she has offered a large sum of money. Getting a loan (*kredit*) in the 1990s from the state bank involved handing over a substantial percentage to the official arranging the loan. Simply to initiate a court case one had to bribe the judge. Clerical workers offered no service without *ryshfet* (a bribe). Some school and university teachers could be bribed and exam passes could be bought. By handing certain LEA personnel officers a sum of 70 dollars, a teacher leaving his/her job to seek work abroad could secure the stamped document that would produce a year's unemployment pay. Officials in high positions might accept bribes in exchange for not dismissing incompetent and/or dishonest heads of municipal departments.

Private Enterprise

Private enterprise was extremely limited. The state shops were sold off in 1991, and in most cases bought by their managers. These acquired the shops at very low prices, which gave them a head start. At this period driving schools were amongst the commonest types of business to be set up all over Albania. Since private cars had been banned under Communism, only professional drivers had licenses. As soon as Communism ended there was a rush to learn to drive accompanied by a rush to open a driving school. Some of the schools were scams where licenses could be bought by the unqualified, but many were genuine, and over-supply led to early bankruptcy for a large number. One in Rrëshen continued to flourish long after most had closed down chiefly because its owner, a mechanical engineer in his late twenties, was a shrewd businessman who not only understood the technical side of his business, but was also scrupulous. He had originally tried to secure a state loan with which to buy a bus. The loan was refused but he eventually succeeded in getting a loan to open a driving school. He enlisted 16 pupils and with the proceeds bought a car; with the next 16 he was able to buy a second car. His instructors were former official communist drivers. With the early profits from the driving school he bought a lorry for transporting wood from Fier in central Albania to Saranda on the west coast; each delivery brought a profit of about $200. With the profits and a state loan he was able to buy a flat in Rrëshen where he installed himself and several of his adult siblings. In 1993 he opened a *gomisteri* (for repairing car tyres) in Rrëshen. For several months his lorry lay idle for lack of a spare part; unobtainability of spare parts was the bane of the early post-communist years. In 1995, he expanded his business to a repairs and spare parts workshop for cars and lorries. His long-term strategy was to build up a number of small safe enterprises, which guaranteed a regular income. Part of his success lay in the treatment of his employees, few of whom, significantly, were related to him either by blood or fictive links. In 1995 he paid his chief mechanic $100 a month, considerably higher than the average salary of $50–60 a month. Workers could thus be depended on, making it possible to guarantee repairs for six months. After the first year, instead of being paid a fixed salary, the employees were paid according to the monthly turnover. Even though this might range from $30 to over $100, the average continued to be above $60 monthly.

In 1994 there were two Rrëshenites who were earning by walking round the streets with Polaroid cameras offering to take photographs of passersby. This was a common profession in a country where there were still very few camera owners. The younger of the photographers, a man in his early 20s, officially worked in the employment department of the town hall. But he rarely went in to work except to pick up his $40 monthly salary paid fortnightly. As he said, anyone who worked in a private capacity could earn much more than a state employee. His income from photography fluctuated considerably, he admitted, but he could often make $200 a month. At one point he acted as interpreter for an Italian sociologist. This eventually brought him the greatest reward of all in the form of a job as a park gardener in Rome, and ultimately legal immigrant status.

By 1995, there was a small furniture workshop and a milk supply business, which imported milk from the northern area of Bushat, Shkodër. There were now two private bakeries though the state bread factory continued to operate for another year. In 1995 there was also a mass bid for commercial success in the form of *bilardo*, snooker halls. Some were opened by people who had decided to re-place their failing cafes or shops with *bilardo*; some by new aspirants to business. *Bilardo* proliferated until there were so many that none could make much of a profit. The following year, 1996, brought variation in the form of bingo halls that, like *bilardo*, started open-ing in large numbers. Another increasingly popular way to eke out or supplement a living was videoing weddings and funerals, even birthday parties. Very few video-makers were at all skilled but de-mand was big and largely uncritical, while at $60 a wedding, the video-camera owner was doing good business in the high season – late summer and early autumn. Weddings and funerals provided the only opportunities for socialising, and hence were occasions for very large gatherings and extravagant expenditure.

The animals that roamed the streets, mainly cows and pigs, were a source of income to quite a lot of flat dwellers who kept their animals at night in makeshift shelters near their apartment blocks. The animals fed off the large quantities of rubbish lying around the streets and grazed from the open containers or areas set aside for rubbish. The cows were kept mainly for the owners' dairy needs rather than for commercial purposes. But where a family had several pigs these would eventually be sold. Ironically, a Rrëshen woman who had been living in Italy since 1997 commented during a visit home in 1999: 'All these animals that the incoming villagers have brought with them; the place is beginning to look like a village.'

'You've forgotten,' her brother told her, 'There have been animals in the streets since 1991.'

Private pharmacies began to open in 1994, but other specialised services like private dentists and hairdressers for women did not appear till later because the capital outlay necessary for equipment was difficult to raise. The first hairdresser set up in a kiosk in 1996 and did very good business right from the start. The same year a jewellery shop opened, as did some kiosks and shops selling new clothes from Turkey. It was hard to see who would be able to afford to patronise these shops, given that from 1995 debt had started to become a widespread problem – debt to food shops and on state loan repayments. The people who had got off right at the start to enterprises such as grocery shops, driving schools and cafes were solvent but certainly not flush with spending money. Anyone benefiting from a pyramid scheme was probably going to spend the money on an apartment or moving away. Those in local government who had siphoned off funds designated for municipal water systems and road improvement into villas on the coast had already moved away; it was not long before the jewellery shop and most of the clothes shops had to close down for lack of clients.

Illegal enterprises included growing marijuana in the case of some villages near Rrëshen, selling timber without a licence, and managing prostitution rings, initially in Italy. To set up as a pimp one started probably with a friend, by taking a couple of girls, perhaps fiancées, to Italy, crossing by one of the infamous *motoskafe*. Once in a big city, one would rent a flat and settle there with the girls. During the first month the young men would arrange for their girl friends to mingle with girls who were already prostitutes in the hopes that they would fall easily into the required way of life. Sometimes getting the girls to start work as prostitutes took a certain amount of '*presion*', though many pimps would deny keeping on girls under duress. Perhaps this is true in some cases. Gradually the young men would build up a larger number of girls. A girl would be expected to have at least 20 clients a night and, depending on the area, this could bring in an income of $1,000 nightly. One pimp, asked what percentage of the takings the girls got, said their expenses and demands were very modest; the pimps, in other words, took the lion's share. If a girl earned enough money and returned home, as some did, she told her family that she had washed dishes, and the parents would pretend to believe this. Some parents early on did believe this to be the truth.

After some time in Italy, during which time there might be fights between pimps over street rights or exchanges of girls, a pimp might decide to move to new ground in search of greater profits, less risk, different laws. For instance, in the Czech Republic brothels are legal. Here it might be possible to arrange with a brothel owner to take over some sex workers and transfer business to Holland where profits would be still greater. There, with bought falsified papers one could work 'legally'.

One problem facing successful pimps was how to launder surplus money once they had built new houses for themselves and their families, and acquired some smart cars. In 1996, if unwise, they could 'invest' money in a pyramid scheme. A safer alternative was to keep it under the mattress. Some pimps claimed to be worried about their souls (as well as *opinion*) and resolved to turn their backs on this dishonourable work '*punëtë pandershme*' after a certain age.

A Mirditan friend who lived in Italy thanks to an arranged marriage to an Italian widow, told me of a young Albanian woman she had recently met on the Bari-Durrës ferry boat. This woman was married with a child, and she and her husband had worked in Italy for four years. Despite working very hard indeed they had been able to save virtually nothing. Finally, with the agreement of her husband, she had spent the last year working as a prostitute. In this year she had earned more than in the previous four, and the family was at last able to return to Albania to buy a flat and settle down.

In subsequent conversations with friends I tried to find out who, in an area where a girl's honour was so carefully guarded, would consider prostitution. Not that there are no cases of forced abduction, but these are comparatively rare. More often a young man would get to know a girl and persuade her that he could find her work in Italy. There were cases where the girl and her parents genuinely believed that a proposed marriage was not just a cover-up for getting the girl to work for a pimp. But there were also cases where girls had gone with the aim of working as prostitutes. These girls tended to come from homes where poverty was combined with an impossible parent, or where the girl had been abused by a stepfather. But in some cases it was simply the living conditions that were intolerable. In one case the entire family lived in one windowless room. In another, the family was technically homeless and squatting in part of a former factory. There were a few cases where a girl had a deformity, which had resulted in a sense of inferiority such that escape of any kind seemed desirable. Over the decade it became more usual to hear of girls who had been prostitutes returning to Albania. Return was now less likely to be the social death it had initially been.

Religion

When we first started living in Rrëshen, locals reasonably enough assumed we were missionaries. No other foreigners except a peace corps member had ever stayed in the town, while the variety and the number of missionising groups were considerable. Apart from two different Catholic groups, there were Bahai, Seventh Day Adventists, Mormons, Lightforce Evangelists and several other evangelical groups, some American, some Swedish. But there was not the run on religion that some of the missionaries seemed to have anticipated. Atheism apparently sat rather comfortably on Mirditans for all they were traditionally Roman Catholic. They liked the definitive identity that being Albania's Roman Catholic minority conferred, but were unenthusiastic about today's brand of Catholicism. Even those who did feel nostalgic for the old form were not attracted by the contemporary version. As for the other brands of religion, Rrëshenites used to ask us why religion was so often purveyed by people who appeared to them either as ridiculous or physically disadvantaged. It was true that an unlikely proportion of English evangelical groups wore thick glasses, had pasty faces, funny clothes and gangly walks. It was also true that the small motley groups of limp English or more energetic American cheerleading types looked absurd as they interspersed sermonising in the central square with campfire type ditties. A few mocking kids and passers-by would hover for a bit. No-one paid any more attention than Cambridge shoppers do when oddball preachers start up in Market Square. I asked some of the groups calling themselves Christian why they had come to an area which was already Christian to missionise. Did they even know that Mirdita was a Catholic area? Why did they exhort Mirditans to turn to Christianity in their speeches? It was impossible to get the missionaries even to engage with the question. Some of the organisers of the longest stay groups were actually there for business purposes though most of the recruits were unaware of this. One Rrëshen cafe owner was unable to resist playing a joke on a fervent Adventist, taking him to see the supposed ruins of an ancient Adventist church, which he pretended had been found just above a village to the north of Rrëshen. The Adventist was immensely excited by the discovery and wrote home to inform the parent church.

On one occasion, returning to Tirana from Fang in 1993, Soula and I were astonished to find three foreigners sitting in front of us in the bus. We listened to their conversation for a bit and just as we were wondering what they were, were struck from above by 'God's Gift to Mankind' printed in Warwick, England, as a large pile of religious pamphlets fell out of the luggage rack on to our heads. We found this so hysterically funny that it was some time before we could get a sufficient grip on ourselves to collect up the literature and hand it over to the missionaries.

Missionaries seemed to have enjoyed more success with Mirditans from Manati, a coastal area of Lezhë. A friend's teenage cousin told us that they were regularly visited by German and black Brazilian evangelists who wanted them to become Christians.' 'But you're Catholics, you *are* Christians,' I said. 'No, they say that we're *Krishteje*, not *Krishtiane* like them, because we worship in churches and have saints. Christians only believe in Jesus. They are very good people,' she went on, 'they have given one of my brothers a scholarship to study Jesus for nine months in Tirana.'

The following year in Rrëshen there was an American group called, *Jeta e Re*, New Life, which spent a lot of time taking off and landing a helicopter in the area. I spoke to the Albanian interpreter, a realistic young man, who said that the missionaries succeeded best where they had the most to offer materially. In Korça in the south-east, for example, where the Greek Orthodox Church was active helping locals materially, this evangelical group had not made many converts. Their biggest difficulties were getting aid through the Albanian customs where bribes were insisted on. Indeed, he claimed that the largest part of aid had been sold by customs personnel on the open market. I asked what lay behind the helicopter's constant activity; were they, as rumoured, dropping aid on all the surrounding villages? No, they were taking their Jesus film and showing it to villagers. He said that they had repaired two village schools, but that when they had got all the materials ready to repair the school in one highland village, the Catholic Church had angrily ordered them off and done the repairs themselves. At this point in our conversation he had to go as the helicopter was once again about to take off. An American photographer was the last to get in and, keeping his door open, was leaning precariously out while filming the town below. One could imagine the voice-over back home: 'This shabby litter-strewn li'l ole communist town wasn't as ready for Jesus as much as some of these li'l ole isolated villages.' Not that we had ever been to a village where a helicopter-borne Jesus film had landed, so the actual impact was anybody's guess.

The Catholic impact was slightly different. Firstly it was official, and representative of the region's faith. It had the backing, financial and spiritual, of the Vatican, and was a source of concrete advantages such as a kindergarten and medical supplies. The attitude of the priest at the Easter service in Orosh, recounted above, was unfortunately characteristic of the Catholic presence in Mirdita – authoritarian and intolerant. At the Orosh mass that spring, I had been asked by one of the priests to take some photographs after his film had run out. This provided me with an excuse to pay a visit to the Catholic headquarters shortly after we had set up base in Rrëshen. The building where the Catholic mission was installed had previously been the reception centre for visiting Communist Party officials, including occasionally Enver Hoxha himself. One side of the three storey building had been turned into a church. The rest housed the nuns and priests running the mission. There were five or six of them, mainly Italian, though one nun was a Kosovan who had lived in Belgrade. On the occasion of our visit we had to call for a long time before anyone heard us. The doors and windows were barred, giving the impression more of a fortress than a drop-in centre for the faithful. Talking to the nun who eventually let us in we understood why. Her horror stories of the local population, its depravity, thieving tendency, number of mental problems, level of drunkenness, violence and unwillingness to follow the straight and narrow path of reason and righteousness, had closed, she told us, the initially open doors of the mission.

It was hard to see how the mission would ever be able to sow the seeds of righteousness given the extent of its members' distaste for the locals. However, notwithstanding a measure of hostility, some Mirditan intellectuals were initially rather drawn to Catholicism. They felt the need for a faith, particularly one as closely associated with Mirditan heritage, to replace Marxism-Leninism. The Catholic Church, as an institution with an established ethic and a long history, could supply a much needed stabilising influence, they felt. Gradually though, the hierarchical nature and authoritarianism of the clergy they met at first hand cooled their early enthusiasm. A friend, an intellectual (in the English sense), a teacher, researcher and poet, was at first very enthused by what he felt the church had to offer. He went to see the priests several years after their arrival in Rrëshen to ask their opinion as to his conclusions after serious thought on religious matters. He told them that he believed in God but that he wanted to take whatever seemed good from the various Christian denominations of which he had now gained some knowledge. The priests, unsurprisingly, completely rejected his ecumenism, insisting on strict acceptance of Catholic dogma and nothing else. 'In that case,' said our friend, 'I won't be coming to your church.' Disillusionment was complete when it became clear that the Catholic Church was only prepared to help Mirditans who were practising Catholics. The clerics refused to cooperate with non-religious aid organisations, which were helping locals to establish improved educational and sports facilities in the province. Cooperation, which would have halved the expense and doubled the numbers benefiting, was not forthcoming. They would support the minds and bodies only of those whose souls were already in their keeping. Older women who had tried the church before rejecting it disliked the authoritarianism of the Italian priests, who were liable to give sharp autocratic orders as to expected behaviour in church, mid-service. The fact that there were as yet no Albanian priests to officiate was another disadvantage.

In 1999, Mirditan Catholicism took on a new dimension. Some thought that Catholicism might be one key to economic and regional development. At the individual level this meant that a professional painter started to paint religious pictures having realised that the Catholic Mission was the most likely buyer for his work. At the national political level, Catholic ethnicity could provide a very acceptable bridge to a European cultural identity. At the provincial level, this regional advantage might be the way forward to win funding not otherwise forthcoming for educational and cultural development. The school founded by Abbot Preng Doçi in 1899 in Grykë Orosh, the second earliest school in Albania, was due to celebrate its hundredth anniversary in the autumn of 1999. Grykë Orosh is a roadless village, very difficult to access and fast losing its population as a result. Funds were found with difficulty for the renovation and refurbishment of the building, its symbolic cachet justifying expenditure despite imminent closure as the local population left for the plains. The day of celebration had to be delayed several times as work did not progress fast enough, partly due to shortage of funds. But finally, on 11 November, preparations complete, the President, the Minister of Education and a team of television cameramen were helicoptered on to a small patch of level ground in front of the school. Speeches were made, a beautifully trained choir of local children sang, and then the distinguished visitors were helicoptered down to Reps, where a ceremonial lunch was held with more speeches concluding this brief day of glory for Orosh.

At a conference held in June 1999 at the Slavonic School of Studies, an English contributor mentioned in his paper that 70 per cent of Albanians are Muslims. A well-known Tiranian intellectual in the audience demanded to know what he meant by this. The speaker looked nonplussed. The point the questioner wanted to make, as I understand it, was that while 70 per cent of the population might be nominally Muslim in as much as their names are Muslim and their funeral celebrations may follow a traditional Muslim pattern, 70 per cent of the population is not Muslim in terms of religious belief. In fact, it is completely misleading to speak of Albanians as mainly Muslim. In my own experience, while plenty of Albanians, if asked, would say they believe there is a God, none that I have met to date associate God with a particular sect or denomination. Moreover, a large number of Albanians are declared atheists. In what was perhaps a further attempt to communicate to Europe that Islam is not a cultural characteristic of Albanian life, an international conference was held in Tirana in the same month entitled *Krishtërimi në Shqipëri* – Christianity in Albania. This was attended on the first day by the President, and on subsequent days by most of Mirdita's LEA, as well as several teachers and the head of Orosh district.

In many respects the picture I have drawn of Rrëshen is representative of numerous small provincial Albanian towns at this period. High unemployment, nearly zero productivity, parasitic public sector jobs, petty commerce, these are typical characteristics of such towns. Geertz's 'agitated stagnancy' conveys the scene. An Albanian might say of such town life: '*Ecim, por jo përpara*', we are moving (walking) but not forwards.

Chapter Thirteen

RRËSHEN: LIFE AND DEATH AND THE BREAKDOWN OF LAW AND ORDER

Town Dwellers

Whether staying in Rrëshen for one month or six, we rarely stayed in the same flat. This meant that we got to know different parts of the town intimately, and met a wide variety of flat-owning families. Each had a very different lifestyle and varying strategies for generating income in addition to renting out their flat. In the spring of 1995 we stayed in a flat belonging to five sisters who had been orphaned in their teens. Two were married and living in Italy. The two youngest were staying with the eldest who was married in Rrëshen. The younger had been to ballet school during the Communist period. She was a talented dancer who often performed with the Mirdita folklore group on its tours abroad. But her eldest sister and brother-in-law were trying to dissuade her from this career. To get on in this capitalist world, they kept telling her, she would be much better off studying accountancy. Ira, the sister who was in charge of us and the flat, was a sports teacher at the school nearby and a member of the Rrëshen volleyball team. Surprisingly, given the disastrous state of communications and infrastructure generally, volleyball teams were still competing with each other round the country. The buildings where the players were put up on their visits to other towns were in an appalling state of disrepair, Ira told us. But the fact that these events could take place at all struck me as a positive sign; a sign that there was still some institution able to overcome the current obstacles to organisation and coordination. We went to watch a return match when Gjirokastër came to play Rrëshen. Large numbers of Rrëshenites were gathered to watch. Occasions for community involvement other than political rallies were very rare and the spectators were obviously relishing this opportunity.

Ira was engaged to a young man from Rrëshen who was working in northern Italy, where she was due to join him at the end of the school year. She told us how hard it had been for orphaned sisters to manage without a brother. One of the sisters living in Italy was married to a Kosovar. Through him the family had met other Kosovars, one of whom became Ira's blood-brother. He was a nice young man, and it was a help to the unmarried sisters to finally have a brother. But one day he scandalised Ira by asking her to marry him. Marrying a person with whom you have drunk blood is to break a sacred law and absolutely unacceptable. The Kanun is very clear on this.[1]

To drink blood – *pi gjak* – was not the outdated institution I had at first imagined. As already related we had come across several instances. Most recently we had discovered that an 18-year-old friend of ours was the blood-sister of a young man from a family of seven brothers and one sister who were now emigrants in Italy. The shortage of sisters in his family was one reason for redressing the imbalance through blood brotherhood. She and the young man corresponded regularly, with the knowledge of her parents, this being an acceptable relationship precisely because there could be no question of marriage. It seems unlikely that the pre-communist Kanun would have considered the possibility of a man and a woman linking themselves in this way, though the male and female offspring of two men linked through blood brotherhood could have mingled freely as a result of the ban on marriage.

Religion, as already indicated, had arrived in Rrëshen in a variety of forms, and Ira was trying them all out. She regularly attended the meetings held by a group of American Evangelists from Tirana who visited Rrëshen each week. They made religion much more accessible than the over-authoritarian Roman Catholics, she said, providing a friendly venue where young people could get together. She also thought well of the Seventh Day Adventists based at the time in Rrëshen, though they might not have approved of her faith in the occurrence of miracles at the Laç pilgrims' church, nor of her feelings towards the Italian Madonna currently in the news for crying tears of blood.

March and April that year were very cold and Ira had told us to use the electric radiator as much as we liked. As a result of the cold snap and an overloaded system there were fairly frequent power cuts, but at other times we were to turn the radiator up as high as we liked. This open-handedness was cost-free since the electricity meter in the flat, as in 99 per cent of flats it emerged, was manipulated so as to record nothing. To guard against detection by the meter reader, a string was cunningly attached to an obstruction that immobilised the hand on the dial. As soon as the meter reader's voice was heard in the building, you pulled the string and threw open the door with a welcoming smile. What happened in our case was that Soula opened the door and, on realising who had knocked, exclaimed: 'Just a moment, I'll get my mother,' closing the door in the meter reader's face and pulling the string. It was one of Soula's great moments. Not, of course, that the meter reader can have been fooled for a second. Later he asked Ira how come the foreigners used so little electricity and she explained that we spent most of our time in the highland villages. I was not at all surprised to read in the papers some months later that Albania was about to invest in a new type of tamper-proof meter imported from Switzerland. Not that this step was ever carried out on a big scale; probably the capital outlay required would have been too big. Numerous attempts of different kinds were made to solve the problem of unpaid for electricity, the most successful being a fixed charge whereby each flat dweller paid a monthly sum regardless of quantity used. Even this did not solve the problem of those who simply defaulted on payments.

Funerals

One night while staying in Ira's flat, we heard a constant tramping up and down the stairs which continued throughout the night and on into the morning. It turned out that the grandmother in one of the top floor flats had died in the night, aged 103. She had been active right up to the last. As soon as a death occurs, certain people close to the family must be alerted to come and help with preparing and dressing the body, to sit with the corpse, and generally provide moral support and practical help. After this initial stage, the household is ready to receive mourners. The ceremonial visits take place throughout the day and constitute the *mort*, the principal part of the funeral rites. No religious clerics are involved in any part of the rites either at home or in the graveyard. I went to the *mort* with a friend of the grandmother's family. In the centre of the far end of one of the rooms the grandmother's body was laid out on a divan. The mourners sat on chairs ranged round three sides of the room. Only women sit in the room with the body; male visitors are received in another room. On entering the flat a woman shakes hands with the male representatives of the family before entering the room where the body is. To each person one says a formulaic phrase of consolation such as '*shëndosh edhe të tjeret*' (good health to the rest). In the room where the body is laid out, one proceeds first to pay one's respect to the dead person, kissing the face if one is a near acquaintance. One then shakes hands with the chief mourners, the closest relations, who are seated nearest to the body. After sitting down, the newly arrived guest is handed a coffee. Having drunk the coffee, the guest returns the cup after placing an appropriate sum of money inside it. The size of the donation depends on the closeness of one's ties with the bereaved family. Funeral expenses are great and include supplying large numbers of guests with coffee, sugar, raki and cigarettes. Relations who have come from a distance may well be staying with the bereaved family, an additional expense.

The grandmother was dressed, as is customary, in Mirditor costume. The costume had the traditional blood red embroidered motifs on a white felted wool background with exceptionally beautiful embroidery on the outer coat sleeves extending right down to the wrists. As we handed back our cups, the *vajtuese* (lament singers) on our left began to sing a lament in which they enumerated the qualities of the dead woman as wife and mother, recalling incidents from her life. They were led by a woman known for her voice and improvising talent. (*Vajtuese* in Mirdita, however well known for their talents, are not professionals in the sense of being paid.) Each verse concluded with a refrain that was taken up by the closest relations who were sitting across the room from the singers. When not echoing the refrain they sobbed aloud. At intervals of 15 minutes or so, visiting mourners would get up and take their leave to be replaced by newcomers. The leading lament singers would be followed by others, more or less talented, throughout the day. The next morning the body was taken down to the open area in front of the block of flats where more Rrëshenites came to pay their last respects and laments were again sung. In this case the grandmother was taken to be buried in her village. Someone who had spent most of their life in Rrëshen would be taken to the Rrëshen graveyard, a kilometre outside the town, accompanied by the mourners walking in procession. At the graveyard, once the grave has been closed, artificial flowers, cigarettes and sometimes money are strewn on the grave. On leaving a graveyard one washes one's hands by the entrance. In the past one washed one's hands in the first river one came to after leaving the graveyard, throwing one's hands three times behind one's back to rid oneself of the graveyard's bad luck.

A tour round Rrëshen's cemetery with a friend to recount the histories of the dead, showed that despite illusions fed by nostalgia, accidental death albeit from different causes (private cars were banned and guns did not circulate freely), was by no means rare in Hoxha's time. The graveyard was strikingly full of young people who had died in factory and mine accidents or by electrocution, as well as of young children killed by falling from upper storey windows or poisoned by contaminated food. The lack of safeguards at work had been graphically illustrated at the Reps copper refinery. And I had met at least half a dozen men who had developed fatal illnesses through working in mines such as the one at Thirra. Today death by electrocution is still common, as is death through gas poisoning in wells.

Discussing the grandmother's costume later with Tom, the musician and head of the Palace of Culture, Tom had wrung his hands at the thought of all these beautiful works of art now mouldering underground. Village women are always buried in Mirditor costume, as are women who have only recently moved to the town. Town women usually have a smart suit laid by for their burial, as do men. But if an unmarried girl dies she is dressed as a bride.[2] An unmarried girl of 32 had died some months before of cancer. One of her brothers, who was working in Italy, brought back a wedding dress of the type specially made for the burial of unmarried girls. The whole of Rrëshen, we were told, attended the funeral, moved by the tragedy of someone everyone had known and liked dying so young. A video was made of the whole procedure, lament singing and burial. For those who can afford it, videoing funerals is as desirable as the videoing of weddings. For those who cannot afford it, photographs of the dead person have to suffice.

A ten-year-old girl who had drowned close to Shëngjin beach while trying to retrieve a ball from the sea was also buried as a bride (she was tall for her age) with lipstick and bridal dress. The logic is that to die unmarried is to die before having fulfilled one's prime role in life. This way the dead person is fulfilled at least in death. This was a particularly poignant case in that, though all the relatives had been at the beach, the paternal grandparents blamed the mother for the tragedy and forbade her to cry at the funeral. The wretched mother wanted her child to be buried in the Rrëshen graveyard so that she could go often to visit the grave. But the grandparents insisted on taking the child to the village graveyard.

At the *mort* in the yard in front of the flat of a 52-year-old vet who had suffered for six months from an undiagnosed illness, one lament singer sang:

> Here's a man who after a life of sacrifice put four of his children into higher education. And now he's well off as his children have in turn enriched him. [Several were earning in Italy.] Now he has two suits at last but has died without the enjoyment of wearing them.

The wife started to cry but her parents-in-law peremptorily hushed her: 'Aren't you ashamed, you can't cry for your husband.' The Kanun has strict guidelines for funeral behaviour though this one is not mentioned in Gjecov's collection which only states that 'men do not lament over women except in the case of a son over his mother or a brother over his sister' (Fox, 1989:218).

Presumably, the ban on crying for your spouse (if indeed there really was one) is dictated by the same rationale as the non-use by a married couple of each other's first name. Namely, that any sign of intimacy is a reminder of sexual relations which, while unfortunately necessary for the production of heirs, are a taboo subject. Hasluck attributes the fact that it was not done for spouses to be seen much in each other's company to a belief, dating back to at least St Paul, that celibacy is seen as superior to marriage throughout the Near East (1954:31). But I doubt that celibacy can be an issue in a clan-based society where the main object of marriage is to produce children; where a wife who fails to produce children is usually divorced. It seems more likely that any demonstration of attachment to a wife (who, it will be recalled, must come from a different clan) would be seen as a weakness, which might undermine a man's clan loyalty and honour.

As self-government and feuds escalated with the deterioration of law and order in the 1990s, there were of course more deaths. Quite often an innocent bystander would get killed as well as the intended victim, since the users of machine guns were not always in complete control, or because within a bus it is difficult to be accurate enough. One woman killed accidentally in crossfire in Rrëshen, was a teacher at the school in Bulshar, and the mother of three young children. The not quite three-year old had been holding her hand when she was killed. He and the middle child, a boy of seven, were taken to the bloodstains on the road in Rrëshen where their mother had been shot, and given plastic flowers to lay on the spot. A photograph was taken of them doing this. The little one was already correcting himself when he referred to 'Mummy and Daddy', saying 'I mean Daddy'. It was an extrovert way of dealing with trauma and possibly much better than suppressing it to fester over time. A video was made of the funeral, and visitors coming to the house to condole over the next few weeks could ask to see the video if they had been unable to come to the funeral itself. Although in some cases a bereaved husband makes a promise at the graveyard never to marry again, no promise had been made in this case. A year or so later, a matchmaker introduced a woman in her early 30s who had been divorced by her husband for failing to produce a child. The couple married to everyone's satisfaction and did in fact eventually produce a sibling for the elder children.

A friend in Rrëshen had devotedly and skilfully helped her neighbour to nurse her mother through the last months of her illness. Throughout the funeral up until the burial she sat by the corpse wiping away the dribbling from the mouth – a devoted last service of caring. I was away at the time of the funeral but was asked to watch the video. While we watched, my friends kept up a constant commentary on which visitors had come, who was who and what the laments were like. There was a nice tragi-comic moment when a friend observed that although the mother's face had begun to degenerate quickly, her body had stayed in first class shape and her new suit was '*ultra*' (terrific). I recalled that shocked criticism which readers of Jane Austen's letters tend to make when they come to the enquiry as to how the corpse of a friend's dead baby looked. No-one in countries where death is treated as openly as in Greece or Albania would think it abnormal to ask how the corpse looked.

Funerals and the duty to attend them are one index of the paramountcy of family ties, clan duty and loyalty. The extreme concern expressed at the non-attendance of *deklasuar* relations' funerals has already been mentioned. Today, post-communism, funerals and weddings are almost the only occasions when Mirditans get together. Whether weddings or funerals, these gatherings provide a much appreciated opportunity for exchanging news and conviviality, as well as sympathy and support. A Mirditan friend observed rather impatiently that Albanians positively enjoy death. In response to my equally critical comment that the English virtually deny the existence of death, he exclaimed: 'Oh, what a vital dynamic people who don't think about death at all, but get on with life.'

We returned to Rrëshen in the summer, Ira's flat had been let to some Italian mineralogists. Ira was now married and, having procured a 'false' passport for $1,500, was about to leave for Italy. Our first week was spent living in a room belonging to a nurse from the hospital. Her room was in a condemned building officially unfit for habitation (*pabanueshme*), which had formerly been the dwelling place for unmarried employees from elsewhere appointed to jobs in Rrëshen. You had to be careful where you walked on the first floor landing as there were holes through to the corridor below. Staying here was a reminder that Rrëshen suffered from a housing shortage. Even before the end of Communism there had been a number of *pastrehur* – people without accommodation (literally without 'shelter'). Each room was now inhabited by families from villages who had moved here about five years before under Communism, having got permission to move, *pasasportizimi*, but nowhere else to live. They paid no rent, only the cost of services. This year there were officially 600 *pastrehur* in Rrëshen. There were 100 families who had been stationed in Rrëshen during Communism and were preparing to leave for their towns of origin as soon as they could find a flat. Fifty flats had already been released by such *jabanxhi* – 'foreigners' – and bought by locals. But the influx of villagers and professionals from towns like Kurbnesh far outstripped the exodus, and new building was minimal. During Communism five new apartment blocks were built in Rrëshen annually. Between 1991 and 1995 only two-and-a-half had been built. The railway station offices were now filled with unhoused villagers, as were the former factory offices and every other building, which had been used for cooperative use or now defunct industry.

Our room was directly above a newly opened *Bilardo* – snooker hall. Before we realised this, we would lie awake wondering what the clicking noises were. *Bilardo* were the favourite new enterprise in Rrëshen this year, and a large number had opened, proliferating in the same way that the cafe-bars had. Productive enterprises were virtually non-existent and debt was becoming a widespread problem – debt to food shops and failure to repay state loans. There was also, unsurprisingly, an increase in tradesmen money lenders charging high interest rates. Concern about the growth of corruption was becoming a major preoccupation, while violent incidents, such as shootings, which went unpunished, increasingly undermined any authority the police might have had.

Whether as a consequence of this somewhat demoralised atmosphere or simply that carelessness of life and limb are often a symptom of poverty, the summer seemed to bring with it an unbroken run of disasters. A speeding lorry carrying 50 people from Lari above Dardhaz to the pilgrimage church of Laç turned over on the way down the mountain just above Rrëshen. The passengers had implored the driver to go more slowly but he had some of his brothers with him, who told the passengers to shut up. Every single passenger had head wounds and four were killed. The driver had unfortunately survived and was now in prison. The doctors from Rrëshen hospital said it was like war. A helicopter was flown on to the football field to take the wounded to Tirana.

In the course of the first two weeks after we had arrived disasters within our circle of acquaintance continued to mount up. Two men, one 22, one 42, died in a well accident. A girl of 19 dropped dead from a heart attack at a wedding dance. A 17 year old fell out of a mulberry tree and was killed. A man dynamited his hand off. Yet another young man was killed in a car accident close to Rrëshen. It reminded me of the appalling accident rate amongst the poor in the Colombian coastal town where I had once lived.

From the condemned building we moved to an apartment owned by a man working in Italy. To get to the flat entrance one had to negotiate a mud track and swathes of festering rubbish in which three or four cows were usually scavenging. The state of repair of much of the stairs and the apartment block entrance recalled the worst slum. The extent of the putrid rubbish below covered several blocks. Inside, however, the flats were well cared for. The owner's aim at the time was to earn enough abroad to buy all the flats on this second floor, since they overlooked the square and were ideally positioned he thought for a restaurant. During our stay, one of the flats did come up for sale, as its owners, convinced that Rrëshen was without *perspektivë*, were moving to Lezhë. The price was $5,500 down, or $6,000 in instalments.

In one of these flats lived the fiancée of a man who had been killed the month before as a result of a longstanding quarrel between two families, one from Rrëshen, one from Ndërfushë. The dead man had been a heftily built bouncer who had more than once been in trouble with the police but whose size and strength had ensured the shortest of stays in custody. He had been shot dead while sitting one morning in a Rrëshen cafe. His father had sworn that he would take revenge, initially preferring the perpetrator, but now declaring that any male member would do. 'The government is not lifting a finger to see justice done, so I shall have to carry out justice myself.' A number of efforts were made by go-between peacemakers to negotiate a reconciliation, but without success. As a result, six of the seven Ndërfushë brothers were staying shut up in their houses while the brother who had killed the bouncer was said to be hiding in the mountains or to have escaped to Macedonia. The police had apparently chosen not to involve themselves. In a recent case in Përlat where they had intervened, they had killed an innocent brother mistaking him for the fugitive killer. Now the family of this victim was in blood with the policeman who had made the mistake.

After two months or so of not being able to go to work, the Ndërfushë brothers asked for *besa* ('word of honour', in this case guarantee of a truce) for working hours. This was possible within the varying (i.e. in some places, at some times) past conventions of the Kanun. For instance, *besa* might be asked for several months so that you could get your fields cultivated. In this case *besa* was refused. One ironic aspect of this affair was the reaction of some of the formerly stalwart communist citizens. They complained that the proceedings were not following the dictates of the Kanun correctly. They were actively concerned to make peace between the parties, but if this could not be achieved, they thought the 'correct' rules should be adhered to. For instance, the feud should be limited to the brothers and their families and not involve the whole *fis* (clan). This combination of conservatism with regard to the Kanun and admiration for the communist period was rather common and not seen as anomalous. Like a lot of contemporary cases of feud (and perhaps earlier ones), this one was not at all clear cut. Both sides included some unsavoury characters acting more as part of a gang than as individuals. There were also some perfectly respectable family members. In another case where I became acquainted with some of those involved on both sides, the situation was not much clearer.

A Tirana friend had asked me to deliver some photographs to two families she had visited while interpreting for an English journalist. The families, who were neighbours, were in blood and had provided the journalist with 'good' blood feud copy. As indicated in an earlier chapter, where property has been restored on a hereditary basis, owners of houses built during the cooperative period often face challenges from the owners of the land on which their house stands. There is no law addressing this problem despite the frequent occurrence of such disputes. In this case, the 'foreign' family's house stands less than 200 metres from that of the hereditary landowner, and the two houses share a well. Following an incident at the well in which the head of the hereditary family was insulted by a member of the 'foreign' family, a son of the hereditary family shot dead the 66-year-old father of the 'foreign' family. The dead man's sons were now obliged to dispatch one of the murderer's male kin, the murderer himself being in prison. Imprisonment is not considered a quid pro quo for murder. The fact that the murderer's imprisonment did not put an end to the dispute is significant and highlights the confusion created by the coexistence of the Kanun and state law. While the State imprisoned murderers, it did not deal with the root cause of the land disputes leading to murders; in this case, the problem of houses built during Communism on land now restored to pre-communist owners. Nor did imprisonment deal with the problem of *opinion*, 'what will people think; will people think we are cowards if we don't take the life of a member of the family responsible for killing one of ours?' The feuding families lived in a village of mainly dispersed houses a few kilometres along the Rrëshen-Përlat road. The area is very beautiful, with rolling hills high enough for extensive views but not so steep as to form ravine-like valleys. It was known under Communism as Mirdita's *myzeqea*, a reference to the very extensive and fertile central Albanian area of this name. However, after the fall of Communism, the entire irrigation system on which the area's fertility depended had been destroyed. It was now difficult to cultivate the land. The Catholics had recently built a church here. The inhabitants would have preferred an irrigation system, though obviously this would have been a much more expensive undertaking. Now, as one villager mockingly observed, you could at least go to church and pray for rain. On the way to the feuding families' houses, we met up with one of the murdered man's sons, Bardhok, a man of about 40 who worked for the electricity board. At home we found various relations, the most voluble and forceful of whom was this man's sister-in-law. We sat around drinking coffee, having delivered the photographs, while Bardhok explained that the only targets from next door would be the two brothers of the murderer who were now *ngujuar*, confined to the house. A third brother doing seasonal work in Greece was not considered implicated. The brothers' father, Frrok, went out regularly, but for some reason did not seem to be a serious target. The sister-in-law, Donika, came across as ready to carry out revenge herself, so impassioned was she on the subject, while Bardhok limited himself to tonelessly repeating 'only blood washes out blood'. I asked him about his post-revenge strategy. How, for instance, would his family manage on their own in the claim shanty he had built on the plain near Durrës to which they were planning to move shortly? Well, he said, once he had got it all organised, he would kill, hide in the mountains where the Kanun obliges families to offer protection to fugitives from vendetta, and ensure that his male kin were taken care of. Throughout our visit the television was on in the background as is normal when guests pay visits. But at this point, we all suddenly noticed that Ariana was on. Ariana has made a lot of programmes aimed at stopping blood feuds. 'She's a very good woman,' said Donika, 'I had her as a teacher at school.' 'Yes,' said Bardhok, 'she's done a lot for peacemaking.' I couldn't help laughing. 'If she's that great, why aren't you listening to her advice?' I asked. 'Blood is washed away with blood,' repeated Bardhok mechanically. After an hour or so of lively conversation we got up to go and Donika presented me with a very nice embroidered pillow case she had made.

Soon after this visit, I found out that only Donika's husband and mother-in-law wanted to take revenge. Bardhok and the rest not only planned no revenge, but had not been on speaking terms with their late father for several years, while they *had* been on friendly terms with the other family. For the benefit of '*opinion*' and the public, however, they had to put up a good show. It was a nice example of the complexity of reality as opposed to a good newspaper story.

One day, Frrok, the head of the family whose sons were unable to leave the house, turned up at our flat in Rrëshen, having heard that I had the photographs. He was an incredibly garrulous man in his 60s and had evidently been a devoted party member. He stayed for hours, going off at innumerable conversational tangents. Two of his chief dislikes, it emerged, were Kosovars and homosexuals. He held no particular brief for blood feud or the Kanun, but if invoked, he liked to see the rules stuck to. He had warned the young man killed by the Ndërfushë family two weeks before he had been killed, telling him to go to Greece for a bit. He was shocked that the young man's family had not granted the other family *besa* for the planting season in April. This was bad, and contravened the Kanun. The brother who wanted to take the life of one of his sons was a coward, he said, and was trying to find someone to do the murder for him. Occasionally, suspicious strangers were seen in Prosek, but Frrok always warned them off and ostentatiously photographed them for the subsequent benefit of the police. The other day he had spotted three men checking electricity pylons. The tools under their arms looked from a distance like machine guns, but in the end he reckoned they were genuine pylon checkers. He concluded that after all there were just as bad goings on in the West, what with war in Ireland and drug gangs and so forth. And we agreed that feud with rules was all right, the present problem being the weak state that sometimes interfered and sometimes did not. As he was leaving, I said that I would be in Prosek some time soon and that I might come and visit him. 'Do,' he said without a trace of irony, 'because even if I'm not there, my sons are always at home.' To my surprise, I heard the following summer that in the end Donika's husband had after all decided to kill Frrok. Discussing it with a friend, it seems that Frrok may have deliberately exposed himself since he was older and had therefore less to lose. Alternatively, the other family may have decided to keep things equal by revenging the death of one elderly man by taking the life of another elderly man. A case in another village, where a young man was chosen to be the victim for the killing of an old man, was the subject of disapproval amongst villagers. Moreover, any suggestion that in some way the two sides are not equal as regards losses, risks perpetuation of the feud.

Growing Insecurity

From the summer of 1995 security was being progressively undermined; neither the law of the state nor the Kanun were being observed effectively. A feeling of insecurity was even stronger amongst Socialists after the passing of the so-called Genocide Law that September. Whereas corruption amongst the police and public sector officials led to non-enforcement of the law, the Genocide Law was both arbitrary and draconianly enforced by the Democrat government. Anyone with a relation who had been a prominent communist was banned from all public sector jobs for the next few years. Socialists could no longer apply for loans to set up or expand a business. The final blow came in 1996 with the general election. The campaign had been aggressive. At one election rally in Rrëshen some Berisha campaigners had a dead hare with them that they hung in a prominent position in the square, declaring: 'This is what we're going to do to Fatos Nano (the opposition leader).' A crowd of Democrat supporters, unemployed youths recruited from Mirditan villages, attended with their guns. When election day arrived, voters in Rrëshen included the dead and the emigrated, while some of the living had voted 15 times. Most farcical of all, when the counted votes produced the desired effect of a win for the Democrats in Mirdita, the President asked the victorious Democrat candidate to be so kind as to stand down in favour of the Republican candidate, a member of the Gjomarkaj family who lived in Shkodra. Too many Democrat MPs in Parliament might look like a lack of pluralism! So Mirdita was now represented by a man for whom 1,000 people had voted, less than a 15th of the province's voters, a man who had never lived in the province and was known to almost no-one.

During the period leading up to the election and thereafter, a number of pyramid schemes had begun to make an impact on public consciousness and pockets irrespective of political affiliation. Two of the biggest pyramid schemes held exhibitions in Tirana to promote themselves and accumulate investors. Their chosen venue was the delightfully apposite Pyramid, former museum to Enver Hoxha on the main Bulevard. Here, Silva on the ground floor, Vefa on the floor above, competed to persuade the public to part with their money. Both fairs were immensely successful in attracting millions of lek from a populace indebted and unemployed, convinced that drugs and arms smuggling guaranteed returns on their money. An architect friend, employed to help set up the fairs, was subsequently struck by the pyramid founders' wasteful use of these funds, a large proportion of which they spent on bodyguards, designer suits and shoes.

The month immediately following the election, we stayed at the top of the town where the apartment blocks had been built in the last years of Communism as the town expanded upwards. Our landlady had been married to a villainous man who had spent six years in prison for embezzlement, probably the least harmful of his misdoings. Communist policy was against divorce unless there were political reasons, and a divorce had not been granted to his wife when he came out of prison in the late 1980s. She left, unable to bear the situation any longer. Her husband kept the house and four children while she had to fend for herself. As the eldest of nine children, she had at least the support of her natal family. Up until 1991, she had worked in the Rrëshen laundry, but this had not survived the end of Communism. Her eldest son had escaped across the border to Greece in 1990, where he had been working ever since. Her second son had followed in 1991. Both broke off relations with their father as soon as they were old enough and supported their mother. They had bought this flat with their Greek earnings in 1994. The two daughters who were still minors stayed with the father. One could see their one storey house from one of the windows of their mother's flat. It was rumoured that the father had forced the girls to work as prostitutes in Greece. Three years later I was in Rrëshen when the truth of this rumour was confirmed by the older daughter shooting her father dead. She had finally summoned the courage to free herself and her sister from the life of prostitution he had forced on them. Some weeks after we had moved into this flat in 1996, the younger son, Zef, returned from Greece to prepare for his marriage, which had been arranged in his absence by a go-between, a neighbour of his mother. The bride-to-be came from a nearby village. The first time we met Zef he had just come back from a mammoth session of clothes buying for his prospective bride. He had been working in the north of Greece for the past five years, earning a daily wage of 4,000 drachmas. Over 1,000 dollars of his Greek earnings, a tenth of his savings over five years, had been spent on shoes, makeup, and dresses for the bride. Given the average Albanian monthly salary this seemed a lot of money, though the sum was not abnormal for bridal expenditure even for non-*refugjate*.

Despite the length of his sojourn in Greece and the fact that he had been working in the same factory job for several years, Zef had not been able to get a visa. So like all the other *refugjate* without legal status, he had to choose whether to risk capture and expulsion or spend significant sums each time he entered or left the country. Entering involved choosing a point where there were no border guards, points at which Greek taxi drivers operated routes often negotiated with the connivance of the police. Returning to Albania, which was more dangerous in that returned migrants who had been working for protracted periods would be carrying large sums of money, the safest solution was to get a Greek taxi right to the border and, once across, to be met by one's relations. That way one stood the best chance of avoiding violent robbery at a time when there was no banking system enabling migrants to avoid carrying large sums of money. Many migrants had no alternative but to walk to and fro across the border with all the attendant risks of beatings by the Greek police, jail, or robbery by fellow Albanians. Even those who had documents risked losing them to Greek border officials who, in their contempt for Albanians, or simply in a show of power, would sometimes rip the papers in pieces. Zef would have liked to take his bride to Greece so that he could continue to work for a few more years to set them up for married life. But thanks to what he saw as the weakness of the Albanian government, there was as yet no agreement between Greece and Albania regarding immigrants and work permits.

In the hopes of starting up some kind of business in Albania, Zef had brought back an electric generator powerful enough to supply a summer camp or perhaps a settlement of squatters with electricity. He was not yet sure where he would settle. Rrëshen, he had heard, had no '*përspektivë*'. He would be consulting with his bride, as marriage is for life and they must make decisions together; nothing patriarchal about Zef. Much more distressing than bridal expenditure which, as he said, is an investment for life, was his plan to invest his entire remaining savings in the pyramid scheme Vefa. This was a terribly tempting proposition for unwary returnees with some capital. Vefa Holdings had especial allure because, in addition to receiving 8–10 per cent interest on their money each month, investors had heard that several government ministers held shares in it. They believed that its security was guaranteed because, unlike some schemes with higher interest rates, Vefa had a genuine financial basis including several supermarkets, hotels and brewing concerns. Some also believed that government investment in illicit enterprises such as drugs and arms was providing an even more substantial basis. Above all, it was difficult to find investment alternatives since it was almost impossible to obtain information on how to set up a business, and still more difficult to obtain credit facilities. Not only did raising a loan entail handing over a substantial percentage of the loan as a kickback to the bank official arranging it, but long term productive enterprises, which were exactly what Albania needed, were far less likely to get loans than quick returns businesses such as buying and selling imports. We discussed the mechanics of pyramid schemes, but Zef knew of enough people who had profited to be unimpressed by the arguments. Vefa's lack of transparency was outweighed by its promise of fabulous returns; why bother with the odds of a lottery when you could be sure of doubling your capital in a year. The following year we went to pay a visit to Zef, his wife and their bouncing baby son. After the initial exchange of pleasantries, Zef surprised us by producing a video camera and filming us with the baby. The video camera was not, alas, a sign of prosperity but, on the contrary, represented Zef's survival strategy after losing almost all his five year's Greek earnings. He had invested 8,000 dollars in Vefa Holdings. But ever resilient Albanian that he was, he had bought a video camera with which to film local weddings and was earning about 50 dollars per wedding as long as the season lasted.

I mentioned this loss to friends, one of whom ruefully revealed that she and her husband had lost $5,000. They had made good on their first investment in the Vlora pyramid scheme, Gjallica, but despite a friend warning them against taking further risks, had not been able to resist putting their newly acquired gains into Vefa. They had even lent a friend $2,000, also lost. 'But at least we didn't sell our apartment like our friends who moved to a rented flat so as to invest the money from the sale in Gjallica.' Our friend's husband was now back in Greece 'starting all over again'. Another friend with $4,000 (the turnover from a state business) lost to Vefa, had been made an offer by an acquaintance: he would rescue her money if she agreed to hand over 1,000 of the four as a recompense for his efforts. Needless to say, no money was rescued. When I told a Tirana friend of these losses she smiled at the size of the sums. Her sister and brother-in-law, who had both been earning well in Greece for several years, had lost 50,000 dollars. On the other hand, we also knew winners. A son of our Mirditan neighbours in Tirana had sold his flat in Lezhë, invested the proceeds in Gjallica, and profited so much that he had been able to buy a flat in Tirana.

We had to move from our flat at the top of Rrëshen after Zef's return, and this time we went to live in the newly built apartment block where the occupants had obtained their flats through the new system of mortgages. Our landlord was a psychiatric doctor whose wife and two children were spending the holidays in his highland village with his widowed mother. Several of his brothers had been working in Italy since the beginning of democracy, and he was better off than most people we knew. The saucepans in the modern kitchen were gold handled; we found two video recorders in the kitchen cupboards, and the furniture was elegant and modern. To our surprise, the doctor was house trained. (We never rented a flat where we had continuous exclusive occupancy, so we often saw our rentiers in action at home.) The doctor not only knew how to work the washing machine – the first we had seen in Rrëshen – but kindly insisted on instructing us how to use it. More impressively, he did his own ironing (on the floor as all Rrëshenites did at the time). Such domestication was said to be usual amongst those men who had gone away to university, where dormitory life had forced them to look after themselves.

On the *xhiro*s of our last evenings of the summer vacation, one of our best friends, the mother of a small boy, kept reminding me that I had promised to go to the Town Council to ask if they would consider building sleeping policemen into Rrëshen's main *xhiro* road. Theoretically, cars were forbidden during *xhiro* hours, but, as in Tirana, the car lobby was asserting itself and making it hazardous for small children. The last thing I would have expected to see in Albania was speed blocks, but to my surprise they had been introduced in the next town, Rubik. So on the last morning my friend Vera and I went together to see the head of the town council. I had always avoided these officials, who had a reputation for corruption, but Vera was insistent that I bring up this matter. It turned out to be well worth the trouble just to hear the uninhibited bigotry of the officials. Having conveyed his importance by writing a lengthy memorandum on our proposition in a large book while we sat in respectful silence for a long time, the mayor finally asked me what changes I had found in Mirditan mountain villages since 1993. The minute he picked up that my impressions were not of burgeoning prosperity and happy family farmers, he interrupted to say: 'How can you say people are not better off than before democracy?' No amount of protestations that this was not under discussion, that I had not been there under Communism, and so forth, had the slightest effect. In the end, half admitting that he knew what I was saying, he shouted: 'If they're not better off after three years of capitalism, it's because they're too lazy to develop *blegtoria* (animal husbandry) and go up to high mountain pastures.' Seeing me about to protest, he cut me off with: 'I, a village boy, had nearly nothing to eat and now my children have three bananas a day.' Misinterpreting my expression, he said: 'I know you're wondering how come I'm such a huge man.' I managed to get in a comment about the trend from mountain village to plain, and what a pity it was that the government had formulated no policy on internal migration so that descending squatters had no security. 'On the contrary,' he said, 'free movement is the policy.' 'What about when they settle on the plain?' I asked. 'What about the bulldozers that have cleared them off? Look at Kamzë, those squatters only got to stay because they blocked the road and captured the government minister, Tritan Shehu.' He was not listening. Long before I had finished he was talking through me: 'Yes, Kamzë, what a beautiful solution, all those lovely villas.' 'But there was a confrontation, a protest,' I said. 'What protest?' he asked incredulously. The head of agriculture for the region who had been summoned as a support-ive chorus, was now enlisted to agree with the Mayor's proposition that Fascism was a greatly superior form of regime to Communism because although free speech was forbidden, commercial activity was freely allowed. The agronomist, who had a bad stammer, did his best to sound supportive.

A sense of insecurity, exacerbated by poorly functioning laws, and worry about increasing debt and corruption were palpable for at least two years before the 1997 crisis. Over the same period, Mirdita, in common with several other provinces, had been losing its communications system. By 1996, the telephone system had not functioned for a year; road surfaces had deteriorated; there was an increase on the roads of armed robberies; the police, badly paid and poorly equipped, were afraid to take action against bandits. The train linking Mirdita with services to the capital as well as to the north had been discontinued, and the sleepers and rails were being appropriated by villagers. The oft repeated cry 'there is no state, there is no law' was on its way to becoming the literal truth. As time went on, the scale of corruption and impotence, laissez-faire or lack of concern on the part of the State to punish crime either violent or financial, led to an increase in the growing trend for *vetëqeverisje/vetëgjyqësije* – self-government or 'taking the law into one's own hands'. For example, in the autumn of 1996, as a result of careless driving, a man's car mounted the pavement and caused the death of a small child in Rrëshen. The driver was imprisoned, but only for three months. When he came out the child's parents, judging the sentence to be wholly inadequate, determined to kill him. A friend of ours was asked to mediate. She suggested that the driver move away from Rrëshen, arguing that it was hard for the parents to come to terms with what had happened if they saw him every day in the street.

A quite different example of *vetëqevërisje* occurred in Kaçinar when a father killed his own son in order to prevent him from committing an injustice. The son, who had just come out of prison, had made up his mind to kill the two men who had testified against him leading to his conviction. His father asked him whether they had in fact told the truth. They had, said the son. Feeling that he was in duty bound to prevent the projected murders, the father shot his son dead. Such incidents indicate the limits of locals' adherence to the state system.

On 13 March 1997 the arms depot just above Rrëshen was raided by locals, mostly boys and the less responsible males of the town. The soldiers guarding the depot withdrew, allowing the weapons to be taken freely. A widespread belief has it that Berisha had ordered arms in the North to be made available in the hopes of engineering a civil war. It is known that members of the Democrat Party were privately issued with arms prior to the depot raids. On 13 March the now armed men and boys, some of whom were only 13, returned from the depot in high spirits, wildly shooting into the air. One boy from the nearby town of Rubik was accidentally killed, another was shot in the leg. The terrifying prospect of all these people having arms in a situation where law and order had ceased to function – by this time the whole of the Albanian population had access to the arms depots – led the rest of Rrëshen's citizens to go themselves and acquire guns the next day. A group of socially concerned arms distributors even went round the villages to ensure that no rural families went without. The realisation by Rrëshenites that as far as the state went they were on their own, led the majority of citizens to shut themselves up at home in terror. The *rrugaç*, that is the potentially criminal, streetwise toughs, roamed outside firing guns and playing with hand grenades. A 13 year old blew himself up with a hand grenade, and another boy lost a hand. But given the number of weapons and their accessibility to all, the accident rate was extraordinarily low.

The depths of terror that these events gave rise to can hardly be conveyed. A student friend said: 'You can't imagine what it feels like to wake up and know that there is no government at all.' On 15 March, an even greater panic hit Rrëshen. A rumour went round that a vast amount of explosive stored in the depot was at risk of blowing up as a result of the turmoil that had occurred in the depot. There really was a large amount of explosive in the depot, but it will probably never be clear how real the danger of an explosion was and whether it would have been of a magnitude to destroy some of the town's buildings. Possibly the group from a nearby village, which raided the grain stores in the absence of the Rrëshenites, had engineered the rumour. Whatever the reality, the already thoroughly unnerved town dwellers were seized by panic, and the entire population fled up the mountain. Most families were convinced that not only would Rrëshen's apartment blocks be razed to the ground, but that the explosion would affect an even larger area beyond the town. It was an apocalyptic scene; one woman fleeing from the maternity ward had to stop at a house half way up the mountain to give birth; an elderly woman, bedridden for three months, rose from her bed and joined the exodus. Her astonished daughter kept exclaiming: 'Look at Mother, she's walking.' In retrospect some citizens mocked their own panic, but it is not hard to imagine that in the terrifying uncertainty already engendered by the realisation that the forces of law and order had completely lost control, even the most staid of citizens was prone to fear the worst.

The first three days after the arms seizure raid were the most melodramatic, though only the prelude to a long period of uncertainty, fear and illicit opportunism. Children had to be kept indoors, schools were closed, shops opened for an hour or so only in the mornings. The group of citizens who had taken it upon themselves to try to reduce the anarchy, sensibly enlisted the *rrugaç* to guard the bank against robbery. The toughs did a good job, and Rrëshen's bank was one of the few that remained intact and lost no money. It was not possible, however, to control certain pre-communist landowners who took advantage of the situation to lay claim to state land such as school, hospital or army property. Thus, the owner of the schoolbooks shop declared it to be his and turned half of it into a *bilardo* – snooker parlour. The ex-owner of the secondary school's dormitory building for boarders from villages demolished it with a view to building something for himself; some of the upper school's playground was appropriated by the former owner, who started to build a house on it. A man whose family had once owned part of the hospital site declared himself director of the hospital. It was several months before the law that state ownership of public buildings supersedes pre-communist ownership was reasserted.

Some Albanians assert that whereas the vandalism of 1991 was caused by resentment towards the previous regime and a wish to start afresh, the vandalism and theft that took place in 1997 was caused by fear for survival – how will we live in a society without a state? In Mirdita, for example, the reserve food depots were ransacked; a mitigating factor here was the fact that these reserves were distributed; it was not just a case of people grabbing for themselves. Whatever the motives, enormous damage was done in 1997, both to existing property and to the future of foreign investment. A significant number of foreign investors gave up trying to work in Albania after 1997.

From Ilir I learnt that the villages above Reps, including his village, had been equally active during the depot-raiding period. There was no arms depot in Reps, but many villagers had gone down to stock up from the Reps' wheat depot, which had likewise been opened. Some villagers, together with Ilir's 14-year-old brother, Ben, had got a lift over to the arms depot in Gjegjan, where they were able to procure guns for their families. According to Ben, the man handing out the guns was very responsible, careful to show all the children how to use them. Meanwhile Ben's father was having trouble getting his wheat back to the village, as anyone with transport was taking advantage of the situation to ask exorbitant fares – one hundred dollars for the half-hour ride, for example. In the end, he had to spend the night in Reps next to his newly acquired wheat, guarded by a friend with a machine gun. At the same time, people from the northern frontier town, Kukës, had got wind of the goings-on and were coming down to trade arms, of which they had large quantities, for wheat, supplies of which were running out in Kukës. Once back home, Mark had been, as usual, very organised and systematic. He taught Ben how to use the gun (type Carabiniere) with daily target practice. When Ilir arrived on the scene, on leave from his waiter's job at the Hotel Rogner, lucrative because the hotel was full of foreign reporters, he was very impressed by Ben's skills, and rather taken aback that his 14-year-old brother was a better shot (initially, he was careful to make clear) than he was.

That summer, we stayed in the flat of a woman who worked at the telephone exchange. Except for the service within Rrëshen, all lines had fallen victim to stolen wires, while the telephone booths in the post office had been destroyed during the worst of the March unrest. Our landlord's income had come from selling groceries from a tiny kiosk. Now a legal dispute over the land on which the kiosk stood had forced him to cease business at least until the dispute was settled, and the family was glad to earn some extra cash by renting to us. In the meantime, the unsold provisions (Turkish chocolate bars, crisps, rice, sugar, spaghetti, fizzy drinks and past-the-use-by-date Bake Rolls) were stored in boxes on the balcony. For Soula, a tuckshop on one's balcony was a dream come true, and her many purchases must have somewhat compensated the owner for the closure of the kiosk. He meanwhile was away at the *llixhat*, thermal springs, having therapy for a rheumatic leg.

Despite the intervention of foreign powers, and a comparatively democratic election establishing the Socialist Party in power, the problem of law and order after a very short period of post-revolutionary quiet resurfaced. There were frequent incidents of robbery with violence, car and bus holdups, machine gun robberies and attacks on police. During the uprising the country had suffered substantial damage to its infrastructure, communications were even worse, the police force was virtually inactive. Unemployment was very high, businesses had been destroyed during the rioting. One Rrëshen friend, who shortly before the uprising had opened a lorry repair workshop in Tirana, lost all his equipment; a number of Mirditan schools and office buildings had once again been badly damaged by vandalism. A bus on its way from Përlat to Rrëshen had been held up by a gang of four men armed with machine guns. The men had robbed all the passengers, including a policeman whose pistol they had taken along with his money. Those who had at first refused to hand over their money had been beaten up, but no one was killed. The driver of a car on the way up to Reps with benefits money was wounded when robbers held up the car soon after Shpal; the policeman with him was killed.

In addition to robbery with violence, violence was escalating at the individual level. The preferred solution to individual conflicts, as in the above example from Rrëshen, was *vetëgjyqësije*, and taking the law into one's own hands was greatly facilitated by the fact that every household now had arms. A number of our friends had as a result been indirectly involved in blood feuds. Some examples will serve to illustrate the sort of situations which were becoming increasingly common during this post-uprising period.

The first case was brought to my attention in April, 1997, when a Mirditan friend I was supposed to be meeting in Tirana failed to turn up. It transpired that, along with the rest of the males in his family, he had had to lie low for 24 hours following the completely unexpected revival of a blood feud dating back 40 years. A cousin of our friend's, the great nephew of the man killed 40 years earlier, had been urged by his grandmother to take revenge now that there were guns to hand. The young man was initially very reluctant, but finally arranged with his brother to intercept the minibus (*furgon* – commonest form of public transport) in which the chosen victim would be travelling from Mirdita to Tirana. The brothers held up the *furgon* in Laç and shot dead their victim, a 28-year-old newly married man. The killer disappeared immediately, leaving even distant male kin at risk for the next 24 hours. A particularly nasty aspect of this senseless revival of an old feud was the choice of victim. The 60-year-old son of the original killer would have been a 'fairer' choice, but the newly married young man was targeted because he was known to be the firiest of his brothers and hence, it was feared, very likely to take revenge back. As calculated, the remaining brothers eventually declared that they would consider the feud closed.

In another case, a cousin of the family from Sang had quarrelled with a neighbour over water access. Having decided to kill his neighbour, and learning that he planned to go to Rrëshen the next day, the cousin got on the village bus shortly before it was due to leave at six am, and aiming his *automatik* at his neighbour shot him dead. But the bus was as usual full, and the shooting accidentally killed an 18-year-old boy as well. The families of both victims were then in blood with every male relation of our friends' family. These had to stay indoors for three days until the head of the family had gone to drink coffee (*pi kafe*)³ with the victims' families, who agreed to give him a guarantee that only the killer's immediate family members would be considered to be in blood with them. In fact, the murderer and his two brothers fled abroad immediately, so were never *ngujuar* – confined indoors, the word used for those shut up at home to escape vengeance. Indicative of the fact that there are no longer standard feud rules within Mirdita are both the variation in time for which those other than the murderer are at risk, and the extensiveness of the kin considered to be fair targets.

A third case involved the niece by marriage of a Bulshar family. She, like the boy in the bus, had been killed accidentally. She had been walking along a Rrëshen street one afternoon with her father and two of her children after a wedding party. A man from the district of Kaçinar had leapt out of a car and fired an automatic rifle at his intended victim. Firing on automatic with repeated bursts of fire had led to the wounding of two bystanders and the death of the wretched woman as well as that of his enemy. The undisciplined way in which the revenge killing had been carried out contravened all accepted norms. It was completely out of order to fire in such a way as to endanger the public. (From a discussion with two friends who knew the killer well, it emerged that he had initially refused to act but that egged on by his relations, had finally given in. By nature he was quite unsuited to any act of aggression and so panic-stricken was he at the moment of firing the gun, he had allegedly closed his eyes; this was the reason that the gun had gone to automatic instead of one-one.) What the Kaçinar man should have done according to one 'expert' was to take hold of the intended victim and despatch him without putting anyone else at risk. Exactly such an exemplary procedure had occurred some weeks earlier at 11 o'clock one morning, when on the bridge between the town and the bazaar, right in front of this expert Rrëshenite, a young man had grabbed his victim by the hair and shot him dead. This expert on the 'correct' way to carry out a feud killing was, ironically, a part-time employee of one of the foreign peace-making organisations, and claimed to have negotiated several agreements to end feuds. Gjeçov's record of the Kanun states:

Involuntary (*padashje*) manslaughter is not avenged by the gun. The murderer pays for the blood and guarantees are given. In this type of killing, the murderer must leave and remain concealed until the affair is clarified. If people of wisdom confirm that the killing was, in fact, involuntary, the murderer pays the blood money and is given guarantees. (1989:176–7)

From the above quotation and the two citations below, it is clear that there has been significant slippage between the original aims of the Kanun to limit killings and later developments.

According to the old Kanun of the mountains of Albania, only the murderer incurs the blood feud. The family of the victim could not pursue or kill any of the brothers, nephews, or cousins of the murderer, but only the actual perpetrator. The later Kanun extends the blood feud to all males in the family of the murderer, even an infant in the cradle; cousins and close nephews, although they may be separated, incur the blood feud during the 24 hours following the murder. (Fox,1989:172)

A prime example of this shift from the Kanun's original aim to limit bloodshed is the latter-day failure to distinguish between *hakmarrje* (to take revenge) and *gjakmarrje* (to take blood). *Gjak* means blood, *hak* means due – what is owed or required by an obligation. The Kanun says that '*Gjaku për faj nuk jet*' – a crime may not be recompensed with blood'. What is meant by a crime becomes clear from the following excerpt:

> The penalty for any crime committed by one Albanian against another Albanian may be adjudicated by Elders and by means of pledges, but bloodshed is not permitted, since 'a crime may not be recompensed with blood'. Neither insult, theft, burning down of a house, a beating, none of these may be resolved by a killing, because if they are a blood feud begins. One should rather look to mediation, with elders and pledges... If someone comes to rob me, even if I see him opening the door and kill him, I incur his blood.... If someone comes to empty my sheepfold, and I see him driving the flock before him and he refuses to release them regardless of what I say, if I kill him I incur the blood feud. (Fox, 1989:173–4)

In other words, because killing in response to injury to property or dignity creates a debt, which leads to a potentially endless chain of killings, it must be avoided at all costs. It seems likely that a lesser adherence to these strict tenets began as the Ottoman Empire fell apart. The diminishing threat of Turkish domination made tribal unity less essential; minimising conflict within the group became less of a priority.

As noted earlier with reference to *besa* (when and for how long this should be granted), Rrëshenites often had views on what were the 'correct' Kanun procedures; even those Rrëshenites who as former devoted Communists might have been expected to have rejected such anachronistic and ideologically unacceptable ideas. It is a mark of how bereft the population felt as regards the lack of a functioning justice system, that the niceties of customary law should have been under debate at all. Ambivalence as regards both customary and state law extended to representatives of the state. On the subject of blood money, a high ranking police officer said: 'It's not like buying animals in a market. You can't buy off a person's spilt blood with money.' And from the point of view of the victim's

family: 'It's *tregti* (commerce) if you accept money. When you die
you will die with a bad name.' His argument was that one should
either achieve a peace without the introduction of money or, if
forgiveness was out of the question, take a life for a life. This was
at odds with the Kanun as quoted above, and certainly at odds
with state law which obviously did not condone vengeance killings
and aimed, albeit often unsuccessfully, to imprison blood feud
murderers.

Another representative of the State, a local judge, aimed to take
the best elements from each legal system. His object was to use
any procedure that would best resolve a conflict. Thus in court,
before getting into the state legal process, he might cross question
two villagers in conflict and then ask: 'Are you prepared to *bën bej*
(swear) that the case is as follows?' Quite often a solution would be
found before the official legal procedure had begun.

On 31 March 1998, a *kuvend* was held in Rrëshen to discuss
the role of the Kanun in contemporary life. As usual on such occasions, the invited speakers monopolised the scene. Presumably
a legacy of Communism, speeches tended to be far too long, and
democratic participation by the audience was restricted to the minimum. Notwithstanding its limited opportunities to contribute, the
audience was evidently hugely enjoying this airing of Kanun laws.
This was especially evident when specific examples of solutions
provided by former elders were cited. Older listeners in particular clearly relished this invocation of past tradition. Despite this
widespread nostalgia for a system that represented cherished past
values, one of the final speakers, a historian of Mirdita, concluded
with the following pithy statement: '*Ku ka ligj, ska Kanun*', literally
'where there's law, there's no Kanun'. In other words: where state
law functions, there's no (call for) Kanun law'.

By the mid–1990s, as we have seen, such sanctions as those
cited by Gjeçov, which had served to control and limit killing, had
been undermined both by the coexistence of two only partially
functioning legal systems and by demographic instability. From
1996, the laws of the Kanun continued to be invoked, but with
an eye to 'self-government' according to a particular individual's
rights, rather than to a system subscribed to and enforced by an
entire group. Even when the Kanun was paramount, it can be
inferred from the advice to the murderer to conceal himself, that
securing a peaceful agreement was never that simple. In 1997, what

constituted 'involuntary' killing (*vrasje padashje*) was changing as machine guns now circulated freely. Where a man fired in a street or in a bus, killing innocent bystanders as well as the intended victim, he was liable to find himself in blood with the relations of the unintended victims. They argued that the user of a machine gun in a restricted space should foresee casualties beyond the person targeted.

However, in the case of the Bulshar teacher, the family told me that had the killer's family attended the woman's funeral, a peaceful solution (*pajtim*) would have been easy to arrange. But they had not come and no solution was in sight. Attendance by members of the killer's family at the victim's funeral is, in fact, an important first step towards reconciliation. In a case in Kurbnesh in 2003, a youth killed his first cousin. The commune head together with older villagers acted as intermediaries. They persuaded the killer's father to agree to 'drink coffee' at the victim's *mort*, and the victim's family to receive him. 'The mourning family's honour and nobility of spirit prevailed over anger and thirst for revenge,' said the commune head. 'A good sign that the spiral of blood feud will not occur in the future, that the two families will be able to shake each other's hands and be reconciled.' The killer's father attended the *mort* with his hands crossed behind his back according to the customary rite signalling deep regret.

One contributor to feud, evident from the voices egging on reluctant revenge-takers, was concern about *opinion* – 'what would people say? would they attribute making peace to cowardice?' As Hasluck had noted in the 1930s:

> If public opinion stresses mediation and avoidance of bloodshed, a man's dignity is not jeopardised. Peace was always made through an intermediary.... 'You've shot enough...Forgive him, we beg you...' At length he replied, 'All right, I've forgiven him.' Then both enemies were safe from gossiping tongues, that bogey of primitive communities, for no one could say that one or the other man was either brave or cowardly... (1954:256)

But in the past there had been a demographically stable community. Elders with the mechanisms for community-wide reasoned debate could, if necessary, impose sanctions such as expulsion or payment of blood money. In the late 1990s depletion of the community and very limited means of communication meant that less reasonable voices could prevail. Moreover, the absence of any reliable justice system, customary or state, combined with the irritant of insufficient resources, further exacerbated by unemployment and a feeling of physical insecurity, positively engendered quarrels. One is reminded of Rapaczynski's comments on law and order:

> This is the old Hobbesian problem: when most people obey the law, the government can enforce it effectively and [relatively] cheaply against the few individuals who break it. But when obedience breaks down on a large enough scale, no authority is strong enough to police everyone. In such a setting, with enforcement becoming less and less effective, individuals have an incentive to follow their own interests, regardless of any paper constraints.[4] (1996:88)

One of the biggest elements in this climate of 'anything goes' was cash. One could break the law if one had cash and one could exact cash even if the people involved were acting perfectly legitimately. Thus, no sheets for a hospital patient's bed could be obtained without a sweetener to the ward nurse. In a public office, the necessary document did not appear till the supplicant greased the bureaucrat's palm. One could pay for an exam pass or a higher grade. A bribe to the would-be employer could further an applicant's chances when applying for a job. A corrupt member of parliament could be bribed to enable an unscrupulous and probably incompetent individual to run a local state utility – water, electricity, forestry, bank. If a scandal were exposed such as selling off state machinery for personal gain, the lawbreaking post-holder had a fair chance of staving off dismissal with a bribe. As a result, any individual who made good, however honest, would be suspected of dishonesty. To avoid such aspersions, a person standing for office planning to buy an apartment or asset of some kind, was well advised to acquire the asset some time before achieving office.

Instances from different institutions in Rrëshen show how this breakdown of faith in the law had affected all spheres of activity. Some employees in the benefits office noticed that a number of dole claimants were receiving benefits despite being employed. They informed the claimants that they would report them for dishonest receipt of unemployment benefits. The claimants threatened to kill them if they reported the matter. In the event, the officials kept quiet because they had reason to believe that these were not empty threats. Examples of such threats being carried out in other parts of the country existed. A buildings regulations official who had ordered the demolition of an illegal kiosk had been killed, while others had received threats from kiosk owners that the officials' children would be killed if demolition took place. Some of these officials as well as some judges had subsequently been allocated bodyguards by the government, a form of protection unlikely to be extended to dole officials. In another case in Rrëshen, a judge (from outside Mirdita) ruled that a man from Fan alleged to have murdered a woman and abused her young daughter was innocent. It emerged that the judge had been bribed by the murderer not to convict him. The judge was dismissed from his post. He may have calculated that the risk of dismissal was less significant, and certainly less life-threatening, than the risk of incurring the murderer's ire if convicted. He has subsequently set up as an advocate in another region.

There was a brief period following the events of 1997 when post-electoral optimism led several respected individuals to take up positions of authority; posts such as school head or local party head. But their initial bursts of energy and enthusiasm were rapidly replaced by frustration and withdrawal from the posts. One doctor who became a political party head said he was used to making diagnoses and producing solutions. Politics, he found, did not lend itself to this approach.

Chapter Fourteen

DESCENT TO THE PLAIN

As will have become clear, one of the commonest survival strategies practised by mountain villagers has been descent to former state farm land. Many villagers went to the coastal plains where the land before communism had been malarial swampland – *kënet*. These swamps had been drained by the communist government in order to increase Albania's arable land area. Many of the *vullnetare* – so-called volunteers – and forced labour conscripts involved in reclaiming the *kënet*, died as a result of the terrible work conditions. In the early 1990s, descent to as yet undistributed state farm land was commonest amongst villagers from the most remote and inaccessible villages of the North, from the provinces of Kukës, Puka and Tropoja. The tripled population and the collapse of state industries including mines and forestry meant that subsistence in land-scarce mountain villages was no longer possible. Out-migration by family members abroad and/or to the plains was the only means of survival. Because the communist policy of population retention had extended to the remotest rural areas, huge numbers have been involved in this post-communist demographic movement. The pattern, as indicated earlier, has been for a family member to descend to an area of undistributed state farm land and cultivate a plot. He, or more often a young couple, would erect a shanty to live in while tending the crop and guarding it from theft. The immediate aim was to get access to arable land sufficient to provide their families with enough wheat to survive. The long-term hope was to build a house and settle permanently on this piece of land.

Until 1995, when a new law was passed, these cultivators had no security of tenure since they were acting without any legal basis; the undistributed land belonged to the State, which could eject them at any time. Despite this insecurity, the present gain of arable land was well worth the risk of future loss. Moreover, there was always the possibility that for electoral ends the government might decide to grant them their plots. Such an outcome was, of course, dependent on who the competing contenders were. On the coastal plain near Lezhë the squatters from highland areas had been sacrificed in favour of local contenders, as we had seen in the case of the Gjoka family.

Some highlanders chose to move further afield than the Lezhë plain, preferring to squat on the plain near the port town of Durrës, where there is the added advantage of being within easy reach of the capital. Still others moved down to southern Albania, to the plains near the coastal town of Saranda. This was a fertile area where northern migrants could count on finding work, since most of the local workforce was in Greece during the 1990s. Here there were jobs in construction, as Sarandiots' remittances began to fuel a building boom as well as agricultural jobs, mainly herding.[1]

The Gjoka family, whose Lezhë plot was bulldozed in 1995, would not have been able to raise the money for *pasaportizimi* ($200–$300) in addition to the cost of building a shanty, even after two of their sons had made several forays to Greece. The plot outside Lezhë had provided them with essential wheat that they now had to buy out of their tiny income from invalid pension and welfare benefits; their monthly food costs alone now exceeded their income. But in 1996 they had a near miraculous stroke of luck. A relation in Durrës heard through a priest at the Catholic church she attended that the Catholic charity Caritas had just bought some land on the plain outside Durrës for the purpose of housing particularly disadvantaged land-poor mountain villagers. The priest's job was to find really needy families. The one-legged Orosh father with six children and almost no land was clearly a deserving case, and the family was duly allocated a plot some 20 kilometres southeast of Durrës close to a village called Shenavlash.

Shenavlash had originally consisted of little more than a ruined Byzantine church and on the hillsides below the church, reed huts. The proximity of the malarial swamplands was a deterrent to permanent habitation, though the area's suitability for grazing had been attracting migrants from all over Albania and parts of Kosova since the nineteenth century. Many of these settlers came initially as transhumants from the high plateaux in Dibra in the north-east and Korça in the southeast, to graze their flocks on the grasslands in the winter. The population remained small and, despite the village's name and church, was largely Muslim culturally. Once the former swamplands had been reclaimed by the Communists in the mid-twentieth century, the drained area of 12,000 hectares became state farm land chiefly planted with maize. A track divided the reclaimed state farm land from the cooperative land, which lay below the village on the hill. In 1991, the cooperative land was decollectivised and distributed to the inhabitants of the village according to state law, per soul – *sipas ligjit, për frymë*. The state farm land, on the other hand, remained uncultivated and undistributed, providing the government with bargaining power for votes, and squatters from mountain villages with an insecure means of survival. Caritas had just bought up a large section of the privatised former cooperative land, and our friends were to receive a plot big enough for a house, vegetable garden and outhouses for their animals. Building materials for a kitchen and bedroom would be supplied at Caritas' expense.

The father of the Orosh family was naturally overjoyed at this unexpected piece of luck, and in particular by the secure official nature of ownership – Caritas beneficiaries would become legal landowners. As he kept joyfully repeating: '*E kemi me dokumentet*' – 'we've got it with the proper papers', evoking the contrast with his own experience in Lezhë and the current insecurity of the squatters on the other side of the track. He told us that the house would have foundations sufficient for a three storey house, that the building materials would be arriving soon and the family should be able to move in by the end of the year. 'We're on what will be the main road. The children will bicycle to school, to work, to town. We have education on our doorstep, employment, *perspektivë*.' A vision of the future which, in view of the actual conditions, did credit to the family's optimism and courage.

In 1996, with the Greek remittances from their eldest son, the family erected a wooden shack in which to live while they built their house. The bleak ex-swamp area, treeless, mosquito-ridden, houseless, without electricity or water, was very desolate indeed, a characterless no man's land. Water had to be fetched from the village pump 2km distant. The nearest neighbours were a group of shanty dwellers, mainly from Puka,[2] on the far side of the track, a

kilometre or so to the South. The claim shanty had to be guarded
continuously from thieves. While waiting for the building materials
to arrive, the father accompanied by one of the children (who took
it in turns) had to camp for several months in the shanty. The rest
of the family, apart from the eldest son in Athens, remained in the
mountain village herding their animals, tending their crops and, in
the case of the two youngest, attending school. The completed log
shack stood totally alone beside a cart track in the parched, sordid
looking prairie, which was punctuated with channels of murky
water in which swam turtles and snakes. On the other side of the
track were the 12,000 hectares of state farm land, uncultivated
and without an irrigation source since the channels dried out in
summer. The scene recalled the experiences of pioneers in frontier
America 150 years earlier.

The contrast with Bulshar brought home to one how much a
mountain village, for all its remoteness, deprivations and austerity, had to offer. Bulshar had trees, springs, electricity, magnificent
views, long-established friends and landmarks. Despite the break-
up of the cooperatives, village life still took place in a familiar landscape. Without the daily life of the cooperative, villagers were more
isolated, but you knew everyone and could exchange gossip with
those you were on good terms with. You had your own home and
kitchen garden, and post-cooperative daily life now had an established routine. The 15-year-old son had gone every day to herd the
family's animals with his school friends, and knew every inch of the
local landscape. Here on the plain there was no occupation for him
apart from water fetching from the pump where one always had
to queue, sometimes for hours. Not that time was at a premium;
there was almost nothing to do at the shack. There were no friends
or family other than his father, while new acquaintances from the
village were a rough lot who shocked by boasting of stealing and
having smoked from infancy.

By the end of 1996, the whole family had moved down and
was camping in the shanty while the house, in theory at least,
was nearing completion. During the 1997 insurrection, anarchy
and raiding of the arms depots left the family feeling vulnerable;
conscious that the shanty walls gave little protection from bullets,
and that the whole population was armed. But in most respects
the move was proving a wise one. The ten year old reported that
the school here was better than the village one. There were enough

teachers and they were properly qualified. The family now had geese, a pig, a new cow and calf, two dogs, two cats and chickens. Most importantly, with the help of church funds and a neighbour expert at well-making, they had sunk a well. The water, though not drinkable, was salt free. The first crops, sown before sinking the well, had dried up but now they had water they could provide most of their subsistence needs; essential if they were to make ends meet. Equally important was the freely available grazing for their cow, which was flourishing on the local grass. There was of course no electricity, but the family was planning to transport a large tree trunk from Bulshar and to buy wires.

By October 1997 the family was installed in their two room house. Not all the promised building materials had reached the intended recipients, but the disappearance of consignments whether for roads, municipal water systems or aid to individuals, was too established a phenomenon to surprise. The weather was unusually cold, and the new cement walls dripped damp. The tree trunks had been brought from the village, and the house now enjoyed sporadic electricity. During the day there was never a strong enough current to bake the daily quota of bread, and someone always had to get up to bake it after midnight. The father had to sleep in the original shanty, now part of the animals' stalls, to ensure that no one stole the animals overnight. Despite these drawbacks, the family was flourishing and most of them visibly weighed more. There was less back-breaking work for the mother who no longer had to go miles in search of forest wood, and water was now close to hand.

Employment

In addition to gradually building up subsistence farming, there were some other sources of income, albeit spasmodic. Able-bodied men looked for work in construction either in Durrës or in the village, where in-migrated settlers were beginning to replace their provisional accommodation with proper houses. About three kilometres along the road that leads to the main Durrës-Tirana road, there was a jean shirt factory. This was a joint Italian-Albanian venture, which operated in a barn-like two storey building formerly the commune headquarters. In 1997 there was no water in or near the building and the light was very poor. One hundred females of varying ages worked there from 7am to 3.30pm, with one break from 9.30 to 10am. Their job was to fulfil the production 'norm' of 350 shirts a day. For some months, the Gjoka family's eldest daughter worked there. Her job was to make the shirt cuffs. She described how she sat hour after hour hunched over a sewing machine always focusing on the stitching till her eyes burned and her head ached. 'By the end of each day we were covered in dust and sweating; I often cried.' Social insurance was paid only after a test period of three months. Slow workers were fired. In periods of low activity many were laid off. On one occasion Elda, who was earning the previously unimaginable sum of $60 a month, was handed $10 after a fortnight. She protested and, to the employer's surprise, produced the record she always kept of the piece work she had done. The employer reluctantly paid her her full entitlement. The shirts were for export to Italy where the prices netted a handsome profit for the sweatshop venturers. As Elda's father said, conditions were much like those in industrialising England. This was evidently one of the well-absorbed anti-capitalist history lessons learnt under Communism, as whenever I described this factory work to Albanian friends, they responded with the same comparison.

Some of the women working with Elda in the factory came from Durrës, others from Shenavlash, but none from the squatter settlements. These girls, when asked by Elda why they did not take advantage of the chance to earn such a good salary, replied that it would be shocking for young girls to go off on their own and work. Those questioned came from remote villages in Puka where family life was very strict, *fanatik*. In fact Elda herself, until she left Bulshar, had rarely been allowed to go anywhere on her own, as we had seen for ourselves, but the family need for income must have banished their scruples; and she herself had always been of an independent turn of mind.

Fortunately for the *fanatik*, there were jobs which could be done at home. Firstly, all families, whether on the ex-cooperative land or the state farm land, had animals to look after. Cows had to be taken to graze and were a source of both food and income; *kos*, a kind of thin yoghurt, has always been a major item in the daily diet, and some families had surplus milk, which they sold in Durrës. All had vegetable gardens to be tended. One could earn by doing piece work at home for an Italian-Albanian shoemaking firm, though the advantage of earning without leaving home was outweighed by the miserably low pay. No one stuck to this particular form of exploitation for very long. One woman who tried it was a neighbour of our Orosh friends. In 1997, her family had been allocated a piece of land on which they had recently completed a one room house. Her husband, despite being prone to epileptic fits, went away to work in Crete together with their eldest son, a boy of 13. For a while, to help feed herself and her other five children in her husband's absence, the mother worked at home for the shoemaking firm. She earned nine US cents for each pair of shoes, an hour's work. Six hours work paid for the cost of the family's daily flour ration. Subsequently, though it meant leaving her young children to fend for themselves, she went to work at the jean shirt factory.

Two other sources of work nearby were a hennery – *puleria* – and a piggery. Until the piggery closed down, a woman whose husband was in prison worked there for a couple of hours in the morning and again in the afternoon. She had originally lived in a shanty next door to her brother-in-law and his family, but had later been allotted some land by Caritas. When she moved to the plot with her small daughter, Caritas gave her the use of one of the container cabins, which had been provided for the Kosovar refugees in 1999. Later she found work in the hennery, leaving her daughter with our friends while she was at work.

On the road before the jean shirt factory, was a larger *puleria*, an Italo-Albanian enterprise called Floryhen. Here a few tried to obtain, and select workers had, a proper contract with social security, but most were casual labour who earned almost nothing and could be fired or hired from day to day. The jean shirt factory eventually slightly improved its working conditions. In the twenty-first century there is now water, and though the workers have a slightly longer day, they get two breaks.

Hopes for a new source of employment were raised when a big Saudi-Arabian firm, Mak Albania, was rumoured in 2000 to have bought several thousand hectares of the state farm land to the north of the squatter area. It was said that an enormous greenhouse development was planned that would provide work for large numbers of locals. But nothing had yet come of this rumour three years later.

For a brief period, a construction boom in the late 1990s led to some new enterprises in Shenavlash itself. These were based in the former state farm buildings. One made breeze blocks, another was a welding business making door and window frames. Two of the welders were from the northern town of Shkodër, and their presence in the soldery reflected a new, if small-scale, national trend. This trend not to return to Greece, despite difficult conditions and very low salaries in Albania, was increasing, as we had noted in Rrëshen. Both these welders had worked in Greece for seven years, during which time, in addition to supporting their families, they had modernised their houses and installed Western style conveniences. Improvements included: a modern kitchen with stainless steel sink units, electric stove, refrigerator and washing machine; modern bathroom with shower, bath tub and European style lavatory; and new sitting-room furniture. Both had decided not to return to Greece again. The psychological toll caused by distance from family and discriminatory treatment by Greeks was simply not worth the slightly higher earnings. At the same time, because Shkodër lacks a hinterland (being close to the Montenegrin border) and has suffered from even greater lack of economic development than other Albanian towns of any size, employment there was particularly difficult to find. So during the week these two men camped in the elder's Volkswagen bus next to the soldery. At the weekends they returned to their families. It seemed a tough fate after all they had endured abroad, but with no employment nearer home, they had little choice.

Domestic Life

In the autumn of 1998, the Gjokas suffered a very serious financial setback. Their cow, which had been a prolific milk producer, died after getting at a sack of wheat and gorging itself. From all around, shanty dwellers and villagers came to condole exactly as they would have done in the event of a human's death. In order to buy a new cow, the family had to use the meagre sum set aside for house improvements as well as selling their calf. The new cow was large but ate more and gave less milk. The welfare of animals is a critical factor in making or failing to make ends meet, and the similarity of response to humans' and animals' births or deaths by the plain's inhabitants highlighted this importance. On a happier occasion, we celebrated the good fortune of some squatters on the other side of the track whose daughter's pig had just given birth to 12 piglets, six of each sex. We went to admire the pigs, saying '*marshallah*', the word which is at once congratulatory and averts the evil eye – the same word used when admiring a baby or someone's beautiful child.

The inadequacy of the father's pension, the death of the cow, the high cost of living, precluded more than a hand-to-mouth existence for the Gjoka family. In 1998 they had not even been able to buy the materials for a Christmas meal until their eldest son arrived from Athens. The son was himself struggling since he was supporting his brother who, not long after moving to Athens, had broken his leg in a motorbike accident. But by taking on a second job delivering pizzas, the elder brother had managed to save enough to reduce the family's financial problems for the immediate future.

Despite very difficult conditions and financial setbacks, the family reiterated that anyone prepared to work could make a living here given the abundance of plains grass. We saw evidence of this every morning during the winter months when several large flocks of sheep and smaller herds of horses would pass along the track in front of the house. These were herded by men who had come from the high Korça plateau or the Dibra highlands to winter their animals. The herders rented the former cooperative barns for their animals, and used these as living quarters for themselves as well.

In December 1998, the eldest Gjoka son, Simon, who had been working continuously in Greece since 1996 and had never seen Shenavlash or the new house, arrived to spend Christmas with his family. His 15-year-old sister, Vjollca, took me and her brother on a tour of the village. The first building we came to as we entered the village was a mosque, built by a Saudi Arabian firm a couple of years earlier. The area is a Muslim one culturally; the villagers have Muslim names and follow the traditional form of Muslim rites of passage, but religious interest is minimal after a quarter of a century of official atheism, and the mosque was said only to be attended by five old men.

All over the village we saw new houses being built, including some large three-storey ones. Two of these were owned by the managers of a prostitution business in Italy. From the top of the village we stopped to look down on the eight-year school, which had just been repaired with World Bank funds. At the top of a hill just above the village, on the site of an ancient Orthodox church, we found a huge new complex funded by the Greek Orthodox Church. This consisted of a theological school, a building for students and staff, an enormous new church, and a house for the monks. 'Think how many houses could have been built for shanty dwellers with all this money,' said Simon bitterly. Several years in Greece had not turned him into a great admirer of the Orthodox Church. On our way back we made a detour to reach the village graveyard where a young woman, a friend of Vjollca's, had recently been buried. The sound of machine gun fire from a nearby house made us jump as we turned off the road to the graveyard. However, gun shots in the area were not uncommon though more usual at night, so we were not unduly alarmed. Vjollca was more frightened at the prospect of the ghosts she expected to find amongst the graves. Here the names on the gravestones were Muslim but, a little removed from the main graveyard on the other side of the path, we found a Catholic section opened up five years earlier. Here Vjollca's friend was buried. In common with every other graveyard I had visited, a disproportionate number of graves contained young men. Hardly surprising in a country where a complete disregard for driving rules on lethal roads was combined with the universal possession of arms.

One reason why the 15 year old Vjollca had been keen to tour the village was the rare chance it gave her to get out of the house and see other people. As soon as the family had moved down from the village, she had had to give up her schooling and stay at home busying herself with housework, clothes washing and growing veg-etables. Although she actively enjoyed the domestic occupations, she minded not continuing her education and particularly missed the company of her classmates. However, it was not long before 'interventions' on behalf of several different suitors were made. One year after settling on the plain she said to me: 'I know some girls think it's enough if their husbands are nice characters and a suitable age. But I want someone who's good-looking too. One of the men was already 29,' she told me in disgust, 'and I was still only 14.' I was glad she was being demanding, because the temptation for a teenage girl to get engaged simply in order to have access to some social life is very great. Respectable young girls on the plain are extremely isolated, virtually incarcerated within the household. In the village, it would have been unusual for a girl to marry at such a young age. On the plain, it was obvious that her parents were keen to get her engaged, though they would not have forced her against her will. Once a girl is engaged she presents much less of a risk either of abduction or of adverse gossip.

The number of young girls forcibly carried off is greatly outnumbered by those misled into going voluntarily, which does not make the girl's ultimate fate any less tragic. The coastal plain near the port of Durrës has attracted very large numbers of young men in need of an income, some of whom do honest work, some of whom are involved in drug smuggling, stolen car dealing or prostitution rackets supplying an Albanian mafia abroad with young girls. Others have set up begging businesses in Athens, recruiting, for example, children maimed by hand grenades. Some young girls have been literally abducted, taken against their will to earn as prostitutes in Italy. But many of those who end up on the streets of Rome or Milan originally left the country either because they thought they were in love with the young man who had perhaps promised marriage or because he had suggested he could find work for them abroad, which would help their families. The monotony and isolation of their home lives may well have weighed in their decision to leave. For these reasons, the girls from self-respecting families could only go out if accompanied by a father or a brother. In the Gjoka's case, the mother was influenced both by a lifetime of preoccupation with *opinion* and a realisation that a good-looking man with a bit of blarney could carry off a girl, perhaps even such well brought up ones as her own. It was also hoped that this evidence of a strict upbringing would attract a better type of suitor.

Despite these precautions, some concessions had already been made to the differing lifestyle and fashions of plains life. Like the formulaic greetings, which took a different form down here, what was considered acceptable dress for young girls was also different. It was all right for these young girls to wear tight trousers or short skirts. This would have been shocking in the mountain villages, where girls' dress was usually skirts over trousers or, for the more liberal, loose fitting trousers or skirts below the knee. One day going out with the father and the two younger girls, who were dressed up according to local fashion, I joked to the father that responsibility for anything that happened to the girls was his. '*Kemi evoluar*,' he said; (we have evolved). When a couple of years later, someone commented on certain non-traditional (that is, non-Mirditan) aspects of his daughter's wedding, he again invoked the family's changed lifestyle: '*Jemi bërë modern tani, evropian.*' (Now we have become modern, European.)

One contributor to this 'modernity' was television. A major change in their lives on the plain once they had installed electricity was access to many of the private television stations, stations that could not be received in Mirdita. These broadcast innumerable musical shows, many of which are decidedly 'adult'. One would have expected *fanatik* fathers and mothers to be shocked by some of these shows. Instead, grandparents and parents (male and female) of young teenagers would watch these programmes like robots, occasionally laughing embarrassedly, but never apparently worried by the impressions the films might be making on their offspring. The explanation seems to be that what is on television is 'modern' and hence must be harmless. Thanks to their extreme isolation, young unmarried girls spend a lot of their time watching these programmes or endlessly surfing the channels. In the early morning, in bed and barely awake, one reaches for the remote control to switch on the television, which stays on until the next electricity failure. In between the music programmes are the advertisements showing expensive cosmetics, clothes and electrical goods, or luxurious Western style sitting-rooms and bedrooms. Ironically, however, the most popular films of all shown by these private television stations, products and purveyors of modern capitalism, are the old Partisan films that dwell fondly on the heroism and triumphs of the communist supporters in the early 1940s.

As time went on, the number of Caritas beneficiaries grew. Most of them came from mountain villages in Mirdita, and all had experienced some misfortune. Some had lost their house through fire, some had a debilitating illness and a large family; others had disabled children, or a family head in prison. All were unemployed and receiving welfare benefits, albeit minimal. The struggle to survive even after receiving a piece of land was uphill work. One day I noticed a newcomer, a sickly looking middle-aged man with a prominent humped back, sticking bits of cardboard over a flimsy frame. He had no nails or tacks, though a neighbour later offered to lend him some, and the construction for the time being at least, looked like something a small child in England might have made to play house in.

During the Kosovo crisis in 1999 large numbers of refugees were put up on the plain further to the North in tents and container cabins. Following the return home of the refugees, some newly descended mountain villagers who had been granted land by Caritas were lent containers from the stocks brought in for the Kosovars. This was an enormous saving, since instead of having to spend time and money (at least $1,500) on constructing a *barakë* for temporary shelter, they could start straight away on permanent house construction while living in the container. One of the tents from the Kosovar camp was set up between the containers and shanties to be used as a Sunday school for the settlers' children. Nuns from Caritas visited from time to time, and at Christmas time brought presents to be distributed amongst the families. This could be an unedifying experience as I discovered just before Christmas one year. All the settlers rushed out, some openly clamouring for presents. After the nuns' departure one or two people were happy, but more were discontented either because they had received nothing or less than a neighbour, or something useless such as baby clothes where there was no baby. Some complained that the nuns had favourites. The Sunday school tent was subsequently vandalised, and Sunday school came to an end.

Squatters

In 1996 the Gjoka's shanty was the only one on the land Caritas had acquired, though another family had started building a house, commuting in from near Durrës where they were staying with relations. For the first six months the nearest neighbours were the 30 or so squatter families who lived in shanties on the state farm land further along on the other side of the track.

In 1995, President Berisha made his *fytyre nga deti* (faces towards the sea) speech that proclaimed freedom of movement such that highland villagers were officially encouraged to settle on the coastal plains. Official encouragement was not, however, accompanied by the introduction of official procedural mechanisms. As a result, various anomalies arose, one of which concerned the passportisation (*pasaportizimi*) procedure. In order to move from one place to another, a citizen must obtain a verification of residence document (*vërtetimi*) from the headman of the new location declaring that he has somewhere to live locally. Because a would-be squatter on undistributed state farm land does not in fact have a place to live locally, he has to pay a bribe to the headman to verify what the headman knows not to be the case. Once the *vërtetim* has been obtained, the applicant proceeds to the *komuna*, the district authority, which then issues the passportisation document on receipt of an official payment. This guarantees with a fair degree of certainty that somewhere on this land area, once it has been distributed, the payer will have the right to 300 square metres of land on which eventually he will be able to build a house.

Shortly before the 1996 election, changes occurred on this part of the plain altering the status of two groups. The squatters, who had mostly been squatting since 1992 and had no passportisation rights, were granted *pàsaportizimi* in a bid by the Democrat government to secure their votes. Thereafter, these squatters were recognized administratively as living in the *komuna*, with the voting rights, access to birth and death registration, schooling for their children, and so on, which this entails. Above all, they now had the right to 300 square metres of land in the area once the land was finally distributed. However, simultaneously, some ex-state farm workers had been granted use rights on the very same stretch of land. These rights allowed them two dylims each of land *në përdorim*, that is, for cultivation use, as distinct from land ownership rights. These state farm workers initially tried to pressurise the squatters to leave but were subsequently allocated land further along the road. Why any one of the surrounding unoccupied areas had not been given to the ex-state farm workers in 1996 was a mystery. Perhaps it was to ensure future electoral bargaining power, perhaps different authorities had simply failed to communicate with each other. Whatever the cause, the result for the shanty dwellers was protracted uncertainty, an insecurity of tenure, which spelt terrible hardship. They had earned enough to build proper houses but could not risk investing in any form of permanence such as tree planting or house building. At the same time, there was no obvious alternative for investing their savings, since a national financial infrastructure, despite the lessons learnt from the pyramid schemes, had yet to develop. Thus, the shanty dwellers were condemned to go on living in conditions were extremely stressful for adults and responsible for a high illness rate amongst their children. The situation was a breeding ground for corruption, disputes and desperate measures; over the years, squatter families would be approached by less scrupulous owners of former cooperative land

and offered land parcels 'free' in exchange for young girls to be put to work abroad as prostitutes.

The material, as opposed to the psychological, conditions in which the squatters lived were no worse than those of the Bulshar family camped in their shack on ex-cooperative land; although the squatters had to go further to get drinking water unless they could afford to buy it from the itinerant water-sellers who delivered by horse and cart. Outside each shanty there would be a small area planted with cabbages, peppers and tomatoes, and, alongside, one or two dome shaped haystacks (*mullar*) of prairie grass and an outhouse for the chickens, pig and cow. The insides of the shacks were arranged as comfortably as ingenuity allowed given the crampedness and provisional nature of the constructions, but no one pretended that they enjoyed life under these circumstances of makeshift impermanence. Someone always had to be around to ward off thieves. The youngest children often looked weak and unhealthy, badly affected by the mosquitoes in summer and poor hygiene all the year round, since little water could be spared for washing and there was no canalisation.

For the most part these squatters came from mountain areas that were too steep and isolated to offer any prospects for survival now that the communist sources of employment – mainly mines – had ceased to exist. Several families came, for example, from Fushë Arrëz in the province of Puka, just north of the Mirditan border. I once asked an acquaintance with a sick baby and two small children (three older ones continued to live with her parents-in-law in Fushë Arrëz): 'Is it really worse for you in Fushë Arrëz?' 'You can't have been to Fushë Arrëz,' she replied. 'It's a terrible place, so steep there's almost no land. My husband's one of seven brothers; they have 70 square metres of land. The mine's closed. We've been down here for two years.' I could see she was right. A missionary group based for a while in Rrëshen, had made Fushë Arrëz one of their prime targets for aid and missionising. The place was so hard to get to, they said, that they usually made the trip by helicopter. A plain with fertile land, close to the port of Durrës, only an hour's drive from the capital, and the hope of a house in the near future, was indisputably preferable.

Another family had moved down from their mountain village as soon as the mine where the husband worked had closed down nearly five years before. The husband now did casual building work wherever he could find it, sometimes in the village where new houses were beginning to be built, sometimes in Durrës. The wife, a lively enterprising woman, had set up the only shop in the shanty settlement. The shop consisted of a couple of shelves of basics such as salt, sugar and washing powder, stocks which she obtained from a supplier close to the Durrës-Tirana road. They were comparatively expensive since the shopkeeper had to pay a man with a horse and cart to bring the goods the 5km to her shanty. In 1997 she had two sons aged six and three, the elder of whom was teaching himself Italian from a booklet distributed at school. Going to school involved expense as the pupils had to pay for their books and exercise books. Some families simply could not afford the necessary outlay. For those families where the father was away working in Greece and the mother went to work early in the morning before school began, it was simply too difficult financially and practically to ensure that small children attended school.

Not all the squatter families had moved because of closed mines and land shortage. A number had moved to escape from property disputes or blood feuds arising from property disputes. One family had decided to move to the plain because their house built under Communism on what was now someone else's land had led to a blood feud. The three brothers had each built a shanty and brought their families down. Hoping to establish security of tenure on the spot where their shanties stood, they had gone to the local deputy in 1998 and asked point blank when the final land distribution would take place. In 2003 they were still waiting for a reply.

One or two better off squatter families who had saved enough money to buy land elsewhere, eventually ran out of patience and bought plots on the more reasonably priced tracts of former cooperative land across the track, preferring to spend their savings on certain tenure than to live with insecurity. Some of these families sold the land they were squatting on (despite having no ownership papers or official rights) to newly arrived squatters.

Prices ran into thousands of dollars, and while passportisation papers provide near certainty of a plot of land somewhere in the area, there could be no question of designated boundaries until final distribution. Notwithstanding, disputes over these purely speculative boundaries were already creating problems between squatters.

Subsequently, thanks to Caritas, some squatters acquired property without having to use their savings. This came about as a result of the influx in the spring of 1999 of Kosovar refugees, many of whom were sheltered in a huge camp on the plain to the northwest of these squatters. In addition to the containers and tents used to shelter Kosovar families, a small complex of prefabricated flats was built for the refugees near the top of the village. When the Kosovar refugees returned to Kosova, everything movable in the camp was appropriated by less scrupulous locals. Nothing but the containers, a couple of tents and the flats remained for Caritas to distribute to the neediest families. Officials made efforts to discover which of the squatter families were most in need. As always, this proved a near impossible task, and some of those involved were not impervious to bribes. As a result, amongst those who were allocated flats, one was the proprietor of a flourishing cafe-bar, another the owner of a newly built house in Durrës. Some of those who moved to the flats sold their shanties or rented them out, a perfectly reasonable procedure. But others, like the ex-shanty dwellers referred to above, sold the land on which their *barakë* stood, despite the fact that the land itself was not only not theirs, but in some cases at risk of being claimed by ex-state farm workers wanting to exercise their usage rights.

A kilometre or so beyond this group of shanty dwellers who are from Puka and Mirdita, there are a number of other groups, mainly from the northeast, and more villagers are moving down to both areas all the time. The state is continuing to delay distributing the land, presumably calculating that land allocation wins votes and that as long as the settlers are still only squatters, no state investment in infrastructure need be made. One of the many negative consequences of this non-action policy is the above mentioned dilemma it poses to the squatters; should they build substantial houses and cultivate their land on a permanent basis, or is this too risky? Another consequence is the escalation of prices of former cooperative land, where owners are asking astronomical sums per plot, beyond the reach of any but millionaires. In fact, the non-cultivation of sizable tracts of land has given rise all over Albania to the suggestion that owners should either be taxed if they do not work their land, or forced to rent out the land to cultivators; a suggestion still unheeded by the present Socialist government in 2003.

In the year 2000 a few squatters fed up with years of discomfort and impermanence, took the risky step of starting to build houses.

A year later, the representative of a German charitable organisation arrived on the scene. His object, apparently, was to provide the squatters in this particular section of the state farm (about 30 families, including those who were already building permanent houses) with free building materials so that they could build themselves brick houses with tiled roofs. The story went round that the German had gained a promise from the *komuna* that these houses would be allowed to stand for the next five years. This in itself struck the squatters as an odd agreement. Suspicion increased when no building rules or regulations were stipulated and families were left to build where and how they liked with no regard for the most basic planning. It was then suspected that the interpreter used by the German had simply acted in the interests of the building firm. However, the squatters decided that the government was unlikely to risk a confrontation with house dwellers, as opposed to mere shack dwellers. Nevertheless, under the leadership of one of the earliest settlers they were prepared to confront the government should their houses be declared illegal; if necessary, along the lines of the Bathorë inhabitants, with force.

While it is not difficult to understand a weak government's reluctance to attempt to organise migration, it would have been a shrewd move to introduce certain official measures for descending migrants, which would have contributed positively to stable settlement. For example, rather than turning a blind eye to the illegal enrichment through bribes of individual local officials, the government could itself have profited financially and used the bribes money as a tax towards establishing basic services in the new settlements. It would have lost some of its pre-election bargaining powers, but it would have saved itself a lot of future social problems.

Chapter Fifteen

CONCLUSION

A growing shortage of hope on the part of Albanians is all that differentiates 2012 from 2003 when I wrote the conclusion to the first edition of this book. Migration, internal and external, continues to be the most significant socio-demographic and economic phenomenon since the end of Communism, as the following update of the families encountered in the book illustrates. I start with the furthest afield, and work down the mountain to Rrëshen, the Durrës plain, Tirana and Athens. Map 1 shows the villages in the bajraks of Fan and Orosh.

It was a long time before Nikolle's family from Dardhaz in the bajrak of Fan found the means to descend from their isolation in the 'depths' to the periphery of Laç, a town half way to Tirana. In the meantime Nikollë used his carpentry skills to make their house in the rapidly disappearing woods comfortable for his still growing family. The eldest daughter married into an Orosh village and subsequently moved to the outskirts of Tirana. In 2007 the family together with their six remaining children (two boys and a girl had been born since the death of Pashka) finally moved down to the Laç plain. They were one of the last families to leave; in 2010 there was only one family left in Dardhaz, too poor to leave.

The family of ten children from Sang who, as descendants of a heroine of the people, qualified under the communist regime to be educated for professions, have all left the village. Some initially lived abroad. Most now live in Tirana. It was easier for those who were already qualified in 1992 to re-establish themselves on their return to Albania. The entrepreneur of the family has set up a business in partnership with a European firm. This has not been easy in a period of world debt crisis. The government's seemingly arbitrary laws regarding taxation and import rules can lead to unintentional infringements and heavy fines.

The Leka family from Bisak made a particularly satisfying exit. It may be recalled that it had always been the father's intention to move to Tirana. He had said: 'Even though I live in a village, I am a *qytetarë*,' (a citizen, but in this context literally 'a city man'). 'My long term plan since 1991 has been to educate all my children out of the village so that they can take up non-village professions. Eventually I will move to the capital myself. I work what little land I've got so as to eat, but I'm not a villager.' A decade after making this plan Mark carried it out. Through an acquaintance he heard that the Old Tractor Factory in Tirana (Uzinë e Vjetër) had become a centre for descended villagers. The entire site derelict and disused was gradually being taken over by villagers from the poorer areas of Albania such as Kukës, Tropoja, Mirdita in the North, Gramsh and Skrapari in the South. Mark took over (with some financial help from his two emigrant sons now based in England) a two-storey partially converted two-room factory space in which the previous occupant, a carpenter, had built a wooden staircase, thus making it a habitable dwelling. This part of the factory extends for about 100m along the road, starting close to the *oxhak*, a huge free standing, now leaning, chimney, memorial to the factory's obsolescence. The converted buildings joined to each other by the factory's skeleton stand beside a muddy track that intersects with other tracks stretching over several hectares of ramshackle dwellings. Each 'house' has a space in front where most inhabitants plant vegetables. In summer, many gardens have an abundance of grapes and as much maize as can be fitted into the limited space. In fact, this cultivation was beginning already by 2003 to affect the availability of water for household use.

In 2001, Mark, in addition to raising the sum required for paying the previous occupant, managed to organise passportisation, thus officially changing his residence from an isolated highland village to the city of Tirana, and entitling his children to attend school in the area. At the time the government had not made a decision as to the status of the factory complex. Any individual could stake a claim and build himself a dwelling using the factory materials to hand. If he wanted, he could then sell the dwelling on to another individual, as in Mark's case. Between 2000 and 2004 prices doubled. As in the case of the squatters on the plain near Durrës no documents existed. Thus, only those who sold on and left with cash in hand had a sure gain. For this reason, Mark invested nothing immovable in his dwelling beyond the necessities for daily convenience. Others, however, were more sanguine and built brick villas sometimes incorporating their houses into parts of the factory, making use of the existing steel girders. Some squatters dismantled parts of the factory skeleton and used the materials to build elsewhere in the complex. It was hoped that if the entire complex was rebuilt by squatters the government would accept the take-over as a fait accompli rather than risking a serious conflict.

The Leka's descent from their poverty-stricken one room in Bisak to the Old Tractor Factory, a ten-minute bus ride from the centre of Tirana, was a real coup socially, geographically, and economically. Mark found himself a night-watchman's job at the German embassy. His eldest daughter, Bardha, found work initially in an Italian shoemaking enterprise organised along the same exploitative lines as the enterprises near the squatters on the Durrës plain. Once she had saved enough money she took a course as an apprentice hairdresser. Now she is married and lives in Saranda, where she has her own hairdressing salon. Another daughter and her *refugjatë* husband live in Greece. Mark no longer has a job, but ever since he arrived in Tirana he has been active on the governing board of the local school, which his youngest child still attends despite being above school leaving age. The effects of malnutrition had stunted this son's growth so badly that for several years during his teens he was too embarrassed to go to school. In 2009 he spent the summer working with his brother-in-law in Greece where, as his father explained it, independence and responsibility caused him to grow up in mind and body.

The family does not receive social welfare and struggles to live on irregular remittances from their sons and the income of the three unmarried daughters who work as flower sellers in the centre of Tirana. When Dava, the mother, was suddenly taken ill recently with a heart problem, it was discovered that she is not registered as living in Tirana. Without passportisation papers she was not entitled to free treatment at a city hospital and had to be treated privately. Yet for all the difficulty of making ends meet, the family rightly feels that they are incomparably better off than they were in Bisak. The houses here remain illegal, but a World Bank project acting together with Tirana's City Council will, it is believed, eventually replace these houses with social housing apartment blocks such that each squatting family will eventually have a flat. Jobs, even for those with political connections (or friendship/kin influence), are few and far between, but being within the city of Tirana increases opportunities for earning, if only sporadically.

Bulshar in the bajrak of Orosh has lost more than four-fifths of its population. The headman has died, his family are dispersed, most living in Greece. The daughter of the schoolteacher 'Heroine of the People' divorced the headman's son and lives in Tirana. The Deda household in Lëgjin, a few kilometres below Bulshar, was somewhat better off than most of the other village families I knew. The grandfather had owned land on the Lezhë plain as well as having a bigger house and more land than most other people in Lëgjin. This has enabled two of the sons, following several stints working in Greece, to leave the highlands for Lezhë. A third son now married to a girl from Mirdita still works in Athens, one married daughter lives in Crete. The parents continue to live in Lëgjin despite its isolation.

Ironically, a super modern four-lane motorway linking the port of Durrës with Kosovo that might have transformed the isolated settlements of Fan and Orosh has for the time being at least had the opposite effect. The 'superstrada' passes through 61km of the mountain remotenesses of Mirdita; its incongruous presence in the so-called 'depths' where locals had once told me I couldn't possibly go looks surreal and has proved a very challenging engineering feat. In 2003 I wrote that if the proposal for a road linking the port of Durrës with Kosovo was realised all the villages within the area would be positively affected. As well as the service sector jobs, which an international road would generate, I suggested that easy access to these mountain villages might even lead to the type of *sommerfrisch* tourism found in Austria and Switzerland. I did not foresee that the road would be a motorway with only two exits over the entire Mirdita stretch. To date, instead of bringing new life to the villages on either side, the new road cuts them off. Indeed, since the old roads between the villages are hardly maintained any more, the villagers' situation has actually worsened. The government has given precedence to facilitating tourism from Kosova to the Durrës coastal area, which it is hoped this highway will generate. The government also hopes that this link will increase commercial activity between Albania and the rest of the Balkans. In June 2009, with much pomp and fanfare Prime Minister Berisha exploited the unfinished road for electioneering purposes, prematurely declaring open the unfinished Thirra tunnel that divides Mirdita from the last lap to the Kosovan border at Morinë. Since then the tunnel and some stretches of the road have repeatedly suffered from construction problems, often leading to partial or complete closure. Nevertheless, despite the lack of advantage for locals at the moment, there is some hope that in the long run linking the country to Kosovo and beyond will prove positive economically.

Continuing the descent down the mountain we reach Rrëshen. The make-up of Rrëshen's population has changed; many villagers have moved into the town (population c.8,000), while many Rrëshenites have moved to Tirana or abroad. Recent administrative changes mean that most of the bureaucracy, including the law courts and the Local Education Authority, has been moved to the bigger town of Lezhë (population c. 27,500). Those who predicted that Rrëshen had no *perspectivë*, no future prospects, claim despondently that they have been proved right. However, many of the intellectuals, teachers, writers, doctors, continue to live, and work and write, in Rrëshen so that one might question what is meant by prospects. There are still the schools, the hospital (though this functions minimally) and the House of Culture. And there is of course, the newly completed large Catholic church with its staff of mainly Italian clerics and nuns. But it is true that manufacturing and agriculture related industry have ceased to exist in the area since the end of Communism. Outside the state sector there are virtually no jobs.

A number of Rrëshen's unmarried women made the decision to marry abroad; some simply to escape the enforced idleness of unemployment. But others left jobs to escape to what they hoped would be a more affluent life within the security of a functioning state. One married an elderly man in need of nursing care in Belgium, another married a divorced Italian whom she helps on his farm as well as looking after his teenage children. By the same means – arranged marriages – women from isolated villages are enabled to escape to Rrëshen. A number of Rrëshenites' now grownup children have moved illegally to Belgium and England.

Accommodation costs make moving to Tirana from Rrëshen very difficult. The price a Rrëshenite gets for selling his or her flat to an incoming villager is a small proportion of the cost of a flat in Tirana. Yet moving to Tirana is a pull for many even though it will likely involve the discomfort of a very small apartment in an unattractive suburb a long way from the city centre. Flats and houses in the centre of Tirana, apart from those inherited from the early 1990s when privatisation occurred, are now only affordable by successful businessmen and women, politicians or foreign organisations. As noted, children of the communist elite from the provinces who had just entered or completed higher education when Communism came to an end have fared better than recently arrived provincials, both in terms of finding jobs and accommodation. One result is that much of the present population in central Tirana comes from the same class as the communist elite families.

For those with an income and lucky enough to live centrally, Tirana is a comparatively appealing place to live. Distances are small; theatres, art galleries, concerts, exhibitions are all within walking distance and, thanks to the communist legacy that promoted culture, both active and affordable. On the downside a lot of the buildings are still shabby and few of the new high rise blocks are aesthetic. The water supply is sporadic except in those apartment blocks where the inhabitants have paid to install water tanks. But the centre of the city has retained its original character even while modernising. The parks have been cleared of illegal buildings; the lakeside park with its woods and wild flowers is a source of pleasure to thousands of Tiranians at the weekends. Tiranians are the beneficiaries of a capital city-centric government whose lack of a regional development policy has forced so many, mainly rural, Albanians to work abroad in difficult circumstances.

Those squatters who moved down from distant mountain villages to the coastal plains near Durrës are at last nearer to ending the long years of insecurity. In Shenavlash on the former state farmland reclaimed from the swamps near Durrës there is now a real prospect of imminent legalisation. The headman of the squatter group tried repeatedly, year after year, to clarify the situation. He spoke to members of the Durrës town council, he spoke to officials at the local *komuna* office. With no result because, as each authority explained, you squatters are registered in Rrashbull, the *komuna* where the passportisation process was carried out, but the land you live on belongs to the town council of Durrës. He tried repeatedly to contact the local MP, again without success. Then he tried applying for information to the regional Qarku, the administrative authority that encompasses both the town council and the *komuna*, but never received a reply.

In 2006, Aluizni, the agency for legalisation, urbanisation and integration of illegal property was established. The law says that where a piece of land of over five hectares has been built on, as is the case for this settlement, the inhabitants' plots will be legalised. Legal ownership will follow a payment by the squatter of a cash sum of around $2,000. Since 2009 the Durrës branch office has been collecting evidence relating to all illegal buildings but had still not reached Shenavlash in 2010. There have been the expected setbacks; for example, four employees of the agency were arrested in April 2010 for accepting bribes relating to the legalisation of property. But the squatters do now believe that they will eventually get ownership papers and have the right to stay where they are permanently.

Those on the other side of the tract, on former cooperative land bought by Caritas, are now well established. The scene since 1996, when the Gjokas from Bulshar were allocated a desolate plot by Caritas, has changed considerably. Near their original lonely shack they have built a small two-room house, which now stands as the Gjoka father had predicted next to an asphalted road with traffic including a valuable bus service to and from Durrës. Many of the makeshift shacks nearby have been replaced by cement houses, some two storeys high. The Gjokas have planted fruit trees and vines, and grow vegetables and maize in season. But like their neighbours they are dependent on their emigrant children for expenses such as medicine and clothes. Their life is lonely despite occasional visits to or from their children and grandchildren, all of whom live abroad. Their three sons and eldest daughter live in Athens, while the other two daughters are married to *refugjate* and live in Italy.

In one respect Albanian emigrants, most of whom work in Europe, are better off than the outflow of Greek and Italian emigrants who left for distant continents; the Albanians are at least much closer to home. But like immigrants everywhere they do the jobs that no one else wants to do, from badly paid work in construction or iron foundries to baking bread in the small hours of the night or delivering food round the city from night till dawn. At the same time, as one immigrant put it: 'In some ways we are spoilt, we have become unused to conditions in Albania. We may be treated here as second class citizens, but at least we can come home after work and take a shower, knowing that there will be water and electricity; knowing that in winter we can heat the house.' But living in Greece or Italy is expensive; saving enough to support one's parents and younger siblings as well as putting money by for the future is impossible. Accidents at work exacerbated by slack safety regulations for foreign workers are not infrequent and result in time off work and debt. The absence of grandparents makes childcare difficult. The eldest Gjoka daughter, Elda, works whenever work is available in a shop. This means leaving her two small children alone in the house for several hours until her husband returns from his job in the afternoon. Raising oneself out of the labourer class is very difficult; the eldest Gjoka son, who lives in Athens, managed to combine studying for a degree in sports journalism with working in a pizzeria. After qualifying he worked for a newspaper as a sports reporter but, after nine months without being paid 'because we don't pay beginners', he was forced to quit.

What incentives are there for migrants to return to Albania, where unemployment is so high?[1] Where law and order are far from under control, where crime and corruption have continued to escalate, and lack of clarity regarding property rights has reached crisis proportions? The supply of electricity and water continues to be irregular. Official communication channels between state institutions and local communities barely exist. The institutions remain the domains of individuals rather than neutral bodies functioning independently of their administrators' personal lives. So what could possibly draw emigrants back? Prime Minister Berisha during a visit to Athens in 2006 made a public statement to Albanians working in Greece. Come back home and we the government will help you to invest in business and put your savings to good use. Nothing has come of this promise according to those few who have returned and put it to the test. And not many of those working in Greece whose lives I have followed for the last 10 to 15 years have accumulated any savings. As we've seen, they send money to their unemployed relatives in Albania despite barely being able to make ends meet themselves. It is very rare for Albanian emigrants without previous higher education or professional skills to raise themselves from a hand-to-mouth existence. Work is often sporadic, and financial security no more than a dream. Even those emigrants with higher education such as the Greek minority

Albanians from Dropull, some of whom do enjoy a decent standard of living in Greece (despite not being able to practise their original professions), cannot return to Albania other than for holidays; there are few jobs for them or their children to return to, and none with salaries comparable to those in Greece. Notably, however, they do feel strong attachment to their villages and return to their homes regularly.

In the autumn of 2010, Albanians were finally granted visaless travel in the Schengen zone. This was trumpeted by Prime Minister Berisha as an indicator of Albania's progress. The triumph looked less glorious the next day when it was learnt that the European Commission had rejected Albania's application for EU candidature. The first reason given for this rejection was the parliamentary impasse that was preventing the proper functioning of state institutions. A second reason was the government's failure to crack down on corrupt behaviour not only in the wider society but more spectacularly within its own ranks and the judiciary.

In an interview for the newspaper *Shekulli* (22 November 2010), Pandeli Majko,[2] a former Socialist Prime Minister, discussed the parliamentary impasse. According to Majko, Berisha's refusal to negotiate with the opposition despite calls from Strasbourg and Brussels, and his cavalier attitude to financial scandals within his own party, were symptomatic of an exhausted 'Postcommunism'. The implication was that 'Postcommunism' as distinct from postcommunism (in the temporal sense) is different both from democracy and from totalitarianism. Majko doesn't develop this interesting observation, but the idea of a Postcommunist Albania is worth closer investigation. Dictatorship achieves 'consensus' by eliminating – be it through imprisonment or death – its opponents. Democracy negotiates and compromises. Postcommunism is intolerant of criticism, doesn't compromise, ignores dissent. But it can't *outlaw* dissent because a feature of Postcommunist government is the absence of dictatorship's terror apparatus. Freedom of speech and an active opposition are established features of the transitional road to democracy, features underwritten by organisations such as the Council of Europe and human rights bodies. Though of course these features can be jeopardised by international players in the 'interests of stability' if the status quo seems like the best bet regardless of its ethical merits.

Right from the start in 1992, when Berisha's Democrat Party came to power, he was famously intolerant of dissent, dismissing some of his ablest ministers when they disagreed with his policies. Because international donors had to be kept onside and a semblance of democracy maintained, these critics were able to establish a rival party. Media critics considered a threat by Berisha might well find themselves in prison, though not on charges relating to their criticisms. This tendency to authoritarianism may have contributed to his loss of the 1994 referendum on a new constitution, which was rejected by the voters as giving him excessive powers. Though he won the 1996 election, a number of foreign powers believed the election to have been rigged. Other members of the international community were prepared to overlook election violations however, preferring a known and tried quantity in the Balkans even at the expense of perpetuating both the weaknesses of Postcommunism and stagnation.

Two months before the 1996 election, Berisha exempted the pyramid schemes from a banking law that would have regulated them – his solution to retaining support. Two months after the election he intervened once more to prevent the schemes from folding despite urgent pleas from the Central Albanian bank to close them down. This reckless intervention led to the catastrophic events of 1997 and further exodus. Berisha's attempted coup d'état in 1998 following the death of Azem Hajdari, a member of the Democrat Party, got no further than occupying the radio and television building for an hour or two. But the willingness to ignore the law, to take reckless steps to maintain or regain power, are in character with his intransigence over the 2009 disputed election and his readiness to condone corruption in his own ranks; further illustration of the development of Postcommunism as a form of governance.

As noted, in the early days of Berisha's premiership media critics of his policies risked imprisonment. Today Berisha's government has successfully insulated itself from outside criticism. Hence it is possible for citizens and journalists to be highly critical of the Prime Minister in print and even face-to-face with him on television (as in the Fevziu interview) with impunity. Not because freedom of speech is a democratic right that can't be denied but because its expression is no longer a threat to the *modus operandi* of Berisha's government.

Berisha has been leader longer than any other individual since the end of Communism. Crucially, he has been at once the beneficiary of emigration, which has removed so many potentially dissenting voices from the country, and a contributor to the exodus thanks to his neglect of economic development and failure to uphold law and order. Nonetheless, it is hard to explain, given his dire record as regards the country's development, how he has managed to make a comeback so often. One factor may be that Berisha has been the one and only Democrat Party leader. The Socialist Party by contrast has had a series of leaders. Does the Democrats' continuity of leadership perhaps speak to a post-communist nostalgia for a cult of personality in preference to a parliamentary system?

Non-functioning state institutions and a culture of impunity with increasingly brazen corruption are two reasons why more Albanians may take advantage of the new opportunity for visa-free travel. Indeed, the European Union fears that visa-free travel within the Schengen zone (albeit only as tourists and with stays limited to three months) may lead to a further exodus by Albanians hoping to evade the ban on working. At the same time, as the economic crisis deepens in Europe and unemployment grows, there may well be a flood of long-term emigrants made jobless returning to Albania. This misfortune, economically disastrous in the immediate term for the Albanian population, may prove the catalyst needed to alarm a corrupt and complaisant government out of postcommunism and stagnancy into action.

SKETCHES FROM A 12-YEAR-OLD'S NOTEBOOK

A Rough Guide to Tirana, Albania, 1992

Arriving in Tirana may be a little daunting, what with the dirt and damage, but if one ventures into further Albania, one will be quite happy to see Tirana again.

It is best to arrange your accommodation before you arrive. Apartments can be rented for negotiable (up to a point) prices, but the Albanians are out to exploit the RICH FOREIGNERS so beware! An able English speaking Albanian, L, will be more than willing to find out about apartments in Tirana if you fax her before arrival. Once one arrives in Tirana airport, if you are British you have to pay a sum of $40. From Rinas airport into Tirana there will be taxis outside the airport, but it's wiser to arrange the car with L.

The conditions vary a lot from winter to summer. In winter it is advisable to bring torches and candles as Tirana guarantees no electricity. But in summer unfortunately, the shortage is water and we are unable to advise any products.

Shopping in Tirana is a time consuming occupation so if you aren't going to have the shopping done for you, but find it hard to go without small food commodities, then we advise you to bring the following: instant coffee; powdered milk; peanut butter (this seems to be a weakness among Tiranian foreigners).

Tirana has few tourist attractions, but in the evenings one can walk down the Boulevard, which is a beautifully wide avenue with trees growing all the way down on either side. Few cars pass here but the few go to President Berisha's office at the end of the Boulevard. Another nice walk is round the former Blloku, the roads where, in communist times, all the top Communists lived and no-one else was allowed to enter. The Blloku has a lot of pretty trees and bushes. The houses are villas now inhabited by foreign officials. The Artificial Lake at the end of 'New Tirana' is the picnic place for Albanians. Now the lake itself is filthy and infested with rowdy boys and rubbish, but the park land is quite pleasant. It isn't a good idea to go to the lake alone as it's never very busy and there are plenty of (possibly) robbers. Then there is the zoo at the end of the lake. This place couldn't be described as a place for entertainment. The zoo has five animals, all of which have very small cages (especially the bear). The animals sit huddled up being chewed by the infestation of rats. The saddest animal is the bear who sits in his tiny cage looking at the ground with sad eyes while the rats scuttle around him eating his food.

Another place to see is the mosque. Though Tiranians are Muslim, they take religion very mildly. Few men go to the mosque and most of those that do go out of curiosity. Women are allowed to stand at the door and watch. Most afternoons you see a small flock of little girls with a long piece of material hiding their hair and legs, but it's only a game to them and will soon blow over. The mosque is elaborately designed with Arabic words and William Morris style designs.

First impressions

Tirana is probably the most grey dirty broken down place I've ever been to. The greyest thing about it is the endless columns of apartment blocks. The entire country has been laden with them. At night one wades through the litter to get to the dark stairs. By the time you've reached your flat and unlocked your door without being set upon by robbers, you heave a sigh of relief and reach for the light switch . . . another evening spent in candlelight. One morning soon after we'd arrived we went out with our landlady. We walked along past the squatting sunflower-seed sellers who were chatting to the shoe polishers about Mrs Hoxha's trial. At the market Mummy stopped to buy vegetables and some 'best before August '92' margarine from the stall next to the man selling destroyed shoes. After the market Vjollca took us to meet a cousin.

We were led into a room with a blaring television and a volouminous pink and brown sofa. The usual Tirana conversation to Mummy: Are you a missionary? No, I'm a social anthropologist. Do you work for Caritas? No, I'm an atheist. Well, my husband's trying to get a job in Italy and needs help, you'd be very useful, I'm so glad you've come. Please have an apple. We Albanians are very hospitable. We know the English are cold. I have a 16 year old daughter who would love to have English lessons. Maybe . . .

A Brief History, 1993

Albania is a small country north of Greece. It's population is three million, that's eighteen times smaller than England. Albania is ex-communist. For nearly 50 years from 1945–91, it was kept tightly under a communist ruler, Enver Hoxha, entirely isolated from all the world except briefly when it was friends with Russia and later China. No Albanian was allowed out of the country and virtually no foreigners were allowed in. Hoxha expected a kind of idolism from the population. For example, you were regarded as a better citizen and partisan if you had pictures of Hoxha all over your house. The first idea of Communism was that everybody was to be equal, so rich landowners had all their land taken away and were on the same level as the peasants. Later, everybody's land however small had to be given to the State. In fact, under this equal right government incredible injustice occurred. People who had had wealthy relations were persecuted. To express a personal opinion or to criticise the government was a great danger. If one had feelings that were either against or challenging Communism, or if one were to merely say one word of criticism, one would be put in prison indefinitely. One's family (even cousins) would not be permitted to have further education.

In 1990 there were riots, vandalisms and every pane of glass was broken as people in a rush of freedom and anger smashed everything up. In 1990 there was no law and order at all and everybody did as they pleased. Now very few things in Albania have been mended or reconstructed and the place still looks pretty bombed. One of the main reasons that all the vandalism took place was that under Communism one wasn't allowed to do virtually anything. So as soon as Albanians didn't have to abide by communist rules they took out their freedom on the buildings.

During Communism, the government lost a lot of money as it made prices so cheap. But now Albania is having to face up to European prices: 70p for a loaf of bread instead of the former 1p. But salaries are still ludicrously low, £15 a month for a well-trained teacher, let alone the fact that 40 per cent in towns and 60 per cent in rural areas are unemployed. The unemployed live off tiny state benefit but this only lasts for a year, then they are pennyless. This is one of the reasons for Albanians to emigrate. Hundreds of thousands of Albanians secretly cross the mountains to get into Greece. If their exodus is not done secretly they have to buy a visa, which may cost around £300. If discovered illegally crossing the border into foreign countries they may be fined, put in prison or even shot. Many Albanian youths take this danger route as they have no visa but desperately need to earn money. Almost every family has a member in either Greece or Italy. After working for several months or years, the emigrants return with their booty. Near the bus station you see them load perhaps a washing machine or a cooker on to a cardboard cart (the better ones are made of bits of old iron) led by a shady looking gypsy. Also bought by emigrants you see broken down Mercedes, sometimes roofless (not because they're chic but because the roof fell off), windowless and most commonly numberplateless. Though it is illegal of course to not have any numberplates on your car, the Albanians have a solution – bribery. Every precautious driver has a collection of natty keyrings that they offer as a bribe to policemen who stop them for being unregistered. The policemen quite readily accept these bribes and allow the driver, after shaking his hand, to drive off very relieved.

As European prices are extremely high for Albanians, they buy and sell dud, out of date, or fallen-off-the-back-of-lorry products. Many times have I been pleased to find a Mars bar for 5p, later to discover it was to be eaten by 1989. A lot of confectionery and products generally are bought from Turkey (where they are manufactured more cheaply). Hilal chocolate bars are sold on every corner, together with sunflower seeds sold by the eggcup, or old shoes that wouldn't be acceptable at a jumble sale. Some earn money with bathroom scales, which you can weigh yourself on for half a p. But not just old age men and eight-year-old boys are in the street selling. There are very respectable geography, maths and history teachers, librarians, opera singers and actors out there selling confectionery and junk. For example, I was walking through the town centre with an Albanian friend when she saw her geography teacher selling a mix of soap, chocolate and tinsel. All around the towns, even the capital, people can be seen leading their cows, goats and sheep through the streets to the market.

Enver Hoxha

Hoxha was Albania's dictator for 47 years. Hoxha himself lived in a vulgar but luxurious mansion while his dictatees, the population of Albania, lived in slum conditions. Hoxha took away everybody's land and turned it all into cooperative farms. Albania didn't produce very much as the workers knew that however little they worked, their pay which was very low, stayed the same. Hoxha had this idea that whatever happens the people must have bread. So he made them terrace every mountainside to grow wheat and maize on.

Every 50–100m Hoxha had concrete mushrooms built. These were bomb shelters where people could hide if there was an invasion. If only they had used all those tons of concrete for building houses, there wouldn't be a terrible housing shortage now. Every year men and women from all over Albania were sent out to practise warfare. This was to keep them busy.

In Hoxha's regime religion was banned. Probably he thought it was enough for the population to have him to worship. On every schoolbook's flypage there was a picture of Hoxha with a little word of worship to him. Hoxha set up a whole museum of himself in Tirana.

The prisons mainly contained political prisoners. These were people who had complained about something or disagreed with his regime. These prisoners have now been let out but have no homes and are living in school dormitories.

Appendix Two

EXTENDED QUOTATIONS FROM THE KANUN OF LEK DUKAGJIN

Below are the quotes in full from the Kanun relating to boundaries and inheritance:

1. 'The boundary stone has witnesses around it. There are six or twelve small rocks which are buried in the earth around the boundary stone. When boundaries are fixed, aside from the households concerned, there must also be present Elders of the village, Elders of the bajrak, and as many young people and children as possible from the villages of the district, so that the boundary will be retained in memory. Every tract of land, whether field or meadow, garden or vineyard, small forest or copse, woodland or pasture or house grounds, village, bajrak or house – all are divided by boundaries.'

'Someone who wishes to set a boundary or restore a forgotten one must take and bear on his shoulder a rock and a clod of earth, and leading the two households or the two villages or the two bajraks, must fix the new boundary or indicate the traces of the old boundaries.

With the rock and earth on his shoulder, the Elder who leads in the division of the old boundaries must swear before he begins.'

Several of the common forms of oath are then cited such as:

1) 'By this rock and earth (or by this weight) with which I charge myself, by what I have heard from my forebears, the boundary points are those that I declare to you now, and to the best of my knowledge, I do not injure anyone's interests.'

2) 'By this weight, here and here were the previous boundaries, and here I set them too. May I bear it in the next life if I deceive you.'

3) 'By this weight which will burden me in the next life [if I lie], these are the old traces of the boundaries as my grandfather informed me; he herded goats in accordance with them when he was a child. He has taken on himself into the next life the burden of truth that the boundaries are here and here, and I too take upon my soul the truth of his word.' (1989:74)

Having duly sworn, the Elder begins:

'If the Elder has been given the stone and the clod of earth, and he has placed them on his shoulder to declare the boundary, no one may stop or hinder him, but he is told: "Go ahead, and if you do not act justly, may you be burdened with this weight in the next life!" When the Elder has set the boundary, he must place his hand on it and say: "If anyone moves this stone, may he be burdened with it in the next life!" If someone moves the boundary in order to cause discord between one household and another, or one village and another, or one bajrak and another, instigated by promises of reward or seeking such, he will be punished with dishonour and will also bear the cost of the damage that he caused by creating this discord. If a murder results from the mischief relating to the moved boundary, the person who caused the mischief must be fined 100 sheep and one ox, and is executed by the village.' (1989:76)

'Land boundaries are not movable'; 'once boundaries are fixed, they are never moved again'. (1989:74)

2. 'The Canon recognizes the son as an heir but not the daughter.

Inheritance belongs to a descendant by filiation or by blood, and not to one related by milk [i.e. a child of different parents suckled by the same mother], nor to the children of daughters.

A wife does not receive a share of inheritance either from her parents or from her husband:

a) To prevent her sons from settling in the home of her uncle who has no heirs;

b) To prevent the woman's parents from settling in the home of her husband who leaves no heirs.

c) To prevent the clan of one bajrak mixing with the clan of another bajrak.

If the male line of a house dies out, even though there may be a hundred daughters, none of them have the right to any share in the inheritance of their parents, nor do any of their sons and daughters. "A descendant in the female line cannot be considered equal to one issuing from uncles."

If a house has only female heirs, the closest relative either goes to live with them or takes them into his home, and from that time he takes ownership of the property and wealth.' (1989:52)

'A father who does not have sons may leave his daughters neither land nor property nor house.' However, 'During his lifetime, a father [without male heirs] may give his daughters money, goods and chattels. After the death of their father, the daughters do not have the right to demand gifts that were promised by him.' (1989:56)

3. 'If the public highway passes across your land and you intend to cultivate that land, you may make the road detour, but you may not divert it through torrents or streams or along the brinks of waters, nor along crags and cliffs.'

'Work moves the path.' If you intend to work land through which runs the village path, work it, but you must find a place for the path. The Canon does not want anyone's land to be damaged; therefore it says that 'the hoe moves the path' but the road and the path must be set in another place.

'Work makes the public highway detour, but it may not be in water where the livestock can drown, nor on rocks where the livestock can break their necks.' (1989:86)

'The path with a stile, or according to the Canon, 'the blind road', is bounded on four sides and opens to the land you work. If this path has always been free to the access of your fellow villagers, but damage has been caused to fields, gardens, vineyards and orchards, you may close it, but you must open another one in the vicinity, not too far away.

If this path has been left as a favour and on the condition that no damage would result, you have the right to close it and to tell the village that it may no longer be used.

If this path has been used for a long time by your fellow villagers, by bride's men and brides, by funeral corteges and by those going to the church or cemetery, then you may not close it.

In order to move any path, the approval of the village is absolutely necessary.' (1989:82)

The above quotations are from:

Fox, L. (1989). *The Code of Lekë Dukagjini*, (Albanian text collected & arranged by Shtjefën Gjeçov, translated & with an introduction by L. Fox) New York: Gjonlekaj Publishing Company.

NOTES

Foreword

1 1999–2002
2 http://cjres.oxfordjournals.org/content/early/2012/04/01/cjres
.rss004.abstract (accessed 2012)
3 http://www.economywatch.com/world_economy/albania/ (accessed 2010 link no longer functional).

Chapter One

1 cf. Giddens, A. (1995). Epilogue. In: Ahmed, A. and Shore, C. (eds.) *The Future of Anthropology*. London: The Athlone Press, p. 274.
2 Clifford, J. & Marcus, E. (eds.) (1986). *Writing Culture*, Berkeley: University of California Press, pp. 112–14.
3 Gellner, E. (1988). *Plough, Sword and Book*, London: Collins Harvill.
4 70–80 per cent of emigrants are without legal documents (Telo, I. (1998). *Mirëqënia dhe Minimumi Jetik*, Tirana: Institut Bashkimi i Sindikatave të Pavarura të Shqipërisë).
5 cf Black-Michaud's thesis on feud (Black-Michaud, J. (1975). *Cohesive Force*, Oxford: Basil Blackwell).
6 By chance in Rrëshen I turned on the television as the take-over occurred. It took a minute to grasp what this act might bring in terms of violence and upheaval. Recalling 1997, the realisation was terrifying.
7 Fortunately, old age pensioners (that is, men and women over 60) are a mere 10.3 per cent of this youthful population. (I. Telo 1998)
8 Post Office advertisements on television in 1999 touchingly began 'Return to Alba Post', such had been the loss of faith in that

institution. While a sad advertisement in the newspaper on 23 October 1999 read: 'Citizens! speed, accuracy, correctness & prices of
the services we offer will leave you satisfied & make you return to
us.'

9 Hasani, A. (1999) *Klan*, 10 October.
10 This was partly in frustration and disappointment when Pandeli
   Majko failed to be elected Party Head and hence had to resign from
   being Prime Minister. The fact that Fatos Nano won the position of
   Party Head was seen as a return to Nano-Berisha confrontational
   politics. Majko was immensely popular as Prime Minister because
   he was not part of this syndrome.
11 The exodus from rural areas of trained teachers had fundamentally
   undermined rural education.
12 It did happen. The first edition in Albanian was published in 2005
   entitled *Mbijetesa* (Survival). The second edition entitled *Shqipëria
   pas rënies së komunizmit* (*Albania after the fall of Communism*) was
   published in 2009.

Chapter Four

1 *Ylli: revistë politiko-shoqërore dhe letraro-artistike viti32-të I botimit*,
  vol. 8 (Tirana: August 1982).

Chapter Five

1 Nor at this stage had they been exposed to NGOs and their donations, or to the relative deprivation and/or dependency and discon-
  tents that accompany such exposure.
2 Catholics make up 10 per cent of Albania's population today.
3 A few were Italian, viz Loka, 1996:58; in 1852 the priest in Fanë was
  Dom Antonio Foderi and in 1878 Niccolo Bianchi, and in the church
  registers for this period all the parishioners names were Italianised.
4 1999:57–65.
5 *Fani del nga Muzgjet* (*Fanë emerges from the twilight*) by a Mirditan
  scholar, Nikollë Loka, 1996.
6 Gregorian.
7 Zmajeviç, V. in *Quellen und Materialen zur Albanischen Geschichte im
  17 und 18 Jahrhundert*, Munchen, 1979:77, cited in Dedaj, 1999.
8 Duodës, P. *Separatum Munchner Zeitschrift fur Balkankunde*, 1,
  Band,1978:51–2, cited in Dedaj, 1999.
9 A timar holder enjoyed the proceeds of the land in exchange for
  military service.

10 Fandi i vogel means Little Fanë, the river passing through Mirdita, and hence the territorial marker.

11 Cited in Loka (1996:22).

12 Names such as Gëzim – joy, Agim – dawn, Bashkim – unity, Besnik – faithful, Ylli – star, were safe and free from religious overtones. Communist names such as Marenglen (telescoped Marx, Engels and Lenin) and Proletar were popular with a certain generation. The communist government tried to get people to choose their children's names from an official list of approved names. In 1982 The Academy of Sciences published a book by A. Kostallari, *Fjalor Emra Njerëzish*, listing 'acceptable' names.

13 A scholar and priest from Kosovë, Father Konstantin Gjeçov was educated in Franciscan schools in northern Albania (Shkodër) and Bosnia, and attended theological college in Kosova. Much of his life as a parish priest was spent teaching his parishioners to read and write Albanian, though Ottoman law forbade the use of Albanian language in the Empire. His most famous work is his systematic study of customary law, which began to come out in a series of articles in the journal *Hylli i Dritës* and was intended to form a book. Tragically, Gjeçov was assassinated in 1929 before completion of the book and much of his unpublished material was lost. The published articles, however, were compiled into a book by fellow Franciscan priests and published posthumously in 1933, as *Kanuni i Lekë Dukagjinit* (*The Canon of Lek Dukagjin*).

14 In the southern and central regions there were also local legal codes such as the Kanun of Laberia (or Papasuli) in the southwest. But in those regions where emigration abroad had been common from the eighteenth century local canons had lost their force by the mid-twentieth century.

15 However, in Gjeçov's Kanun there are some interesting insights into differences between Lek and Kastriot's approach to people, law and democracy. Lek maintained that all people are equal before God; handsome or ugly, poor or rich. He considered that the good are born from the bad and the bad from the good (1989:130, 170, 240, 242). 'If distinctions of blood were permitted, the ugly and the poor could be killed with impunity.' 'Whoever kills a human being, whether man or woman, boy or girl, or even an infant, handsome or deformed... rich or poor, noble or baseborn, must pay the same penalty: 6 purses, 100 sheep and half an ox fine' (1989:170). Lek and Kastriot also differ on vengeance law, with Lek once again more focused on the individual. In the territory governed by Kastriot vengeance for blood could be taken on any member of the brotherhood, the clan, and the progeny: 'Pursue the clan for blood,

fire your gun at a member of the clan.' In the territory governed by Lek Dukagjin, by contrast, the law remained in force: 'Blood follows the finger (i.e. vengeance may only be taken on the murderer, the man who pulled the trigger) and after twenty-four hours (following the murder) vengeance may not be taken on the relatives (of the murderer)' (Fox, 1989:242).

16 All the accounts of nineteenth and early twentieth century observers such as Nopcsa, Hahn, Cozzi, Durham and Hasluck, comment on the centrality of the Kanun in northern Albania.

17 A *mal*, or mountain district, comprised several villages forming an independent territorial and economic unit, governing itself and providing its own defence system. This political organisation was the basis for tribal unity. The *kuvend* members were known as *krere* – chiefs. Their common object was to protect their freedom, their families and their property. Through the council of elected village heads, military leaders were elected. The power of these leaders was limited, and individuals could easily be removed by the village councils if seen to be incompetent. Long-term resistance to Ottoman penetration had endowed the *mal* with a distinctly military character. Taking advantage of the similarity between the existing local form of territorially-based administration and their own, the Turks (according to Pal Doci) simply exchanged the name *mal* or *dheu* for the Turkish word, bajrak. Bajrak means banner or standard as borne by a standard bearer in a military operation; the standard bearer is the *bajraktar*. Mirditans in the seventeenth century were required to supply the Porte with fighting men, a form of tribute that suited them well and brought the region valuable income. They only had to serve as soldiers when the empire was at war and continued to enjoy administrative autonomy. Although through military exploits, a bajraktar could become a heroic figure and hence a figure of local authority, bajraktars are said never to have taken on roles as law and decision makers in Mirdita.

A 'bajraktar' was the head of a bajrak, a territorial division within which there were smaller divisions each with a headman. He and the elders regulated grazing rights and wood-cutting rights, and controlled the supply of water for irrigation. But it is clear from observers' accounts that the bajraktars were closely controlled by the tribe with little freedom of political or judicial action. Should the locals disapprove of one of his decisions, they could make him reassess it. And although the position was theoretically hereditary, an incompetent heir could be passed over, and quite often was, for someone more suitable. Edith Durham observed: 'Of old the bajraktar is said to have been important. In my time he had lost ground and was quite often cut out in council by abler men' (Durham, 1928:16). In the 1930s Hasluck notes: 'In all areas the jurisdiction of the bajraktar was subject to certain limitations. If the commoners did not like one of his decisions, even if made in concert with the headmen and elders, they were not bound to abide by it and could compel him to reexamine the case. Neither he nor a headman could singly or in combination, fine a tribesman without first securing authority from the tribe.' [Hasluck, 1954:121–122]

18 There are various theories about the provenance and date of the Gjomarkaj family in Mirdita, just as there are various versions of the nature of their role in Mirditan society. Naturally, the Communists claimed that Mirditans were enslaved to the family in a system of feudal relations, with Mirdita effectively the family's property. For the reasons already mentioned, relating to the terrain, this is implausible. The limited evidence available indicates that it was not until the eighteenth century that the family began to play a significant role. One theory has it that the family moved from Has (a region to the northeast in the province of Kukës) to Orosh in Mirdita in order to escape from a blood feud; that through the talents and astuteness of various family heads over the years, the family was able to establish itself as a significant influence throughout the region. An interesting variation of this theory hypothesises that the Turks may have deliberately placed the family here once they had realised Mirdita could not be conquered. Useless for raising taxes, the province would remain independent in exchange for a ready supply of soldiers to be mobilised by the Captain of Mirdita. (personal communication, Ndue Dedaj)

19 'To place under ban in the language of the Canon means: to separate, to ostracise, and to sever a family from the community, depriving it of all rights, favour and honour with respect both to the village and the bajrak. If a family is placed under ban, no one from the village may have any relations with it; and if someone does have relations with it, that person receives the same punishment and is also placed under ban. The formula of placing under ban is this: "to be excluded from funerals and from feasts. To be banned from funerals and from weddings and from the borrowing of flour."' (Kanuni i Leke Dukagjinit, 1989:208).

20 Gjomarkaj is the alternative rendering of the name Gjonmarkagjon

21 This substantiates the point that despite Gjon Marka Gjon's status of Captain, he was not in any sense in a feudal relationship with the inhabitants of Mirdita. His right was simply to call up fighters if the Porte required his engagement in a war.

22 I experienced a similar phenomenon in the 1980s doing research in southern Greece, when Athenians would ask me how I managed

'the cold down there'; the prejudice against village life attributing every form of discomfort to it.

23 Ismail Kadare's novel *Dasma* describes the tension at a marriage when a girl from the North, despite being promised as a child to a fellow northerner, marries a man met during the construction of a new town. Will the abandoned groom kill the new one? The book is an indictment of the Kanun, blood feud and the Catholic clergy. Although the story manifestly relays communist propaganda, it is an excellent novel, acutely observed and gripping.

24 Doçi, who was Abbot for 29 years, was a remarkable character, exceptionally intelligent and energetic in his care for his parishioners. He opened a school in Orosh in 1899. He radically improved the existing Albanian alphabet, substituting Roman letters for those which were from non-Roman scripts.

25 It tends to be forgotten that there are also extensive southern areas that were no more 'sophisticated' than the poor areas of the North; areas with good scope for pastoralism but without land suitable for feudal type relations of production and consequent emigration by those without land.

26 The film *Njeriu i mire*, in which an elder brother tries to prevent his sister from marrying the man she loves promotes two morals. One, that a woman must be allowed to decide for herself whom she marries, that such patriarchal relations are unacceptable; two, that decisons should not be based on the career success the partner enjoys in society, the lack of which was the reason in this case for the brother's disapproval. In fact, the message from a non-communist point of view is very immoral since the brother convinces his sister that the young man has concealed the fact that his uncle had fought against the Partisans. This turns out to be a distortion, and once it is clear that the youth has no relations who had fought on the 'wrong' side, the couple is reconciled. No question of pluralism here. The young man ends up being promoted to a high government position such that the brother welcomes him as a brother-in-law only to be insulted and very reasonably condemned for his hypocrisy. This and the condemnation of patriarchalism is the moral message to viewers.

27 The film *Çiftë i lumtur* sets out to ridicule the father of a young man who wants to marry a girl from a different faith. The father is tricked into agreement against his will.

28 Since Hairja's parents had refused their permission, they could not of course negotiate with the groom's parents for brideprice (viz section on marriage).

Chapter Six

1 *Deklasuar* – literally 'declassed' – those stripped of privileges as a result of politically unacceptable behaviour ranging from hereditary position to criticising the communist government implicitly (as in mentioning food shortages) or of belonging to a family one of whose members was politically unacceptable.

2 See Appendix Two for full citation.

3 Two interesting points about *ndarje*: 1) one can be geographically separate, e.g. my parents and brothers live in a flat in Reps while I live with my wife in Laç, but we are not *ndarë*, separated, because we still have a shared budget; 2) but in another flat-dwelling example, a couple with a small child are now *ndarë* from the parents and siblings who live in the same flat because financially they are operating independently. *Ndarje* occurs with an official ceremony that makes public the separation.

4 See Appendix Two for full citation.

5 Viz e.g. Prifti, B. in *Etnografia Shqiptare* 15, 1987, p. 125.

6 Verdery, Katherine 'The Elasticity of Land' in *What Was Socialism and What Comes Next?* 1996:148–9.

7 The Myzeqea is an extensive area of arable land in central Albania.

8 See Appendix Two for full citation.

Chapter Seven

1 Statistics from a conference paper by Nikollë Doda (2001): Lëvizjet e sotme të popullsisë së Mirditës. In: *Mirdita në histori dhe etnokulture*, Rrëshen: Shtëpi Botuese Mirdita, p. 190.

2 Passengers unknown to each other sitting together on provincial Greek buses keep questioning until they have found common relatives or fictive kin links.

3 A common complaint was that most of the aid clothes given to headmen for distribution failed to get further than the headmen's family and cronies.

4 As recently as 2003, the road leading to a school in the village of Lurth above Rrëshen, was closed to foot and wheeled traffic by a family claiming it as part of their property.

5 Mirditans are buried in clothes that have been prepared for the occasion; men in suits, village women in the exceptionally beautiful local costume elaborately embroidered. Unmarried girls over the age of 11 or 12 are buried in bridal dress. Mirditan townswomen usually set aside a smart suit for their death clothes.

6 In 2003, Mirditans who had descended to the coastal plain near Durrës were doing the same.

Chapter Eight

1 The other category of cooperative personnel best placed to enrich themselves after the end of Communism were those who had worked in the store houses of the head cooperatives and those with responsibility for the reserves of goods held against war. They simply helped themselves.

2 Liri Lubonja has an account of just such an expedition in her biography, *Larg dhe mes njerëzve*, of trying to get a lift from the Ura e Fanit up to Spaç prison to see her son.

Chapter Ten

1 A lightning poster displayed in a public place to shame the wrongdoers

2 Mercedes Benz – the most desired car in Albania at the time. People were astonished to learn that the roads of Western Europe were not crowded with Benzes.

3 Vakuf – Church owned land.

4 strict, patriarchal.

5 I mentioned this custom to an Uzbek acquaintance who said: 'That's the custom everywhere.'

6 Welfare benefits were assessed by family, how many members were out of work and how many children there were.

Chapter Twelve

1 The death of a patient would lead to the doctor in charge facing a tribunal.

2 As usual with languages with some Latin roots in common, there are a number of 'false friends', for example: *fanatik, ordiner, origjinal, intelektual*. Sometimes popular usage may not reflect the meaning as used by an Albanian intellectual (in the English sense of the term) and it is as well to be aware of both usages. '*Feminist*', for example, in popular usage means a philanderer/Don Juan! While '*fanatik*' refers to the kind of patriarchal rule that keeps young girls

under strictest surveillance; in rural areas insisting on their wearing national costume and never going anywhere unaccompanied.

3 1999 was no exception: amongst other deficiencies, the new text books for the middle school had not even been published a month-and-a-half after school had begun.

Chapter Thirteen

1 Law 704: 'Brotherhood, which is effected by two men drinking a few drops of each other's blood, causes a permanent prohibition on intermarriage between the brothers, their families and their descendants.' (Fox, 1989:144)

2 cf. Gail Kligman's Romanian study: Kligman, G. (1988). *The Wedding of the Dead*, Berkeley: University of California Press.

3 To 'drink coffee' refers to a ceremony that signifies an agreement between people, whether in this context of feud or, for example, to confirm the engagement of a young couple. It is also the term used when one goes to offer sympathy/consolation (*ngushellime*) to a family in mourning.

4 Rapaczynski, A. (1996). 'The Roles of the State and the Market in Establishing Property Rights'. *Journal of Economic Perspectives* 10 (2), Spring 1996, p. 88

Chapter Fourteen

1 Several years later, when squatters in Saranda wanted to send their children to school, absence of documents meant effectively that their children, whose births had not been registered, did not exist. Similarly, the parents could not vote. When locals who had been working in Greece throughout the 1990s began to return, they wanted to turn the squatters off the land that the latter had been cultivating for nearly a decade.

2 The nearest group of squatters was mainly from that part of Puka, which had formerly been part of Mirdita, and hence culturally Catholic. There were also a few families from Mirdita itself. Some kilometres further along the track towards Durrës, there were groups of squatters from Kukës, mainly Muslim culturally.

Chapter Fifteen

1 The official unemployment rate (est. 2011) is 13.3 per cent. The actual rate according to CIA statistics may exceed 30 per cent,

due to the preponderance of near-subsistence farming. https://www
.cia.gov/library/publications/the-world-factbook/geos/al.html/

2 Pandeli Majko was Prime Minister 1998–9 and for six months in
2002 (accessed 2011. Link no longer functional)

Bibliography

1 The affirmation of new norms and customs in family and social life
becomes a war against backward concepts and customs.

BIBLIOGRAPHY

Ahmed, A. and Shore, C. (eds.) (1995). *The Future of Anthropology*, London: The Athlone Press.

Almanak Mirdita 3, 1975.

Black-Michaud, J. (1975). *Cohesive Force: feud in the Mediterranean and the Middle East*, Oxford: Basil Blackwell.

Burawoy, M. and Verdery, K. (eds.) (1999). *Uncertain Transition*, Lanham: Rowman & Littlefield.

Clifford, J. and Marcus, E. (eds.) (1986). *Writing Culture*, Berkeley: University of California Press.

Dedaj, N. (1999). *Toka e Katedraleve*, Rrëshen: Shtëpi Botuese Mirdita.

Doçi, P. (1999). *Mirdita*, Rrëshen: Shtëpi Botuese Mirdita.

Doda, N. (2001). Lëvizjet e sotme të popullsisë së Mirditës. In: *Mirdita në histori dhe etnokulturë*, Rrëshen: Shtëpi Botuese Mirdita.

Durham, M.E. (1909). *High Albania*, London: Edward Arnold.

Durham, M.E. (1928). *Some Tribal Origins, Laws and Customs of the Balkans*, London: George Allen & Unwin.

Economist Intelligence Unit, *Country Report, 2000*.

Fjalori Enciklopedik Shqiptar, 1985, Tirana: Akademia e Shkencave.

Fox, L. (1989). *The Code of Lekë Dukagjini* (Albanian text collected and arranged by Gjeçov, S., translated and with an introduction by Fox, L.) New York: Gjonlekaj Publishing Company.

Frasheri, S. (1930). *Përmes Mirditës në Dimër*, Korça: Shtyp & Kartoleria Peppo-Marko.

Gellner, E. (1988). *Plough, Sword and Book*, London: Collins Harvill.

Giddens, A. (1995). Epilogue. In: Ahmed, A. and Shore, C. (eds.) *The Future of Anthropology*. London: The Athlone Press.

Gjeçov, S., translated and with an introduction by Fox, L.) New York: Gjonlekaj Publishing Company.

Gjeçov, S. and Fox, L. (1989). *Kanuni i Lekë Dukagjinit*, New York: Gjonlekaj Publishing Co.

Gjeçov, S. (1993). *Kanuni I Lekë Dukagjinit*, Tirana: Albinform.

Hasani, A. (1999). In *Klan*, 10th October.

Hasluck, M. (1954). *The Unwritten Law of Albania*, Cambridge: Cambridge University Press.

Hobsbawm, E. with Polito, A. (2000). *The New Century*, London: Little Brown & Co.

Kadare, I. (1968). *Dasma*, Tirana: Naim Frasheri.

Kligman G. (1988). *The Wedding of the Dead*, Berkeley: University of California Press.

Kostallari, A. (1982). *Fjalor me emra njerëzish*, Tirana: Akademia e Shkencave.

Lalaj, M. (1996). *Kapërcyell*, Tirana: Morava.

Liri, L. (1995). *Larg dhe mes Njerëzve*, Tirana: Dora d'Istria.

Loka, N. (1996). *Fani del nga Muzgjet*, Tirana: Shtëpi Botuese Faik Konica.

Marcus, G.E. and Fischer, M.J. (eds.) (1986). *Anthropology as Cultural Critique*, Chicago: University of Chicago Press.

Mato, E., Mita, N. and Grillo, K. (1995). *Edukata Qytetare* No.7, Tirana: Shtëpia Botuese Librit Shkollor.

Pollo, S. and Puto, A. (1981). *The History of Albania*, London: Routledge & Kegan Paul.

Prifti B. (1987). In *Etnografia Shqiptare* 15, p. 125

Rapaczynski, A. (1996). 'The Roles of the State and the Market in Establishing Property Rights'. *Journal of Economic Perspectives* 10 (2), Spring 1996, p. 88

Stavro, S. (1968). *Skenderbeg and Albanian National Consciousness*, Sudost-Forschungen, Munich: R. Oldenbourg.

Telo, I. (1998). *Mirëqënia dhe Minimumi Jetik*, Tirana: Institut Bashkimi i Sindikatave të Pavarura të Shqipërisë.

Tusha, N. (1975). 'Afirmimi i normave dhe zakonëve të reja në jetën familjare e shoqërore bëhet në luftë kundër koncepteve e zakonëve prapanike'.[1] *Almanak Mirdita* 3.

Verdery, K. (1996). *What Was Socialism, and What Comes Next?* Princeton: Princeton University Press.

Ylli: *Revistë Politiko-Shoqërore dhe Letraro-Artistike viti32-të I botimit*, 8 (Tirana: August 1982).

INDEX